Caterpillar Girl and Bad Texter Boy

SANZO

D1318325

c o n t e n t s

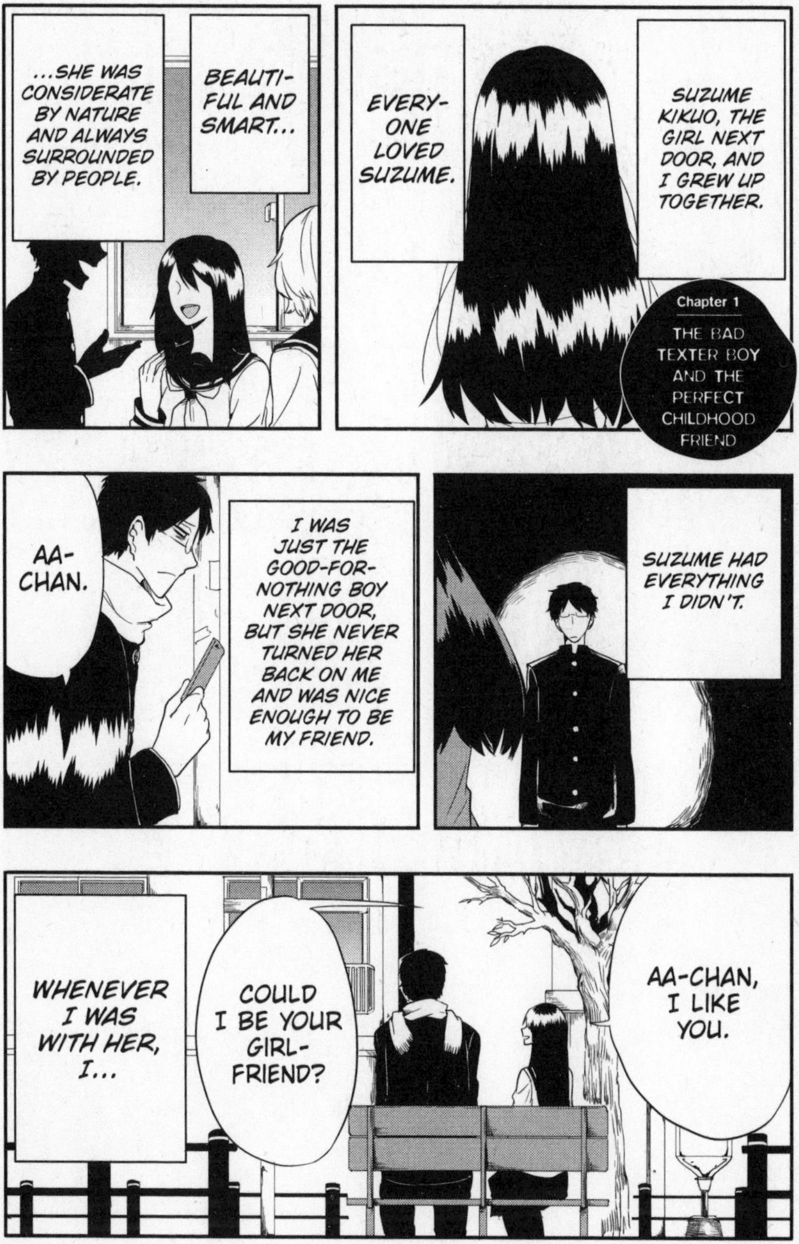
SUZUME KIKUO, THE GIRL NEXT DOOR, AND I GREW UP TOGETHER.
EVERY-ONE LOVED SUZUME.
Chapter 1
THE BAD TEXTER BOY AND THE PERFECT CHILDHOOD FRIEND
BEAUTI-FUL AND SMART...
...SHE WAS CONSIDERATE BY NATURE AND ALWAYS SURROUNDED BY PEOPLE.
SUZUME HAD EVERYTHING I DIDN'T.
I WAS JUST THE GOOD-FOR-NOTHING BOY NEXT DOOR, BUT SHE NEVER TURNED HER BACK ON ME AND WAS NICE ENOUGH TO BE MY FRIEND.
AA-CHAN.
AA-CHAN, I LIKE YOU.
COULD I BE YOUR GIRL-FRIEND?
WHENEVER I WAS WITH HER, I...

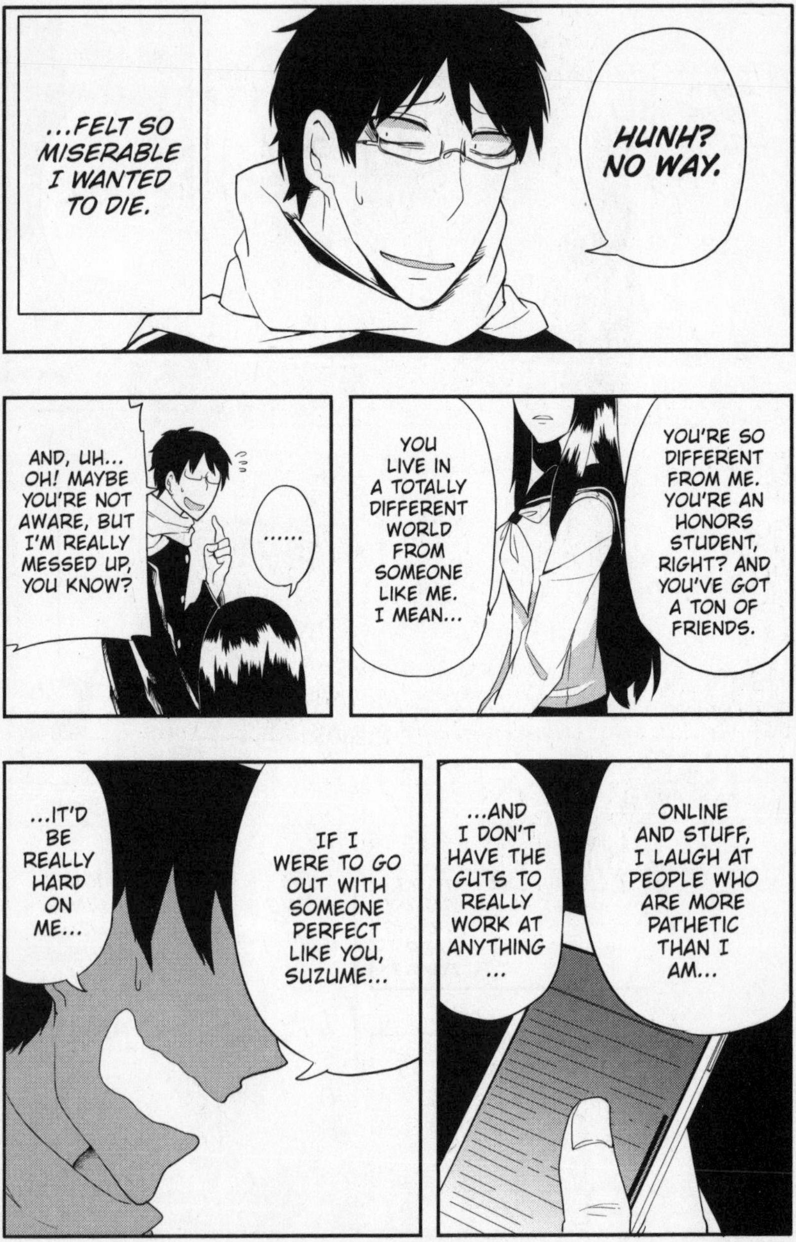
HUNH? NO WAY.
...FELT SO MISERABLE I WANTED TO DIE.
YOU'RE SO DIFFERENT FROM ME. YOU'RE AN HONORS STUDENT, RIGHT? AND YOU'VE GOT A TON OF FRIENDS.
YOU LIVE IN A TOTALLY DIFFERENT WORLD FROM SOMEONE LIKE ME. I MEAN...
......
AND, UH... OH! MAYBE YOU'RE NOT AWARE, BUT I'M REALLY MESSED UP, YOU KNOW?
ONLINE AND STUFF, I LAUGH AT PEOPLE WHO ARE MORE PATHETIC THAN I AM...
...AND I DON'T HAVE THE GUTS TO REALLY WORK AT ANYTHING...
IF I WERE TO GO OUT WITH SOMEONE PERFECT LIKE YOU, SUZUME...
...IT'D BE REALLY HARD ON ME...

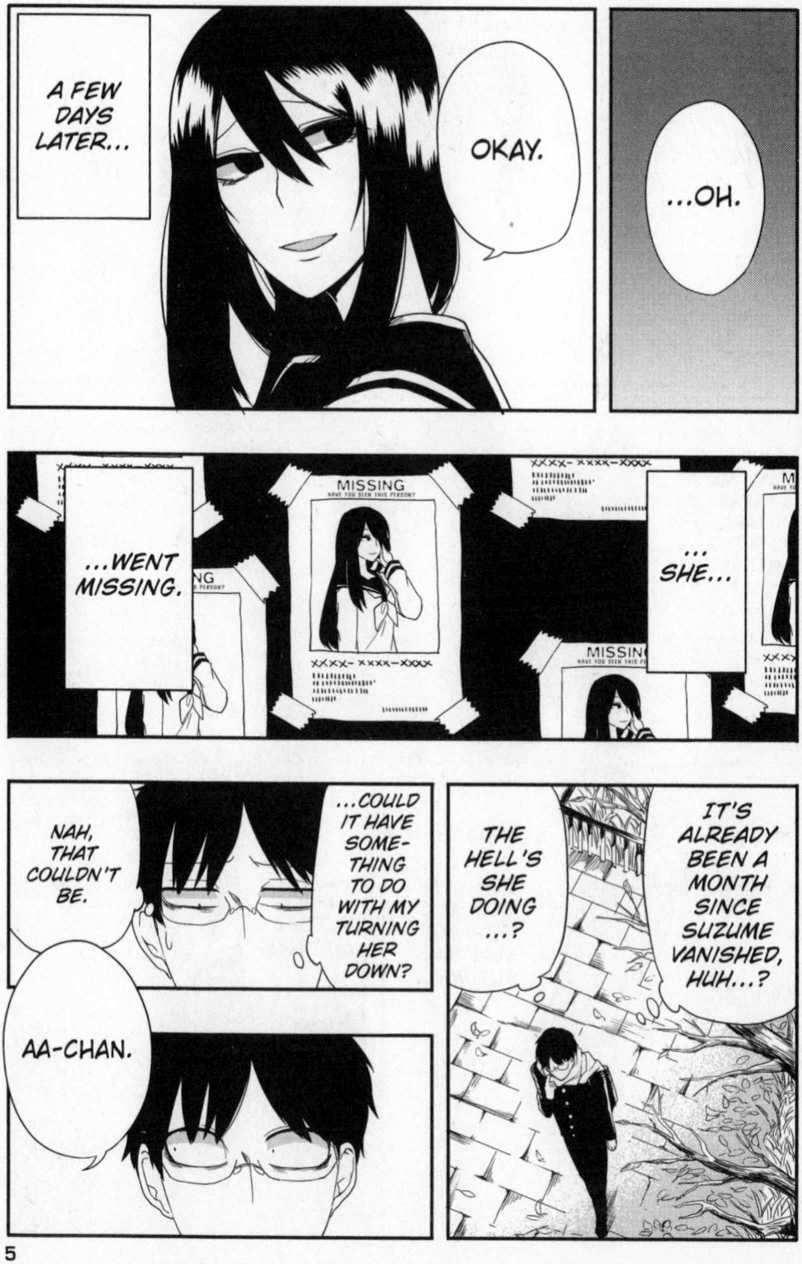
...OH.
OKAY.
A FEW DAYS LATER...
... SHE...
MISSING
HAVE YOU SEEN THIS PERSON?
...WENT MISSING.
IT'S ALREADY BEEN A MONTH SINCE SUZUME VANISHED, HUH...?
THE HELL'S SHE DOING ...?
...COULD IT HAVE SOMETHING TO DO WITH MY TURNING HER DOWN?
NAH, THAT COULDN'T BE.
AA-CHAN.

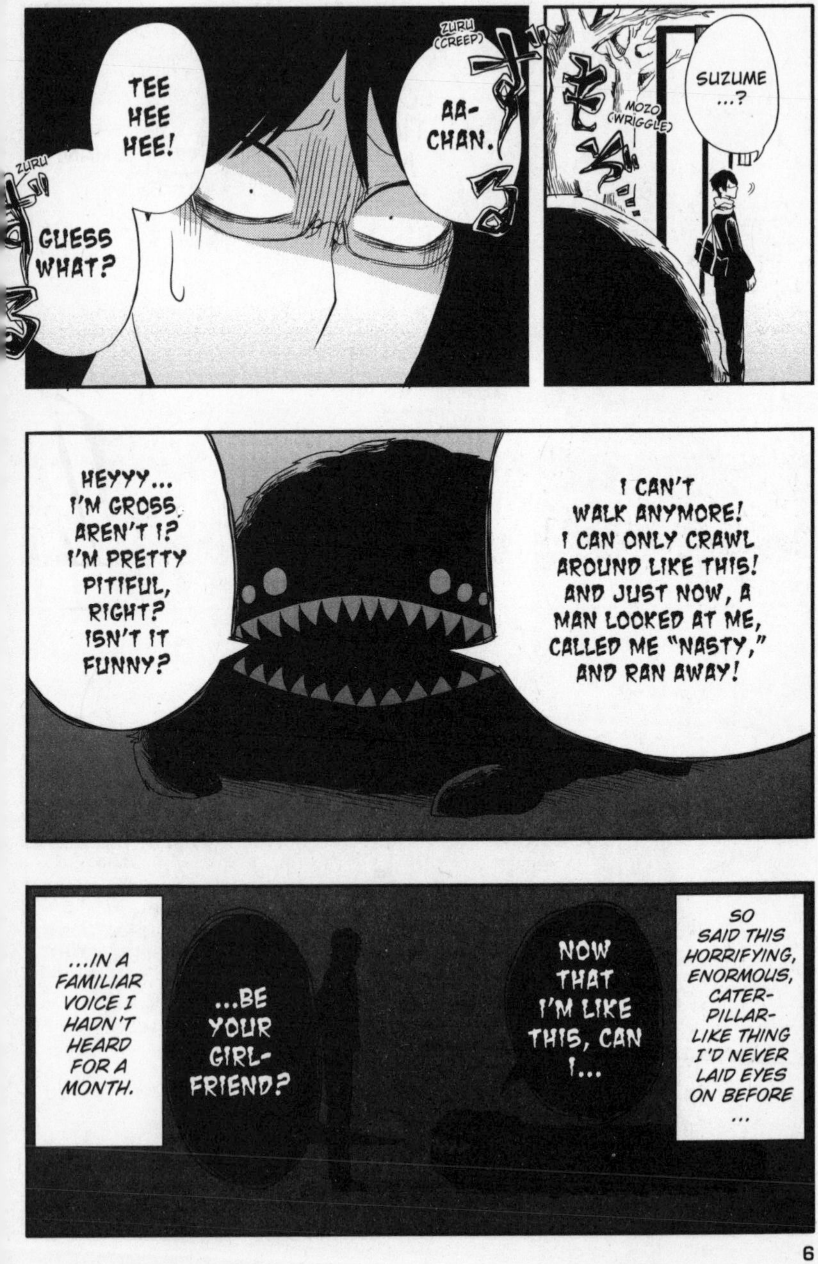
SUZUME ...?
MOZO (WRIGGLE)
ZURU (CREEP)
AA-CHAN.
TEE HEE HEE!
ZURU
GUESS WHAT?
I CAN'T WALK ANYMORE! I CAN ONLY CRAWL AROUND LIKE THIS! AND JUST NOW, A MAN LOOKED AT ME, CALLED ME "NASTY," AND RAN AWAY!
HEYYY... I'M GROSS, AREN'T I? I'M PRETTY PITIFUL, RIGHT? ISN'T IT FUNNY?
SO SAID THIS HORRIFYING, ENORMOUS, CATER-PILLAR-LIKE THING I'D NEVER LAID EYES ON BEFORE ...
NOW THAT I'M LIKE THIS, CAN I...
...BE YOUR GIRL-FRIEND?
...IN A FAMILIAR VOICE I HADN'T HEARD FOR A MONTH.

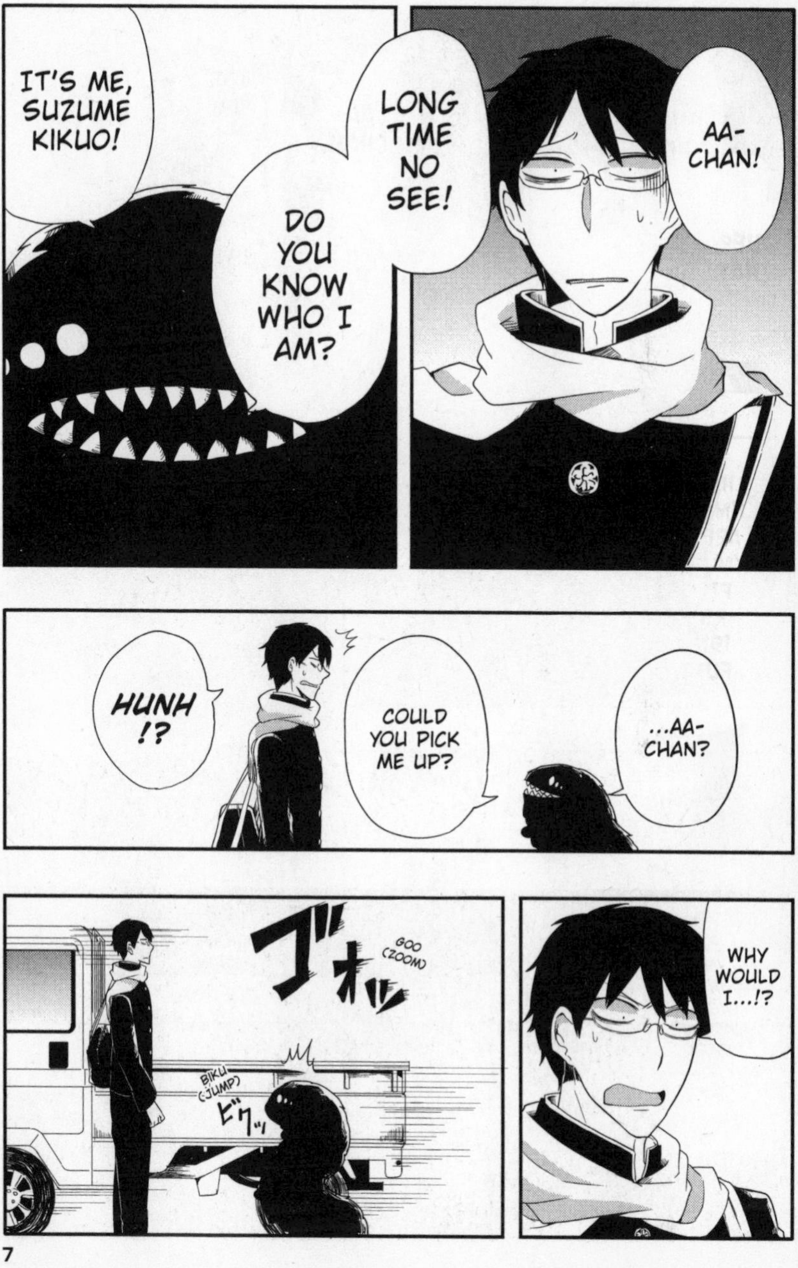
AA-CHAN!
LONG TIME NO SEE!
DO YOU KNOW WHO I AM?
IT'S ME, SUZUME KIKUO!
...AA-CHAN?
COULD YOU PICK ME UP?
HUNH!?
WHY WOULD I...!?
GOO (ZOOM)
BIKU (JUMP)

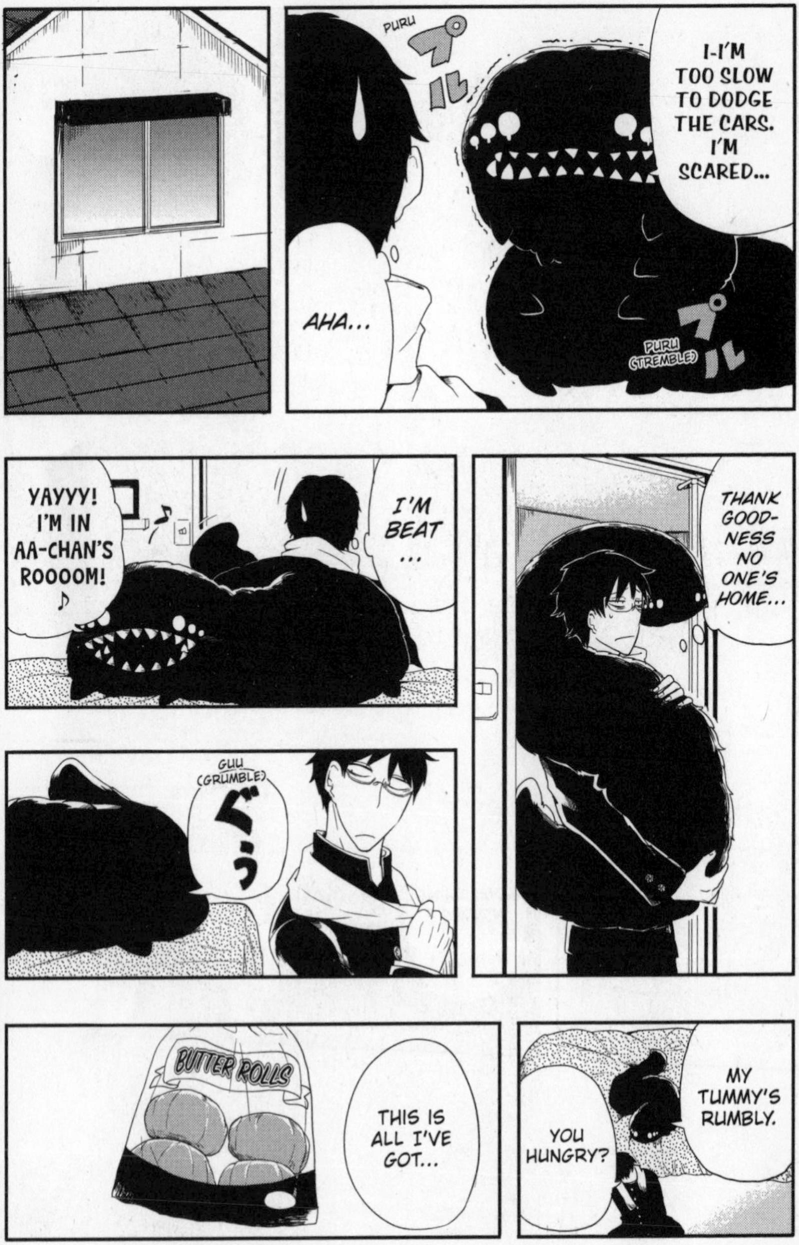
I-I'M TOO SLOW TO DODGE THE CARS. I'M SCARED...
PURU
PURU (TREMBLE)
AHA...
THANK GOODNESS NO ONE'S HOME...
I'M BEAT ...
YAYYY! I'M IN AA-CHAN'S ROOOOM! ♪
GUU (GRUMBLE)
MY TUMMY'S RUMBLY.
YOU HUNGRY?
THIS IS ALL I'VE GOT...
BUTTER ROLLS

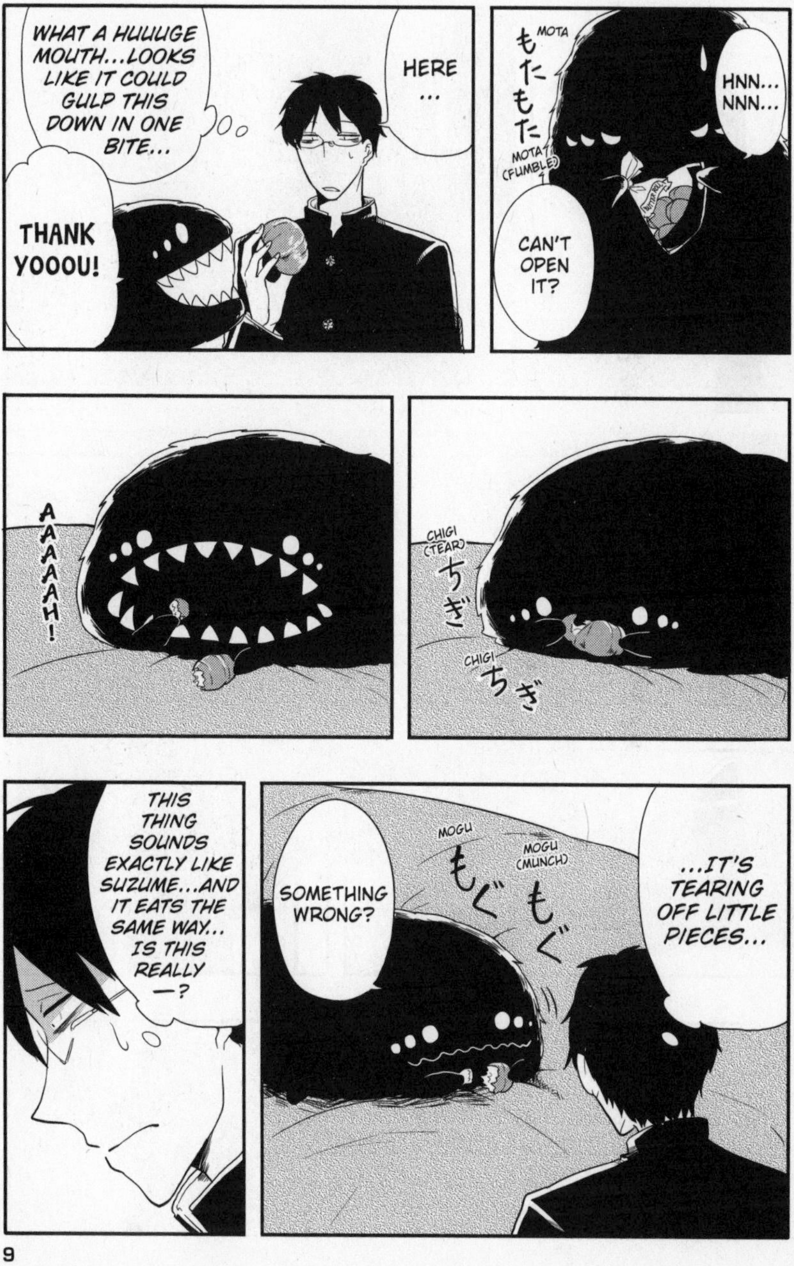
HNN... NNN...
MOTA
もたもた
MOTA (FUMBLE)
CAN'T OPEN IT?
HERE ...
WHAT A HUUUGE MOUTH...LOOKS LIKE IT COULD GULP THIS DOWN IN ONE BITE...
THANK YOOOU!
CHIGI (TEAR)
ちぎ
CHIGI
ちぎ
AAAAAAH!
...IT'S TEARING OFF LITTLE PIECES...
MOGU (MUNCH)
もぐ
MOGU
もぐ
SOMETHING WRONG?
THIS THING SOUNDS EXACTLY LIKE SUZUME...AND IT EATS THE SAME WAY... IS THIS REALLY —?

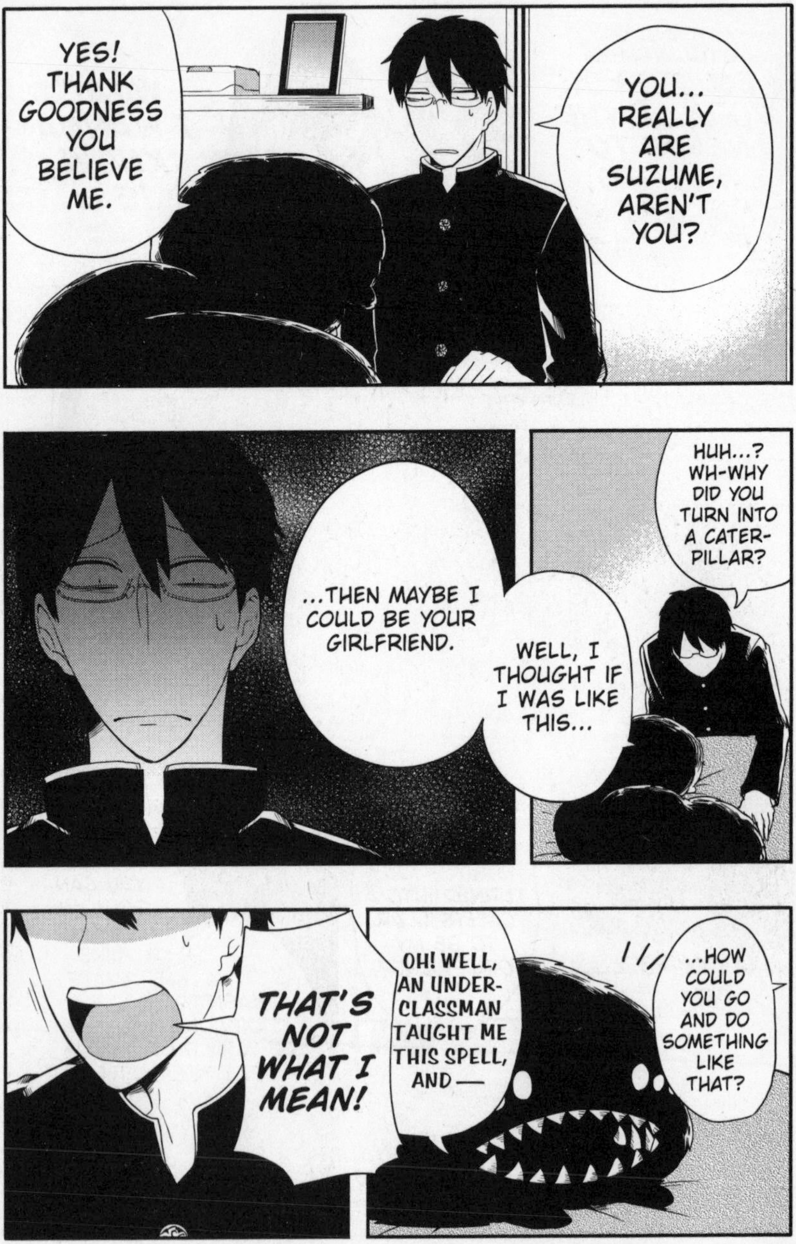
YOU... REALLY ARE SUZUME, AREN'T YOU?
YES! THANK GOODNESS YOU BELIEVE ME.
HUH...? WH-WHY DID YOU TURN INTO A CATER-PILLAR?
WELL, I THOUGHT IF I WAS LIKE THIS...
...THEN MAYBE I COULD BE YOUR GIRLFRIEND.
...HOW COULD YOU GO AND DO SOMETHING LIKE THAT?
OH! WELL, AN UNDER-CLASSMAN TAUGHT ME THIS SPELL, AND—
THAT'S NOT WHAT I MEAN!

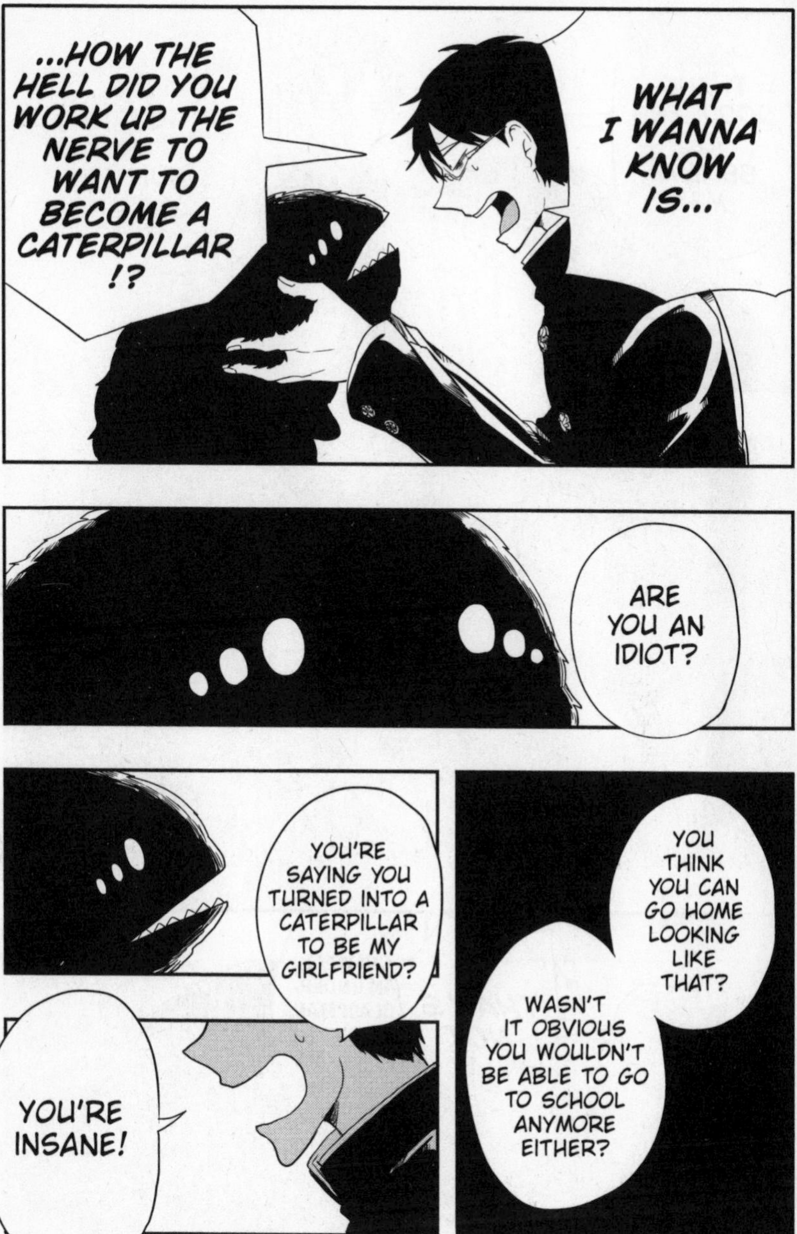
WHAT I WANNA KNOW IS...
...HOW THE HELL DID YOU WORK UP THE NERVE TO WANT TO BECOME A CATERPILLAR!?
ARE YOU AN IDIOT?
YOU THINK YOU CAN GO HOME LOOKING LIKE THAT?
WASN'T IT OBVIOUS YOU WOULDN'T BE ABLE TO GO TO SCHOOL ANYMORE EITHER?
YOU'RE SAYING YOU TURNED INTO A CATERPILLAR TO BE MY GIRLFRIEND?
YOU'RE INSANE!

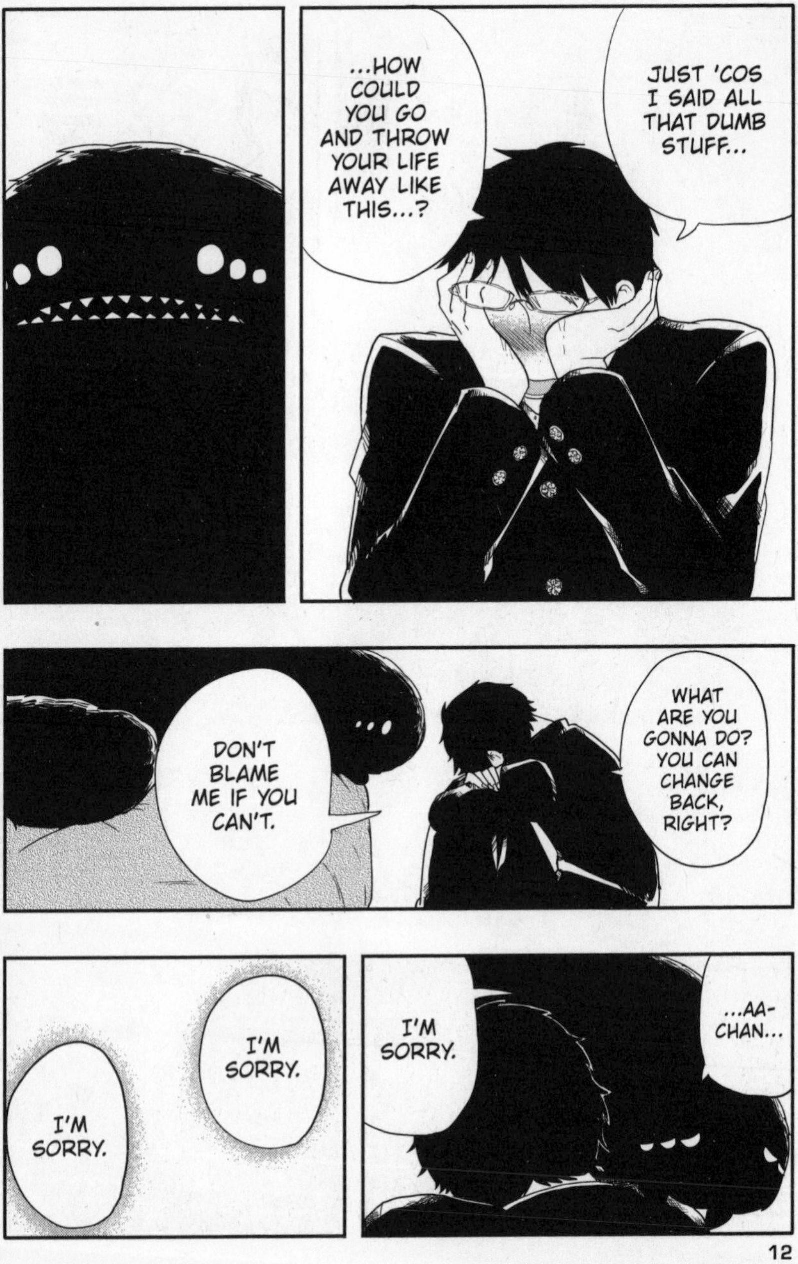
JUST 'COS I SAID ALL THAT DUMB STUFF...
...HOW COULD YOU GO AND THROW YOUR LIFE AWAY LIKE THIS...?
WHAT ARE YOU GONNA DO? YOU CAN CHANGE BACK, RIGHT?
DON'T BLAME ME IF YOU CAN'T.
...AA-CHAN...
I'M SORRY.
I'M SORRY.
I'M SORRY.

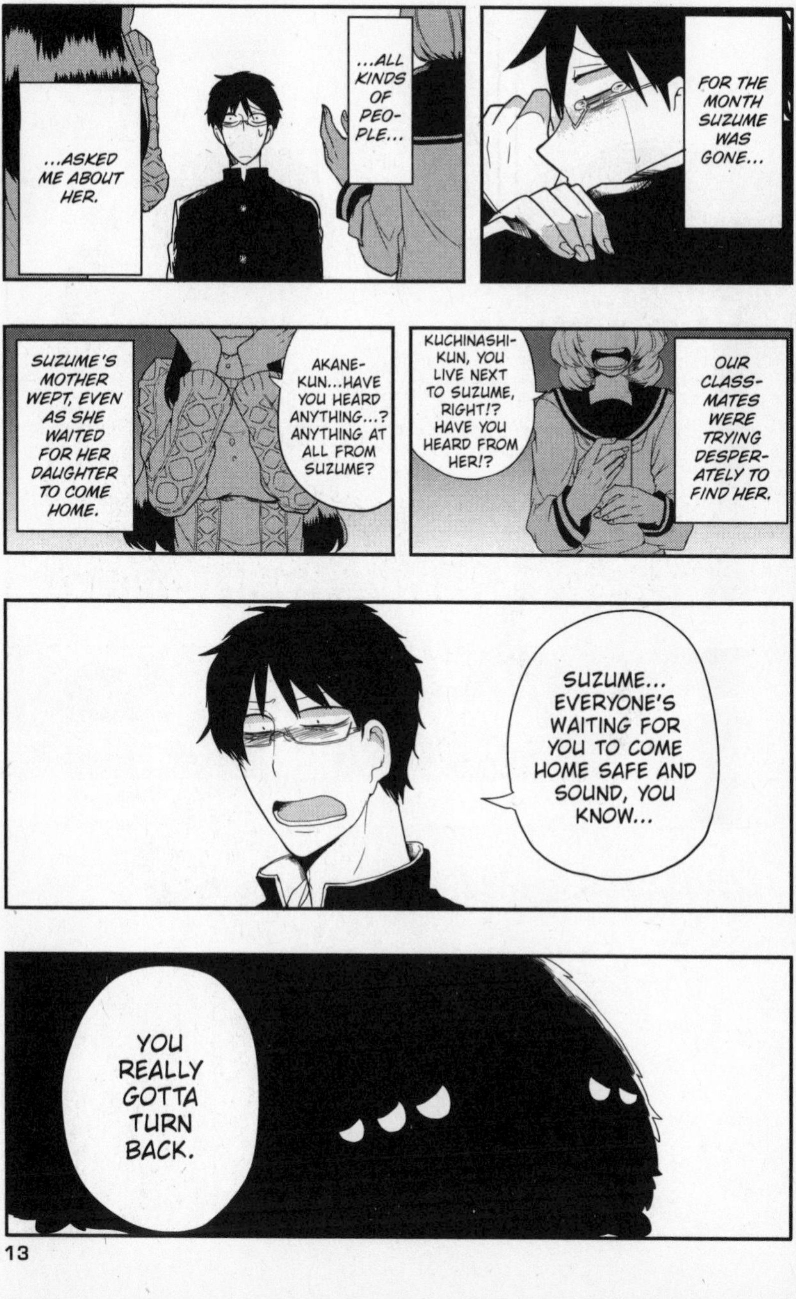
FOR THE MONTH SUZUME WAS GONE...
...ALL KINDS OF PEO-PLE...
...ASKED ME ABOUT HER.
OUR CLASS-MATES WERE TRYING DESPER-ATELY TO FIND HER.
KUCHINASHI-KUN, YOU LIVE NEXT TO SUZUME, RIGHT!? HAVE YOU HEARD FROM HER!?
AKANE-KUN...HAVE YOU HEARD ANYTHING...? ANYTHING AT ALL FROM SUZUME?
SUZUME'S MOTHER WEPT, EVEN AS SHE WAITED FOR HER DAUGHTER TO COME HOME.
SUZUME... EVERYONE'S WAITING FOR YOU TO COME HOME SAFE AND SOUND, YOU KNOW...
YOU REALLY GOTTA TURN BACK.

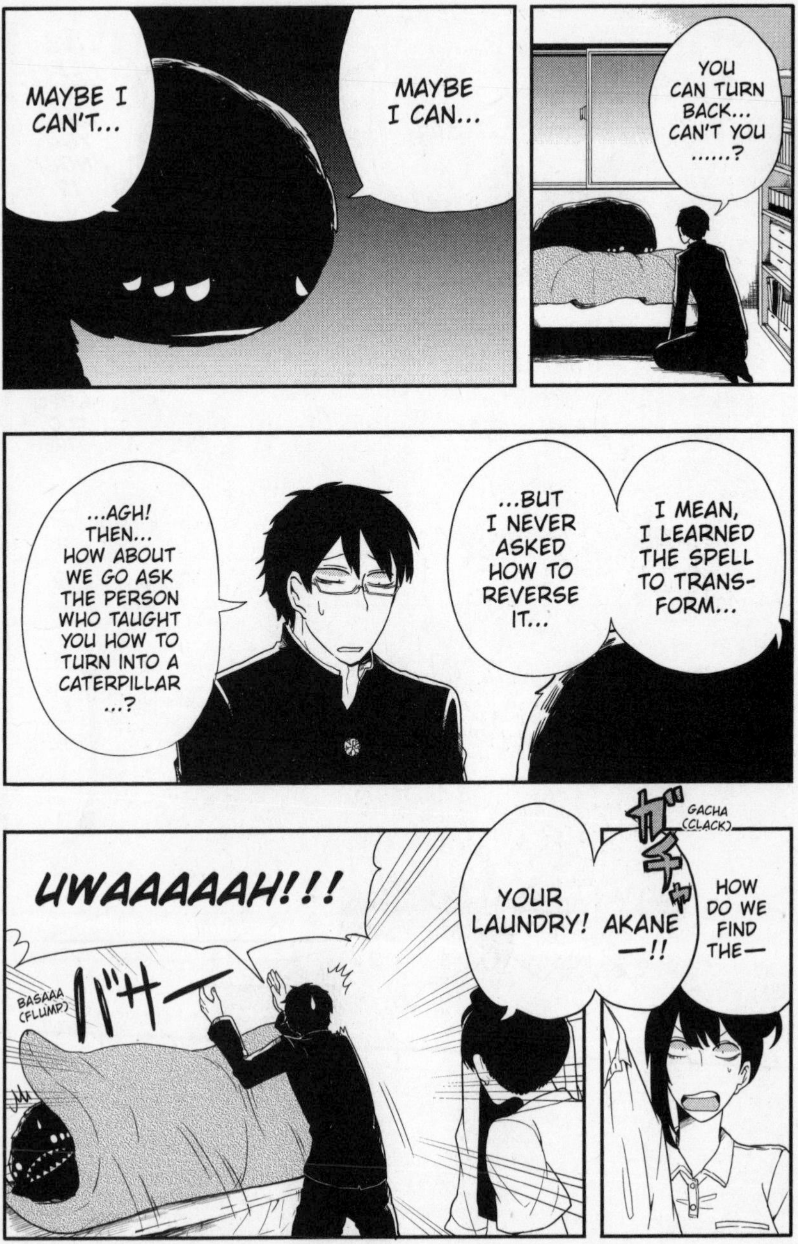
YOU CAN TURN BACK... CAN'T YOU ......?
MAYBE I CAN...
MAYBE I CAN'T...
I MEAN, I LEARNED THE SPELL TO TRANS-FORM...
...BUT I NEVER ASKED HOW TO REVERSE IT...
...AGH! THEN... HOW ABOUT WE GO ASK THE PERSON WHO TAUGHT YOU HOW TO TURN INTO A CATERPILLAR ...?
HOW DO WE FIND THE—
ガチャ
GACHA (CLACK)
AKANE —!!
YOUR LAUNDRY!
UWAAAAAAH!!!
バサー
BASAAA (FLUMP)

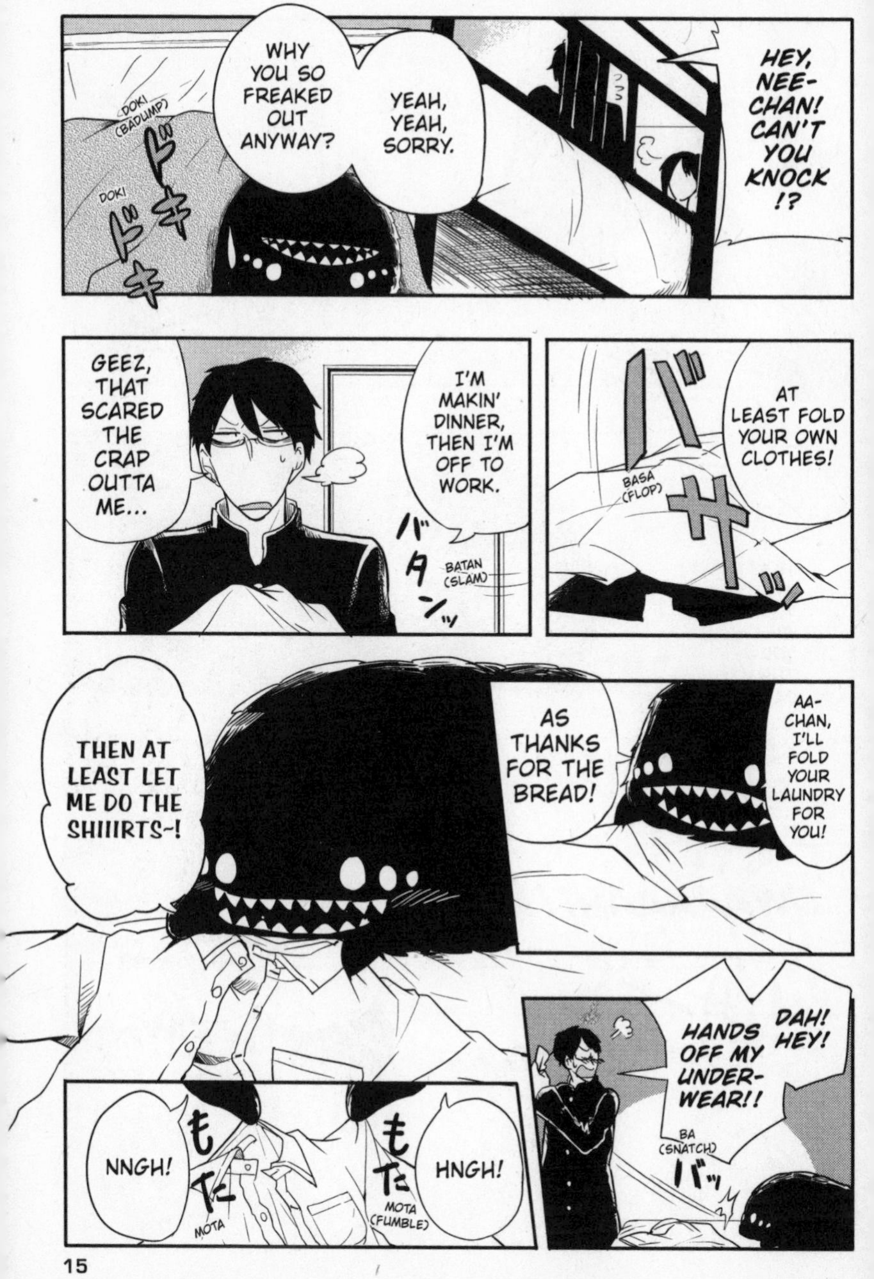
HEY, NEE-CHAN! CAN'T YOU KNOCK!?
YEAH, YEAH, SORRY.
WHY YOU SO FREAKED OUT ANYWAY?
DOKI (BADUMP)
DOKI
AT LEAST FOLD YOUR OWN CLOTHES!
BASA (FLOP)
I'M MAKIN' DINNER, THEN I'M OFF TO WORK.
BATAN (SLAM)
GEEZ, THAT SCARED THE CRAP OUTTA ME...
AA-CHAN, I'LL FOLD YOUR LAUNDRY FOR YOU!
AS THANKS FOR THE BREAD!
THEN AT LEAST LET ME DO THE SHIIIRTS~!
DAH! HEY!
HANDS OFF MY UNDER-WEAR!!
BA (SNATCH)
HNGH!
MOTA (FUMBLE)
NNGH!
MOTA

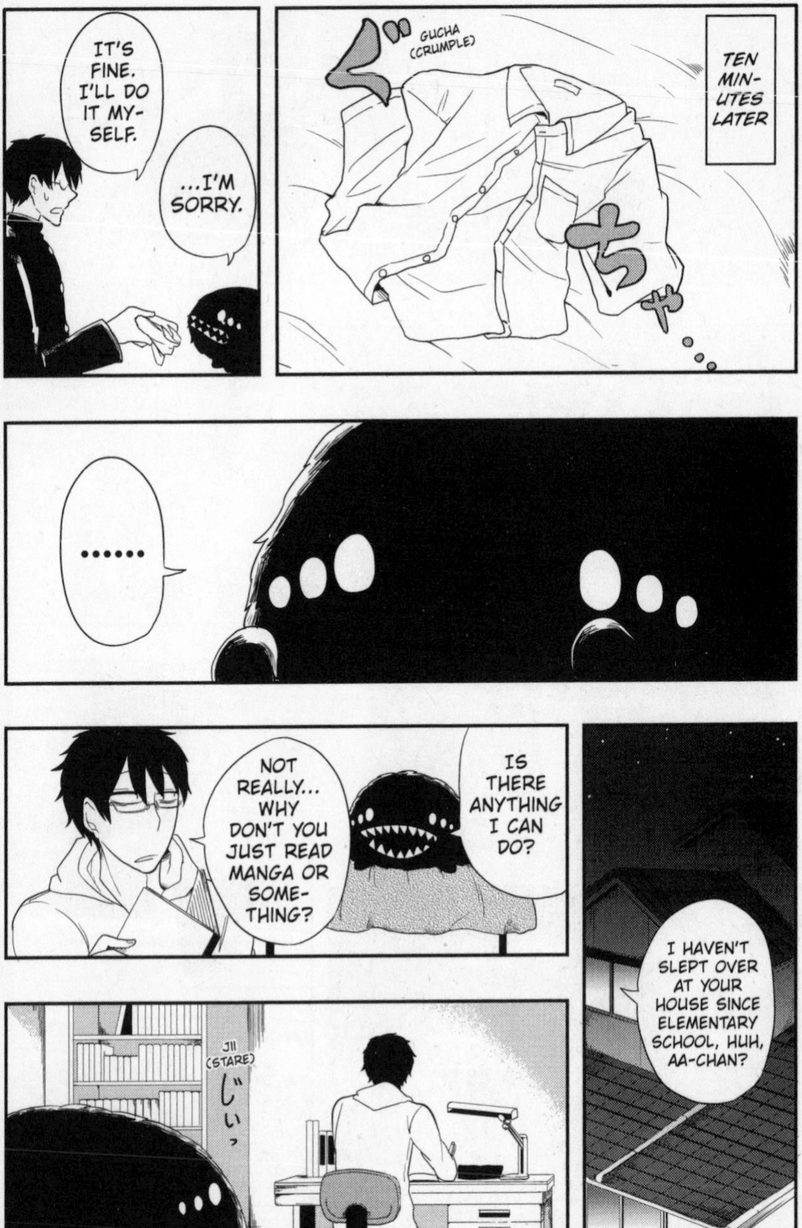
TEN MIN-UTES LATER
GUCHA (CRUMPLE)
...I'M SORRY.
IT'S FINE. I'LL DO IT MY-SELF.
......
I HAVEN'T SLEPT OVER AT YOUR HOUSE SINCE ELEMENTARY SCHOOL, HUH, AA-CHAN?
IS THERE ANYTHING I CAN DO?
NOT REALLY... WHY DON'T YOU JUST READ MANGA OR SOME-THING?
JII (STARE)

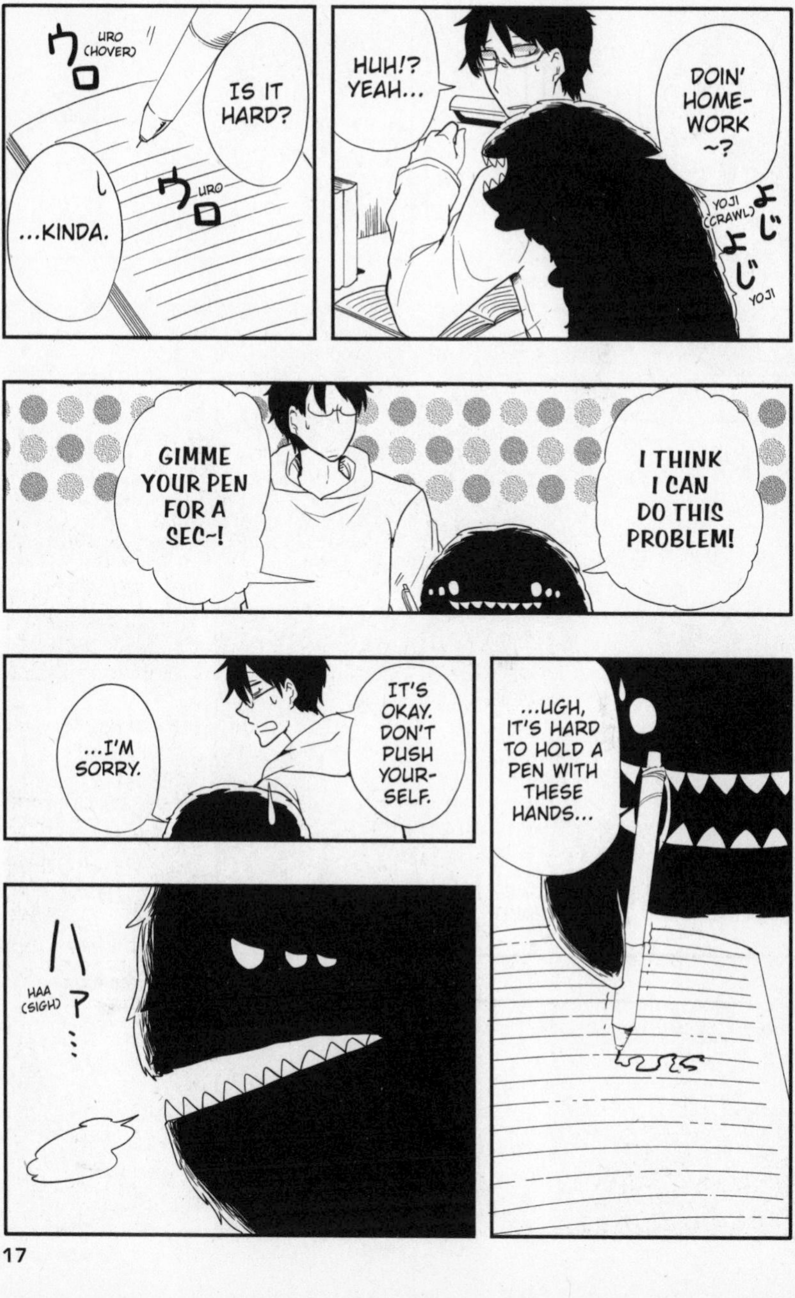
DOIN' HOMEWORK ~?
YOJI (CRAWL) よじ
よじ YOJI
HUH!? YEAH...
IS IT HARD?
URO (HOVER) ウロ
URO ウロ
...KINDA.
I THINK I CAN DO THIS PROBLEM!
GIMME YOUR PEN FOR A SEC~!
...UGH, IT'S HARD TO HOLD A PEN WITH THESE HANDS...
IT'S OKAY. DON'T PUSH YOURSELF.
...I'M SORRY.
HAA (SIGH) ハア…

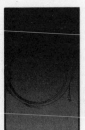

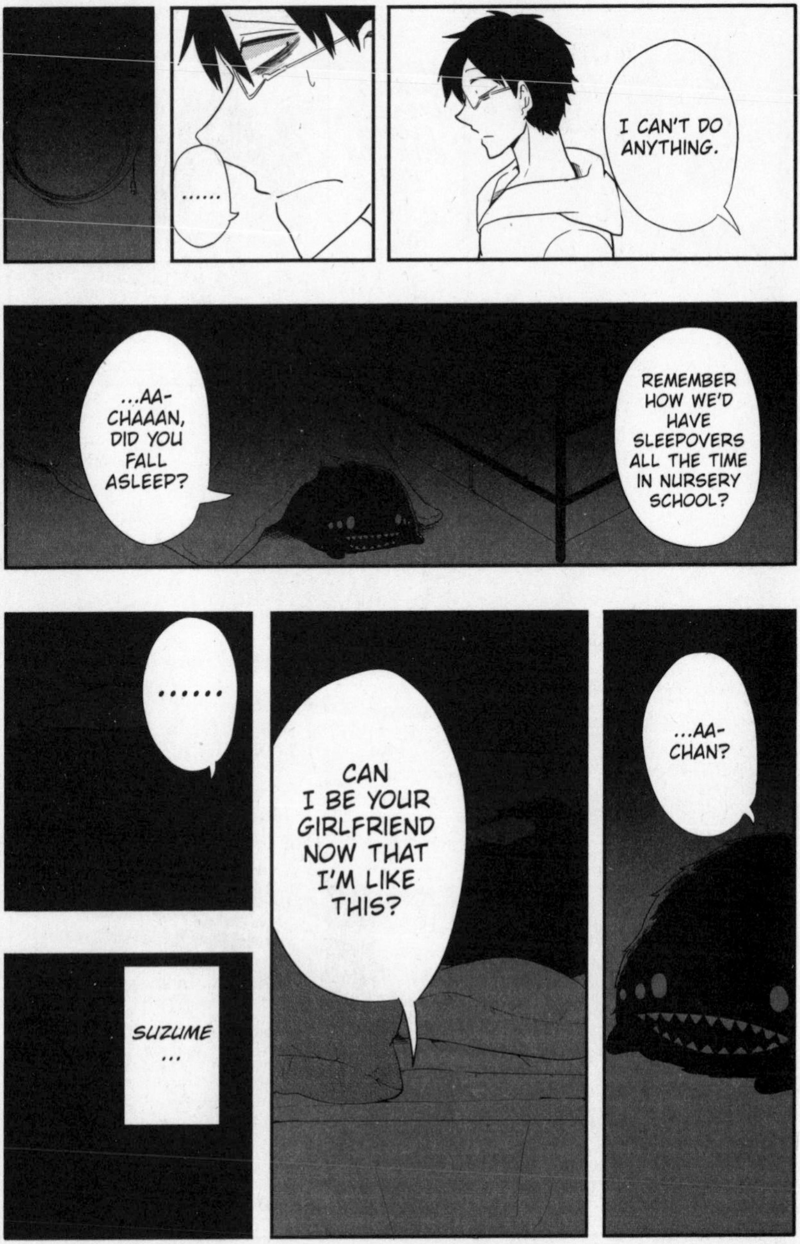
I CAN'T DO ANYTHING.
......
REMEMBER HOW WE'D HAVE SLEEPOVERS ALL THE TIME IN NURSERY SCHOOL?
...AA-CHAAAN, DID YOU FALL ASLEEP?
...AA-CHAN?
CAN I BE YOUR GIRLFRIEND NOW THAT I'M LIKE THIS?
......
SUZUME ...

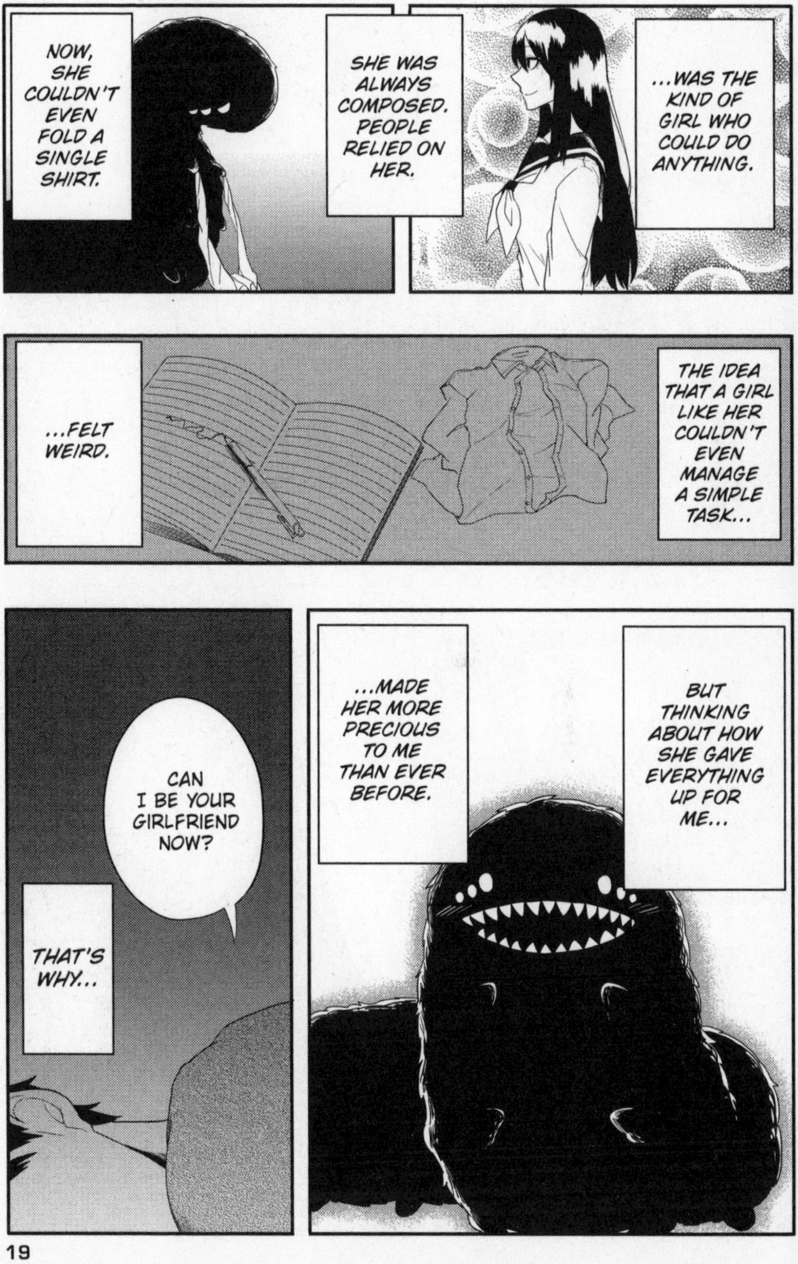
...WAS THE KIND OF GIRL WHO COULD DO ANYTHING.
SHE WAS ALWAYS COMPOSED. PEOPLE RELIED ON HER.
NOW, SHE COULDN'T EVEN FOLD A SINGLE SHIRT.
THE IDEA THAT A GIRL LIKE HER COULDN'T EVEN MANAGE A SIMPLE TASK...
...FELT WEIRD.
BUT THINKING ABOUT HOW SHE GAVE EVERYTHING UP FOR ME...
...MADE HER MORE PRECIOUS TO ME THAN EVER BEFORE.
CAN I BE YOUR GIRLFRIEND NOW?
THAT'S WHY...

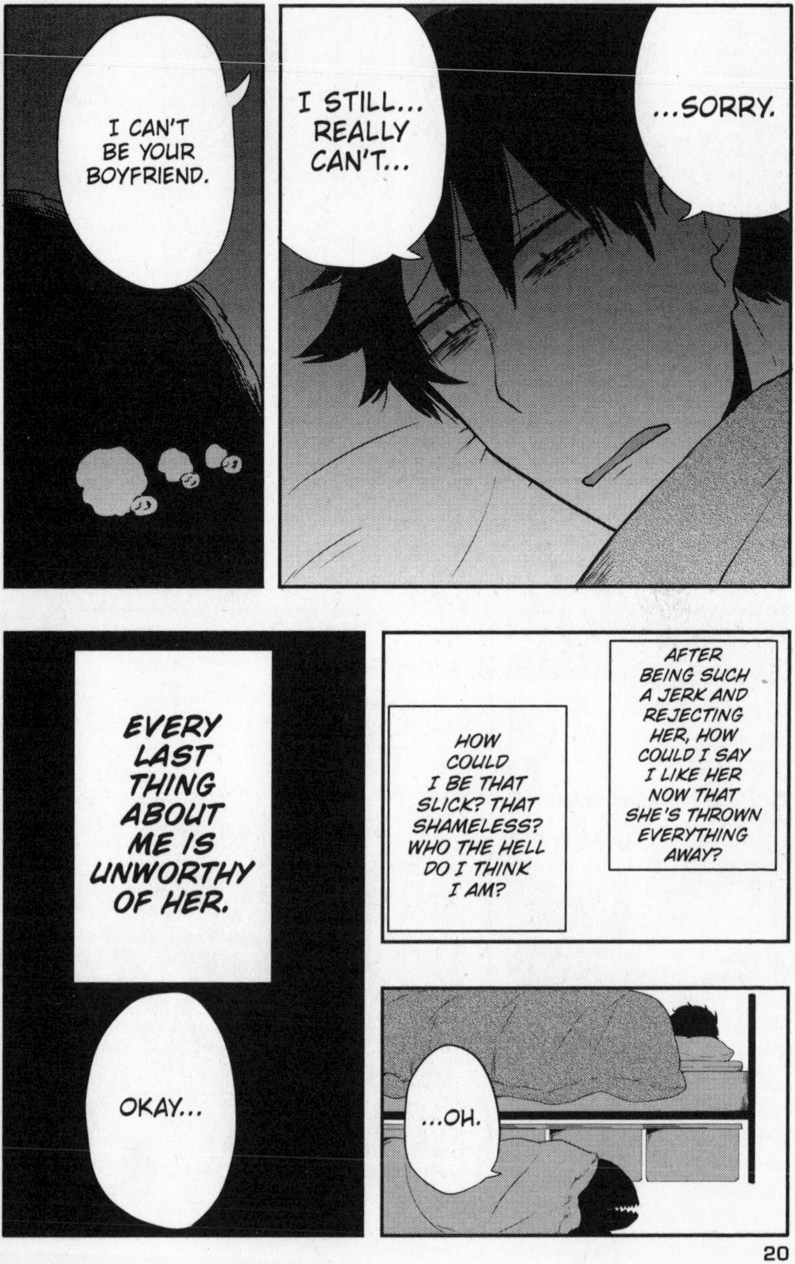
...SORRY.
I STILL... REALLY CAN'T...
I CAN'T BE YOUR BOYFRIEND.
AFTER BEING SUCH A JERK AND REJECTING HER, HOW COULD I SAY I LIKE HER NOW THAT SHE'S THROWN EVERYTHING AWAY?
HOW COULD I BE THAT SLICK? THAT SHAMELESS? WHO THE HELL DO I THINK I AM?
...OH.
EVERY LAST THING ABOUT ME IS UNWORTHY OF HER.
OKAY...

......

SNFF! ...HIC! SNFF!

...UU.

....

SU (SLIDE)

......SHE STOPPED CRYING.

GYUUU (CHUG)

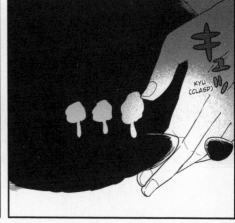

KYU (CLASP)

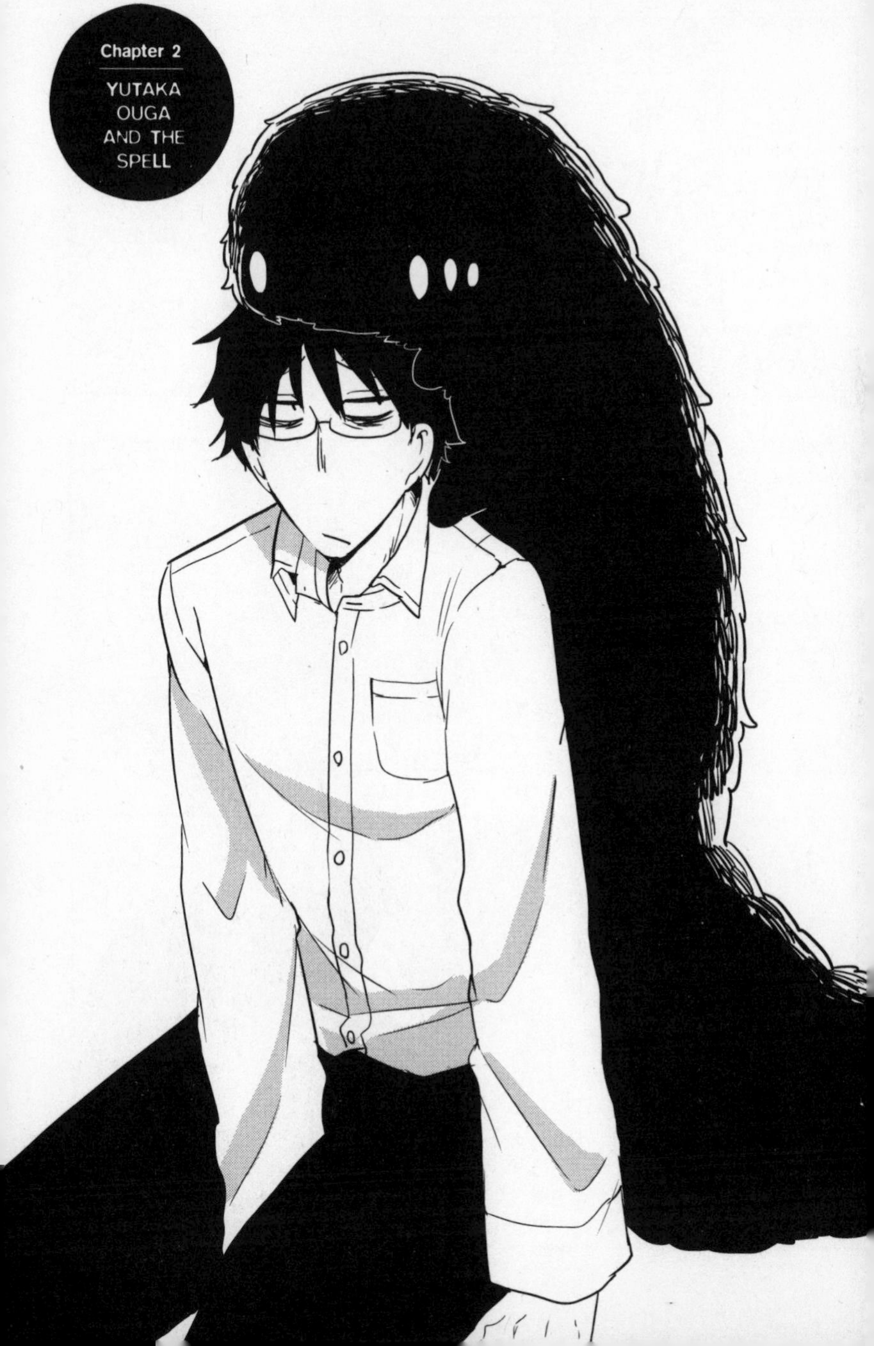
Chapter 2
YUTAKA OUGA AND THE SPELL

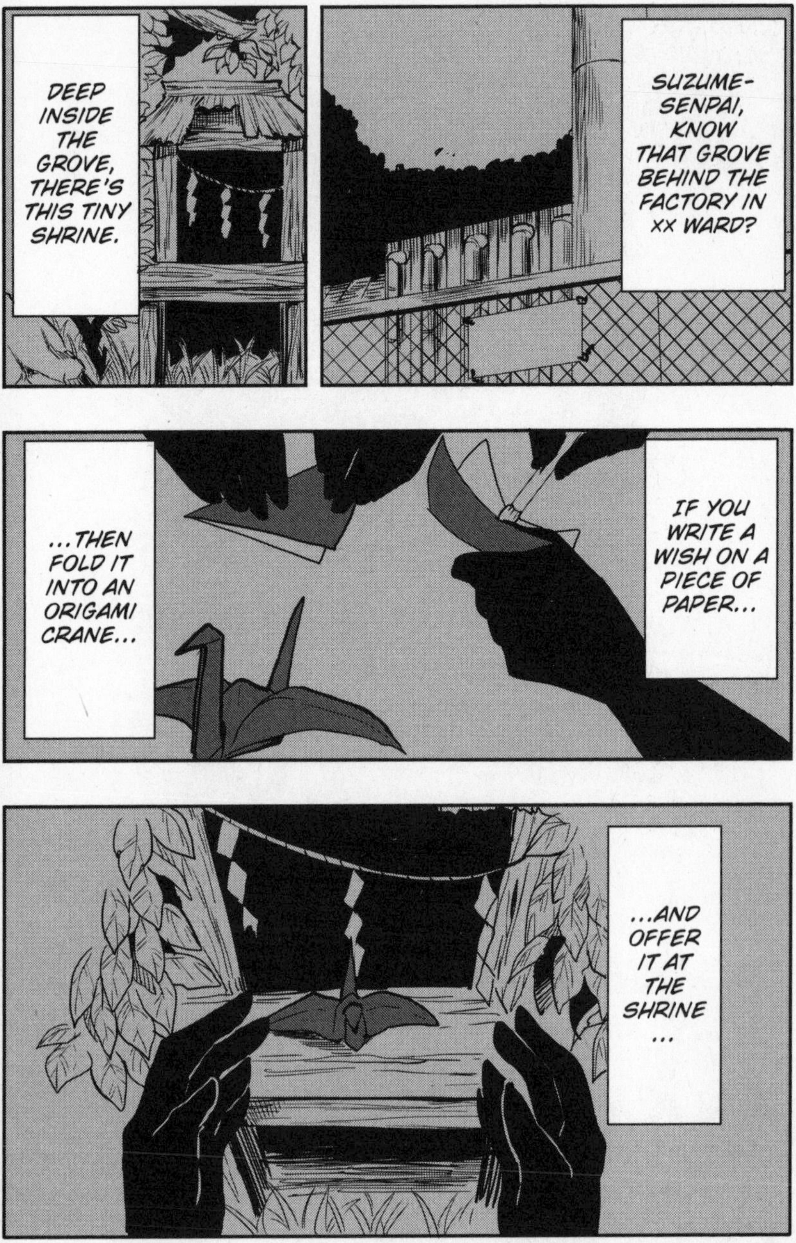
SUZUME-SENPAI, KNOW THAT GROVE BEHIND THE FACTORY IN XX WARD?
DEEP INSIDE THE GROVE, THERE'S THIS TINY SHRINE.
IF YOU WRITE A WISH ON A PIECE OF PAPER...
...THEN FOLD IT INTO AN ORIGAMI CRANE...
...AND OFFER IT AT THE SHRINE...

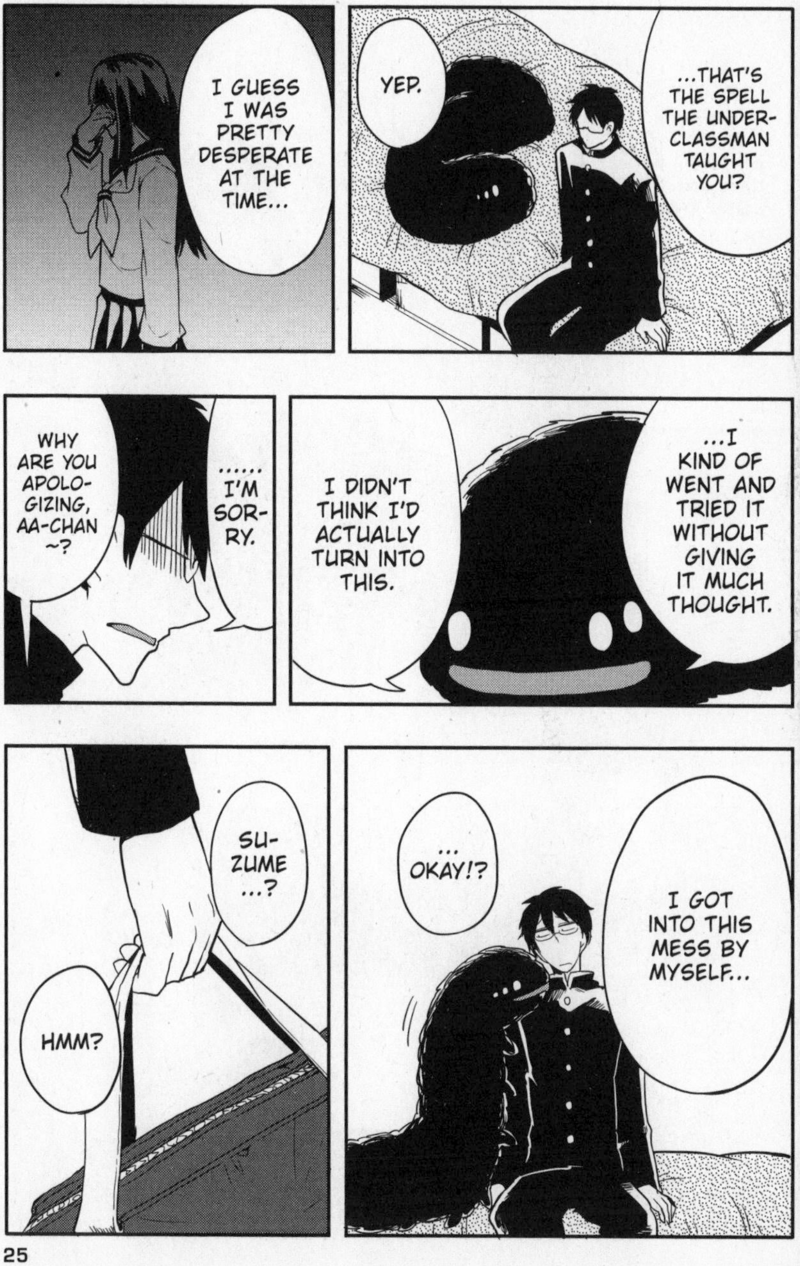
...THAT'S THE SPELL THE UNDER-CLASSMAN TAUGHT YOU?
YEP.
I GUESS I WAS PRETTY DESPERATE AT THE TIME...
...I KIND OF WENT AND TRIED IT WITHOUT GIVING IT MUCH THOUGHT.
I DIDN'T THINK I'D ACTUALLY TURN INTO THIS.
...... I'M SOR-RY.
WHY ARE YOU APOLO-GIZING, AA-CHAN ~?
I GOT INTO THIS MESS BY MYSELF...
... OKAY!?
SU-ZUME ...?
HMM?

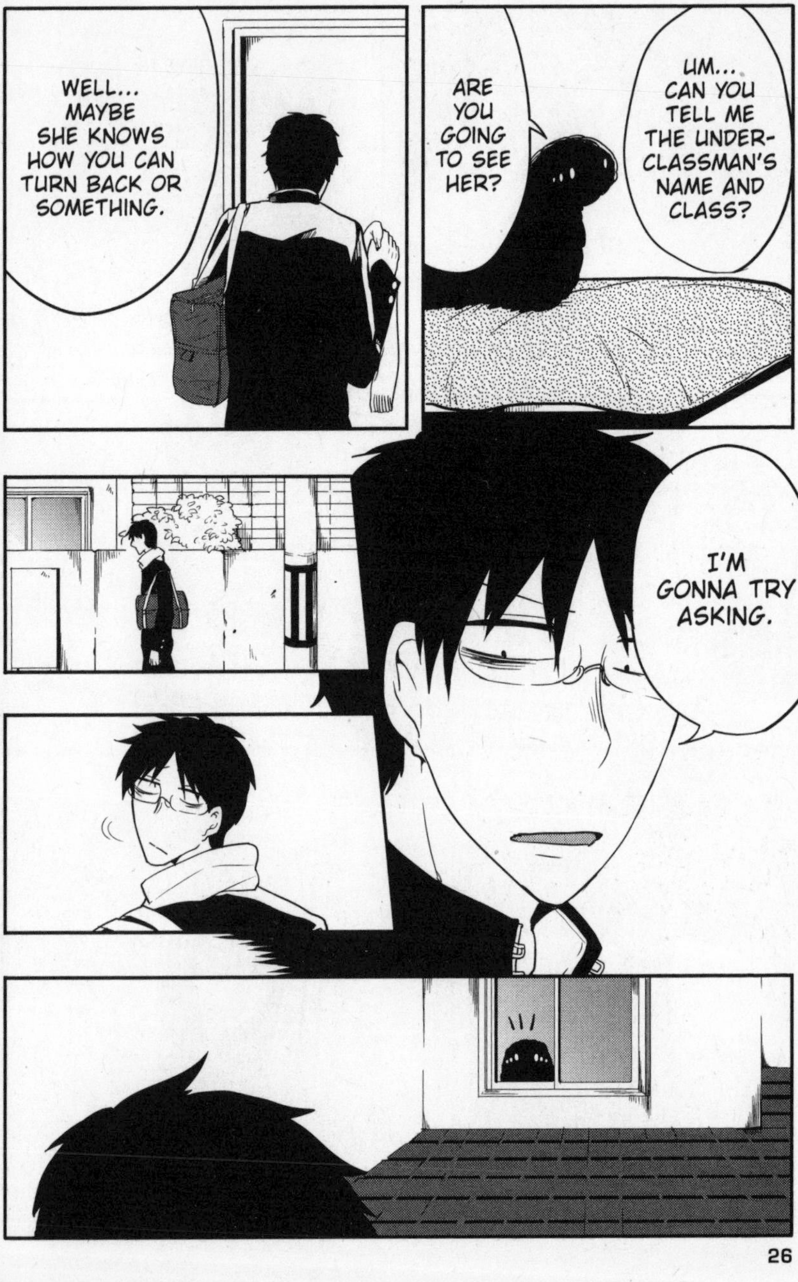
UM... CAN YOU TELL ME THE UNDER-CLASSMAN'S NAME AND CLASS?
ARE YOU GOING TO SEE HER?
WELL... MAYBE SHE KNOWS HOW YOU CAN TURN BACK OR SOMETHING.
I'M GONNA TRY ASKING.

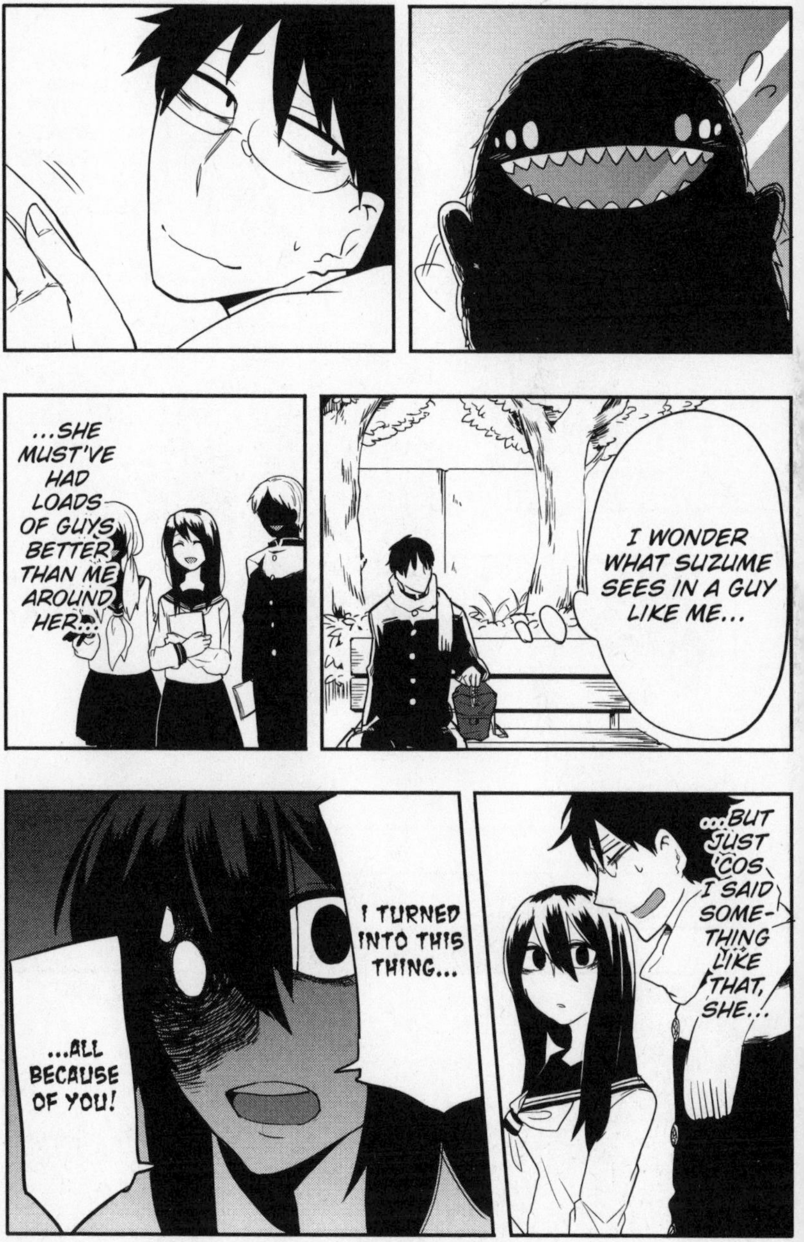
I WONDER WHAT SUZUME SEES IN A GUY LIKE ME...
...SHE MUST'VE HAD LOADS OF GUYS BETTER THAN ME AROUND HER...
...BUT JUST 'COS I SAID SOME-THING LIKE THAT, SHE...
I TURNED INTO THIS THING...
...ALL BECAUSE OF YOU!

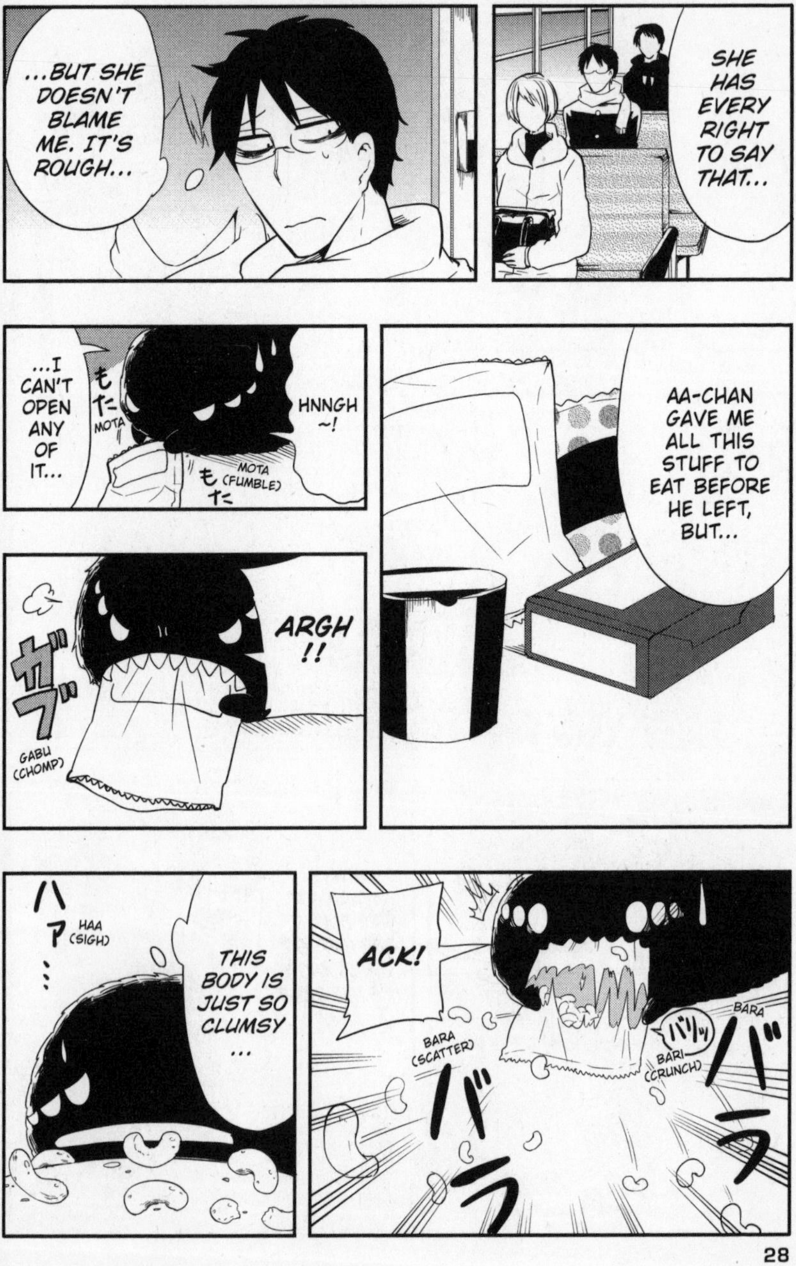
SHE HAS EVERY RIGHT TO SAY THAT...
...BUT SHE DOESN'T BLAME ME. IT'S ROUGH...
AA-CHAN GAVE ME ALL THIS STUFF TO EAT BEFORE HE LEFT, BUT...
HNNGH ~!
MOTA
MOTA (FUMBLE)
...I CAN'T OPEN ANY OF IT...
ARGH !!
GABU (CHOMP)
ACK!
BARA
BARI (CRUNCH)
BARA (SCATTER)
THIS BODY IS JUST SO CLUMSY ...
HAA (SIGH)

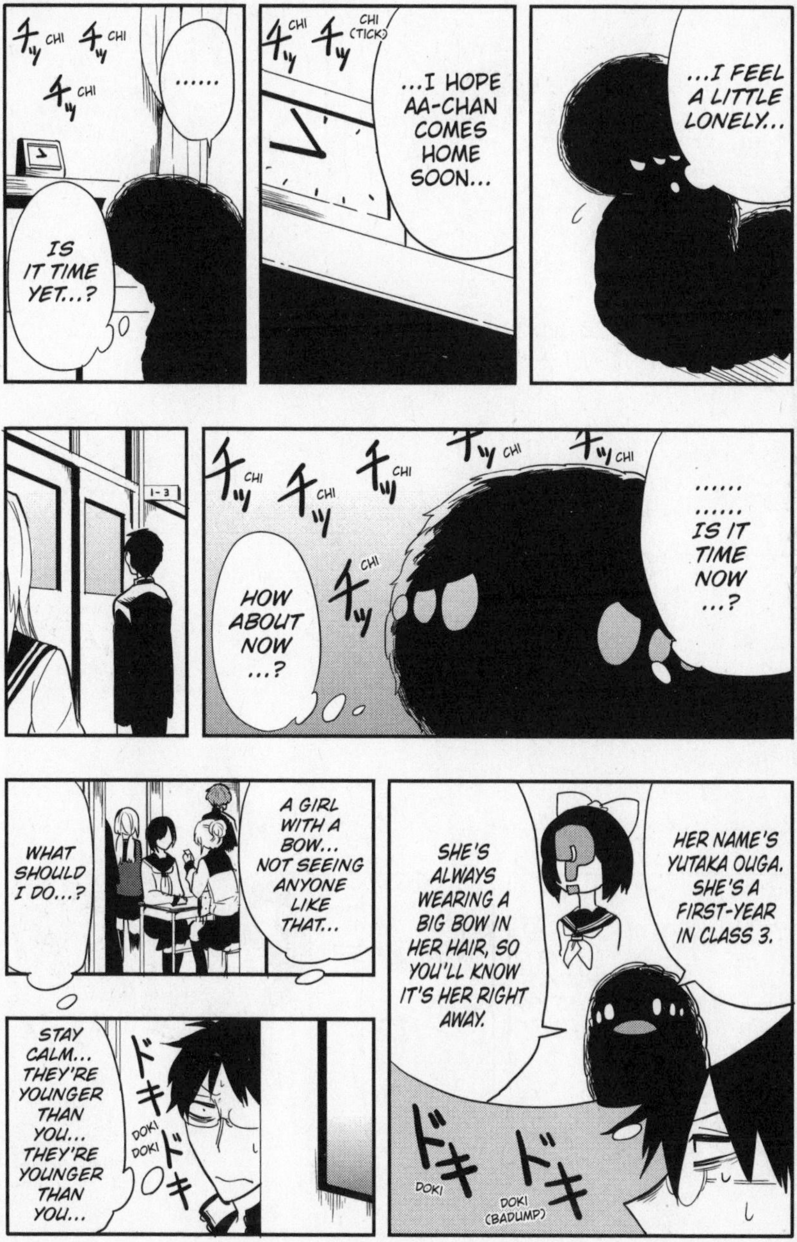
...I FEEL A LITTLE LONELY...
チッ CHI (TICK)
チッ CHI
...I HOPE AA-CHAN COMES HOME SOON...
チッ CHI
チッ CHI
......
チッ CHI
IS IT TIME YET...?
チッ CHI
チッ CHI
.... IS IT TIME NOW ...?
チッ CHI
チッ CHI
チッ CHI
チッ CHI
HOW ABOUT NOW ...?
1-3
HER NAME'S YUTAKA OUGA. SHE'S A FIRST-YEAR IN CLASS 3.
SHE'S ALWAYS WEARING A BIG BOW IN HER HAIR, SO YOU'LL KNOW IT'S HER RIGHT AWAY.
ドキ DOKI (BADUMP)
ドキ DOKI
A GIRL WITH A BOW... NOT SEEING ANYONE LIKE THAT...
WHAT SHOULD I DO...?
ドキ DOKI
ドキ DOKI
STAY CALM... THEY'RE YOUNGER THAN YOU... THEY'RE YOUNGER THAN YOU...

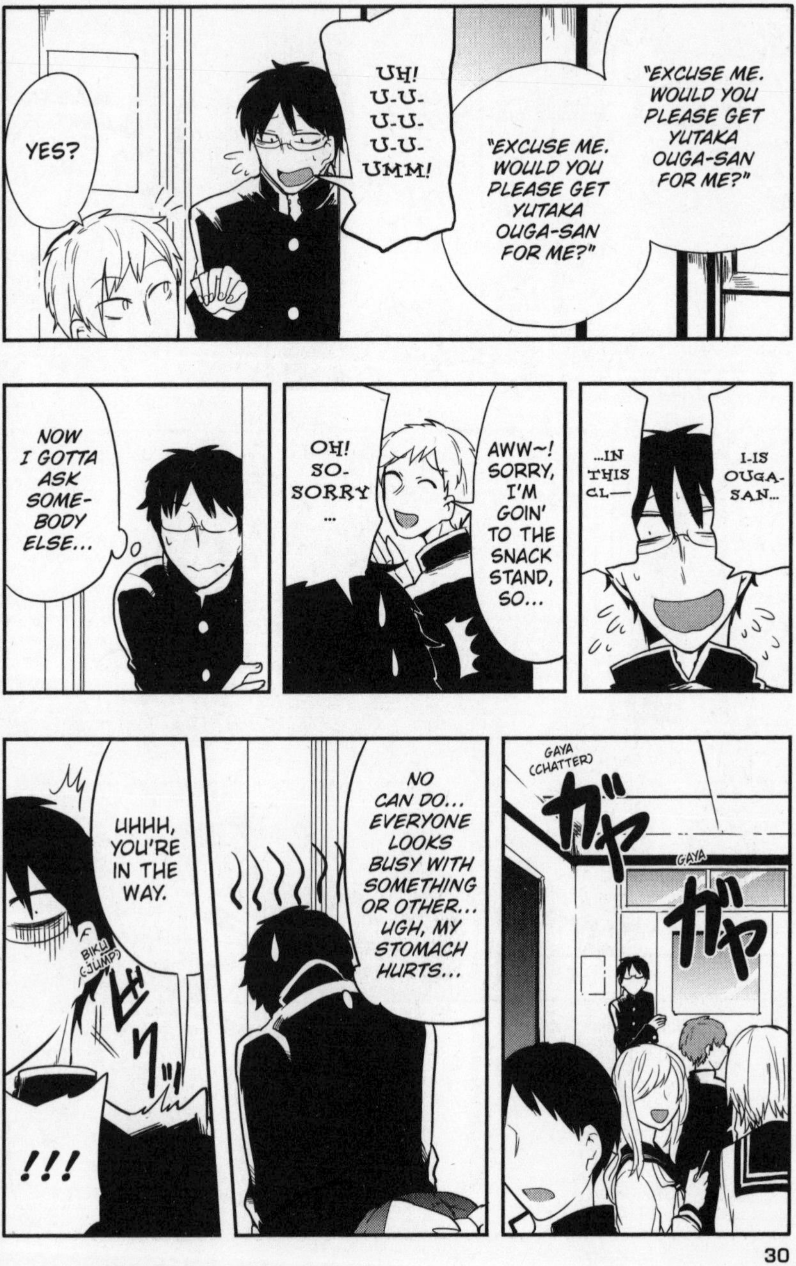
"EXCUSE ME. WOULD YOU PLEASE GET YUTAKA OUGA-SAN FOR ME?"
"EXCUSE ME. WOULD YOU PLEASE GET YUTAKA OUGA-SAN FOR ME?"
UH! U-U-U-U-U-U-UMM!
YES?
I-IS OUGA-SAN...
...IN THIS CL—
AWW~! SORRY, I'M GOIN' TO THE SNACK STAND, SO...
OH! SO-SORRY ...
NOW I GOTTA ASK SOME-BODY ELSE...
GAYA (CHATTER)
ガヤ
GAYA
ガヤ
NO CAN DO... EVERYONE LOOKS BUSY WITH SOMETHING OR OTHER... UGH, MY STOMACH HURTS...
UHHH, YOU'RE IN THE WAY.
BIKU (JUMP)
ビクッ
!!!

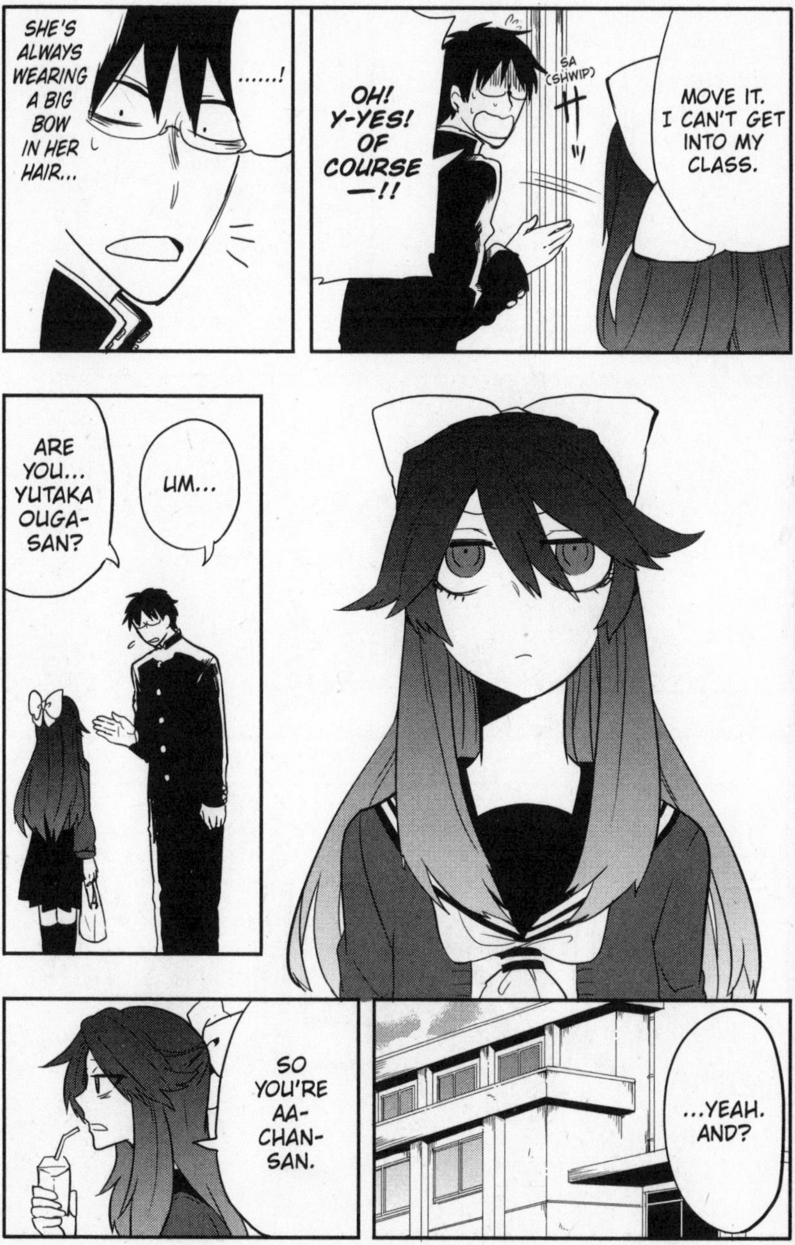
MOVE IT. I CAN'T GET INTO MY CLASS.
SA (SHWIP)
OH! Y-YES! OF COURSE—!!
......!
SHE'S ALWAYS WEARING A BIG BOW IN HER HAIR...
UM...
ARE YOU... YUTAKA OUGA-SAN?
...YEAH. AND?
SO YOU'RE AA-CHAN-SAN.

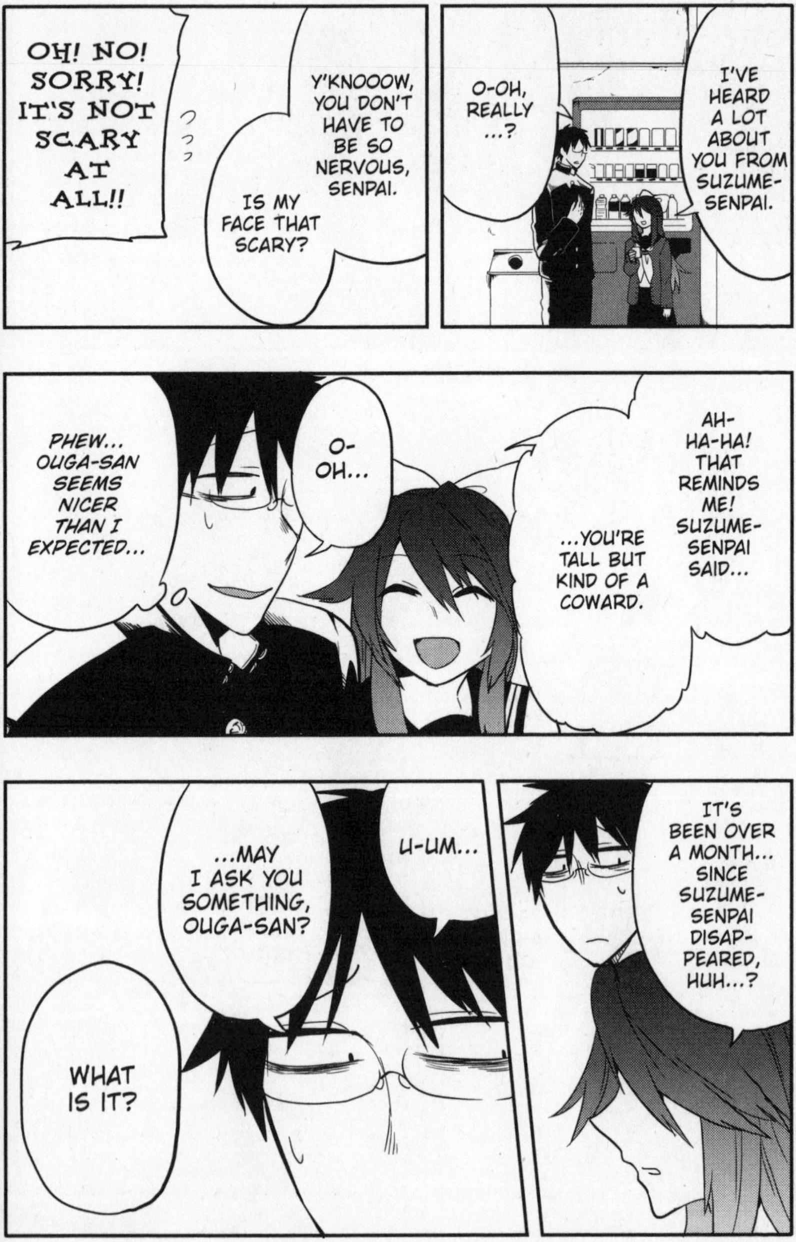
I'VE HEARD A LOT ABOUT YOU FROM SUZUME-SENPAI.
O-OH, REALLY ...?
Y'KNOOOW, YOU DON'T HAVE TO BE SO NERVOUS, SENPAI.
IS MY FACE THAT SCARY?
OH! NO! SORRY! IT'S NOT SCARY AT ALL!!
AH-HA-HA! THAT REMINDS ME! SUZUME-SENPAI SAID...
...YOU'RE TALL BUT KIND OF A COWARD.
O-OH...
PHEW... OUGA-SAN SEEMS NICER THAN I EXPECTED...
IT'S BEEN OVER A MONTH... SINCE SUZUME-SENPAI DISAPPEARED, HUH...?
U-UM...
...MAY I ASK YOU SOMETHING, OUGA-SAN?
WHAT IS IT?

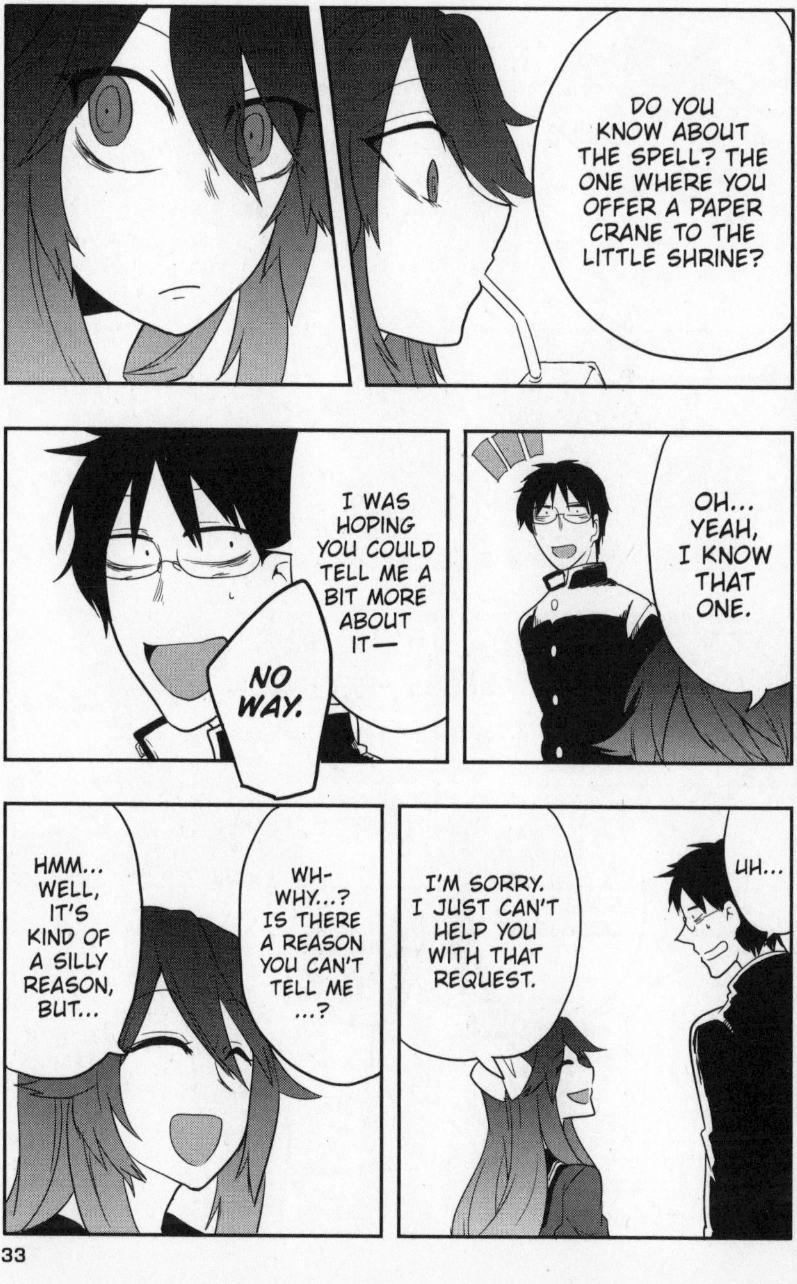
DO YOU KNOW ABOUT THE SPELL? THE ONE WHERE YOU OFFER A PAPER CRANE TO THE LITTLE SHRINE?
OH... YEAH, I KNOW THAT ONE.
I WAS HOPING YOU COULD TELL ME A BIT MORE ABOUT IT—
NO WAY.
UH...
I'M SORRY. I JUST CAN'T HELP YOU WITH THAT REQUEST.
WH- WHY...? IS THERE A REASON YOU CAN'T TELL ME ...?
HMM... WELL, IT'S KIND OF A SILLY REASON, BUT...

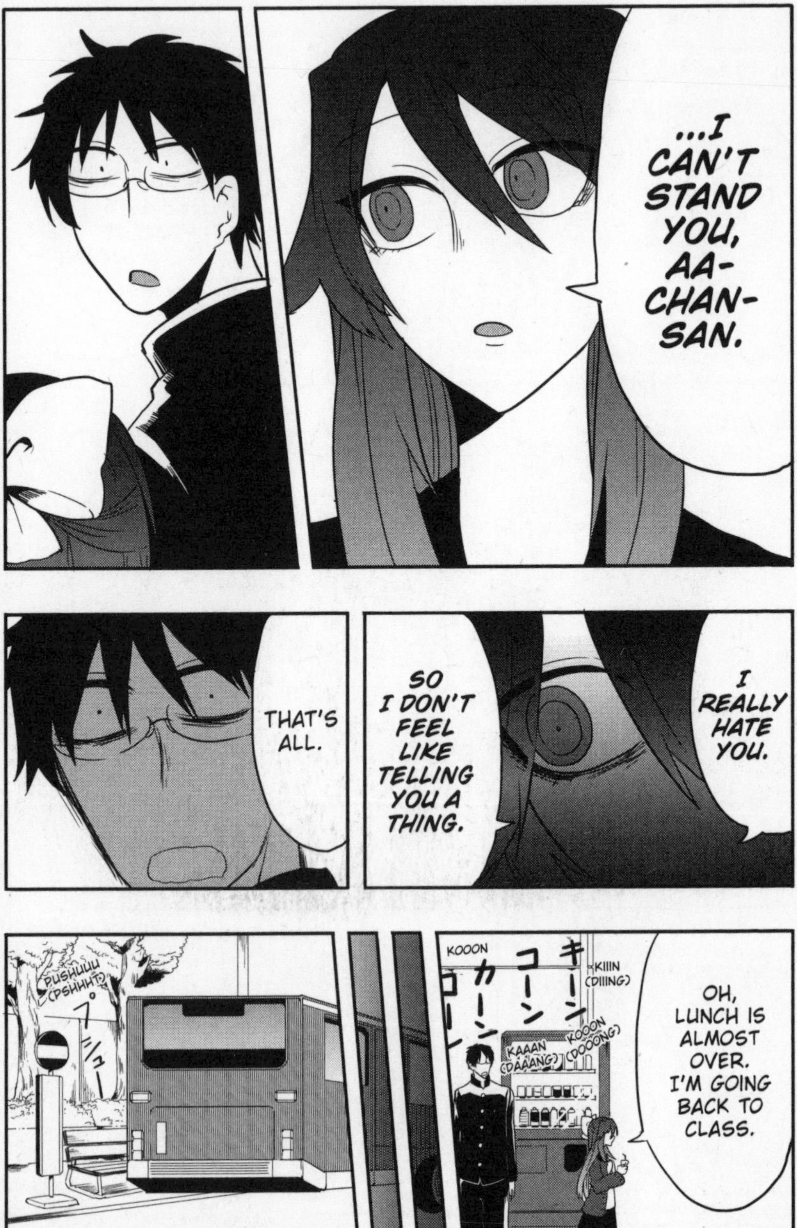
...I CAN'T STAND YOU, AA-CHAN-SAN.
I REALLY HATE YOU.
SO I DON'T FEEL LIKE TELLING YOU A THING.
THAT'S ALL.
OH, LUNCH IS ALMOST OVER. I'M GOING BACK TO CLASS.
キーン
KIIIN (DIIING)
コーン
KOOON (DOOONG)
カーン
KAAAN (DAAANG)
ローン
KOOON
プシュー
PUSHUUU (PSHHHT)

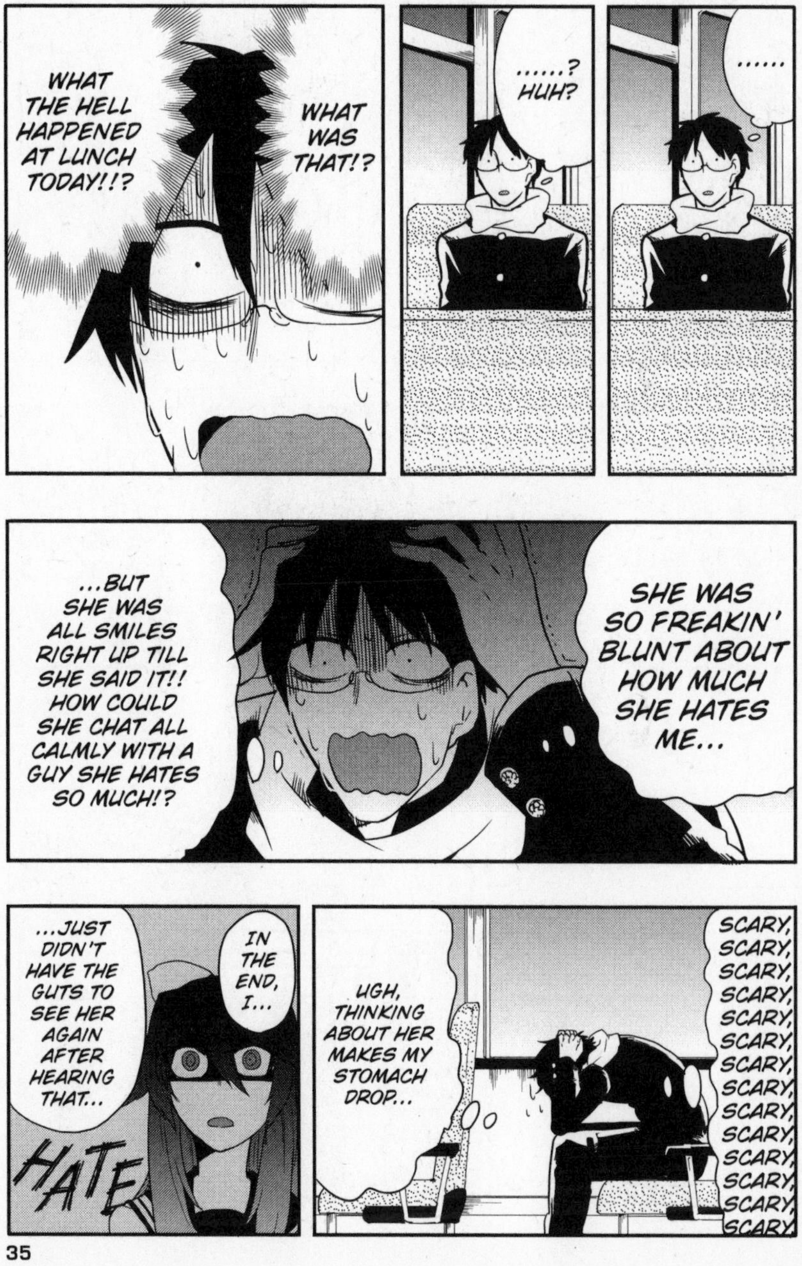
......
......? HUH?
WHAT WAS THAT!?
WHAT THE HELL HAPPENED AT LUNCH TODAY!!?
SHE WAS SO FREAKIN' BLUNT ABOUT HOW MUCH SHE HATES ME...
...BUT SHE WAS ALL SMILES RIGHT UP TILL SHE SAID IT!! HOW COULD SHE CHAT ALL CALMLY WITH A GUY SHE HATES SO MUCH!?
SCARY, SCARY, SCARY, SCARY, SCARY, SCARY, SCARY, SCARY, SCARY, SCARY, SCARY, SCARY, SCARY, SCARY, SCARY
UGH, THINKING ABOUT HER MAKES MY STOMACH DROP...
IN THE END, I...
...JUST DIDN'T HAVE THE GUTS TO SEE HER AGAIN AFTER HEARING THAT...
HATE

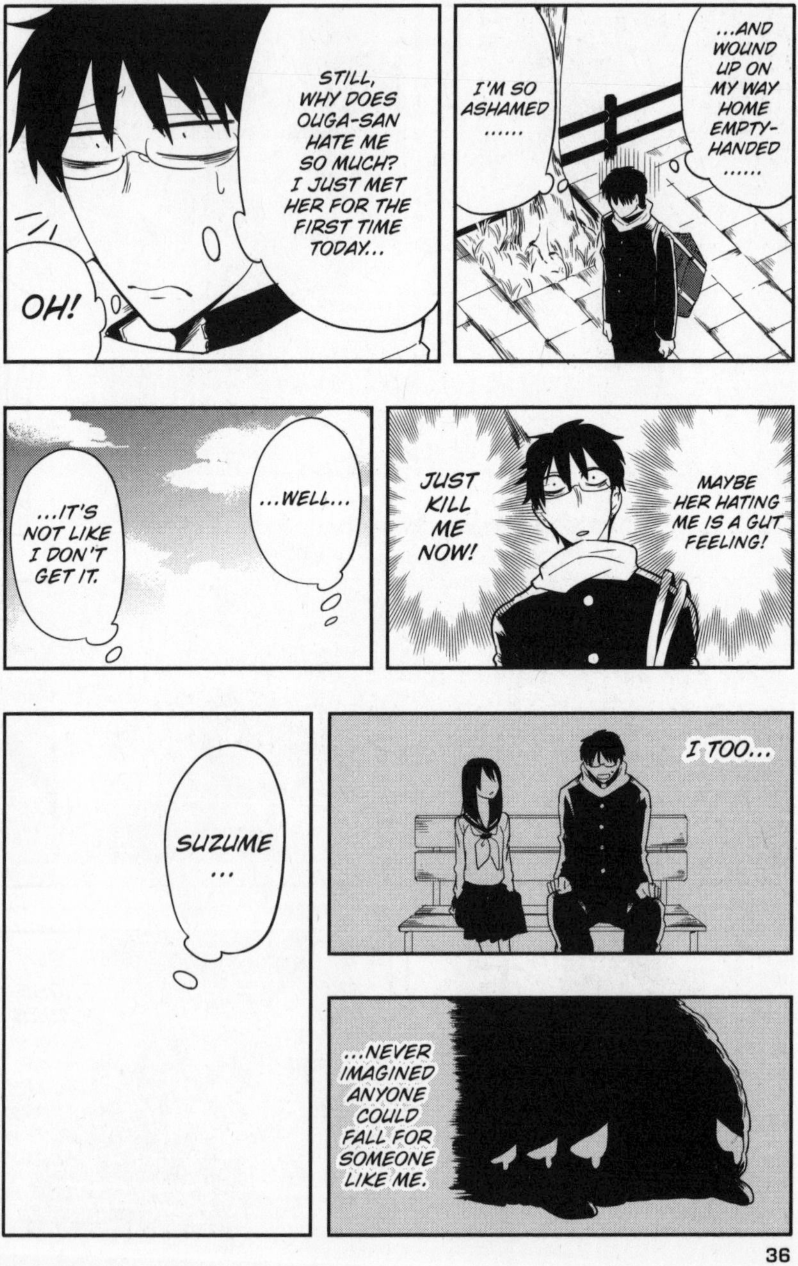
...AND WOUND UP ON MY WAY HOME EMPTY-HANDED......
I'M SO ASHAMED......
STILL, WHY DOES OUGA-SAN HATE ME SO MUCH? I JUST MET HER FOR THE FIRST TIME TODAY...
OH!
MAYBE HER HATING ME IS A GUT FEELING!
JUST KILL ME NOW!
...WELL...
...IT'S NOT LIKE I DON'T GET IT.
I TOO...
...NEVER IMAGINED ANYONE COULD FALL FOR SOMEONE LIKE ME.
SUZUME...

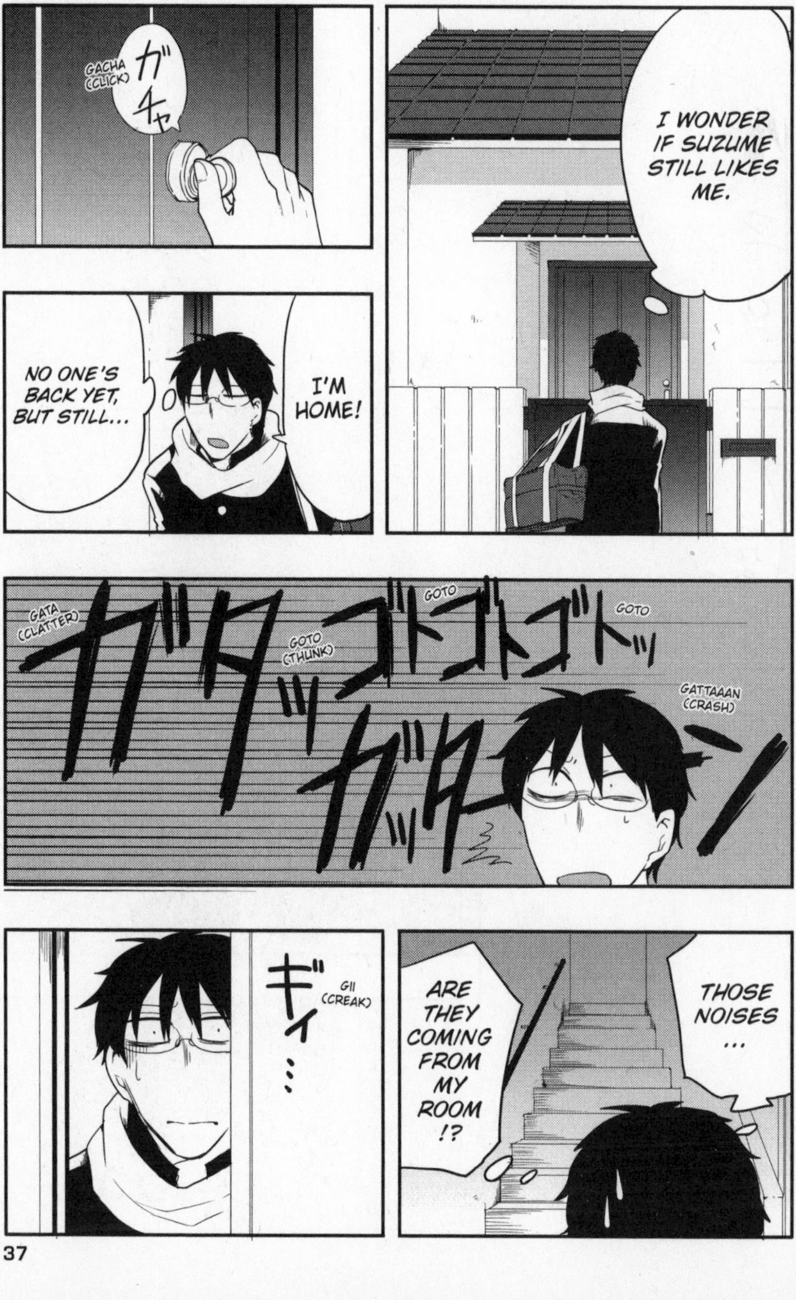
I WONDER IF SUZUME STILL LIKES ME.
ガチャ
GACHA (CLICK)
I'M HOME!
NO ONE'S BACK YET, BUT STILL...
GOTO
GATTAAAN (CRASH)
ゴトゴトゴトッ
GOTO
GOTO (THUNK)
ガタッ
GATA (CLATTER)
ガターン
THOSE NOISES...
ARE THEY COMING FROM MY ROOM!?
ギィ…
GII (CREAK)

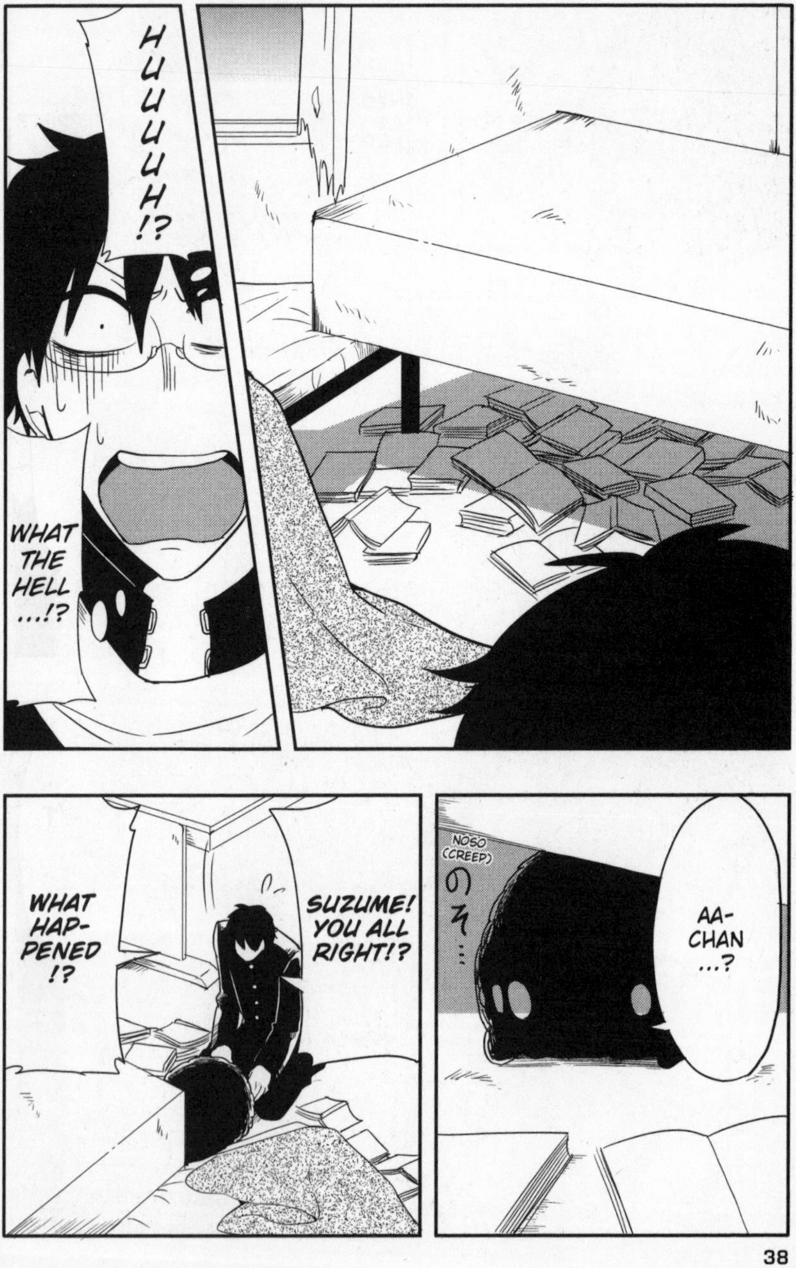
HUUUUUH!?
WHAT THE HELL...!?
NOSO (CREEP)
のそ…
AA-CHAN...?
SUZUME! YOU ALL RIGHT!?
WHAT HAPPENED!?

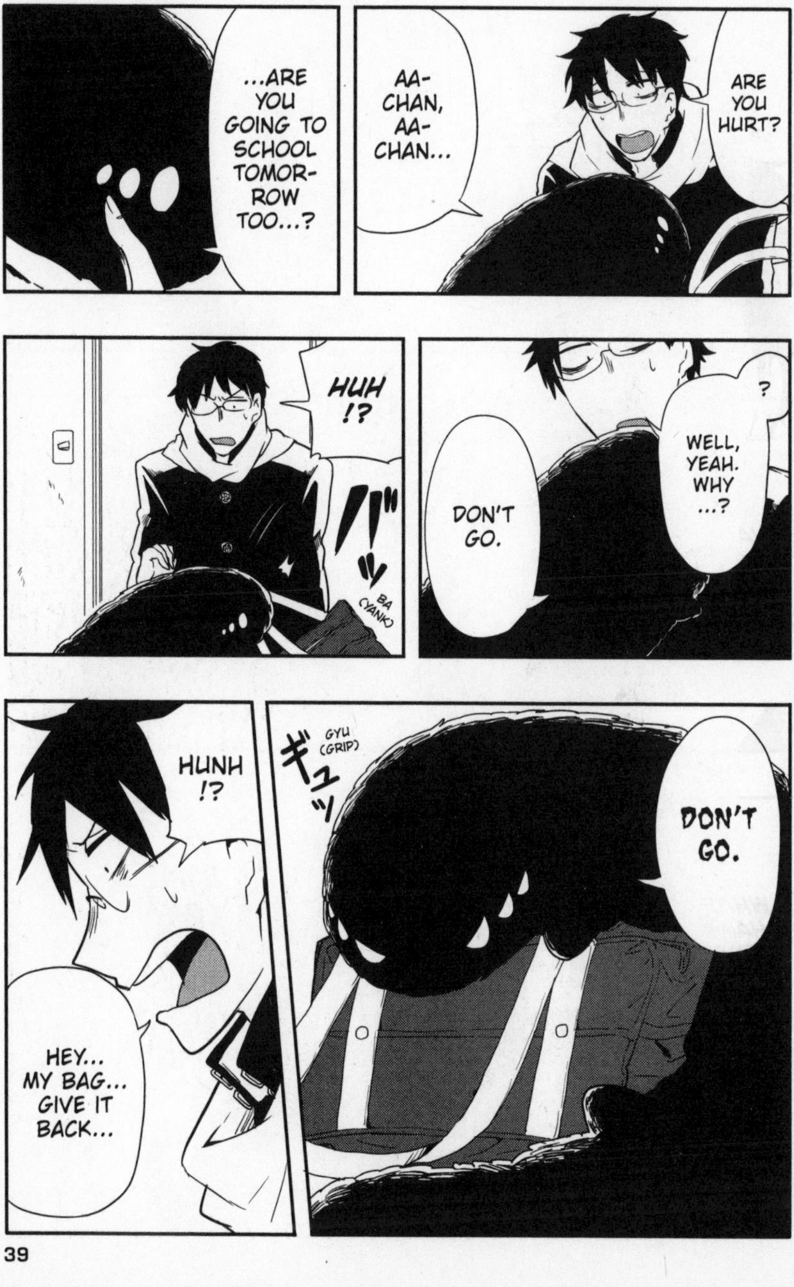
ARE YOU HURT?
AA-CHAN, AA-CHAN...
...ARE YOU GOING TO SCHOOL TOMORROW TOO...?
?
WELL, YEAH. WHY...?
DON'T GO.
HUH!?
BA (YANK)
ギュッ
GYU (GRIP)
DON'T GO.
HUNH!?
HEY... MY BAG... GIVE IT BACK...

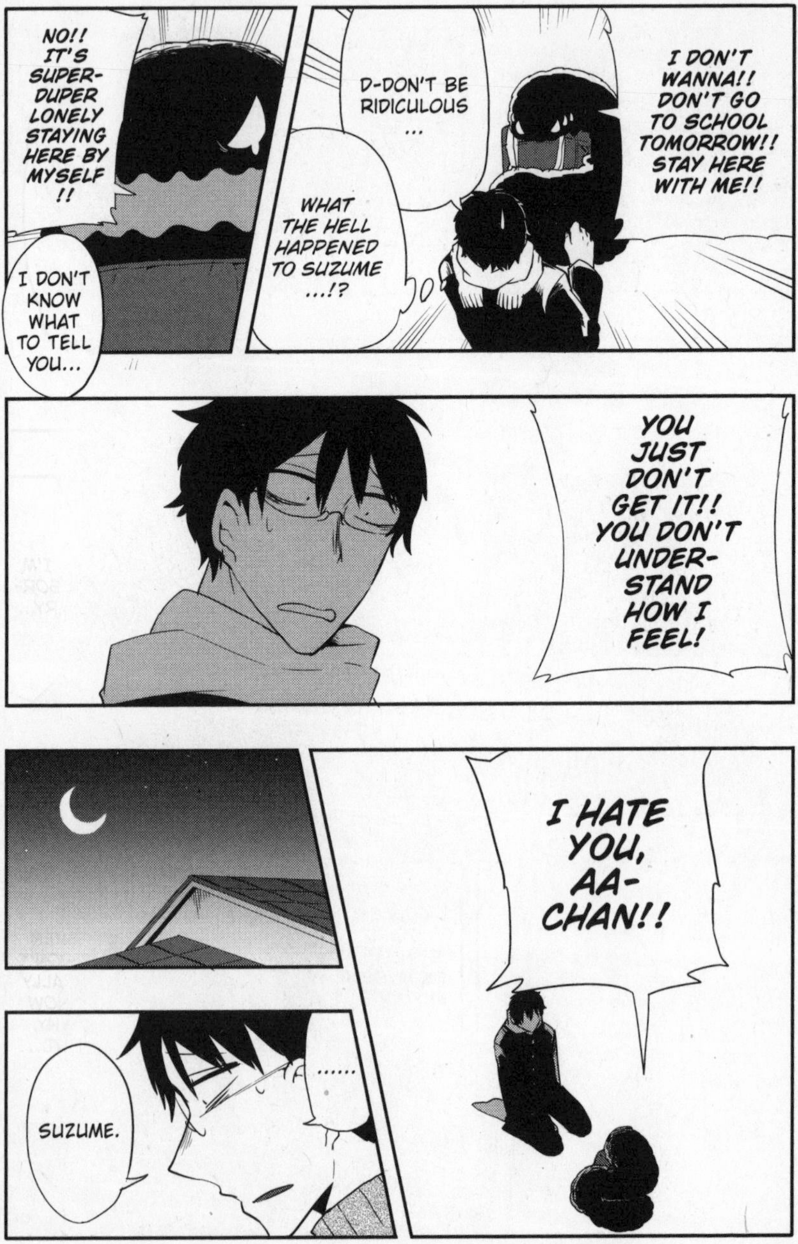

I DON'T WANNA!! DON'T GO TO SCHOOL TOMORROW!! STAY HERE WITH ME!!
D-DON'T BE RIDICULOUS ...
WHAT THE HELL HAPPENED TO SUZUME ...!?
NO!! IT'S SUPER-DUPER LONELY STAYING HERE BY MYSELF !!
I DON'T KNOW WHAT TO TELL YOU...
YOU JUST DON'T GET IT!! YOU DON'T UNDERSTAND HOW I FEEL!
I HATE YOU, AA-CHAN!!
......
SUZUME.

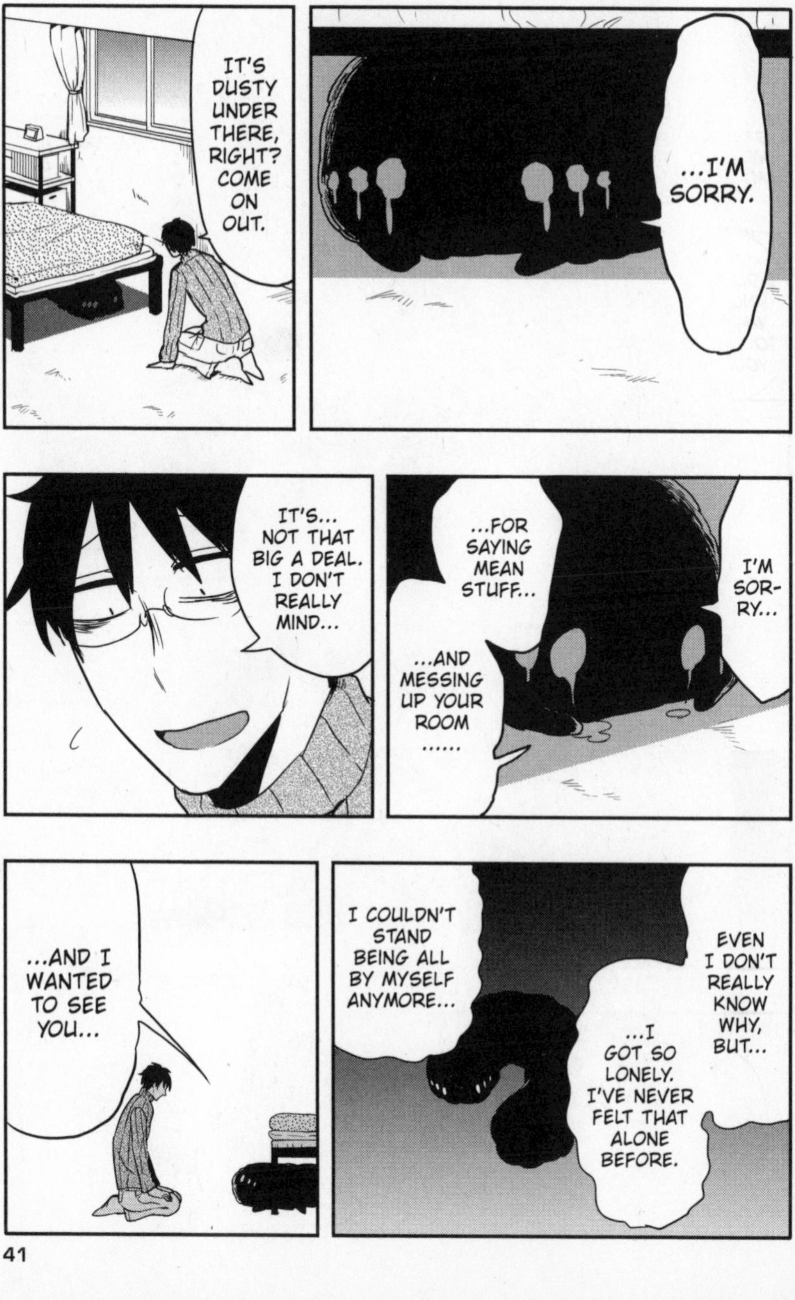
...I'M SORRY.
IT'S DUSTY UNDER THERE, RIGHT? COME ON OUT.
I'M SORRY...
...FOR SAYING MEAN STUFF...
...AND MESSING UP YOUR ROOM ......
IT'S... NOT THAT BIG A DEAL. I DON'T REALLY MIND...
EVEN I DON'T REALLY KNOW WHY, BUT...
...I GOT SO LONELY. I'VE NEVER FELT THAT ALONE BEFORE.
I COULDN'T STAND BEING ALL BY MYSELF ANYMORE...
...AND I WANTED TO SEE YOU...

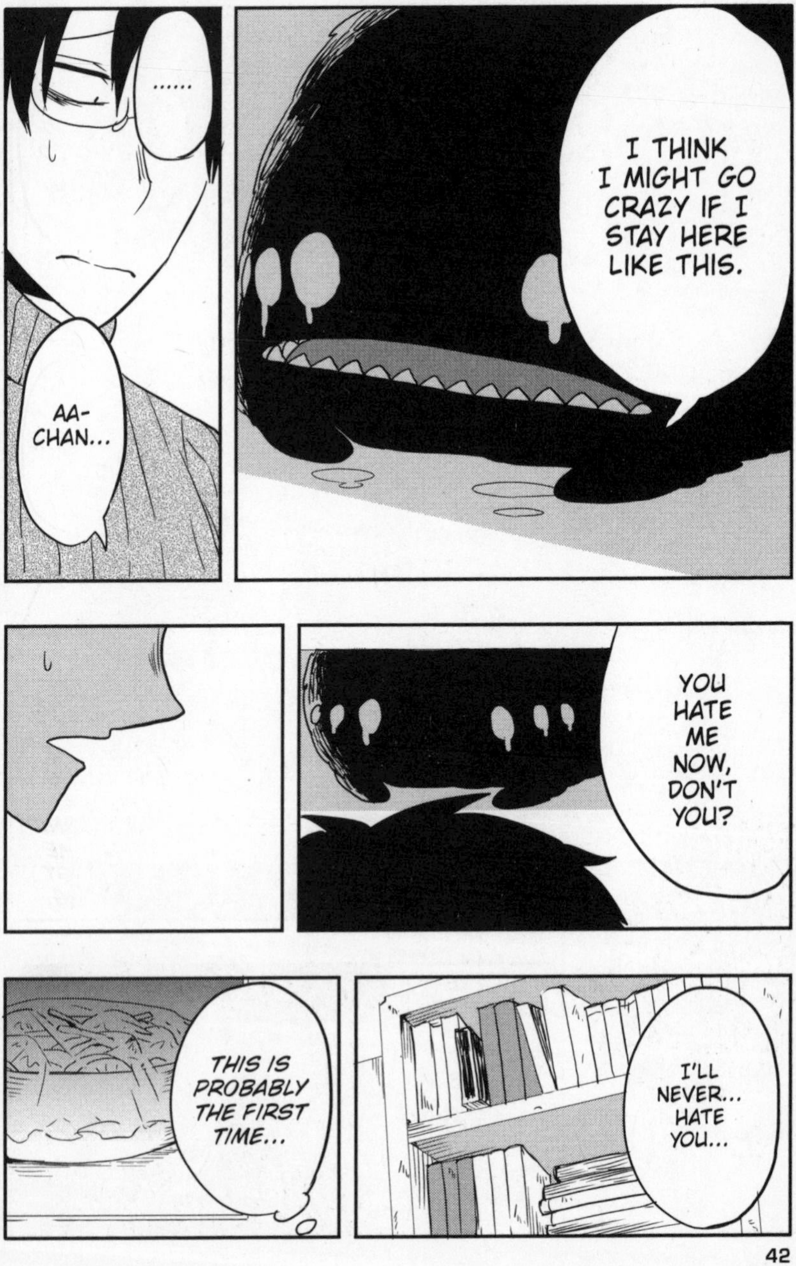
I THINK I MIGHT GO CRAZY IF I STAY HERE LIKE THIS.
......
AA-CHAN...
YOU HATE ME NOW, DON'T YOU?
I'LL NEVER... HATE YOU...
THIS IS PROBABLY THE FIRST TIME...

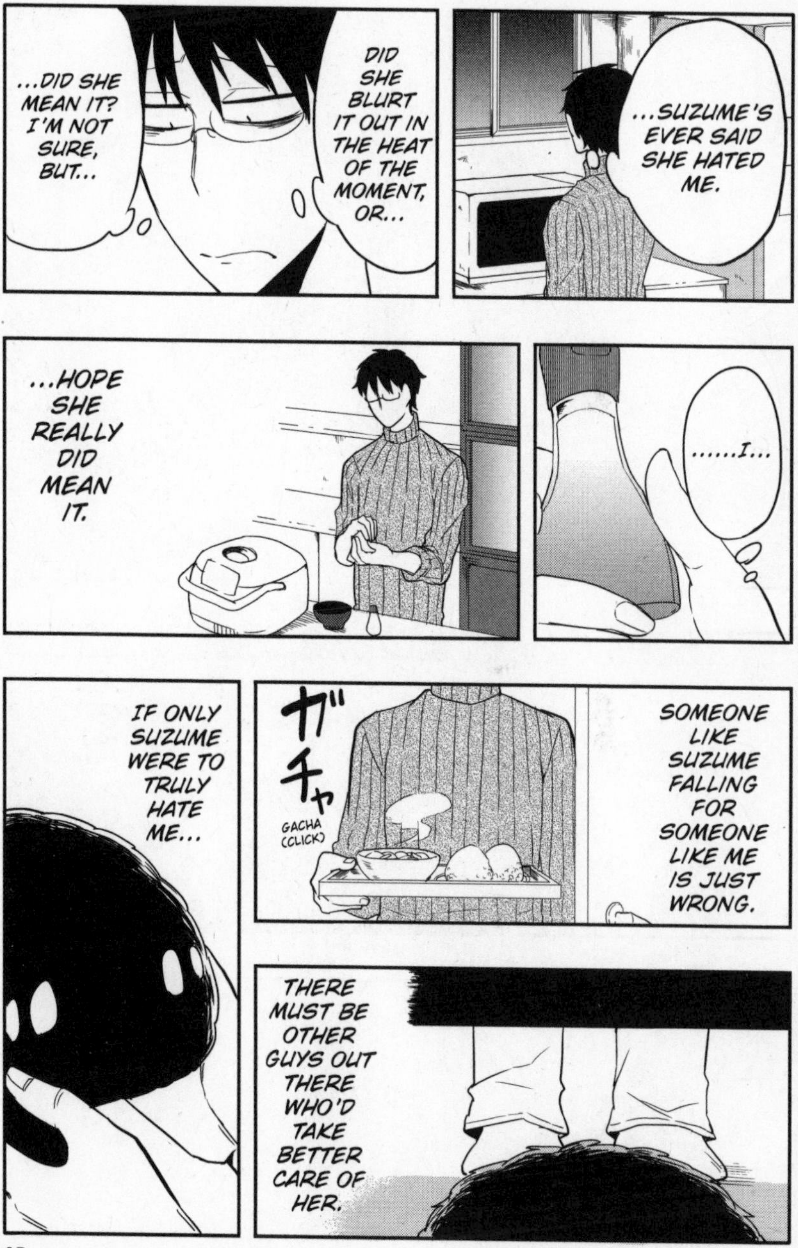
...SUZUME'S EVER SAID SHE HATED ME.
DID SHE BLURT IT OUT IN THE HEAT OF THE MOMENT, OR...
...DID SHE MEAN IT? I'M NOT SURE, BUT...
......I...
...HOPE SHE REALLY DID MEAN IT.
SOMEONE LIKE SUZUME FALLING FOR SOMEONE LIKE ME IS JUST WRONG.
ガチャ
GACHA (CLICK)
THERE MUST BE OTHER GUYS OUT THERE WHO'D TAKE BETTER CARE OF HER.
IF ONLY SUZUME WERE TO TRULY HATE ME...

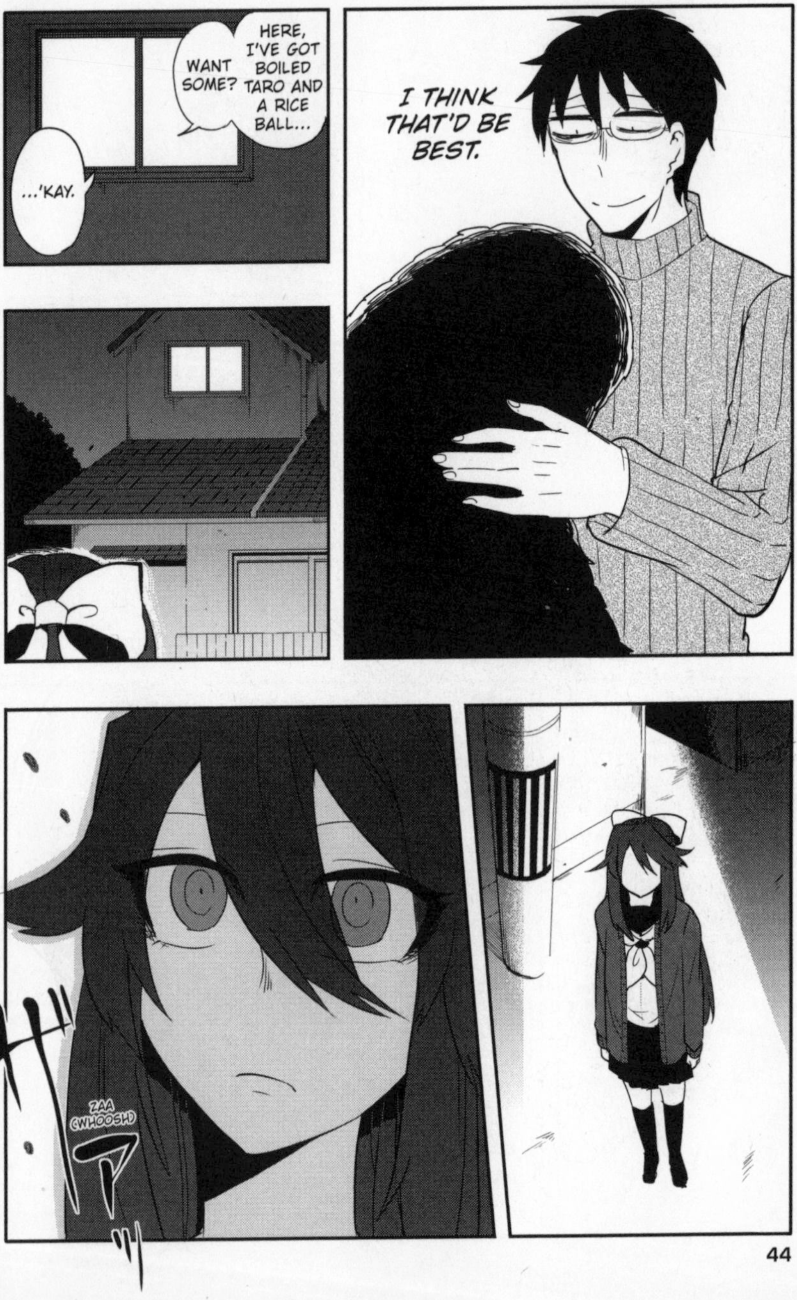
I THINK THAT'D BE BEST.
HERE, I'VE GOT BOILED TARO AND A RICE BALL...
WANT SOME?
...'KAY.
ZAA (WHOOSH)

Chapter 3

THE WAYSIDE SHRINE AND BEING HUMAN

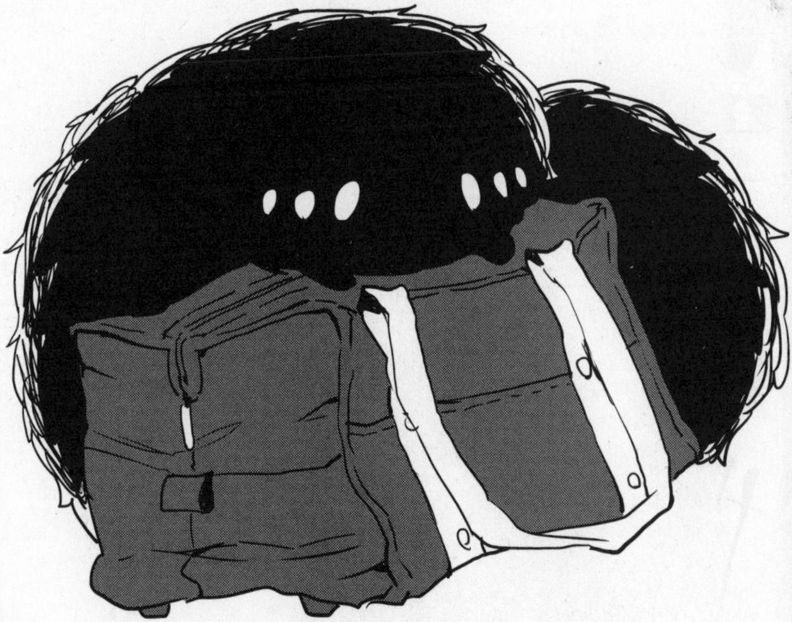

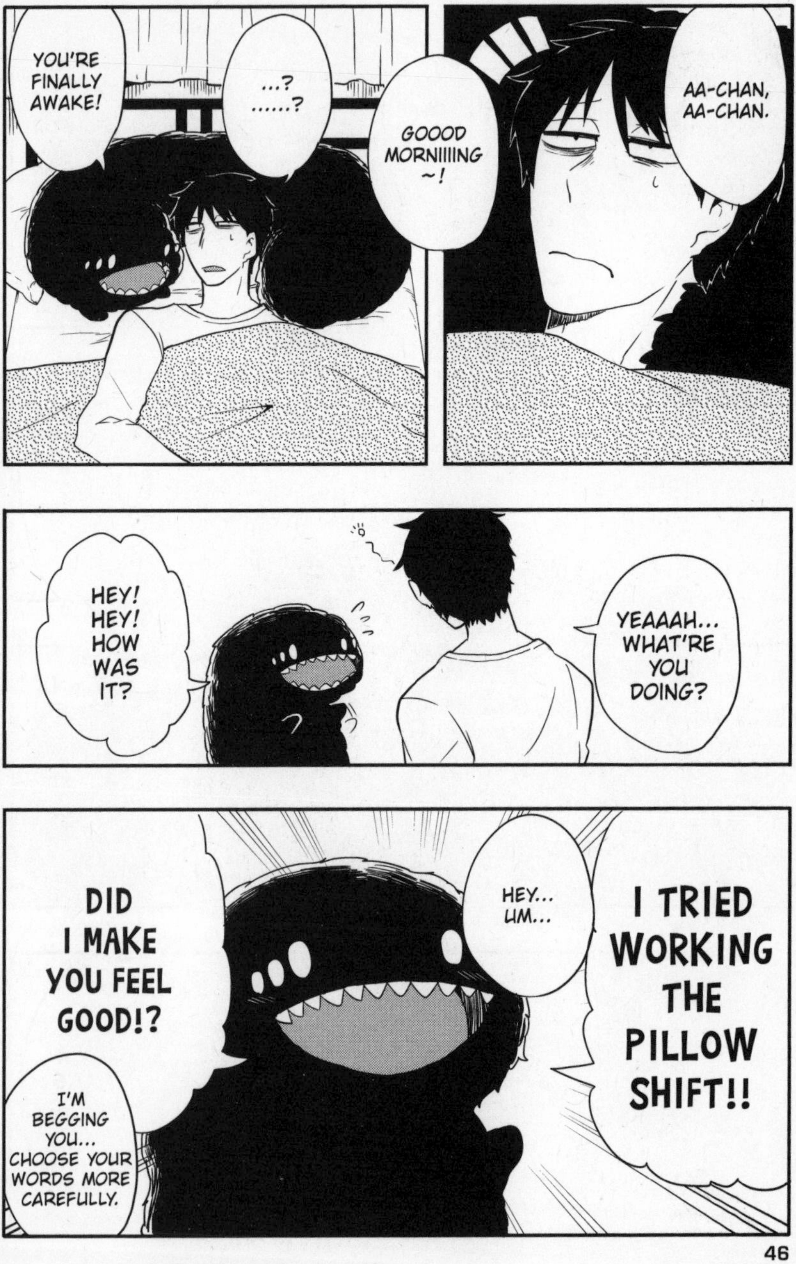
AA-CHAN, AA-CHAN.
GOOOD MORNIIIING ~!
...? ......?
YOU'RE FINALLY AWAKE!
YEAAAH... WHAT'RE YOU DOING?
HEY! HEY! HOW WAS IT?
I TRIED WORKING THE PILLOW SHIFT!!
HEY... UM...
DID I MAKE YOU FEEL GOOD!?
I'M BEGGING YOU... CHOOSE YOUR WORDS MORE CAREFULLY.

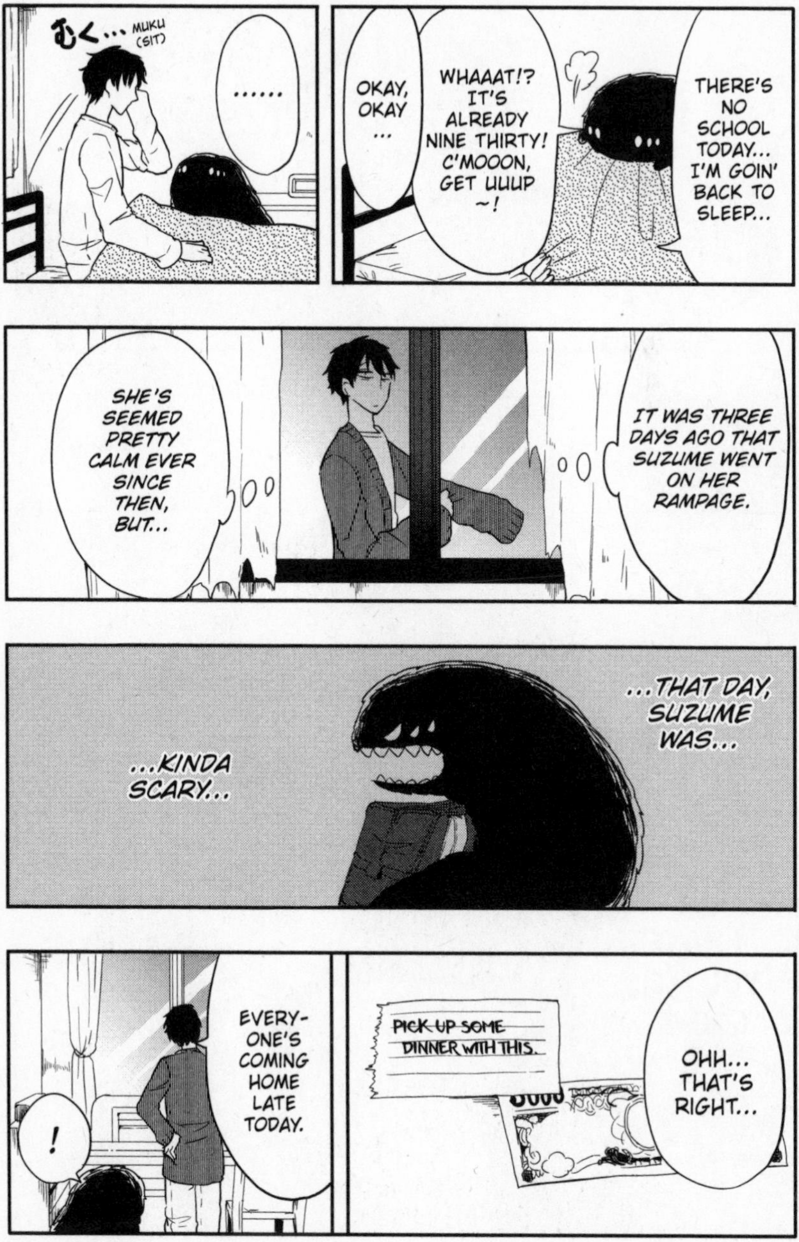
THERE'S NO SCHOOL TODAY... I'M GOIN' BACK TO SLEEP...
WHAAAT!? IT'S ALREADY NINE THIRTY! C'MOOON, GET UUUP ~!
OKAY, OKAY ...
むく… MUKU (SIT)
......
IT WAS THREE DAYS AGO THAT SUZUME WENT ON HER RAMPAGE.
SHE'S SEEMED PRETTY CALM EVER SINCE THEN, BUT...
...THAT DAY, SUZUME WAS...
...KINDA SCARY...
OHH... THAT'S RIGHT...
PICK UP SOME DINNER WITH THIS.
EVERY-ONE'S COMING HOME LATE TODAY.
!

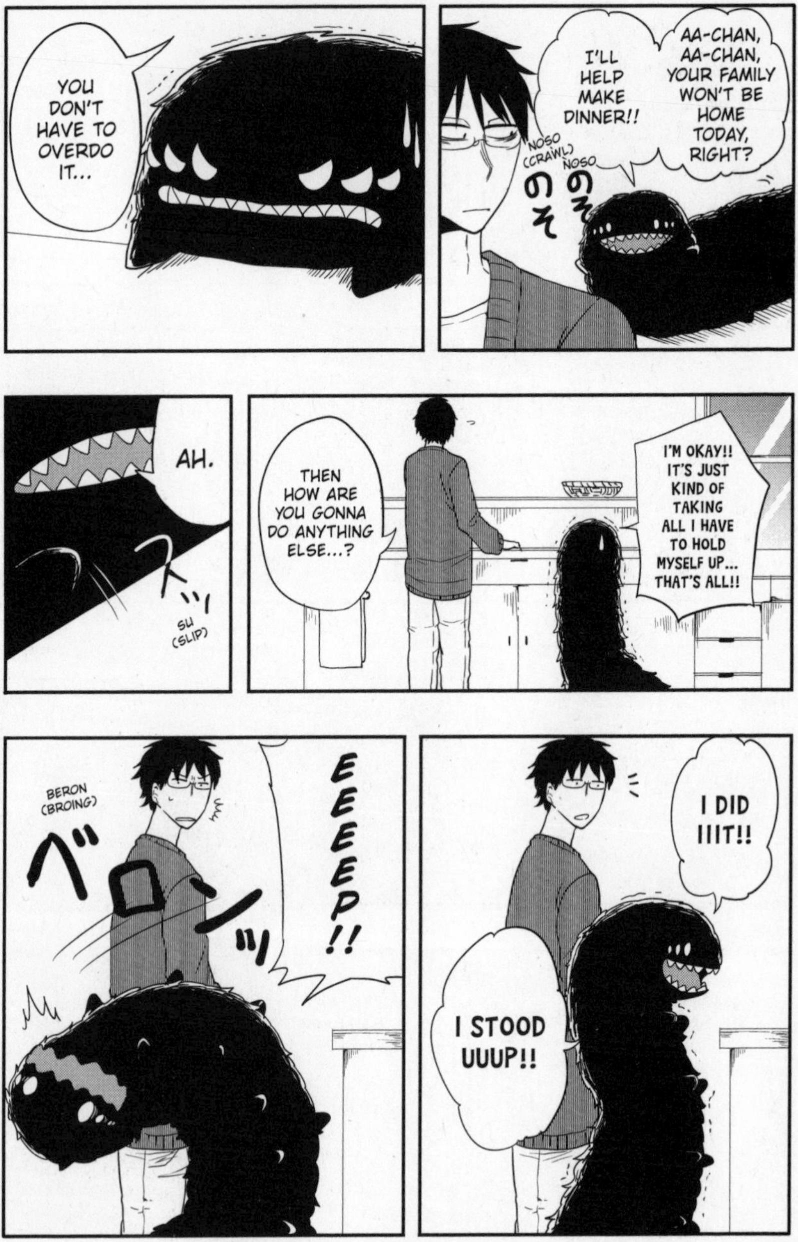
AA-CHAN, AA-CHAN, YOUR FAMILY WON'T BE HOME TODAY, RIGHT?
I'LL HELP MAKE DINNER!!
NOSO (CRAWL) NOSO
のそのそ
YOU DON'T HAVE TO OVERDO IT...
I'M OKAY!! IT'S JUST KIND OF TAKING ALL I HAVE TO HOLD MYSELF UP... THAT'S ALL!!
THEN HOW ARE YOU GONNA DO ANYTHING ELSE...?
AH.
スッ
SU (SLIP)
I DID IIIT!!
I STOOD UUUP!!
EEEEP!!
BERON (BROING)
べローンッ

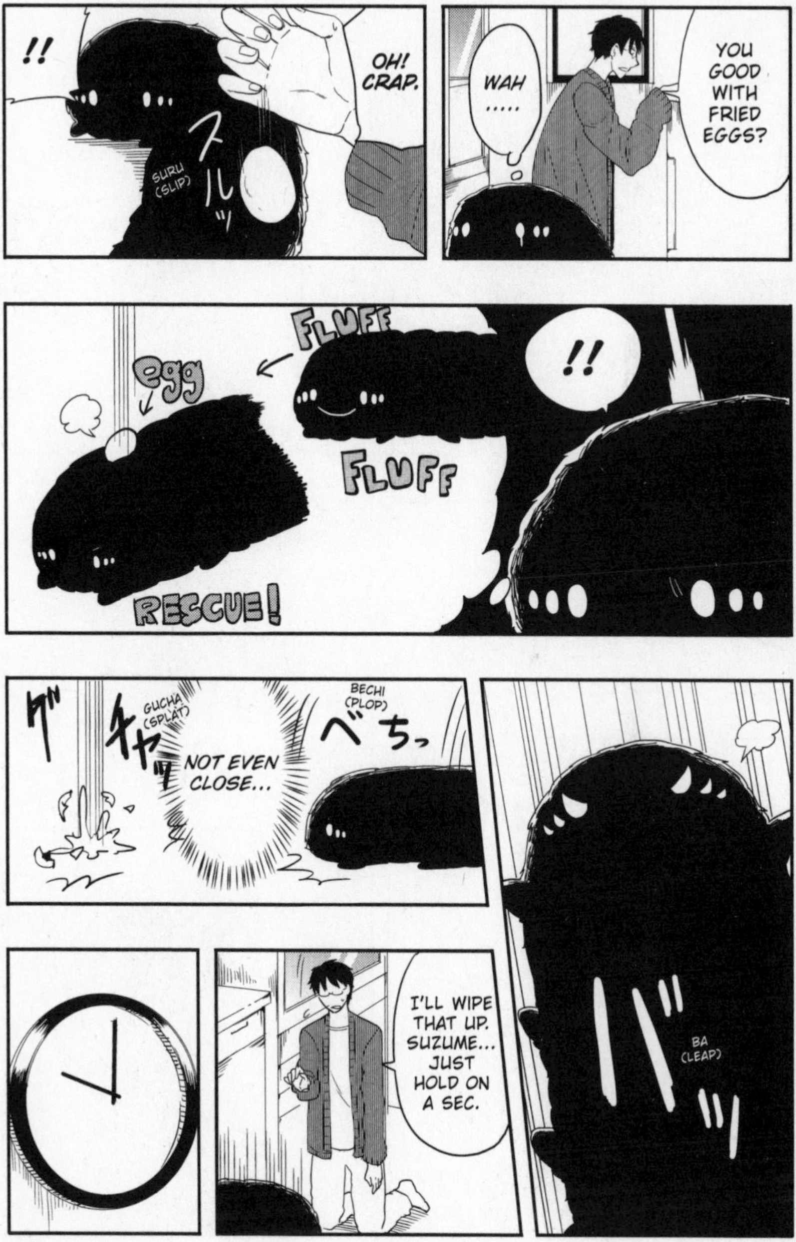
YOU GOOD WITH FRIED EGGS?
WAH .....
!!
OH! CRAP.
SURU (SLIP)
!!
FLUFF
egg
FLUFF
RESCUE!
BA (LEAP)
BECHI (PLOP)
NOT EVEN CLOSE...
GUCHA (SPLAT)
I'LL WIPE THAT UP. SUZUME... JUST HOLD ON A SEC.

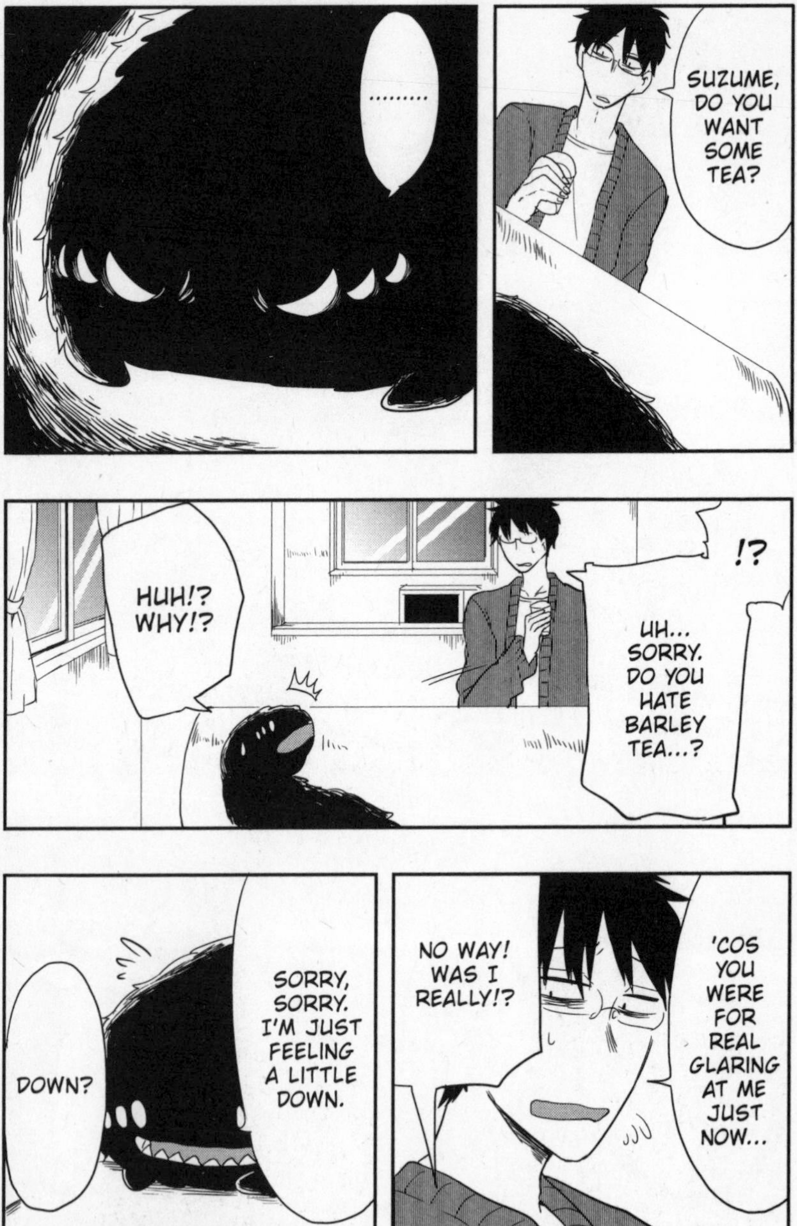
SUZUME, DO YOU WANT SOME TEA?
....
!?
UH... SORRY. DO YOU HATE BARLEY TEA...?
HUH!? WHY!?
'COS YOU WERE FOR REAL GLARING AT ME JUST NOW...
NO WAY! WAS I REALLY!?
SORRY, SORRY. I'M JUST FEELING A LITTLE DOWN.
DOWN?

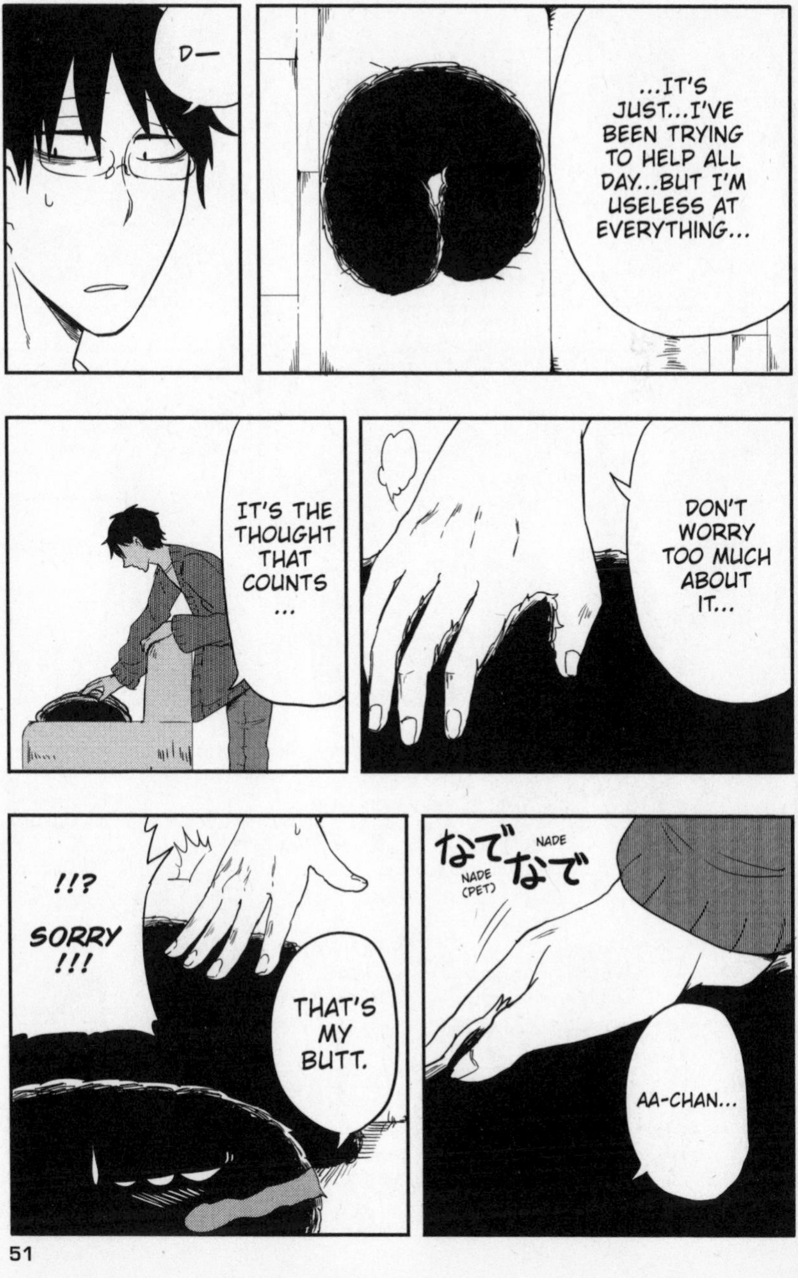
...IT'S JUST...I'VE BEEN TRYING TO HELP ALL DAY...BUT I'M USELESS AT EVERYTHING...
D—
DON'T WORRY TOO MUCH ABOUT IT...
IT'S THE THOUGHT THAT COUNTS...
なでなで
NADE
NADE (PET)
AA-CHAN...
THAT'S MY BUTT.
!!?
SORRY!!!

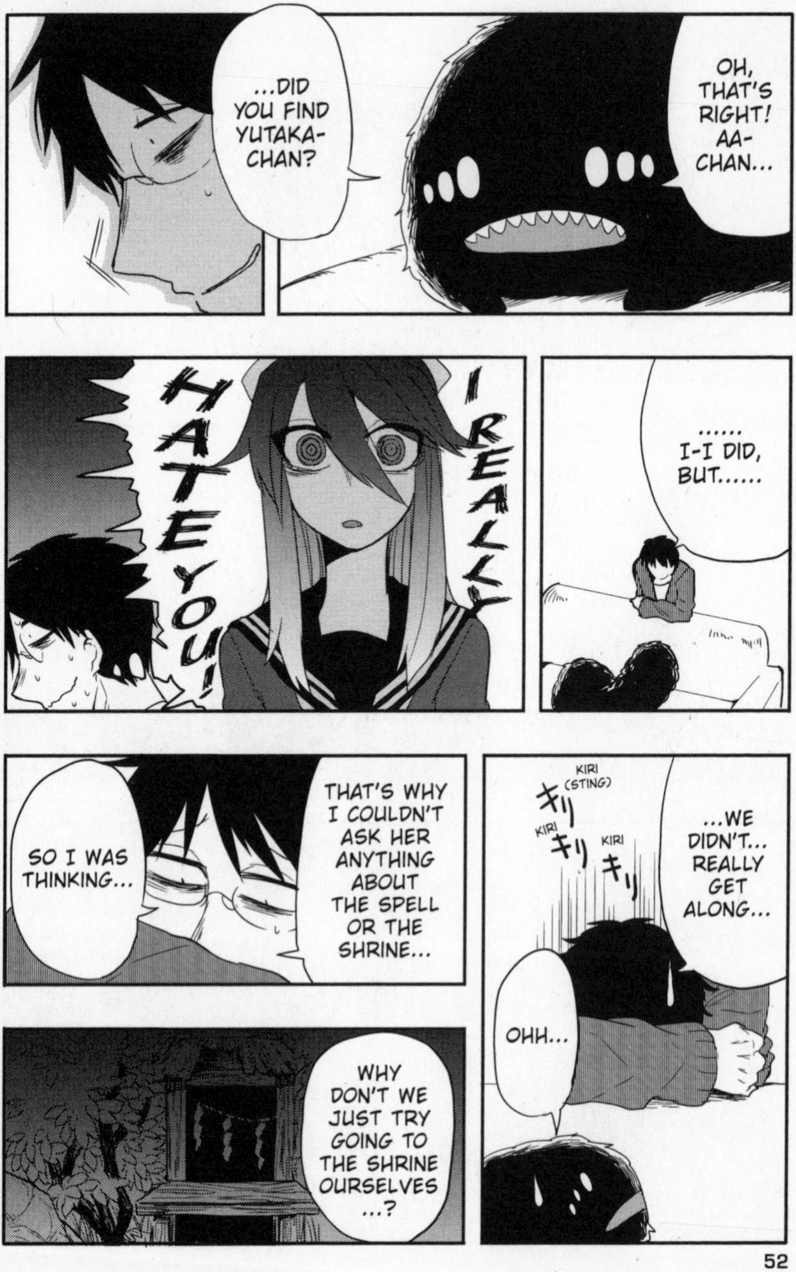
OH, THAT'S RIGHT! AA-CHAN...
...DID YOU FIND YUTAKA-CHAN?
...... I-I DID, BUT......
I REALLY HATE YOU!
KIRI (STING)
キリ
KIRI
キリ
KIRI
キリ
...WE DIDN'T... REALLY GET ALONG...
OHH...
THAT'S WHY I COULDN'T ASK HER ANYTHING ABOUT THE SPELL OR THE SHRINE...
SO I WAS THINKING...
WHY DON'T WE JUST TRY GOING TO THE SHRINE OURSELVES ...?

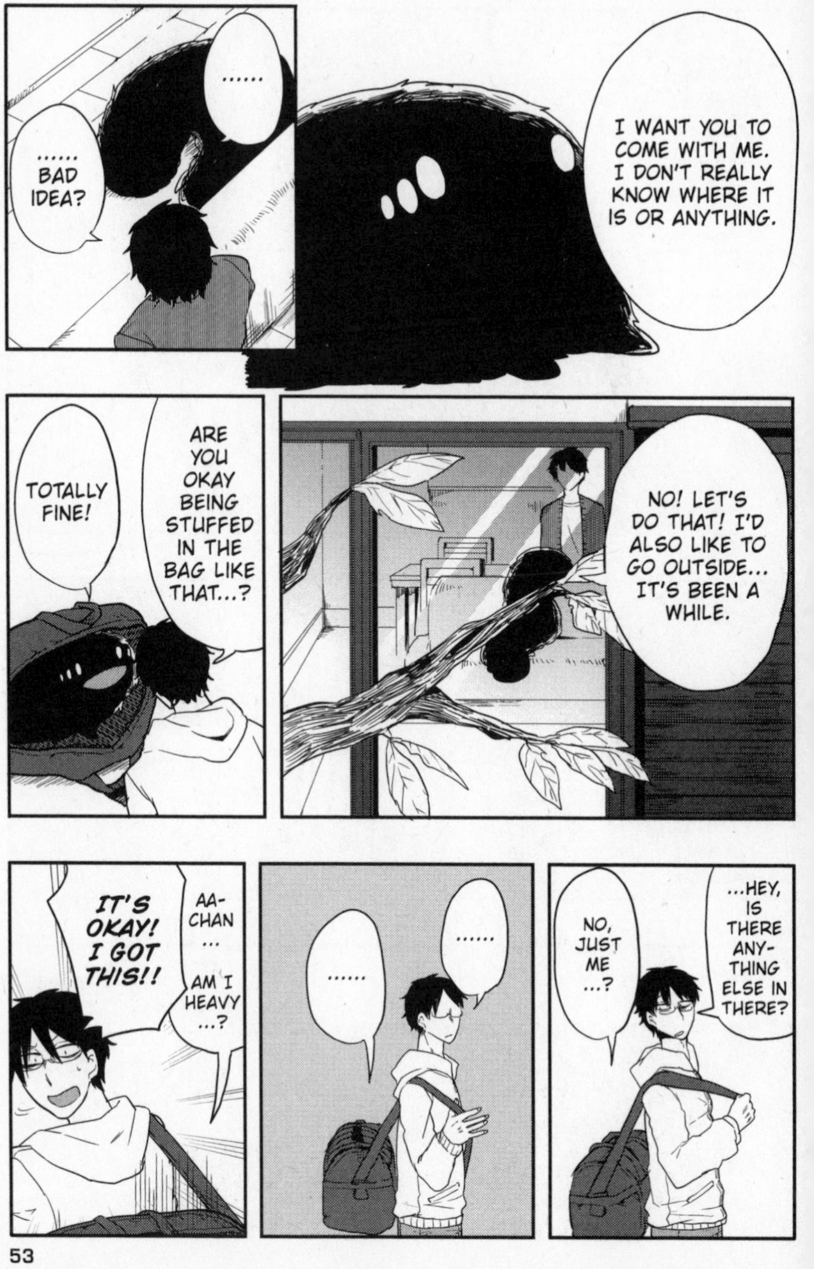
I WANT YOU TO COME WITH ME. I DON'T REALLY KNOW WHERE IT IS OR ANYTHING.
......
...... BAD IDEA?
NO! LET'S DO THAT! I'D ALSO LIKE TO GO OUTSIDE... IT'S BEEN A WHILE.
ARE YOU OKAY BEING STUFFED IN THE BAG LIKE THAT...?
TOTALLY FINE!
...HEY, IS THERE ANYTHING ELSE IN THERE?
NO, JUST ME ...?
......
......
AA-CHAN ... AM I HEAVY ...?
IT'S OKAY! I GOT THIS!!

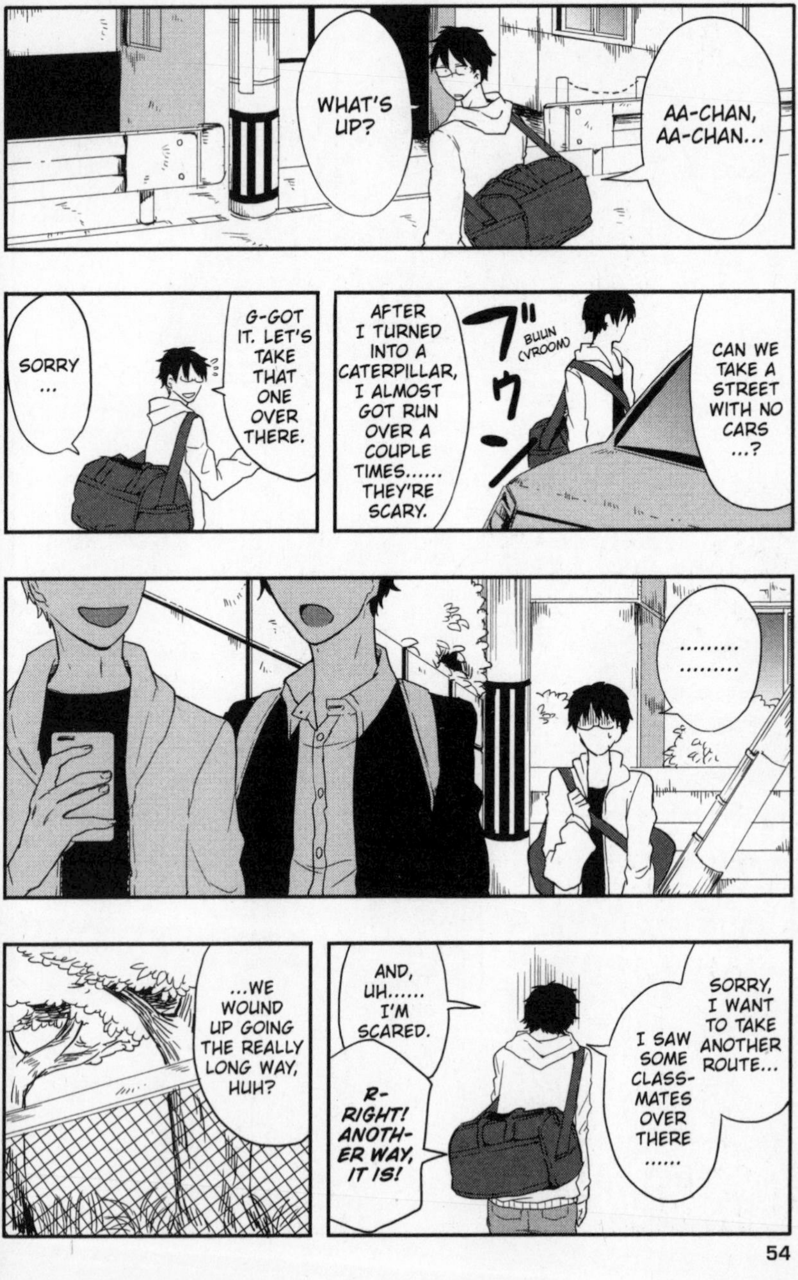
AA-CHAN, AA-CHAN...
WHAT'S UP?
CAN WE TAKE A STREET WITH NO CARS ...?
ブウー
BUUN (VROOM)
AFTER I TURNED INTO A CATERPILLAR, I ALMOST GOT RUN OVER A COUPLE TIMES...... THEY'RE SCARY.
G-GOT IT. LET'S TAKE THAT ONE OVER THERE.
SORRY ...
....
SORRY, I WANT TO TAKE ANOTHER ROUTE...
I SAW SOME CLASS-MATES OVER THERE ......
AND, UH...... I'M SCARED.
R-RIGHT! ANOTHER WAY, IT IS!
...WE WOUND UP GOING THE REALLY LONG WAY, HUH?

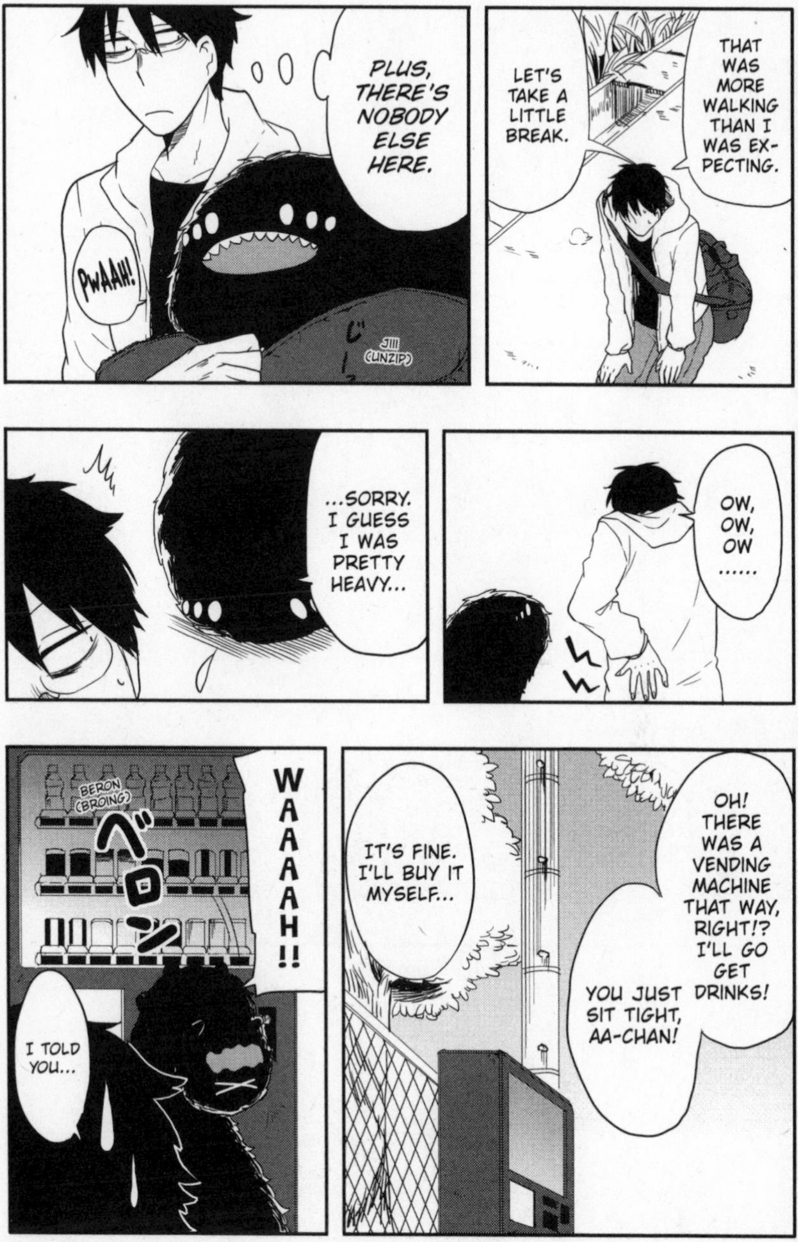
THAT WAS MORE WALKING THAN I WAS EX-PECTING.
LET'S TAKE A LITTLE BREAK.
PLUS, THERE'S NOBODY ELSE HERE.
PwAAH!
JIII (UNZIP)
OW, OW, OW ......
...SORRY. I GUESS I WAS PRETTY HEAVY...
OH! THERE WAS A VENDING MACHINE THAT WAY, RIGHT!? I'LL GO GET DRINKS!
YOU JUST SIT TIGHT, AA-CHAN!
IT'S FINE. I'LL BUY IT MYSELF...
WAAAAAH!!
BERON (BROING)
ベロン
I TOLD YOU...

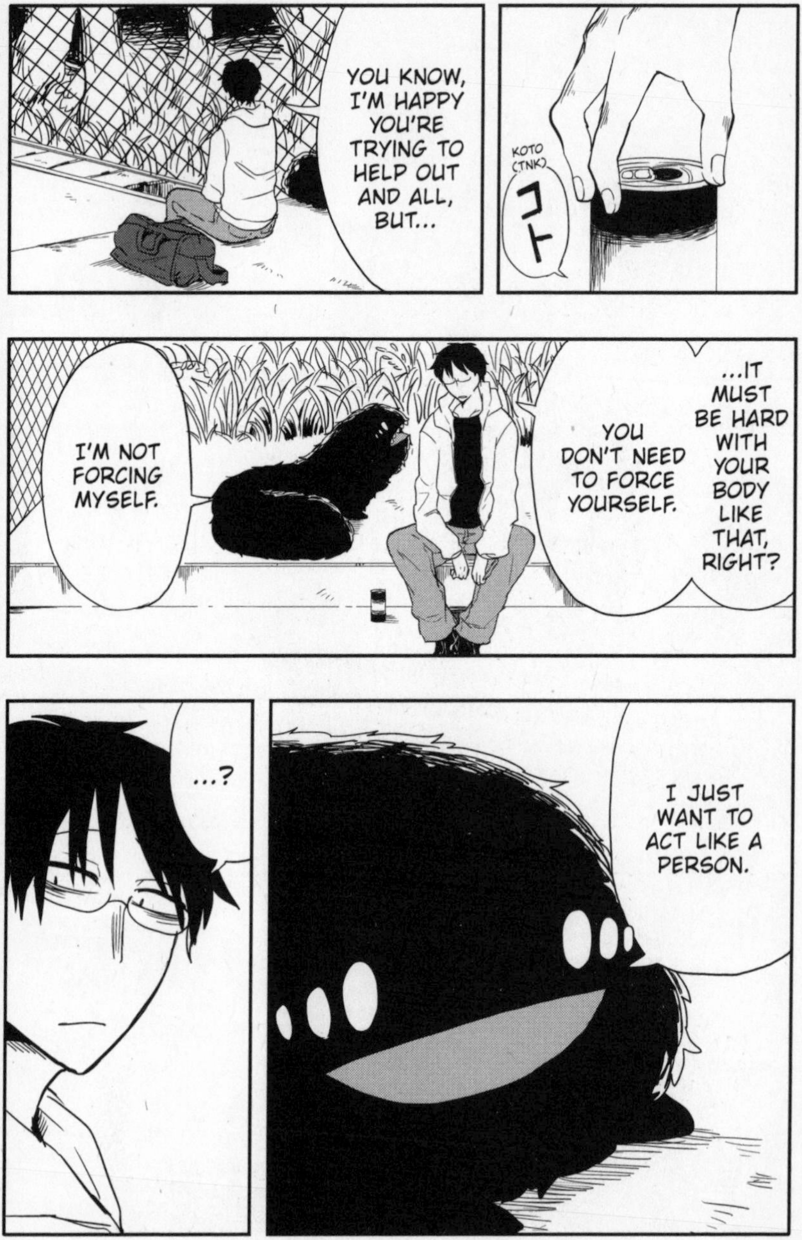
KOTO (TNK)
コト
YOU KNOW, I'M HAPPY YOU'RE TRYING TO HELP OUT AND ALL, BUT...
...IT MUST BE HARD WITH YOUR BODY LIKE THAT, RIGHT?
YOU DON'T NEED TO FORCE YOURSELF.
I'M NOT FORCING MYSELF.
I JUST WANT TO ACT LIKE A PERSON.
...?

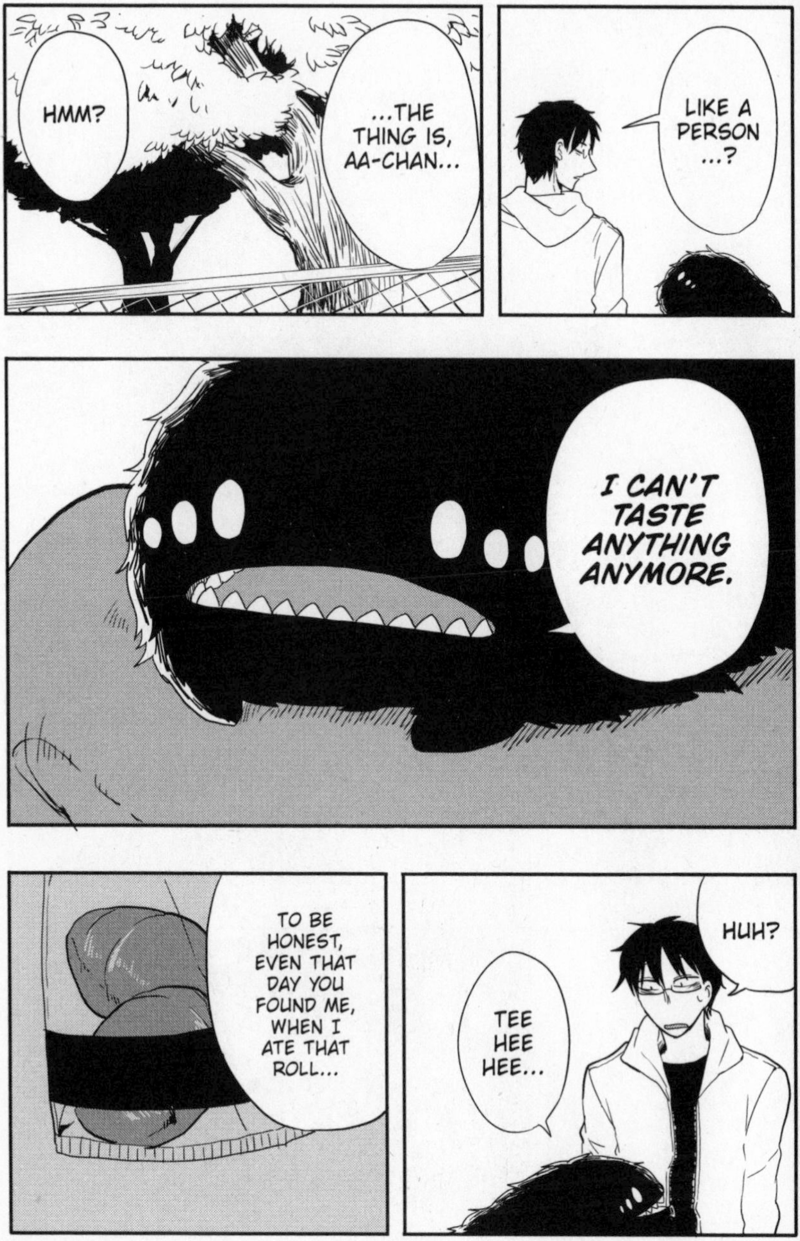
LIKE A PERSON ...?
...THE THING IS, AA-CHAN...
HMM?
I CAN'T TASTE ANYTHING ANYMORE.
HUH?
TEE HEE HEE...
TO BE HONEST, EVEN THAT DAY YOU FOUND ME, WHEN I ATE THAT ROLL...

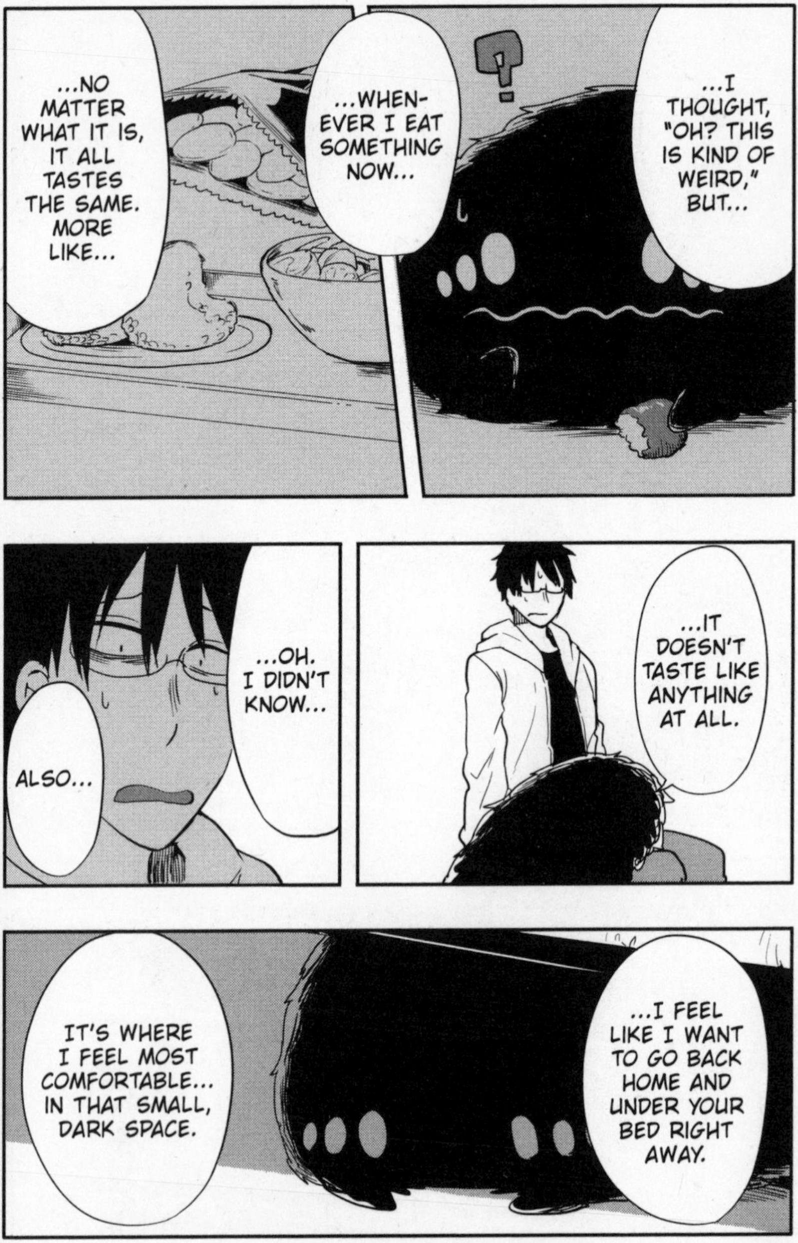
?
...I THOUGHT, "OH? THIS IS KIND OF WEIRD," BUT...
...WHEN-EVER I EAT SOMETHING NOW...
...NO MATTER WHAT IT IS, IT ALL TASTES THE SAME. MORE LIKE...
...IT DOESN'T TASTE LIKE ANYTHING AT ALL.
...OH. I DIDN'T KNOW...
ALSO...
...I FEEL LIKE I WANT TO GO BACK HOME AND UNDER YOUR BED RIGHT AWAY.
IT'S WHERE I FEEL MOST COMFORTABLE... IN THAT SMALL, DARK SPACE.

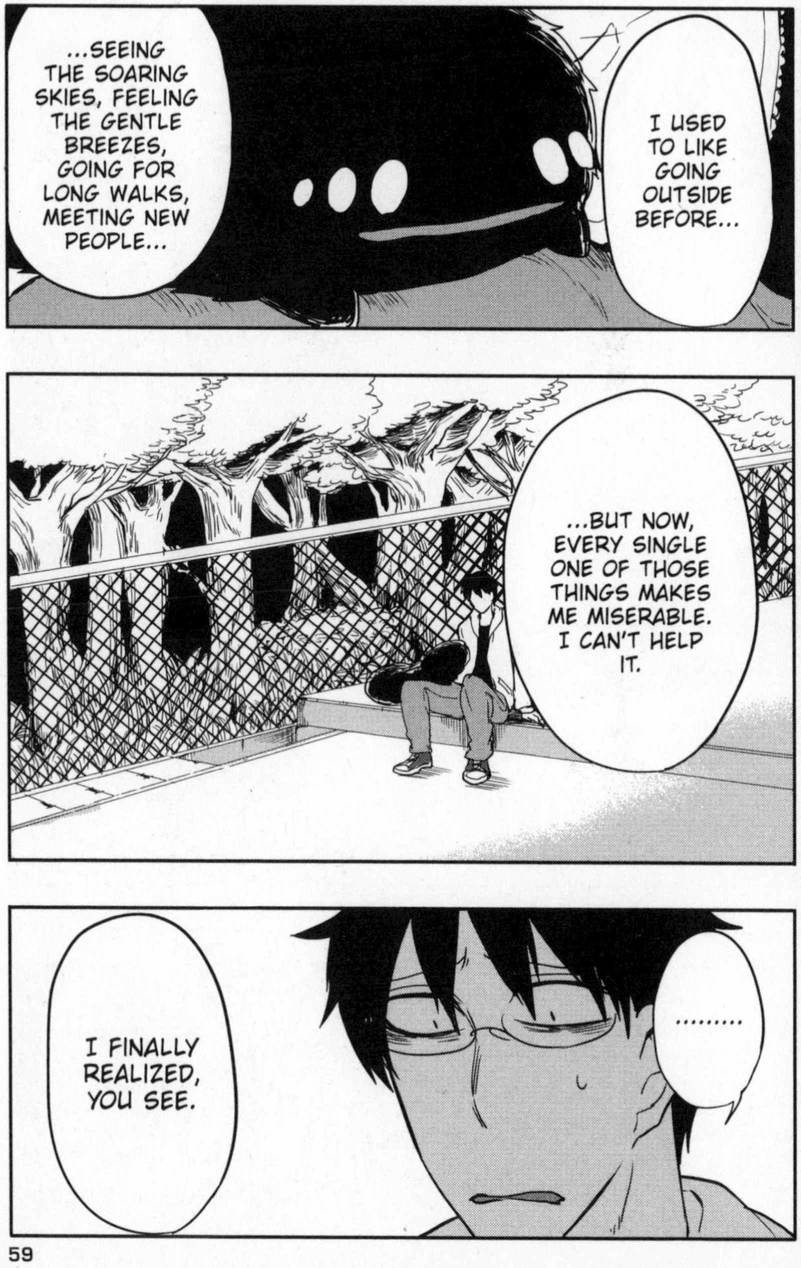
I USED TO LIKE GOING OUTSIDE BEFORE...
...SEEING THE SOARING SKIES, FEELING THE GENTLE BREEZES, GOING FOR LONG WALKS, MEETING NEW PEOPLE...
...BUT NOW, EVERY SINGLE ONE OF THOSE THINGS MAKES ME MISERABLE. I CAN'T HELP IT.
....
I FINALLY REALIZED, YOU SEE.

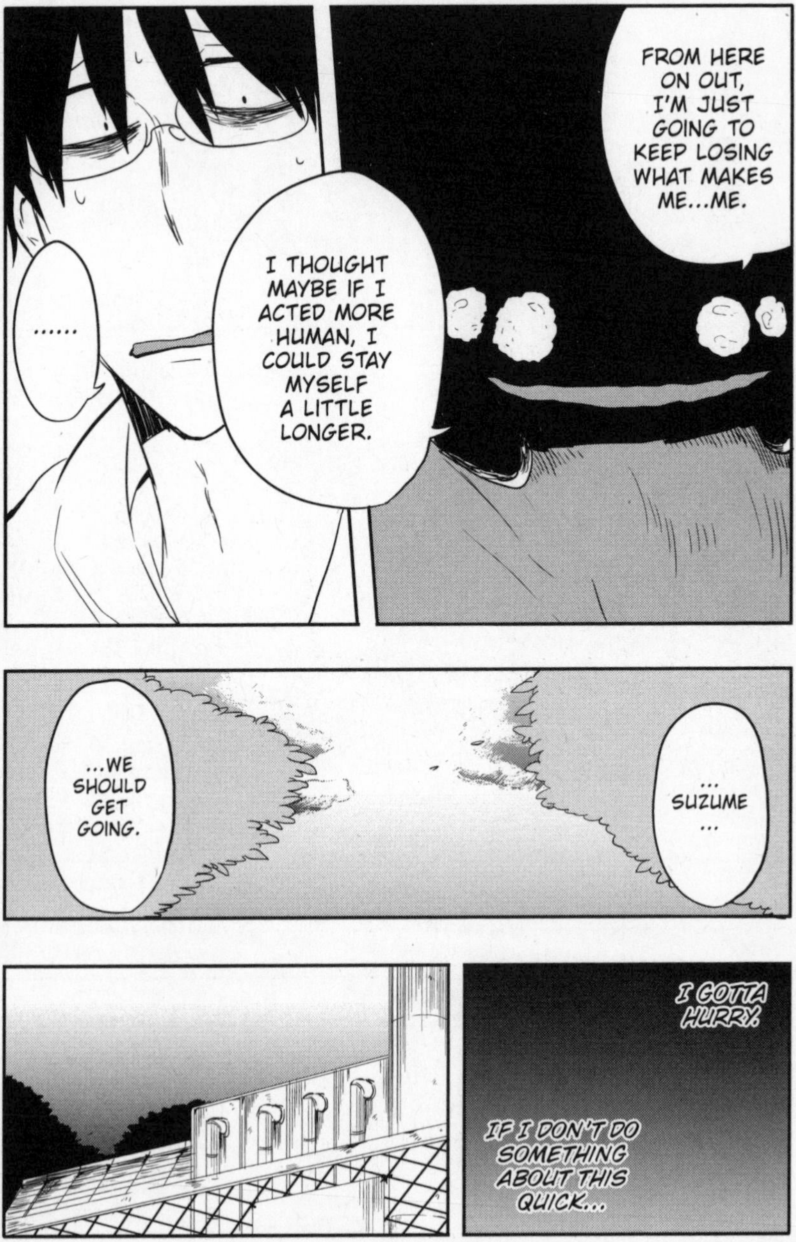
FROM HERE ON OUT, I'M JUST GOING TO KEEP LOSING WHAT MAKES ME...ME.
I THOUGHT MAYBE IF I ACTED MORE HUMAN, I COULD STAY MYSELF A LITTLE LONGER.
......
... SUZUME ...
...WE SHOULD GET GOING.
I GOTTA HURRY.
IF I DON'T DO SOMETHING ABOUT THIS QUICK...

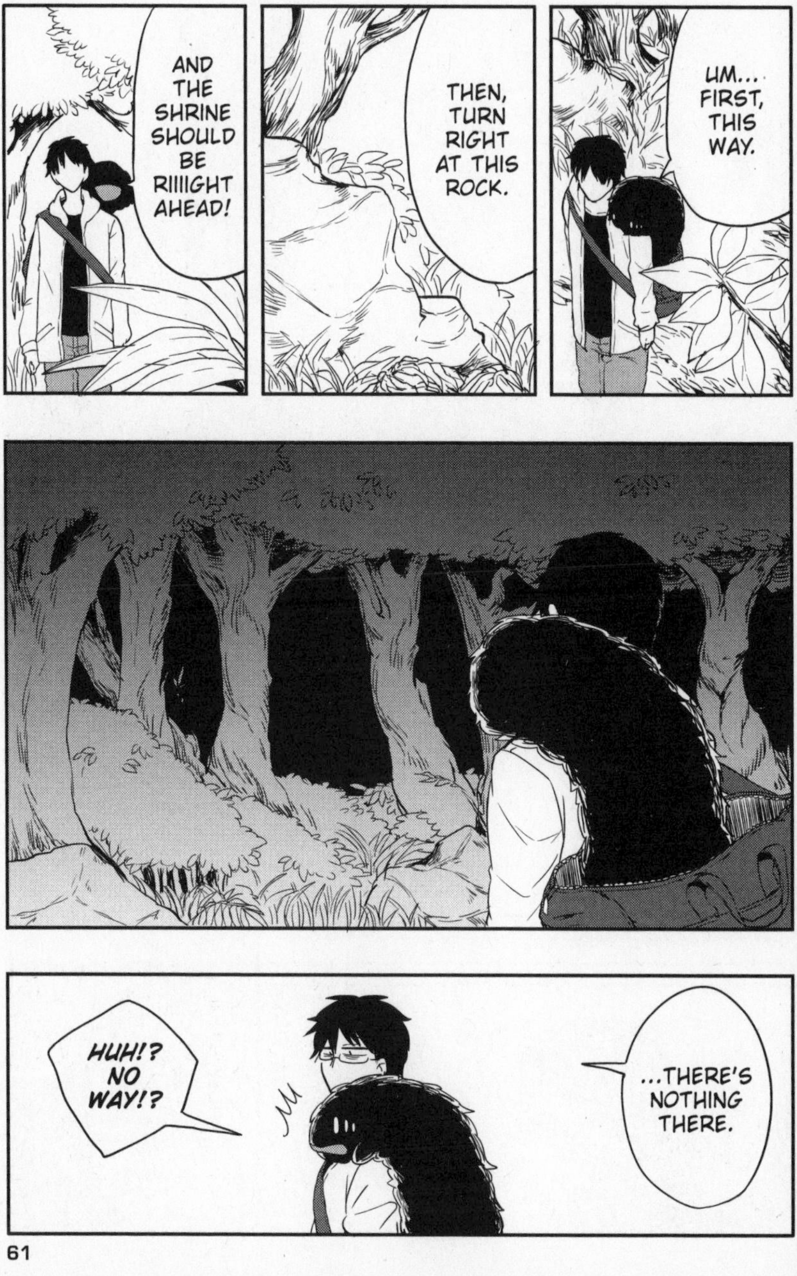
UM... FIRST, THIS WAY.
THEN, TURN RIGHT AT THIS ROCK.
AND THE SHRINE SHOULD BE RIIIIGHT AHEAD!
...THERE'S NOTHING THERE.
HUH!? NO WAY!?

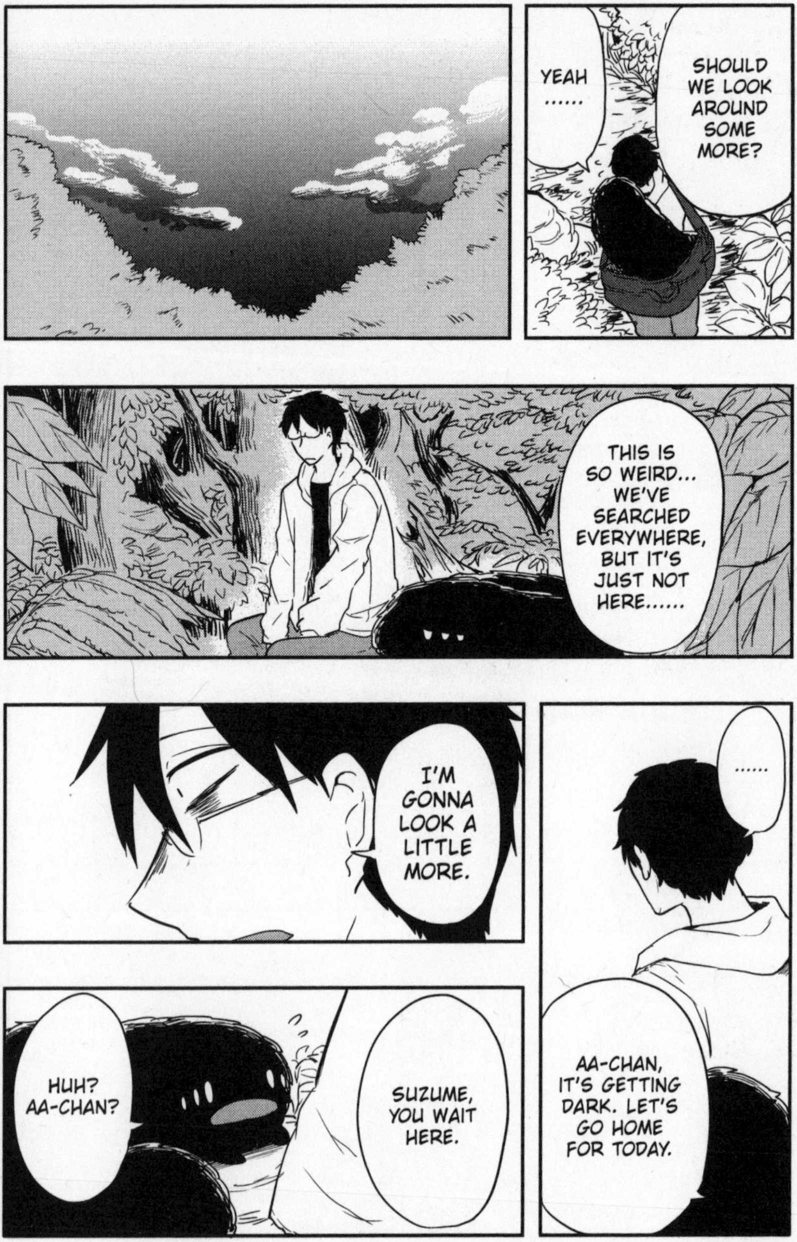
SHOULD WE LOOK AROUND SOME MORE?
YEAH ......
THIS IS SO WEIRD... WE'VE SEARCHED EVERYWHERE, BUT IT'S JUST NOT HERE......
......
AA-CHAN, IT'S GETTING DARK. LET'S GO HOME FOR TODAY.
I'M GONNA LOOK A LITTLE MORE.
SUZUME, YOU WAIT HERE.
HUH? AA-CHAN?

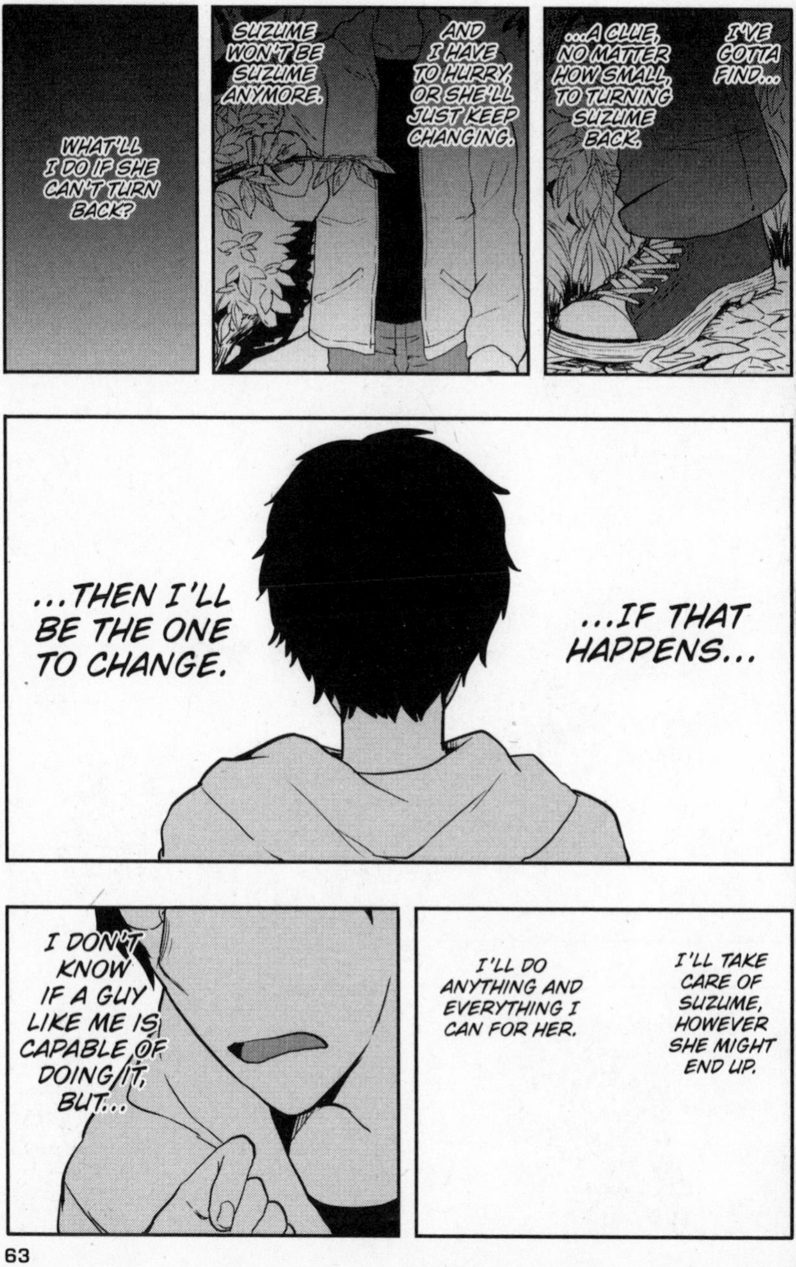
I'VE GOTTA FIND...
...A CLUE, NO MATTER HOW SMALL, TO TURNING SUZUME BACK.
AND I HAVE TO HURRY, OR SHE'LL JUST KEEP CHANGING.
SUZUME WON'T BE SUZUME ANYMORE.
WHAT'LL I DO IF SHE CAN'T TURN BACK?
...IF THAT HAPPENS...
...THEN I'LL BE THE ONE TO CHANGE.
I'LL TAKE CARE OF SUZUME, HOWEVER SHE MIGHT END UP.
I'LL DO ANYTHING AND EVERYTHING I CAN FOR HER.
I DON'T KNOW IF A GUY LIKE ME IS CAPABLE OF DOING IT, BUT...

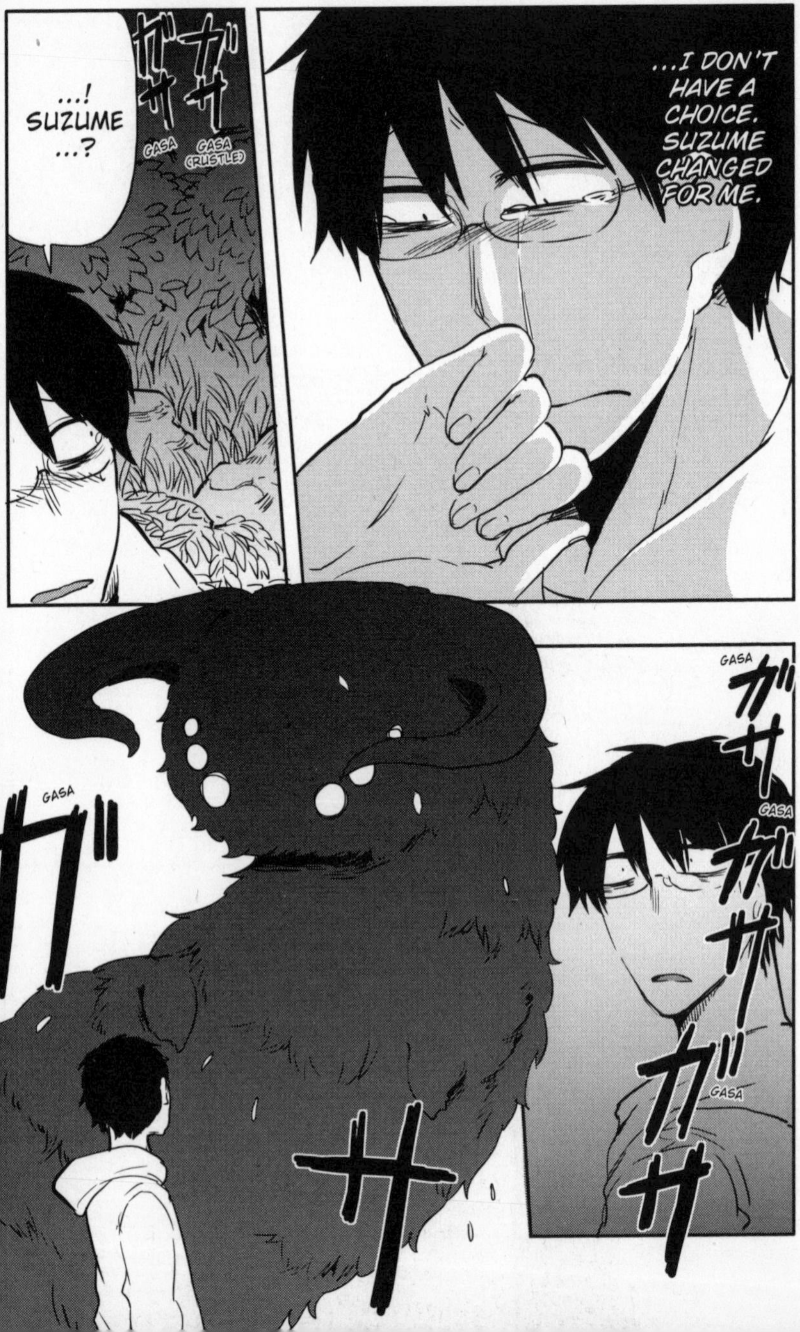
...I DON'T HAVE A CHOICE. SUZUME CHANGED FOR ME.
GASA
GASA (RUSTLE)
...! SUZUME ...?
GASA
GASA
GASA
GASA

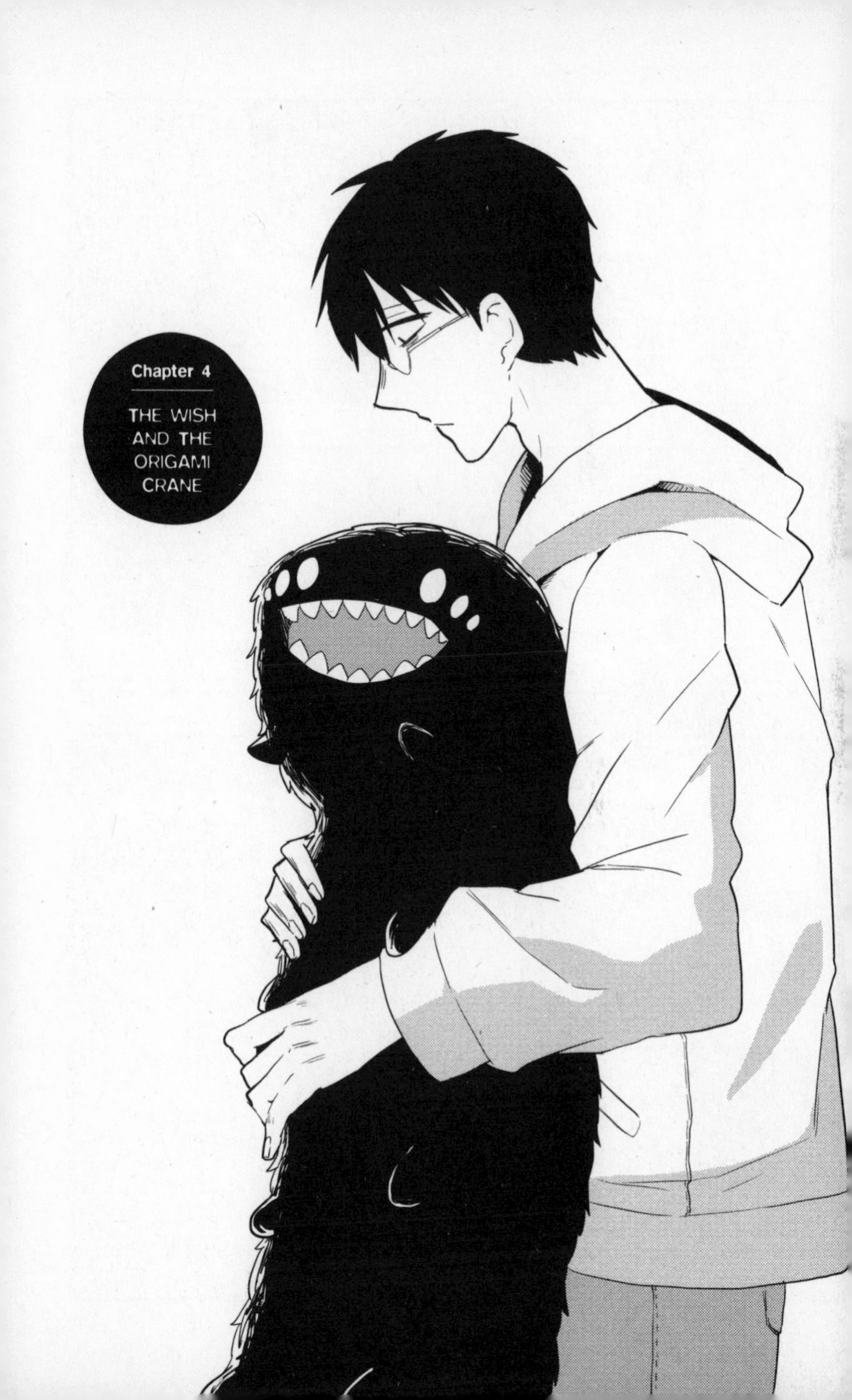
Chapter 4
THE WISH AND THE ORIGAMI CRANE

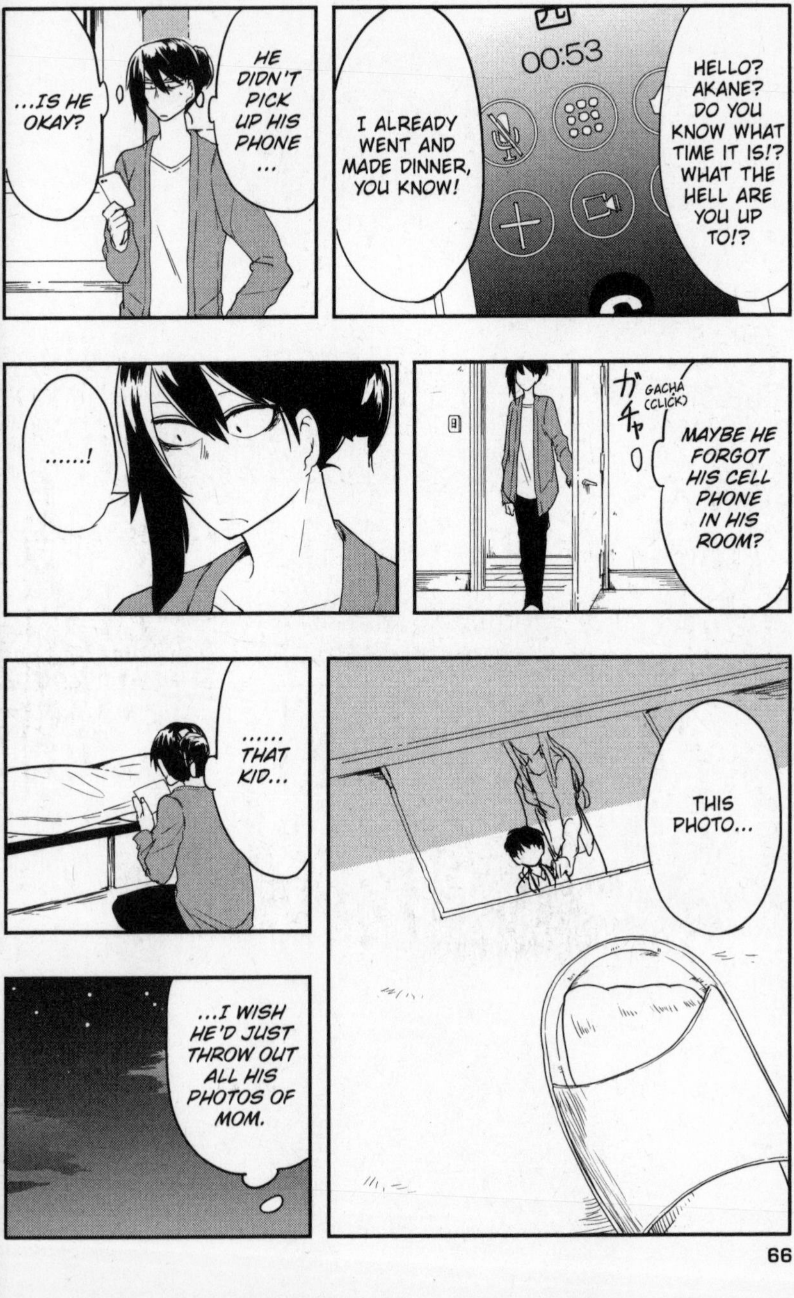

00:53
HELLO? AKANE? DO YOU KNOW WHAT TIME IT IS!? WHAT THE HELL ARE YOU UP TO!?
I ALREADY WENT AND MADE DINNER, YOU KNOW!
HE DIDN'T PICK UP HIS PHONE ...
...IS HE OKAY?
ガチャ
GACHA (CLICK)
MAYBE HE FORGOT HIS CELL PHONE IN HIS ROOM?
......!
THIS PHOTO...
...... THAT KID...
...I WISH HE'D JUST THROW OUT ALL HIS PHOTOS OF MOM.

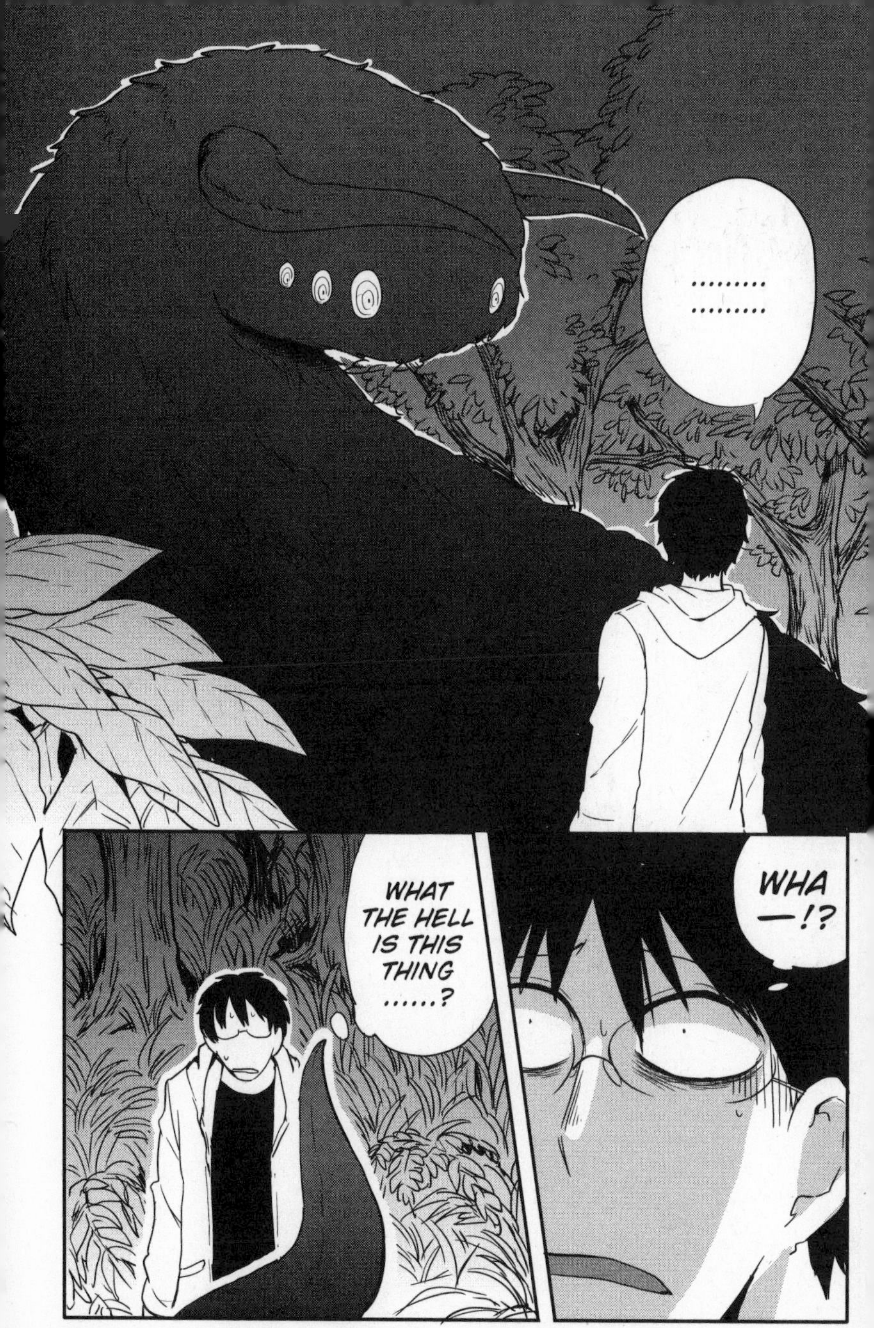
....
WHA —!?
WHAT THE HELL IS THIS THING ......?

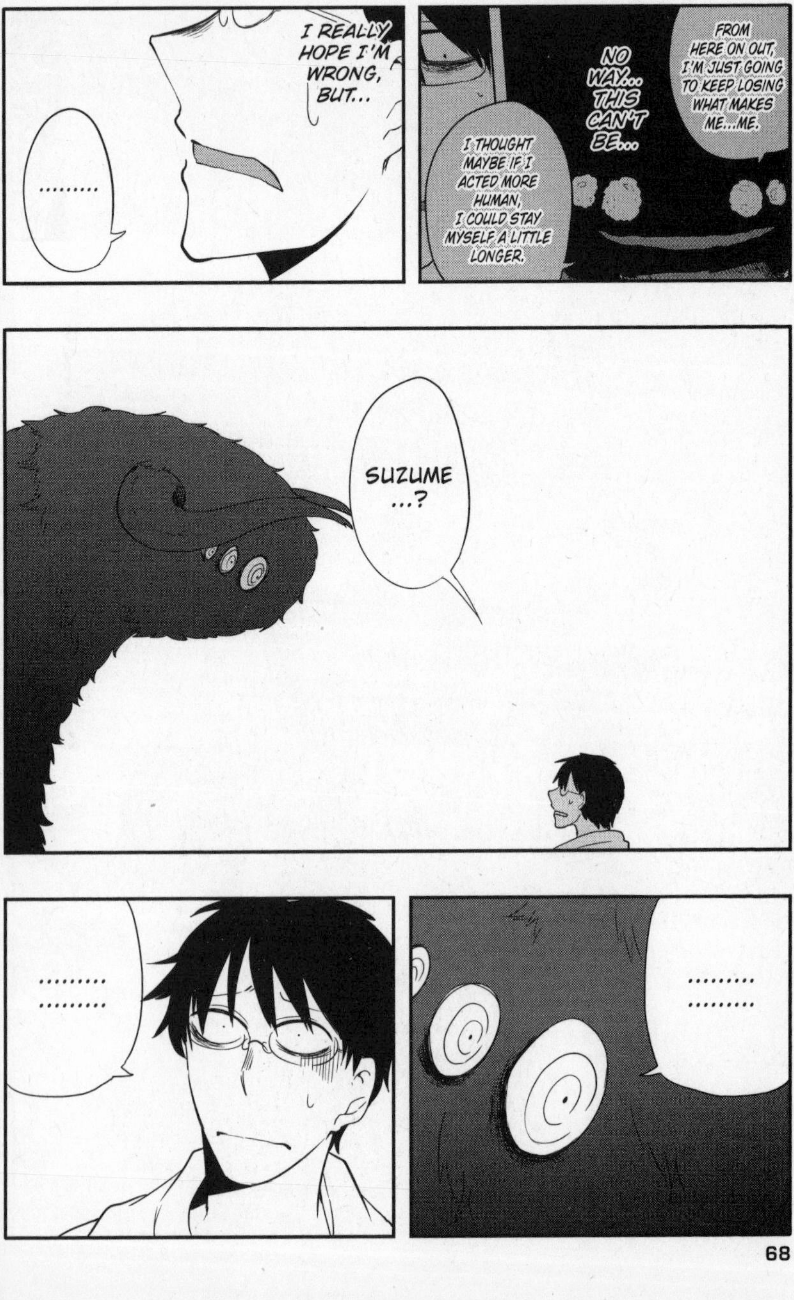
FROM HERE ON OUT, I'M JUST GOING TO KEEP LOSING WHAT MAKES ME...ME.
NO WAY... THIS CAN'T BE...
I THOUGHT MAYBE IF I ACTED MORE HUMAN, I COULD STAY MYSELF A LITTLE LONGER.
I REALLY HOPE I'M WRONG, BUT...
....
SUZUME ...?
....
....

GASA

W-WAIT!!

GASA (RUSTLE)

!!

KURU (WHIP)

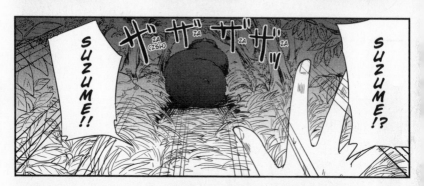

SUZUME!!

ZA (ZSH) ZA ZA ZA

SUZUME!?

!!

IS THAT...

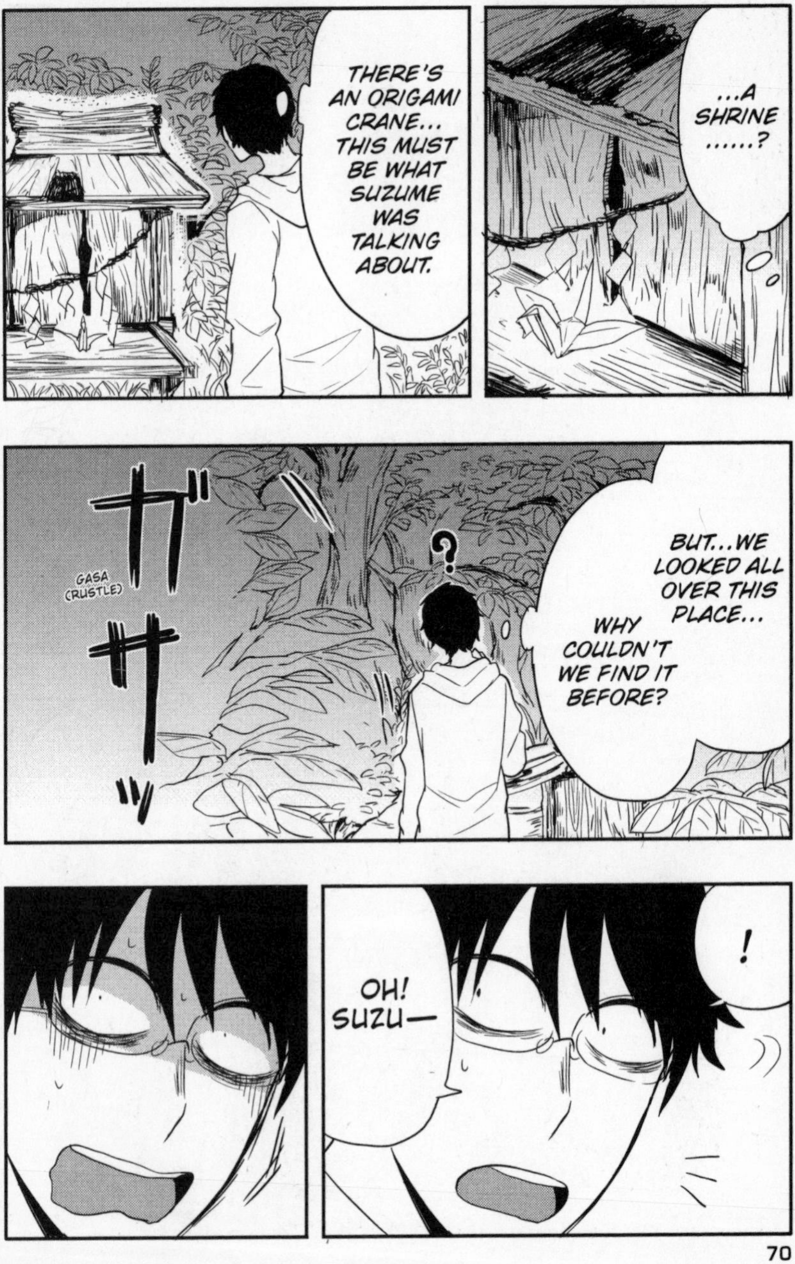
...A SHRINE ......?
THERE'S AN ORIGAMI CRANE... THIS MUST BE WHAT SUZUME WAS TALKING ABOUT.
BUT...WE LOOKED ALL OVER THIS PLACE...
WHY COULDN'T WE FIND IT BEFORE?
GASA (RUSTLE)
!
OH! SUZU—

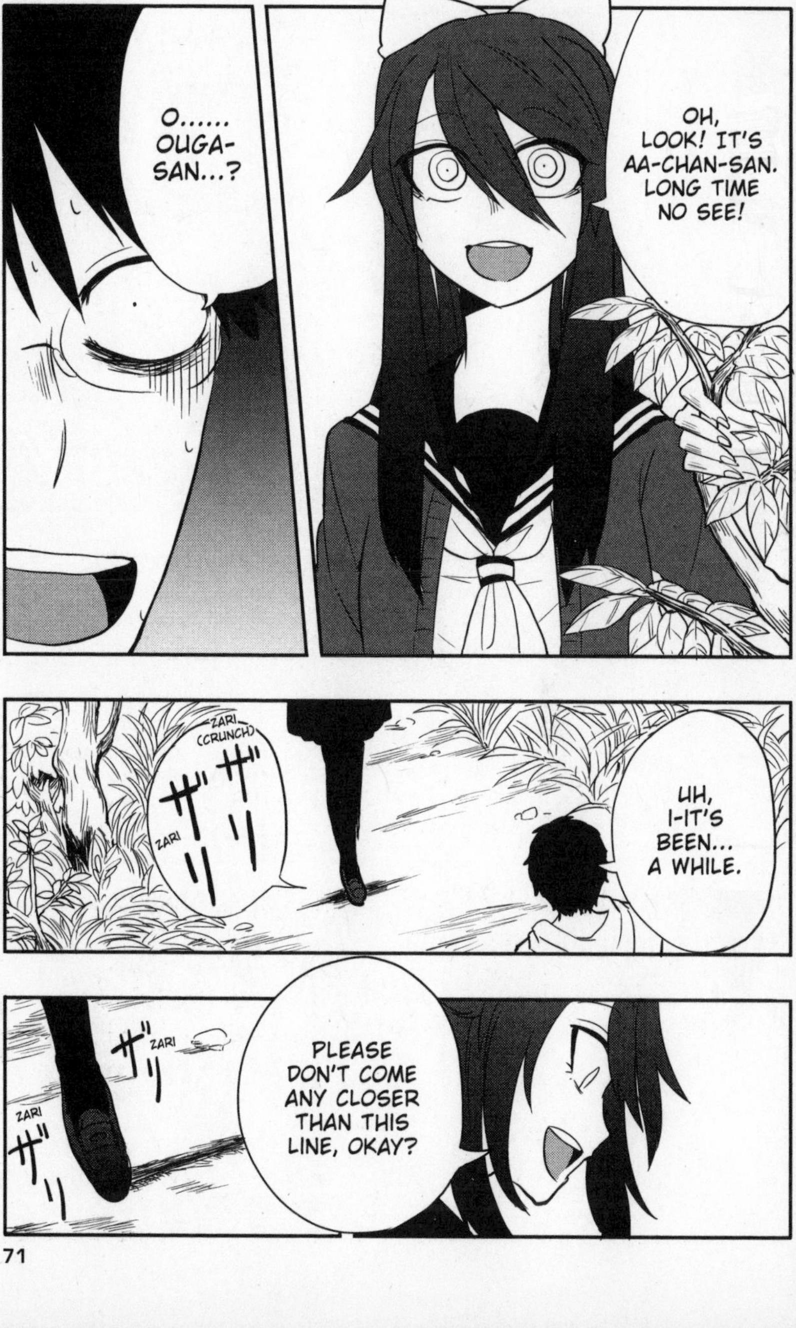
OH, LOOK! IT'S AA-CHAN-SAN. LONG TIME NO SEE!
O...... OUGA-SAN...?
UH, I-IT'S BEEN... A WHILE.
ザリ
ZARI (CRUNCH)
ザリ
ZARI
PLEASE DON'T COME ANY CLOSER THAN THIS LINE, OKAY?
ザリ
ZARI
ザリ
ZARI

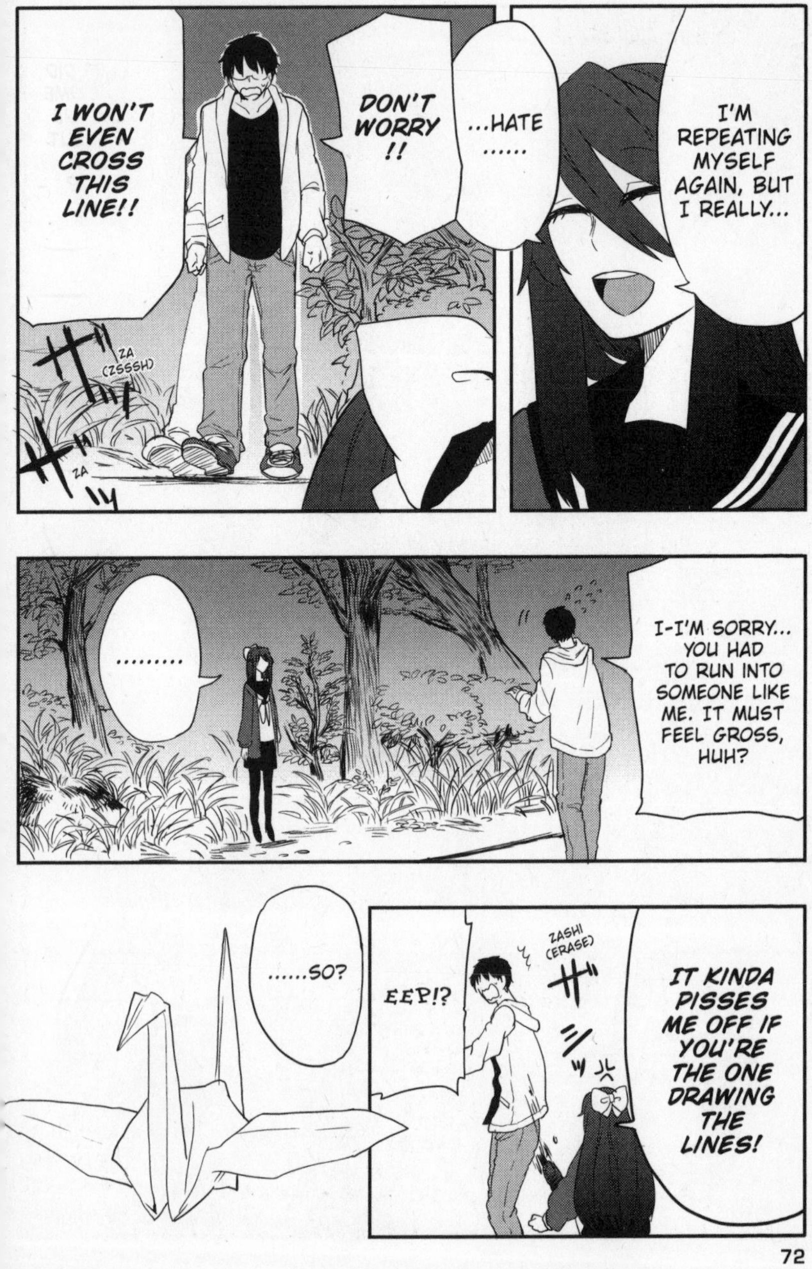

I'M REPEATING MYSELF AGAIN, BUT I REALLY...
...HATE ......
DON'T WORRY !!
I WON'T EVEN CROSS THIS LINE!!
ZA (ZSSSH)
ZA
I-I'M SORRY... YOU HAD TO RUN INTO SOMEONE LIKE ME. IT MUST FEEL GROSS, HUH?
....
IT KINDA PISSES ME OFF IF YOU'RE THE ONE DRAWING THE LINES!
ZASHI (ERASE)
EEP!?
......SO?

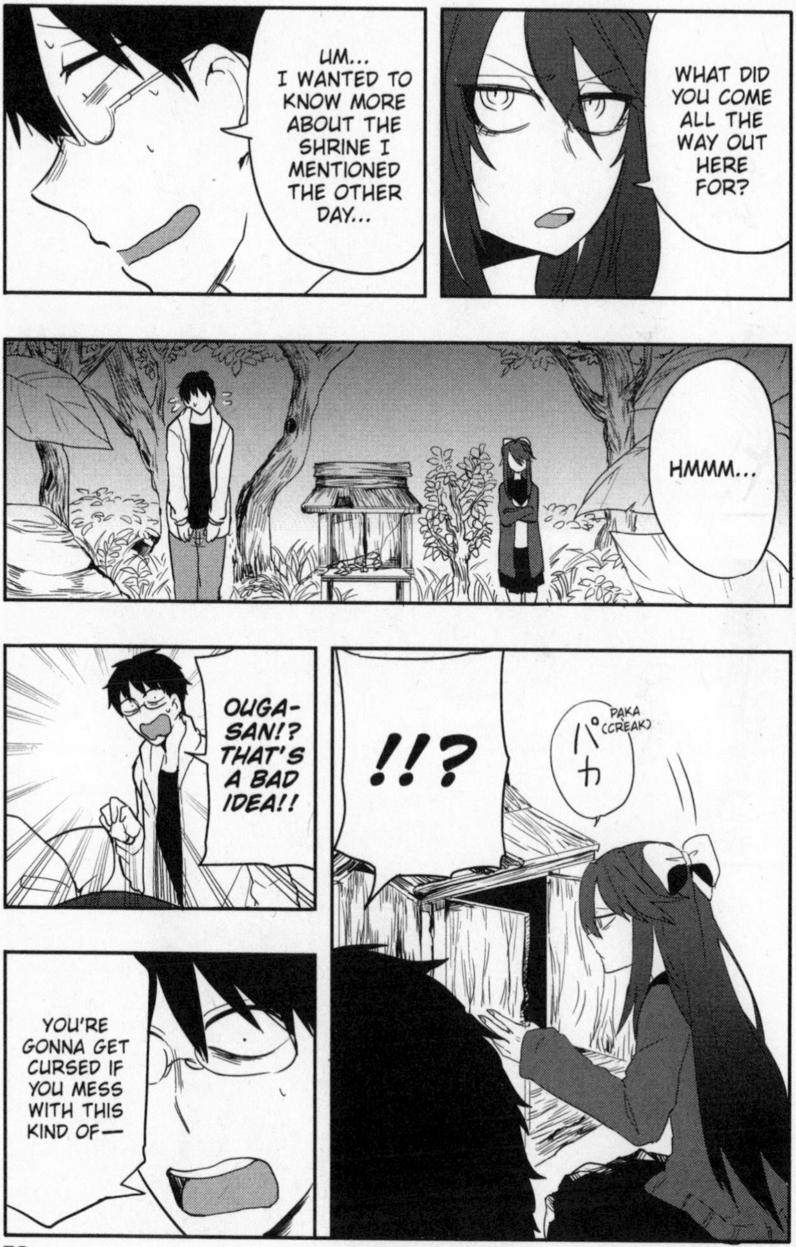
WHAT DID YOU COME ALL THE WAY OUT HERE FOR?
UM... I WANTED TO KNOW MORE ABOUT THE SHRINE I MENTIONED THE OTHER DAY...
HMMM...
パカ
PAKA (CREAK)
!!?
OUGA-SAN!? THAT'S A BAD IDEA!!
YOU'RE GONNA GET CURSED IF YOU MESS WITH THIS KIND OF—

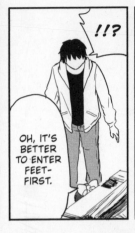

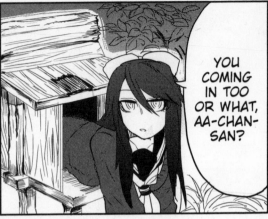

YOU COMING IN TOO OR WHAT, AA-CHAN-SAN?
!!?
OH, IT'S BETTER TO ENTER FEET-FIRST.
H-HUH?? HOW CAN YOU FIT IN THERE!? THAT'S NOT PHYSICALLY POSSIBLE...
....
I'M ASKING IF YOU'RE COMING IN OR NOT.
PLEASE QUIT YOUR BLUBBERING AND DECIDE IF YOU'RE GOING TO COME IN OR FOLLOW ME.
"NO" ISN'T EVEN AN OPTION ......

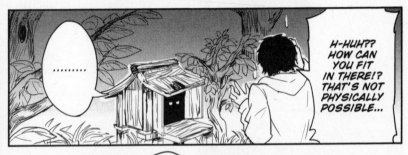

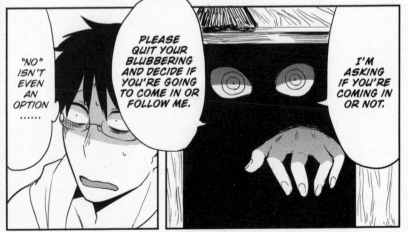

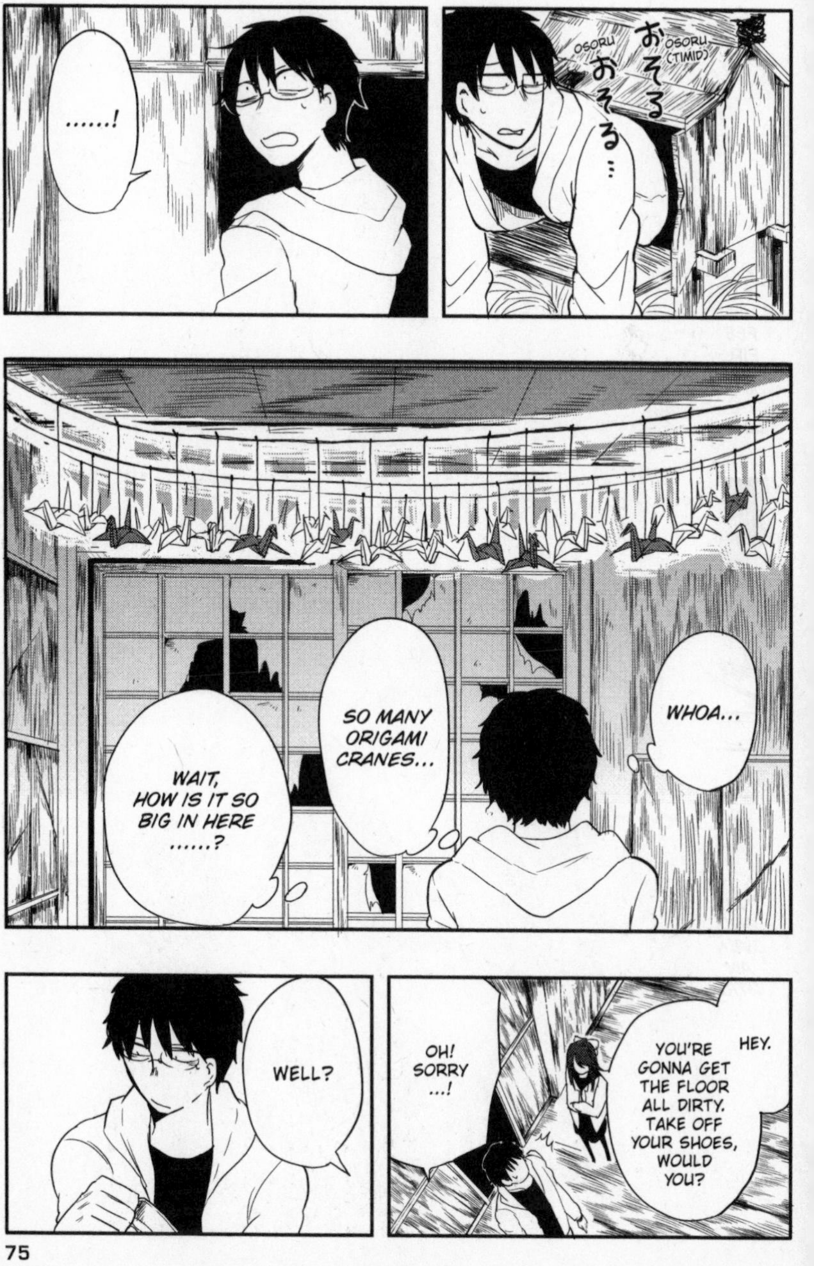

おそるおそる…
OSORU (TIMID)
OSORU
......!
WHOA...
SO MANY ORIGAMI CRANES...
WAIT, HOW IS IT SO BIG IN HERE ......?
HEY.
YOU'RE GONNA GET THE FLOOR ALL DIRTY. TAKE OFF YOUR SHOES, WOULD YOU?
OH! SORRY ...!
WELL?

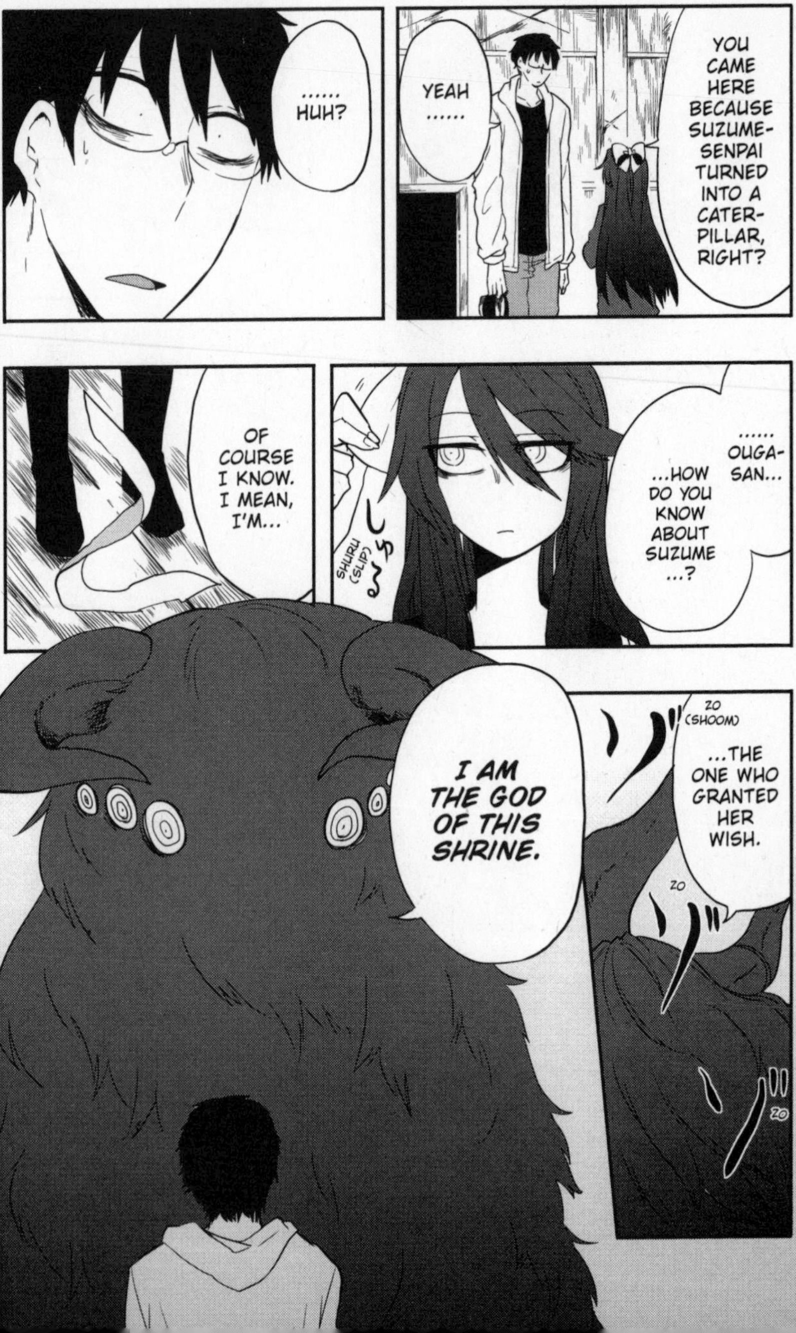

YOU CAME HERE BECAUSE SUZUME-SENPAI TURNED INTO A CATER-PILLAR, RIGHT?
YEAH ......
...... HUH?
...... OUGA-SAN...
...HOW DO YOU KNOW ABOUT SUZUME ...?
SHURU (SLIP)
OF COURSE I KNOW. I MEAN, I'M...
ZO (SHOOM)
...THE ONE WHO GRANTED HER WISH.
ZO
ZO
I AM THE GOD OF THIS SHRINE.

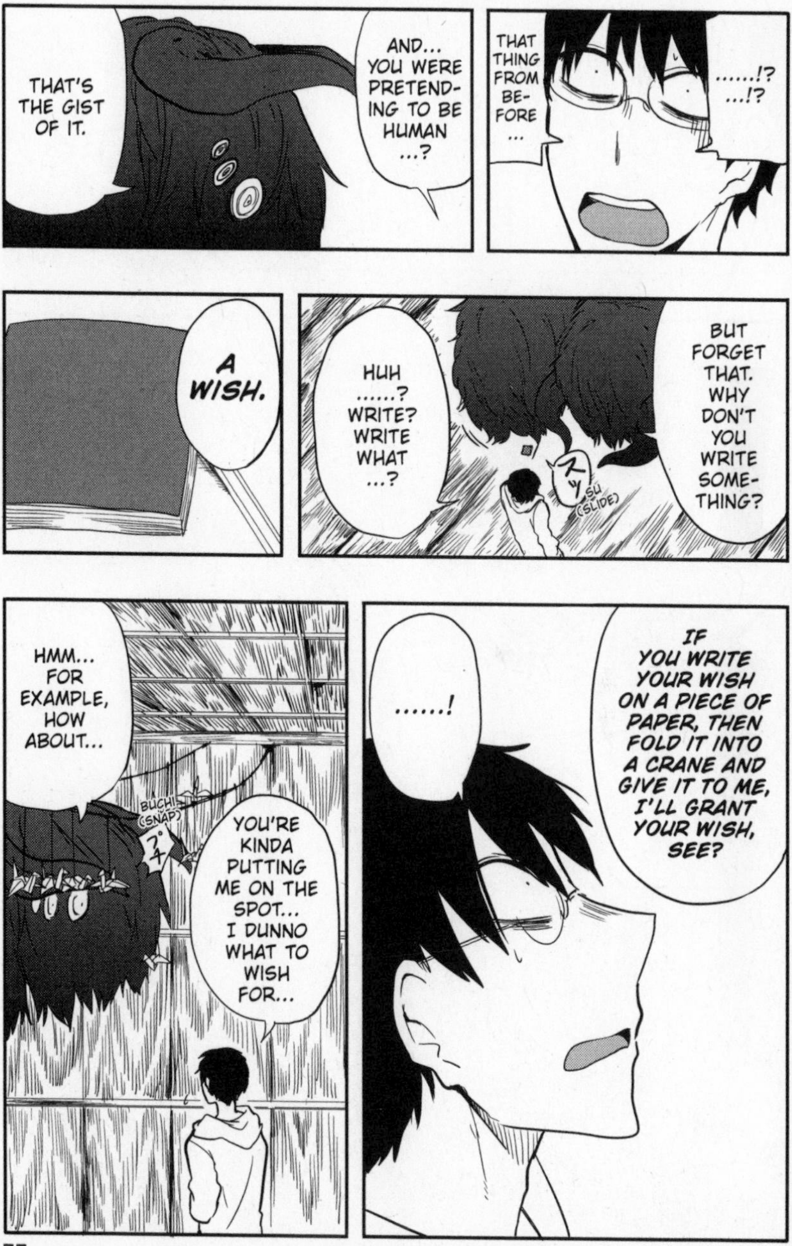
......!? ...!?
THAT THING FROM BE-FORE...
AND... YOU WERE PRETEND-ING TO BE HUMAN...?
THAT'S THE GIST OF IT.
BUT FORGET THAT. WHY DON'T YOU WRITE SOME-THING?
スッ
SU (SLIDE)
HUH......? WRITE? WRITE WHAT...?
A WISH.
IF YOU WRITE YOUR WISH ON A PIECE OF PAPER, THEN FOLD IT INTO A CRANE AND GIVE IT TO ME, I'LL GRANT YOUR WISH, SEE?
......!
YOU'RE KINDA PUTTING ME ON THE SPOT... I DUNNO WHAT TO WISH FOR...
HMM... FOR EXAMPLE, HOW ABOUT...
ブチ
BUCHI (SNAP)

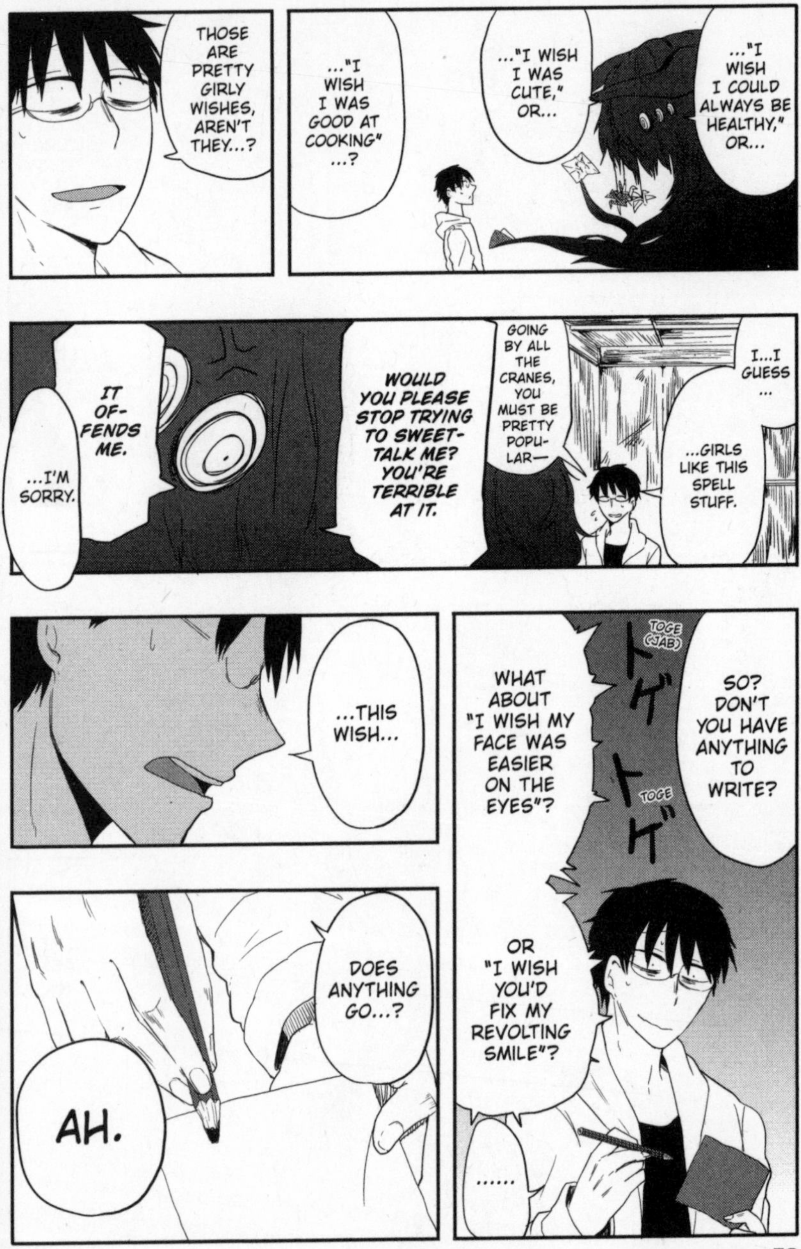
..."I WISH I COULD ALWAYS BE HEALTHY," OR...
..."I WISH I WAS CUTE," OR...
..."I WISH I WAS GOOD AT COOKING" ...?
THOSE ARE PRETTY GIRLY WISHES, AREN'T THEY...?
I...I GUESS ...
...GIRLS LIKE THIS SPELL STUFF.
GOING BY ALL THE CRANES, YOU MUST BE PRETTY POPU-LAR—
WOULD YOU PLEASE STOP TRYING TO SWEET-TALK ME? YOU'RE TERRIBLE AT IT.
IT OF-FENDS ME.
...I'M SORRY.
TOGE (JAB)
TOGE
SO? DON'T YOU HAVE ANYTHING TO WRITE?
WHAT ABOUT "I WISH MY FACE WAS EASIER ON THE EYES"?
OR "I WISH YOU'D FIX MY REVOLTING SMILE"?
......
...THIS WISH...
DOES ANYTHING GO...?
AH.

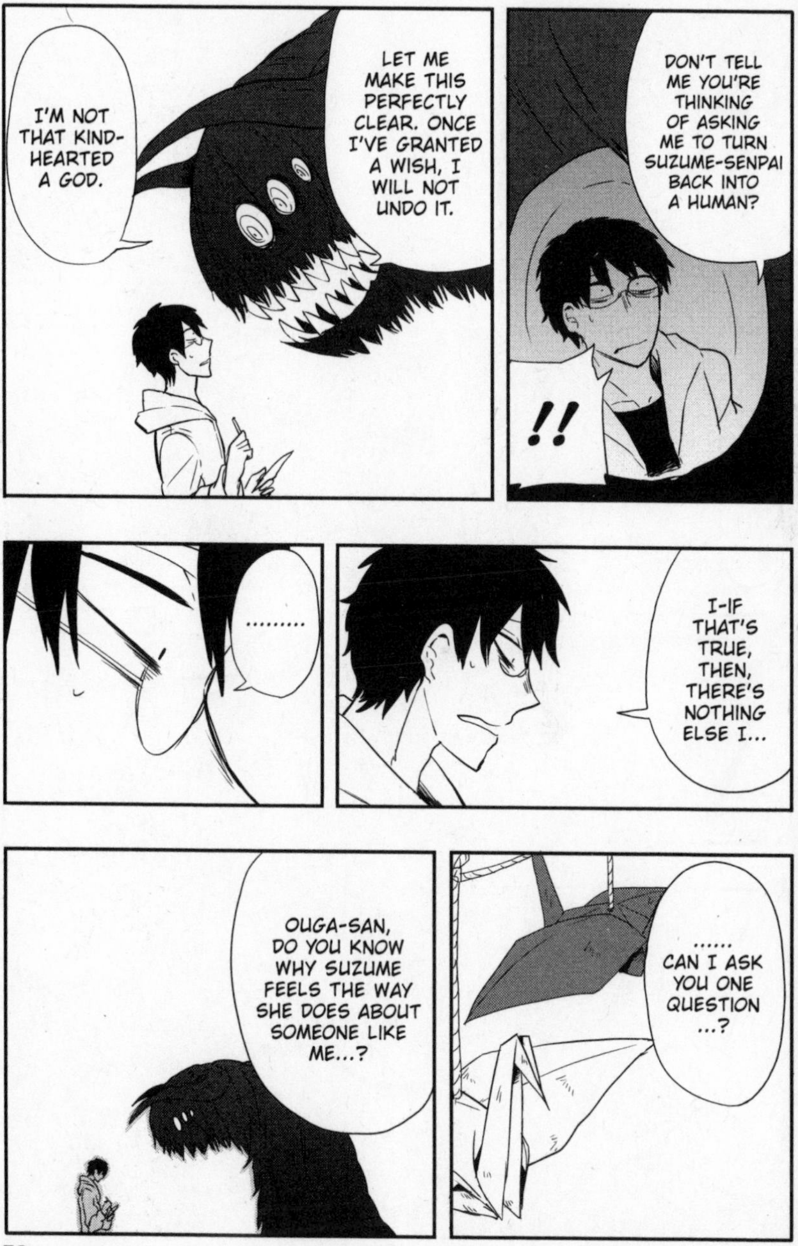
DON'T TELL ME YOU'RE THINKING OF ASKING ME TO TURN SUZUME-SENPAI BACK INTO A HUMAN?
!!
LET ME MAKE THIS PERFECTLY CLEAR. ONCE I'VE GRANTED A WISH, I WILL NOT UNDO IT.
I'M NOT THAT KIND-HEARTED A GOD.
I-IF THAT'S TRUE, THEN, THERE'S NOTHING ELSE I...
....
...... CAN I ASK YOU ONE QUESTION ...?
OUGA-SAN, DO YOU KNOW WHY SUZUME FEELS THE WAY SHE DOES ABOUT SOMEONE LIKE ME...?

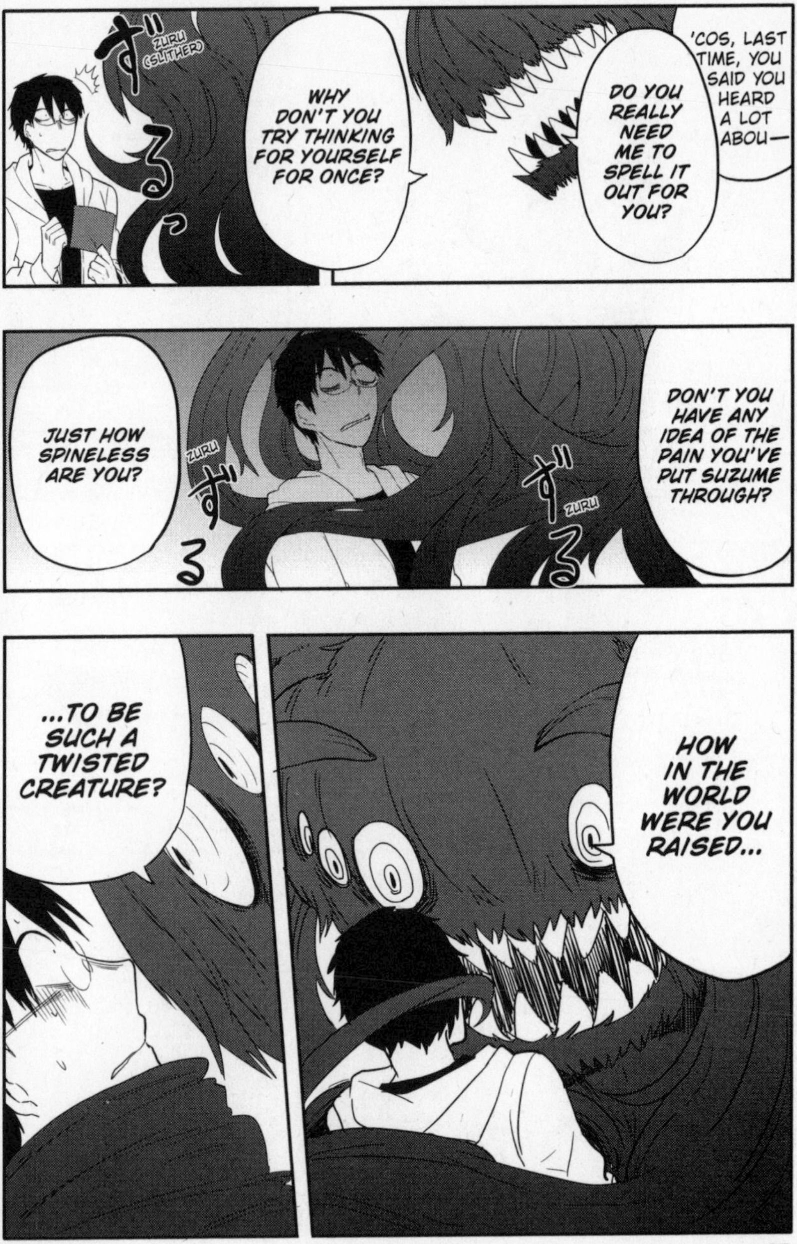
'COS, LAST TIME, YOU SAID YOU HEARD A LOT ABOU—
DO YOU REALLY NEED ME TO SPELL IT OUT FOR YOU?
WHY DON'T YOU TRY THINKING FOR YOURSELF FOR ONCE?
ZURU (SLITHER)
DON'T YOU HAVE ANY IDEA OF THE PAIN YOU'VE PUT SUZUME THROUGH?
ZURU
ZURU
JUST HOW SPINELESS ARE YOU?
HOW IN THE WORLD WERE YOU RAISED...
...TO BE SUCH A TWISTED CREATURE?

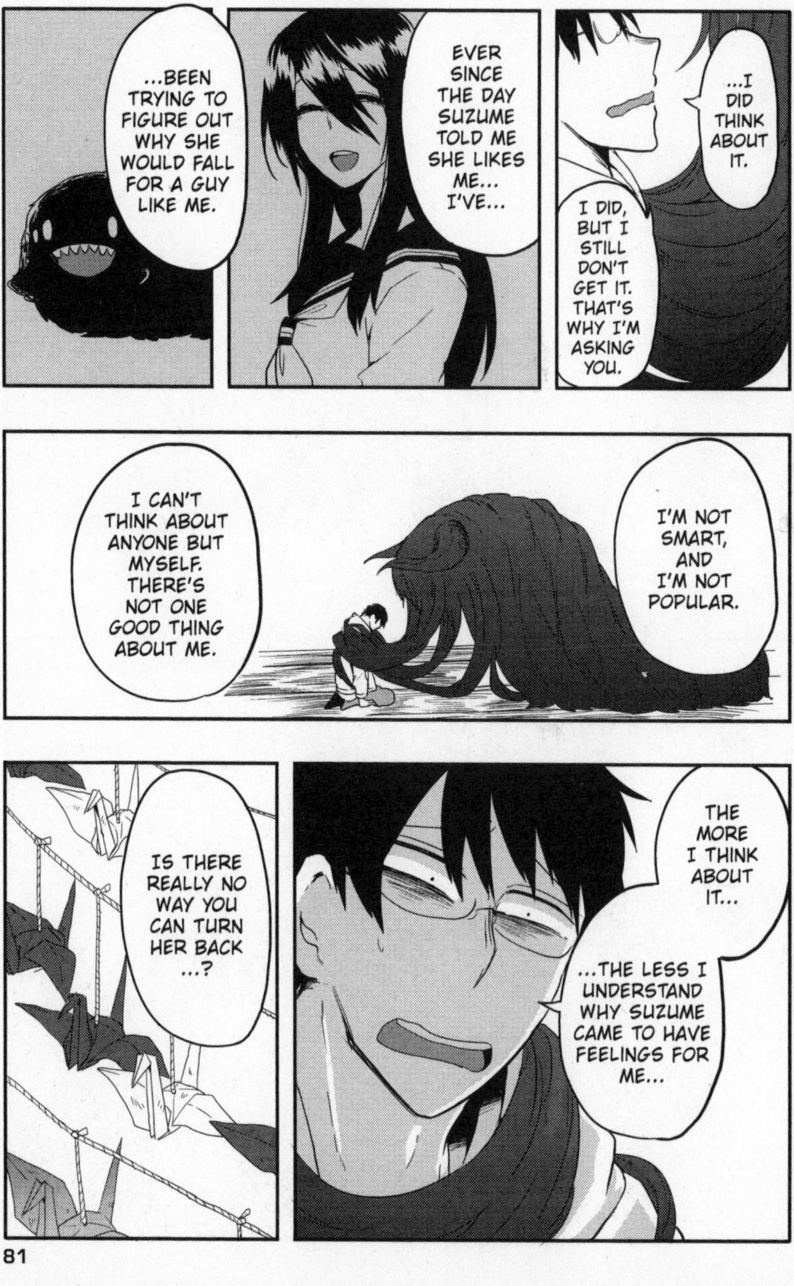
...I DID THINK ABOUT IT.
I DID, BUT I STILL DON'T GET IT. THAT'S WHY I'M ASKING YOU.
EVER SINCE THE DAY SUZUME TOLD ME SHE LIKES ME... I'VE...
...BEEN TRYING TO FIGURE OUT WHY SHE WOULD FALL FOR A GUY LIKE ME.
I'M NOT SMART, AND I'M NOT POPULAR.
I CAN'T THINK ABOUT ANYONE BUT MYSELF. THERE'S NOT ONE GOOD THING ABOUT ME.
THE MORE I THINK ABOUT IT...
...THE LESS I UNDERSTAND WHY SUZUME CAME TO HAVE FEELINGS FOR ME...
IS THERE REALLY NO WAY YOU CAN TURN HER BACK ...?

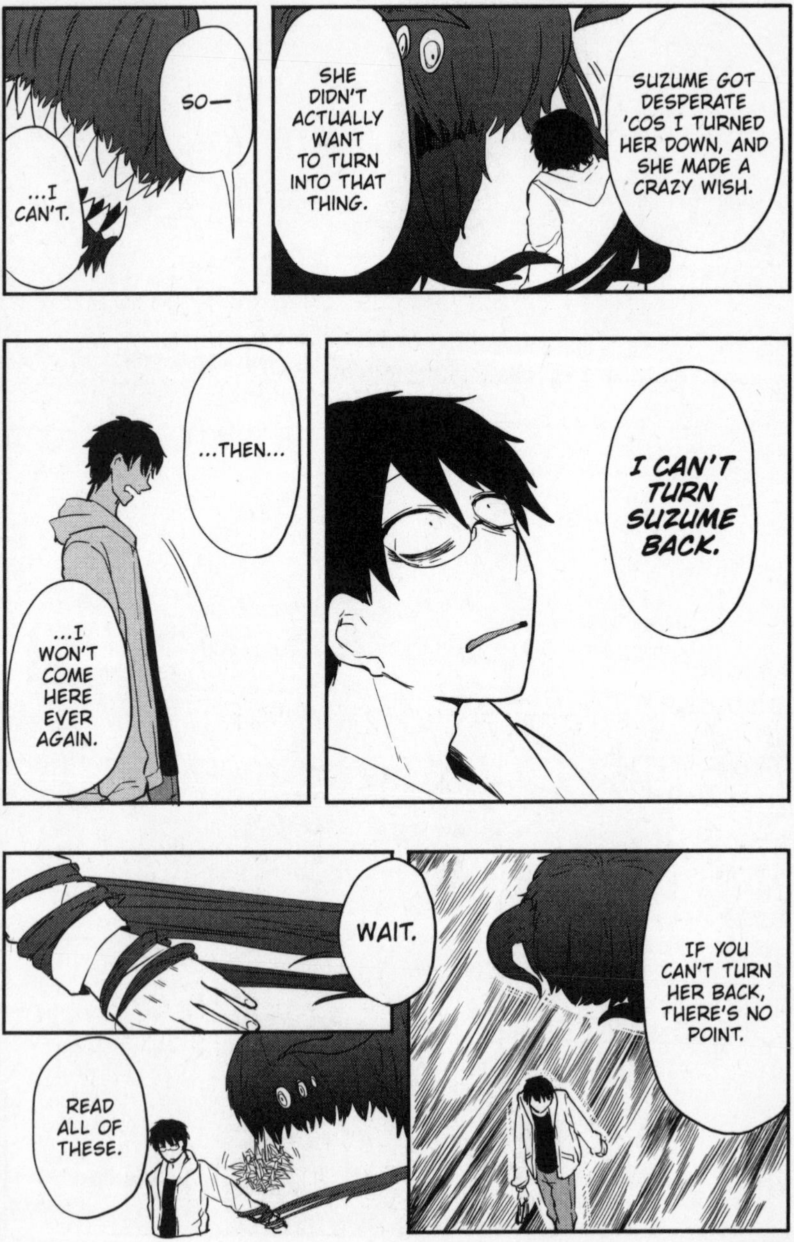
SUZUME GOT DESPERATE 'COS I TURNED HER DOWN, AND SHE MADE A CRAZY WISH.
SHE DIDN'T ACTUALLY WANT TO TURN INTO THAT THING.
SO—
...I CAN'T.
I CAN'T TURN SUZUME BACK.
...THEN...
...I WON'T COME HERE EVER AGAIN.
IF YOU CAN'T TURN HER BACK, THERE'S NO POINT.
WAIT.
READ ALL OF THESE.

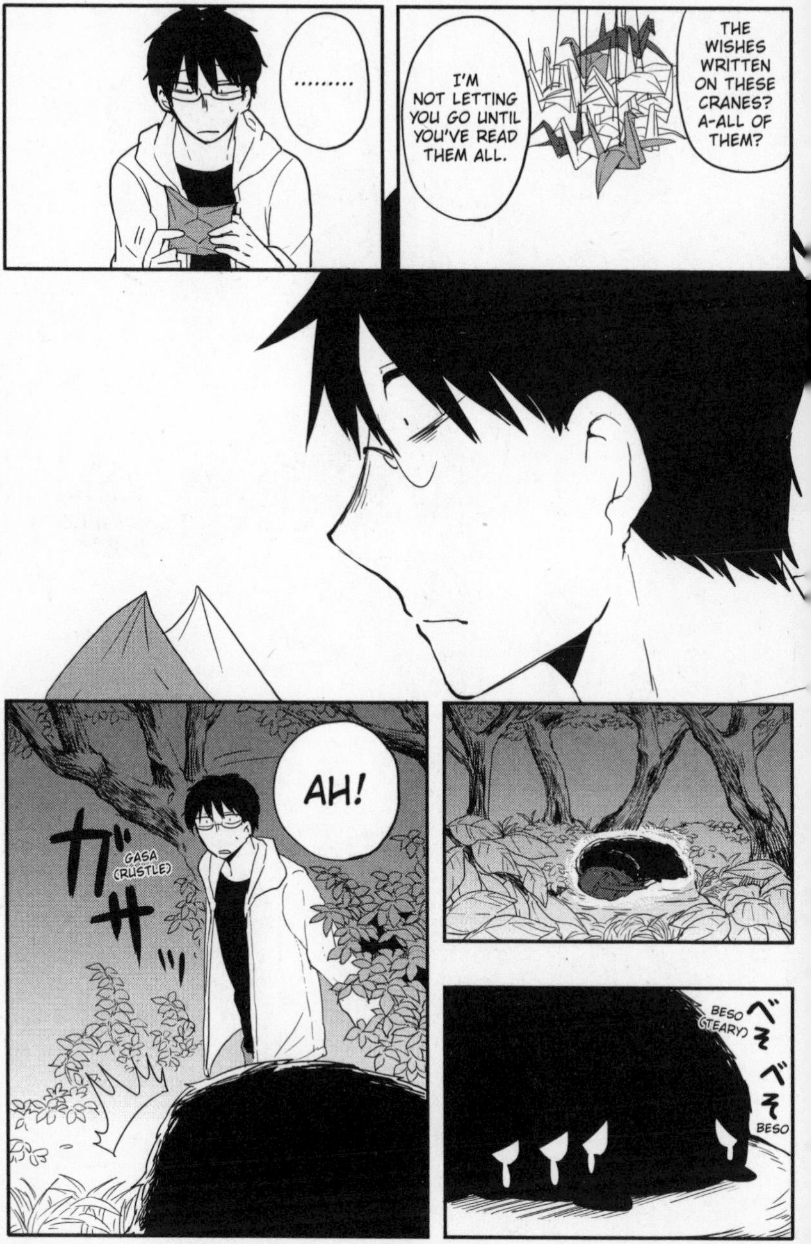
THE WISHES WRITTEN ON THESE CRANES? A-ALL OF THEM?
I'M NOT LETTING YOU GO UNTIL YOU'VE READ THEM ALL.
....
べそ
BESO (TEARY)
べそ
BESO
ガサッ
GASA (RUSTLE)
AH!

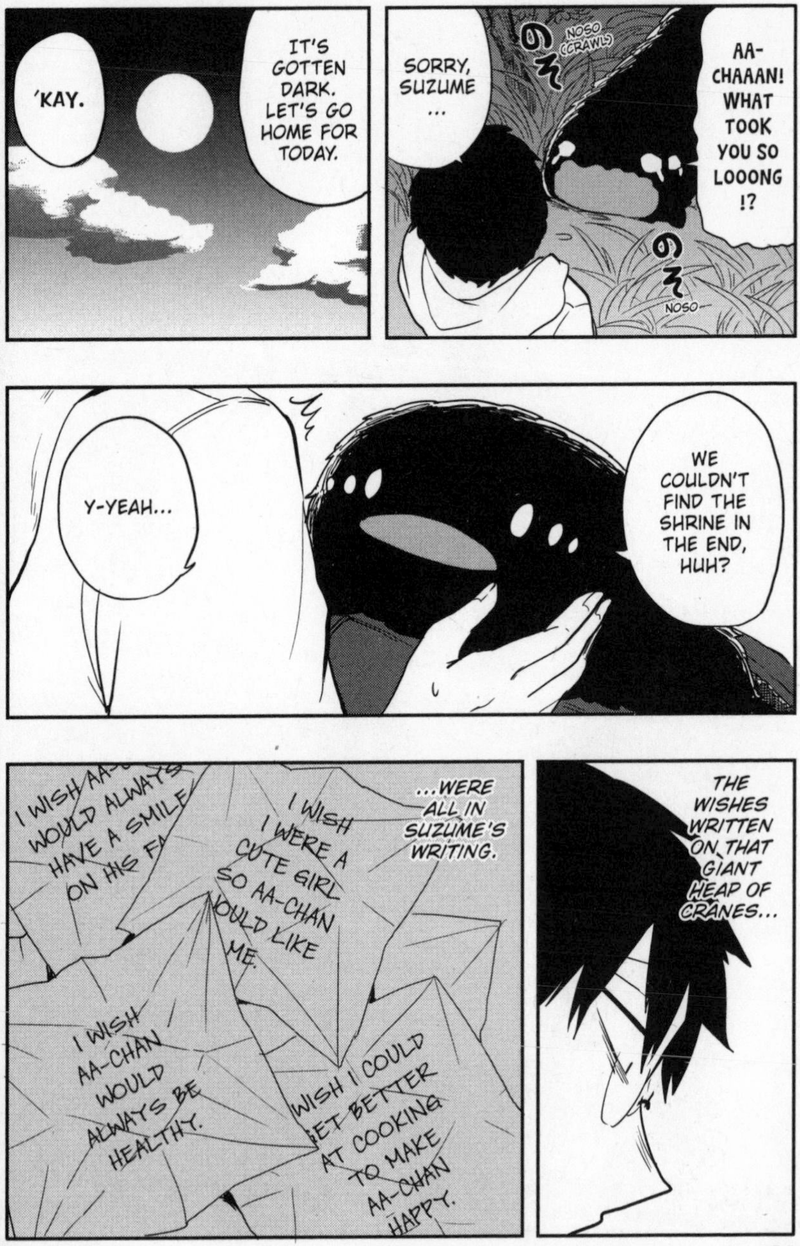
AA-CHAAAN! WHAT TOOK YOU SO LOOONG !?
NOSO (CRAWL)
NOSO
SORRY, SUZUME ...
IT'S GOTTEN DARK. LET'S GO HOME FOR TODAY.
'KAY.
WE COULDN'T FIND THE SHRINE IN THE END, HUH?
Y-YEAH...
THE WISHES WRITTEN ON THAT GIANT HEAP OF CRANES...
...WERE ALL IN SUZUME'S WRITING.
I WISH I WERE A CUTE GIRL SO AA-CHAN WOULD LIKE ME.
I WISH AA- WOULD ALWAYS HAVE A SMILE ON HIS FA
WISH I COULD ET BETTER AT COOKING TO MAKE AA-CHAN HAPPY.
I WISH AA-CHAN WOULD ALWAYS BE HEALTHY.

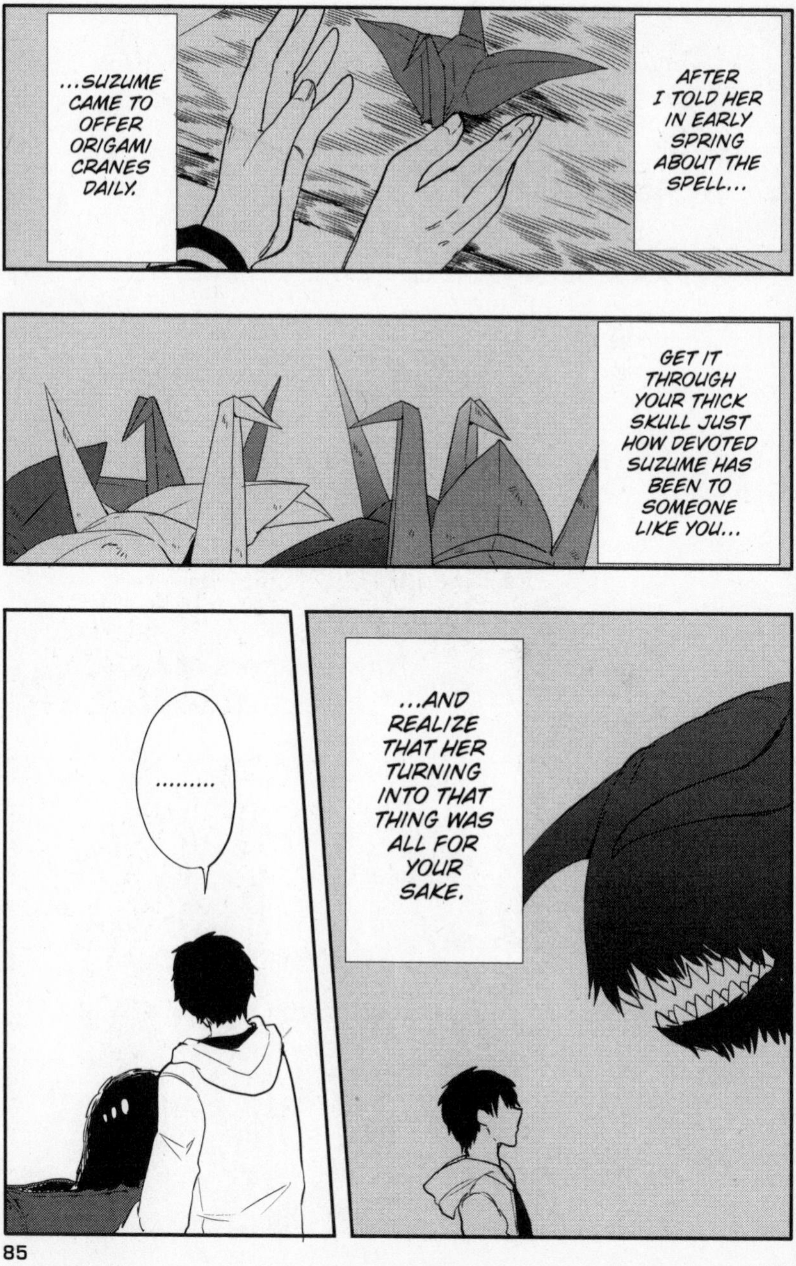
AFTER I TOLD HER IN EARLY SPRING ABOUT THE SPELL...
...SUZUME CAME TO OFFER ORIGAMI CRANES DAILY.
GET IT THROUGH YOUR THICK SKULL JUST HOW DEVOTED SUZUME HAS BEEN TO SOMEONE LIKE YOU...
...AND REALIZE THAT HER TURNING INTO THAT THING WAS ALL FOR YOUR SAKE.
....

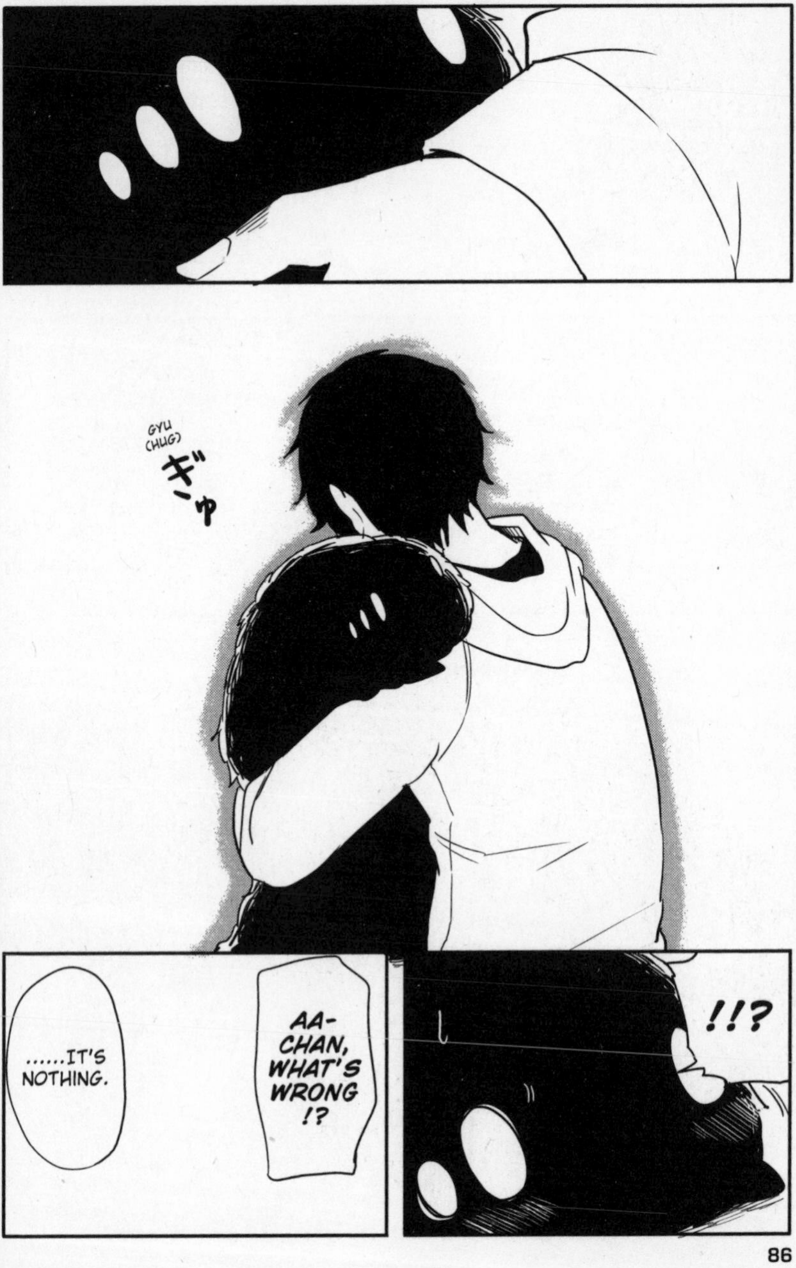
GYU (HUG)
ギュ
!!?
AA-CHAN, WHAT'S WRONG!?
......IT'S NOTHING.

Chapter 5

THE MOTHER AND THE ALLY

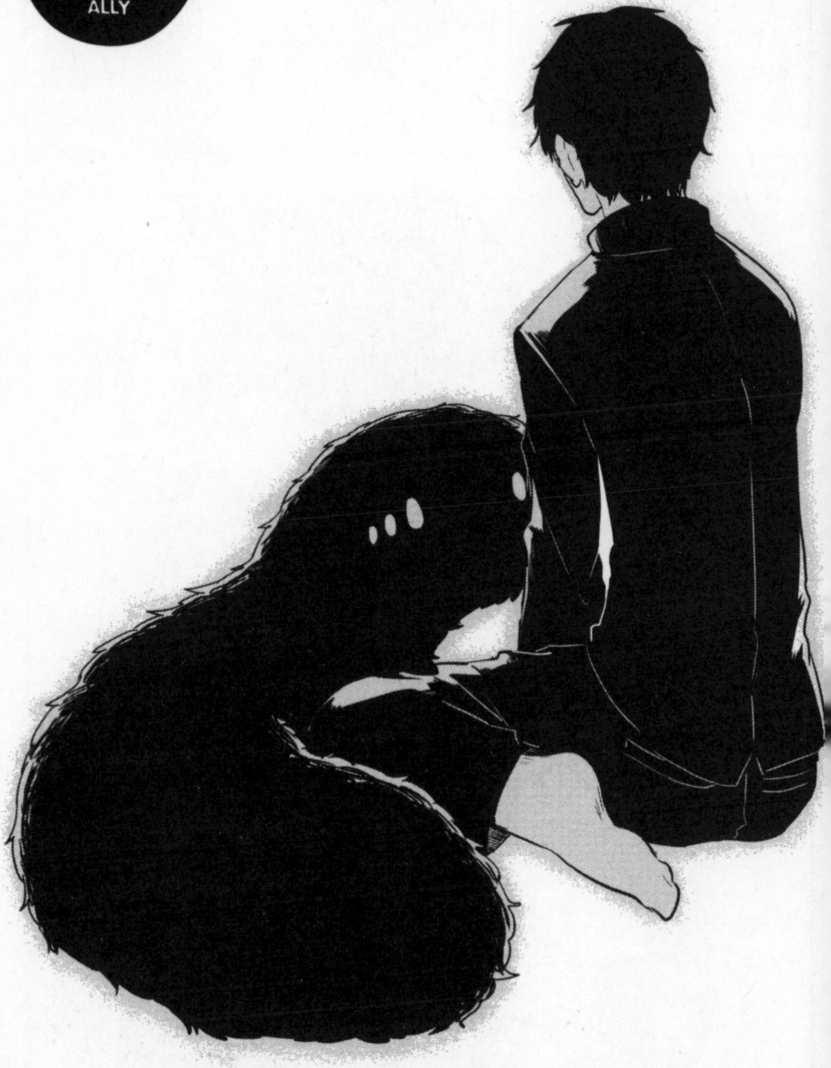

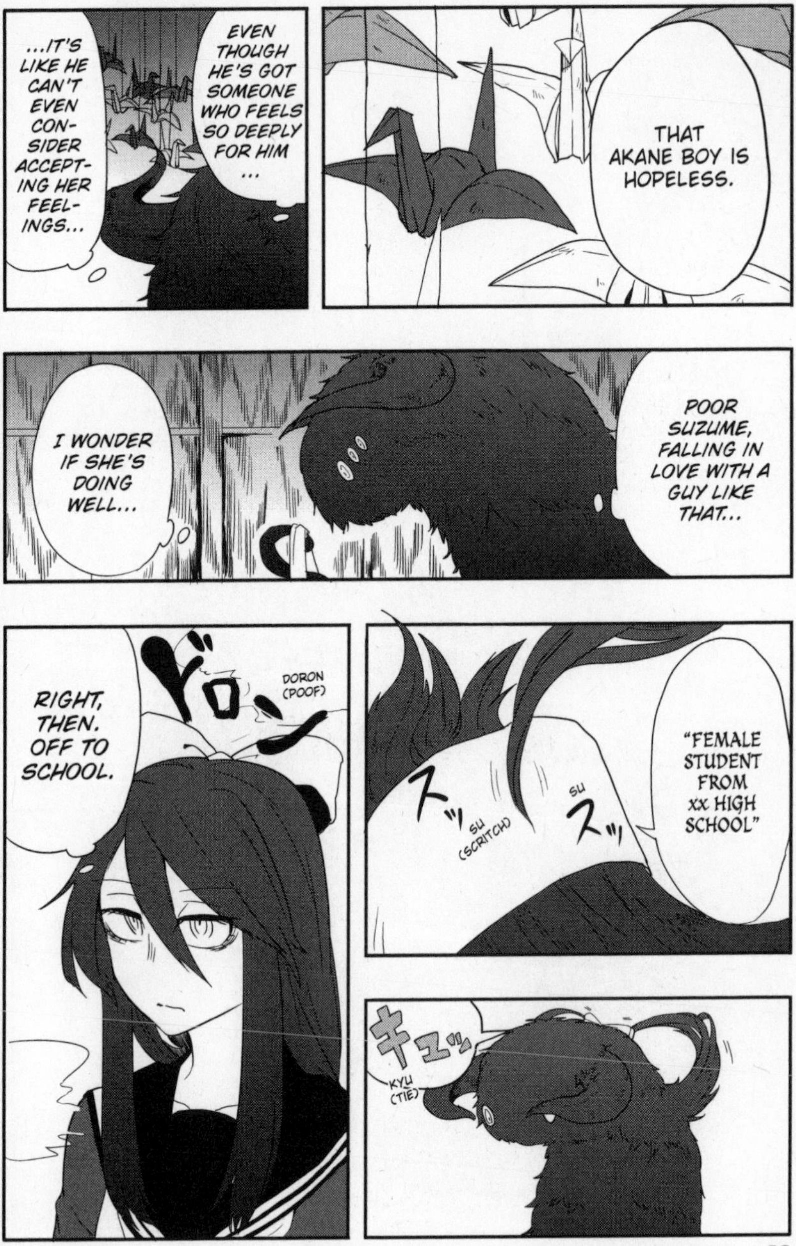
THAT AKANE BOY IS HOPELESS.
EVEN THOUGH HE'S GOT SOMEONE WHO FEELS SO DEEPLY FOR HIM ...
...IT'S LIKE HE CAN'T EVEN CON-SIDER ACCEPT-ING HER FEEL-INGS...
POOR SUZUME, FALLING IN LOVE WITH A GUY LIKE THAT...
I WONDER IF SHE'S DOING WELL...
"FEMALE STUDENT FROM xx HIGH SCHOOL"
SU
SU (SCRITCH)
KYU (TIE)
DORON (POOF)
RIGHT, THEN. OFF TO SCHOOL.

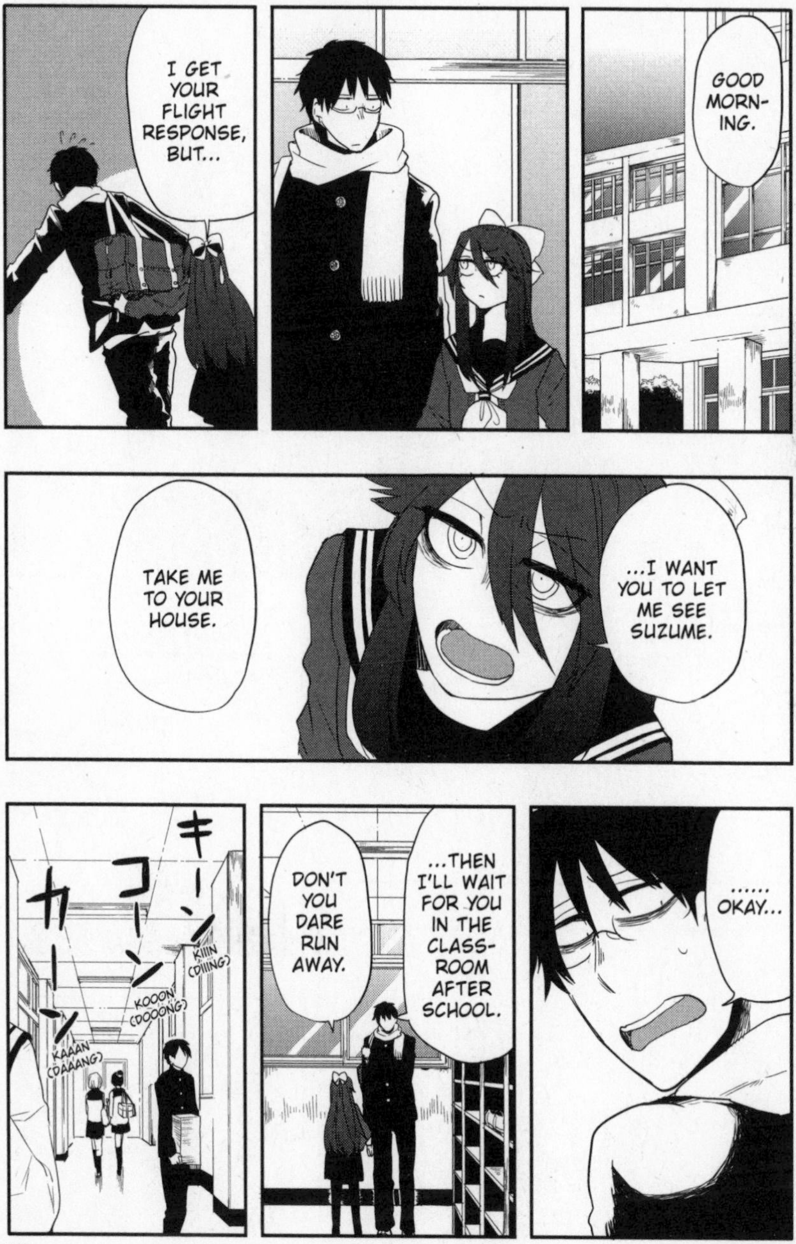
GOOD MORNING-ING.
I GET YOUR FLIGHT RESPONSE, BUT...
...I WANT YOU TO LET ME SEE SUZUME.
TAKE ME TO YOUR HOUSE.
......OKAY...
...THEN I'LL WAIT FOR YOU IN THE CLASS-ROOM AFTER SCHOOL.
DON'T YOU DARE RUN AWAY.
キーン
KIIIN (DIIING)
コーン
KOOON (DOOONG)
カーン
KAAAN (DAAANG)

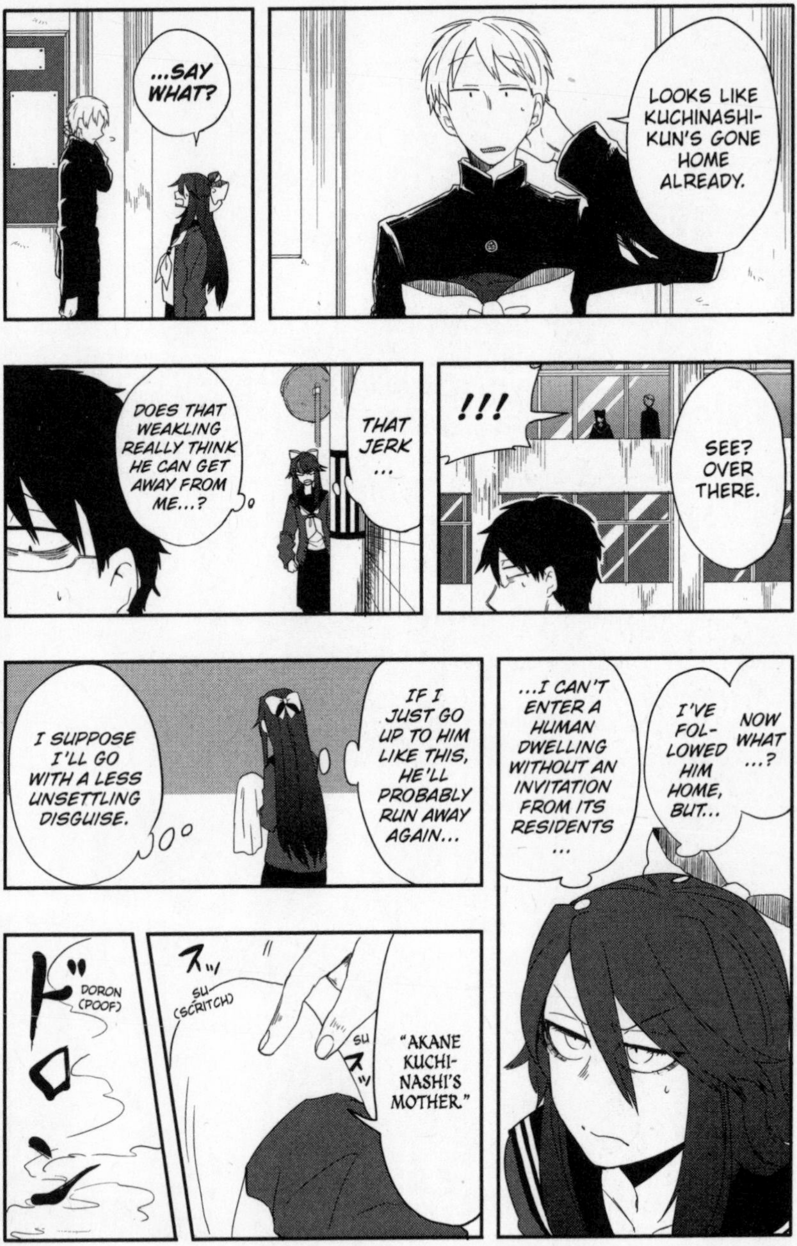
LOOKS LIKE KUCHINASHI-KUN'S GONE HOME ALREADY.
...SAY WHAT?
SEE? OVER THERE.
!!!
THAT JERK ...
DOES THAT WEAKLING REALLY THINK HE CAN GET AWAY FROM ME...?
NOW WHAT ...?
I'VE FOL-LOWED HIM HOME, BUT...
...I CAN'T ENTER A HUMAN DWELLING WITHOUT AN INVITATION FROM ITS RESIDENTS ...
IF I JUST GO UP TO HIM LIKE THIS, HE'LL PROBABLY RUN AWAY AGAIN...
I SUPPOSE I'LL GO WITH A LESS UNSETTLING DISGUISE.
スッ
SU (SCRITCH)
スッ
SU
"AKANE KUCHI-NASHI'S MOTHER."
ドロン
DORON (POOF)

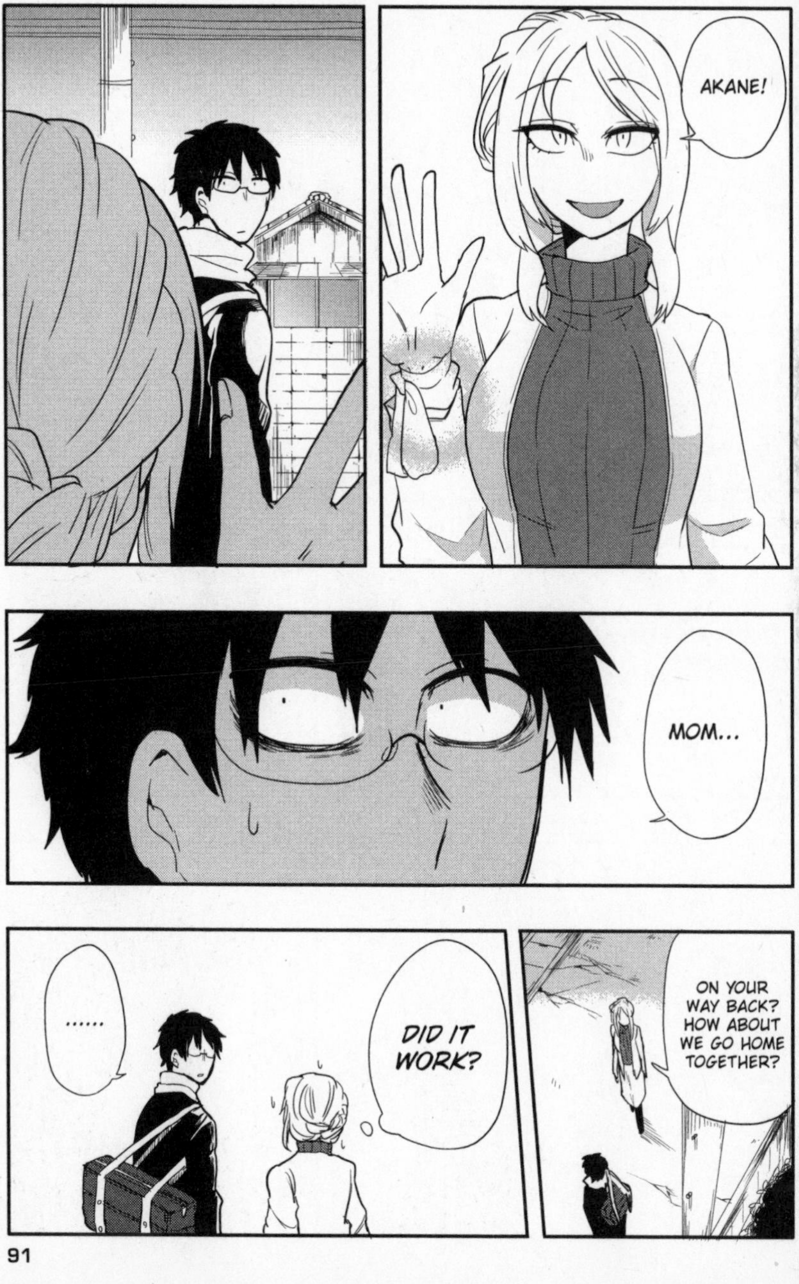
AKANE!
MOM...
ON YOUR WAY BACK? HOW ABOUT WE GO HOME TOGETHER?
DID IT WORK?
......

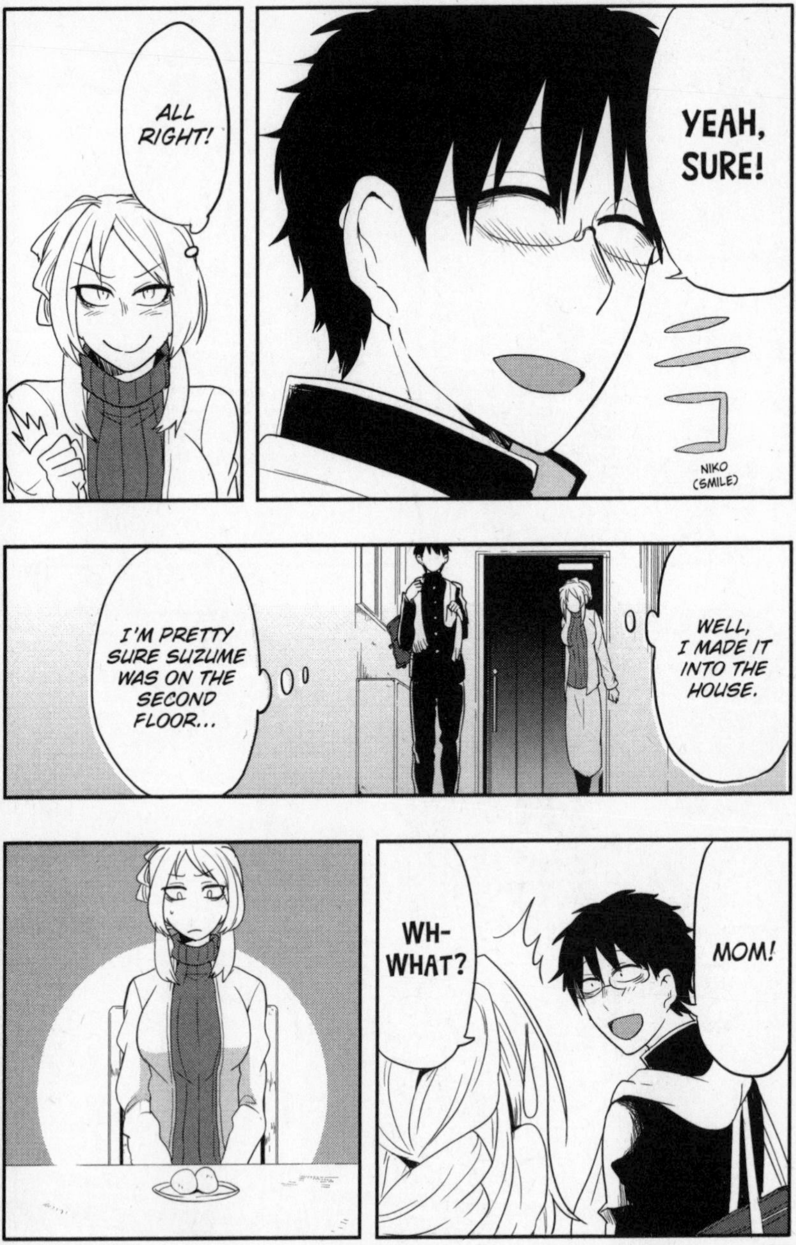
YEAH, SURE!
NIKO (SMILE)
ALL RIGHT!
WELL, I MADE IT INTO THE HOUSE.
I'M PRETTY SURE SUZUME WAS ON THE SECOND FLOOR...
MOM!
WH-WHAT?

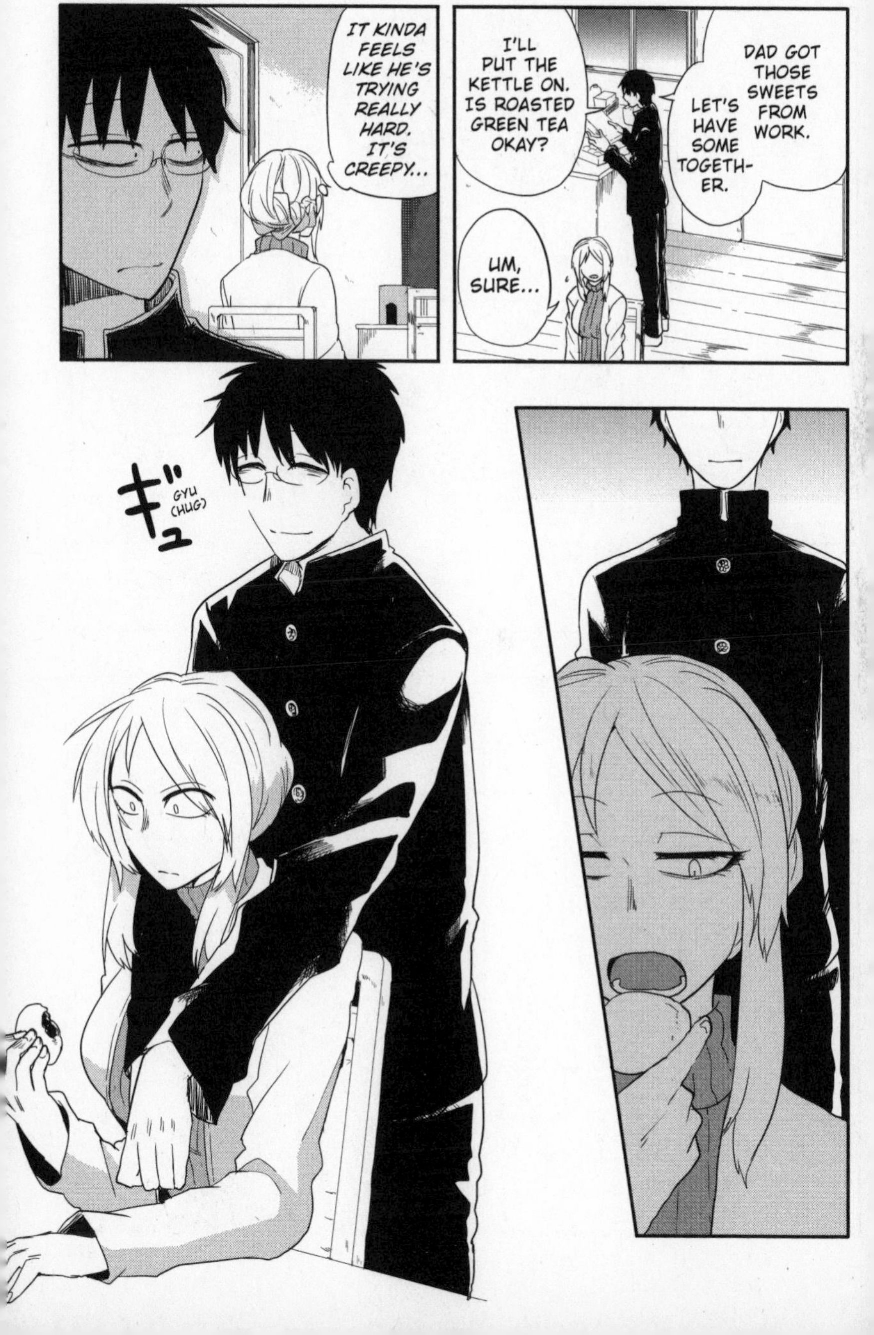
DAD GOT THOSE SWEETS FROM WORK.
LET'S HAVE SOME TOGETH-ER.
I'LL PUT THE KETTLE ON. IS ROASTED GREEN TEA OKAY?
UM, SURE...
IT KINDA FEELS LIKE HE'S TRYING REALLY HARD. IT'S CREEPY...
ギュ
GYU (HUG)

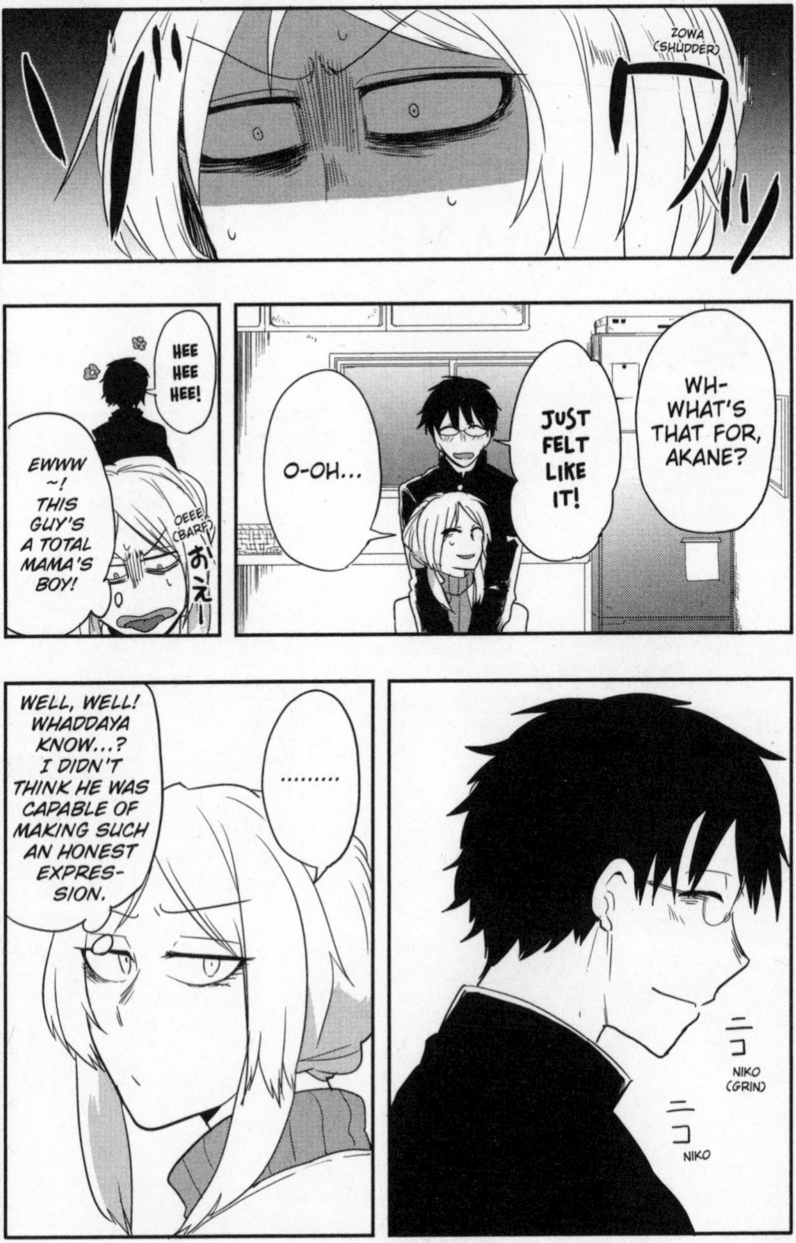
ゾワッ
ZOWA (SHUDDER)
WH- WHAT'S THAT FOR, AKANE?
JUST FELT LIKE IT!
O-OH...
HEE HEE HEE!
EWWW ~! THIS GUY'S A TOTAL MAMA'S BOY!
おえー
OEEE (BARF)
ニコ
NIKO (GRIN)
ニコ
NIKO
....
WELL, WELL! WHADDAYA KNOW...? I DIDN'T THINK HE WAS CAPABLE OF MAKING SUCH AN HONEST EXPRESSION.

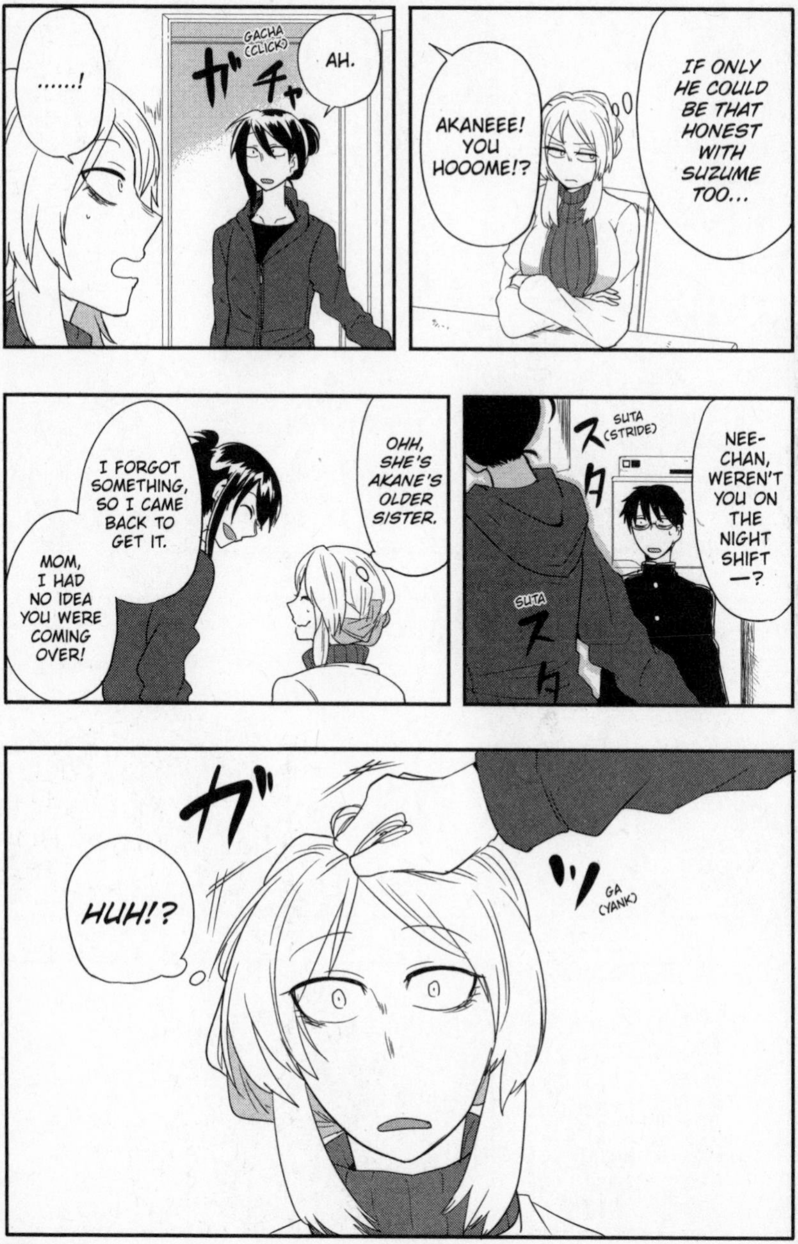
IF ONLY HE COULD BE THAT HONEST WITH SUZUME TOO...
AKANEEE! YOU HOOOME!?
AH.
GACHA (CLICK)
......!
NEE-CHAN, WEREN'T YOU ON THE NIGHT SHIFT—?
SUTA (STRIDE)
SUTA
OHH, SHE'S AKANE'S OLDER SISTER.
I FORGOT SOMETHING, SO I CAME BACK TO GET IT.
MOM, I HAD NO IDEA YOU WERE COMING OVER!
GA (YANK)
HUH!?

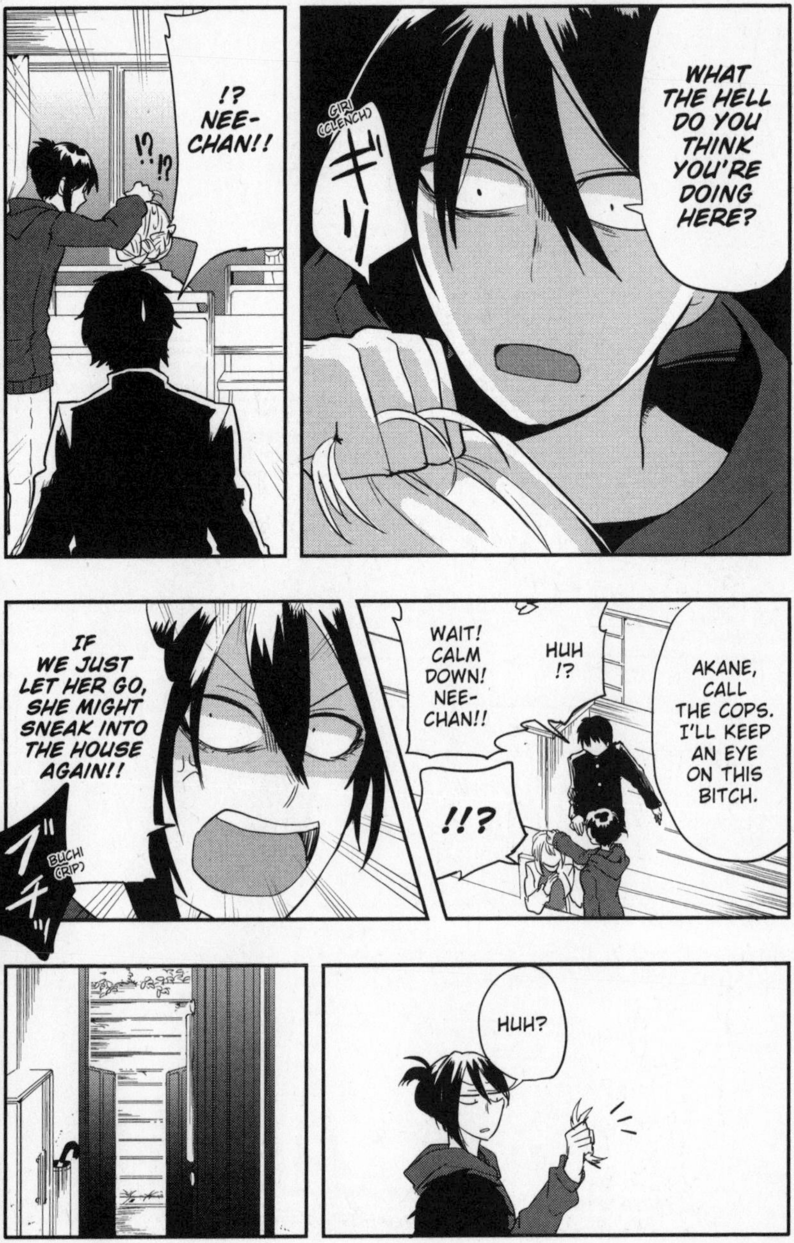
GIRI (CLENCH)
WHAT THE HELL DO YOU THINK YOU'RE DOING HERE?
!? NEE-CHAN!!
!? !?
AKANE, CALL THE COPS. I'LL KEEP AN EYE ON THIS BITCH.
HUH !?
WAIT! CALM DOWN! NEE-CHAN!!
!!?
IF WE JUST LET HER GO, SHE MIGHT SNEAK INTO THE HOUSE AGAIN!!
BUCHI (RIP)
HUH?

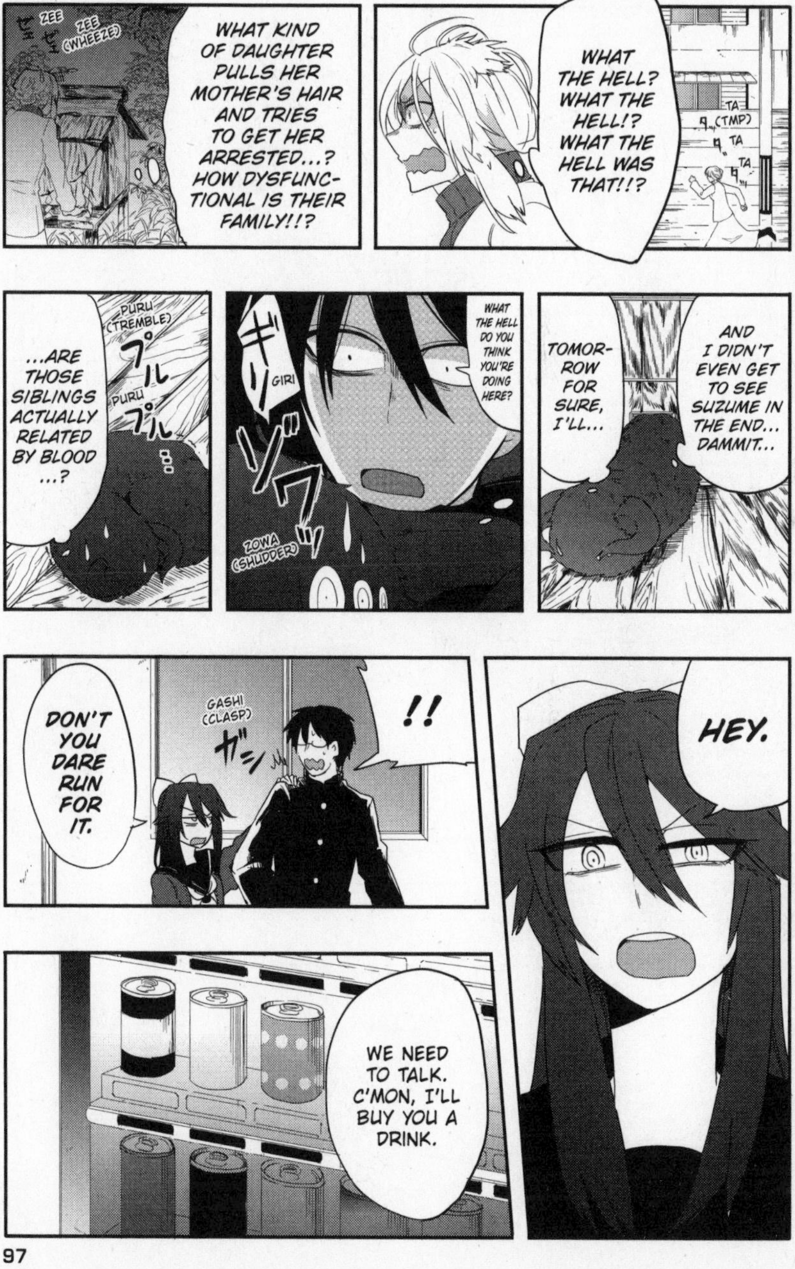
WHAT THE HELL? WHAT THE HELL!? WHAT THE HELL WAS THAT!!?
TA (TMP) TA TA
WHAT KIND OF DAUGHTER PULLS HER MOTHER'S HAIR AND TRIES TO GET HER ARRESTED...? HOW DYSFUNCTIONAL IS THEIR FAMILY!!?
ZEE ZEE (WHEEZE)
AND I DIDN'T EVEN GET TO SEE SUZUME IN THE END... DAMMIT...
TOMORROW FOR SURE, I'LL...
WHAT THE HELL DO YOU THINK YOU'RE DOING HERE?
GIRI
ZOWA (SHUDDER)
PURU (TREMBLE) PURU
...ARE THOSE SIBLINGS ACTUALLY RELATED BY BLOOD ...?
HEY.
!!
GASHI (CLASP)
DON'T YOU DARE RUN FOR IT.
WE NEED TO TALK. C'MON, I'LL BUY YOU A DRINK.

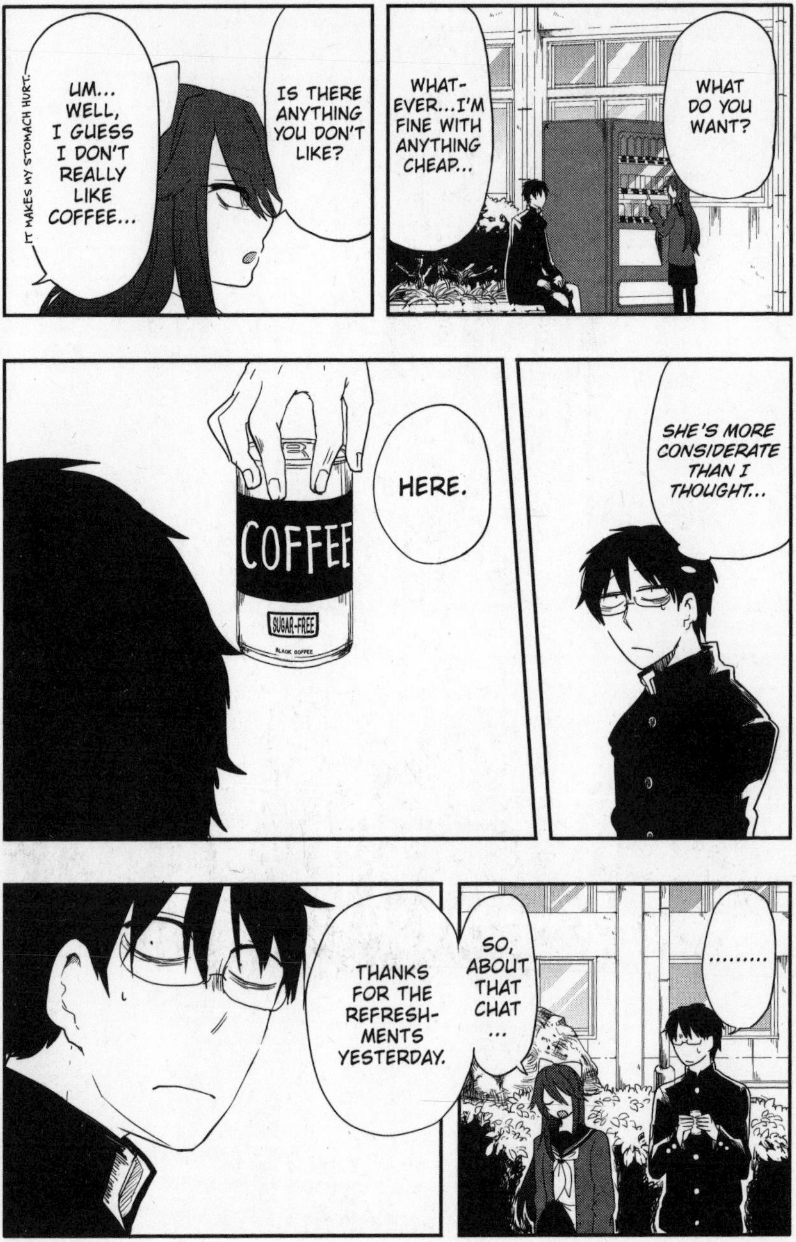
WHAT DO YOU WANT?
WHAT-EVER...I'M FINE WITH ANYTHING CHEAP...
IS THERE ANYTHING YOU DON'T LIKE?
UM... WELL, I GUESS I DON'T REALLY LIKE COFFEE...
IT MAKES MY STOMACH HURT.
SHE'S MORE CONSIDERATE THAN I THOUGHT...
HERE.
COFFEE
SUGAR-FREE
BLACK COFFEE
....
SO, ABOUT THAT CHAT ...
THANKS FOR THE REFRESH-MENTS YESTERDAY.

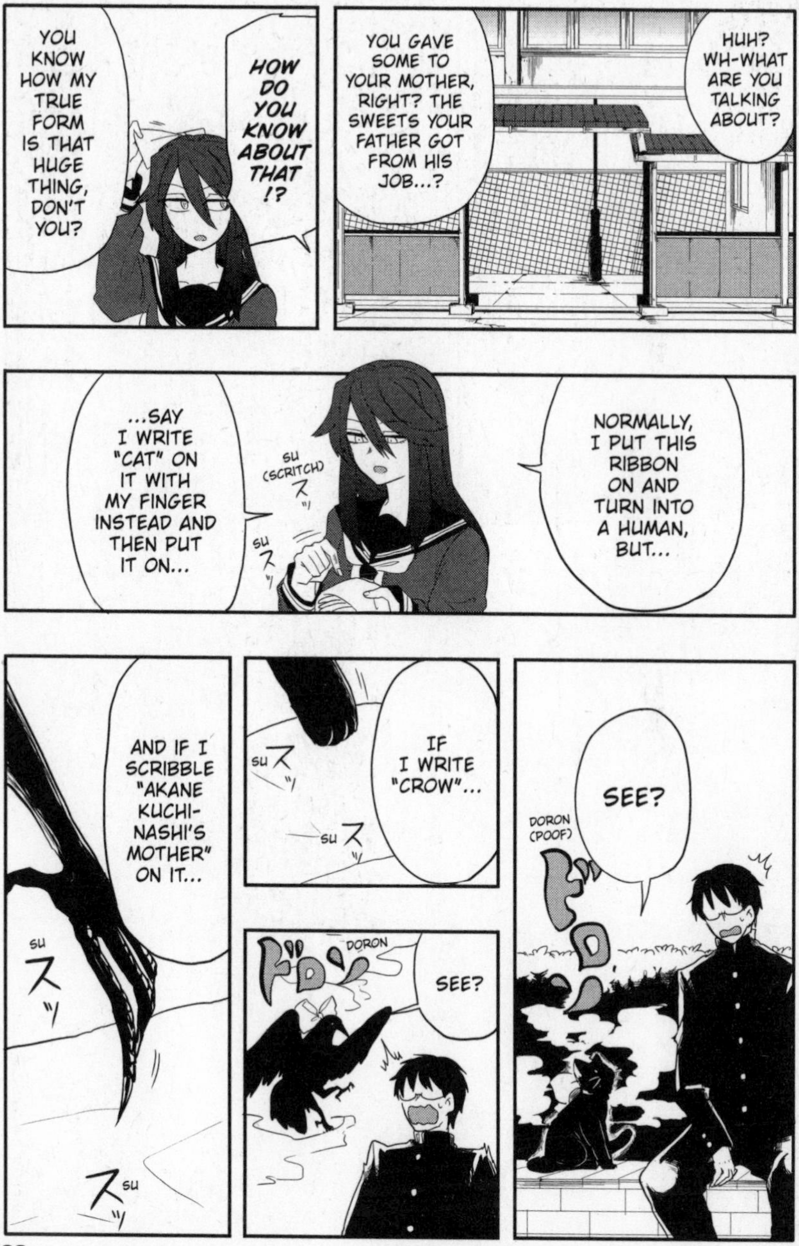
HUH? WH-WHAT ARE YOU TALKING ABOUT?
YOU GAVE SOME TO YOUR MOTHER, RIGHT? THE SWEETS YOUR FATHER GOT FROM HIS JOB...?
HOW DO YOU KNOW ABOUT THAT!?
YOU KNOW HOW MY TRUE FORM IS THAT HUGE THING, DON'T YOU?
NORMALLY, I PUT THIS RIBBON ON AND TURN INTO A HUMAN, BUT...
SU (SCRITCH) ス
SU ス
...SAY I WRITE "CAT" ON IT WITH MY FINGER INSTEAD AND THEN PUT IT ON...
SEE?
DORON (POOF)
SU ス
IF I WRITE "CROW"...
SU ス
DORON
SEE?
SU ス
AND IF I SCRIBBLE "AKANE KUCHI-NASHI'S MOTHER" ON IT...
SU ス

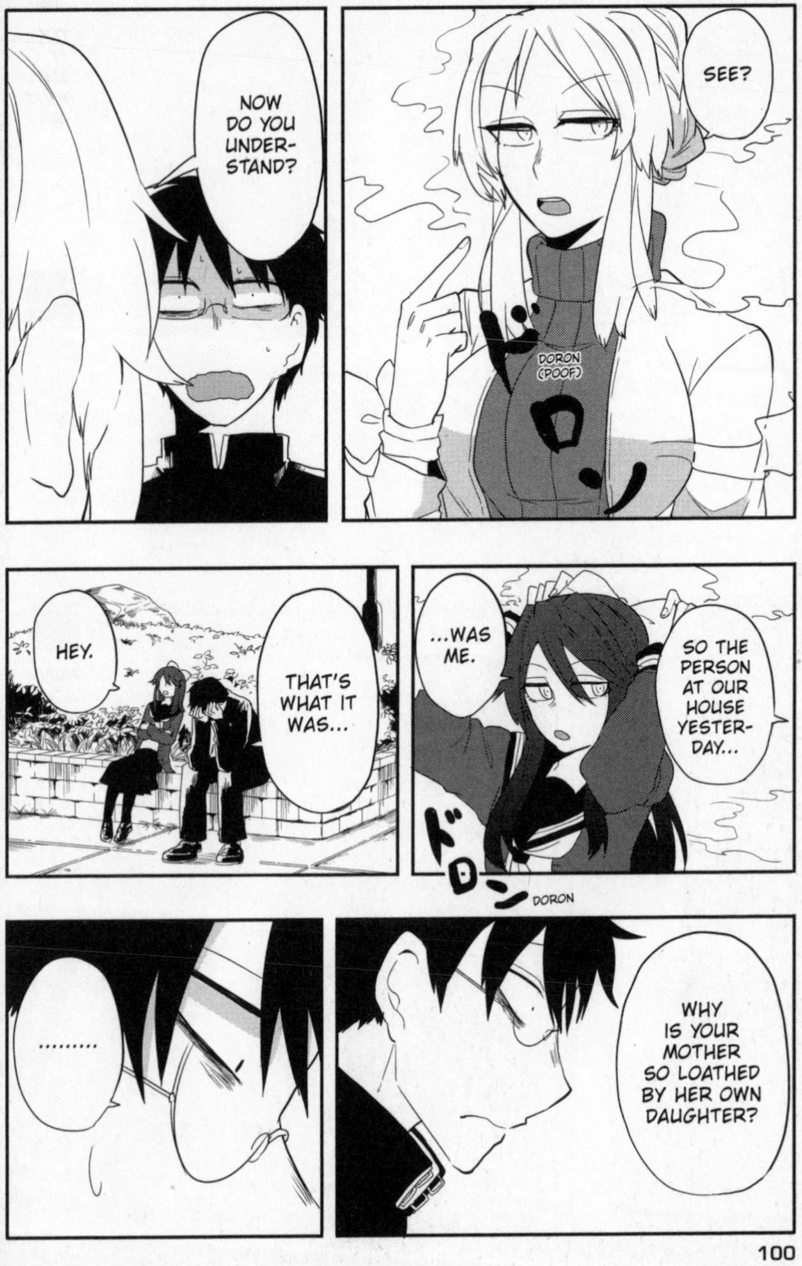
SEE?
DORON (POOF)
NOW DO YOU UNDER-STAND?
SO THE PERSON AT OUR HOUSE YESTER-DAY...
...WAS ME.
DORON
THAT'S WHAT IT WAS...
HEY.
WHY IS YOUR MOTHER SO LOATHED BY HER OWN DAUGHTER?
....

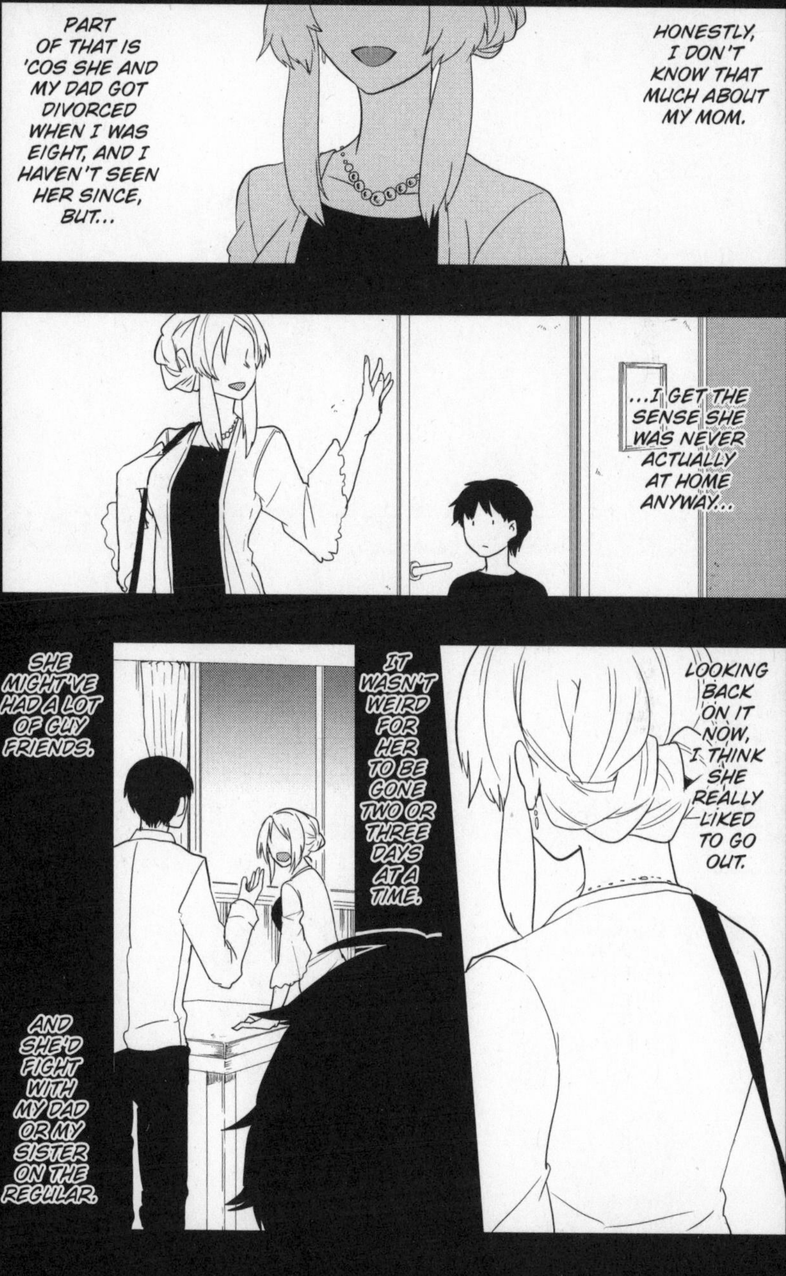
HONESTLY, I DON'T KNOW THAT MUCH ABOUT MY MOM.
PART OF THAT IS 'COS SHE AND MY DAD GOT DIVORCED WHEN I WAS EIGHT, AND I HAVEN'T SEEN HER SINCE, BUT...
...I GET THE SENSE SHE WAS NEVER ACTUALLY AT HOME ANYWAY...
LOOKING BACK ON IT NOW, I THINK SHE REALLY LIKED TO GO OUT.
IT WASN'T WEIRD FOR HER TO BE GONE TWO OR THREE DAYS AT A TIME.
SHE MIGHT'VE HAD A LOT OF GUY FRIENDS.
AND SHE'D FIGHT WITH MY DAD OR MY SISTER ON THE REGULAR.

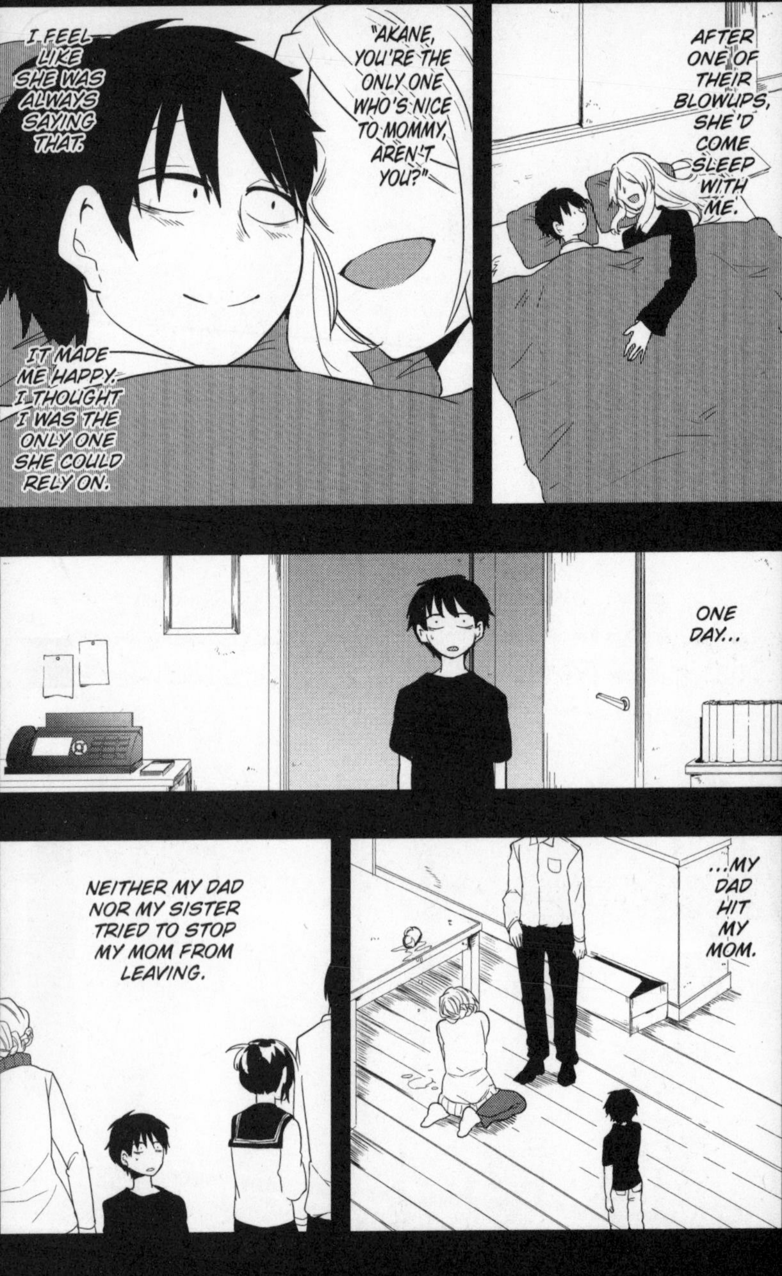
AFTER ONE OF THEIR BLOWUPS, SHE'D COME SLEEP WITH ME.
"AKANE, YOU'RE THE ONLY ONE WHO'S NICE TO MOMMY, AREN'T YOU?"
I FEEL LIKE SHE WAS ALWAYS SAYING THAT.
IT MADE ME HAPPY. I THOUGHT I WAS THE ONLY ONE SHE COULD RELY ON.
ONE DAY...
...MY DAD HIT MY MOM.
NEITHER MY DAD NOR MY SISTER TRIED TO STOP MY MOM FROM LEAVING.

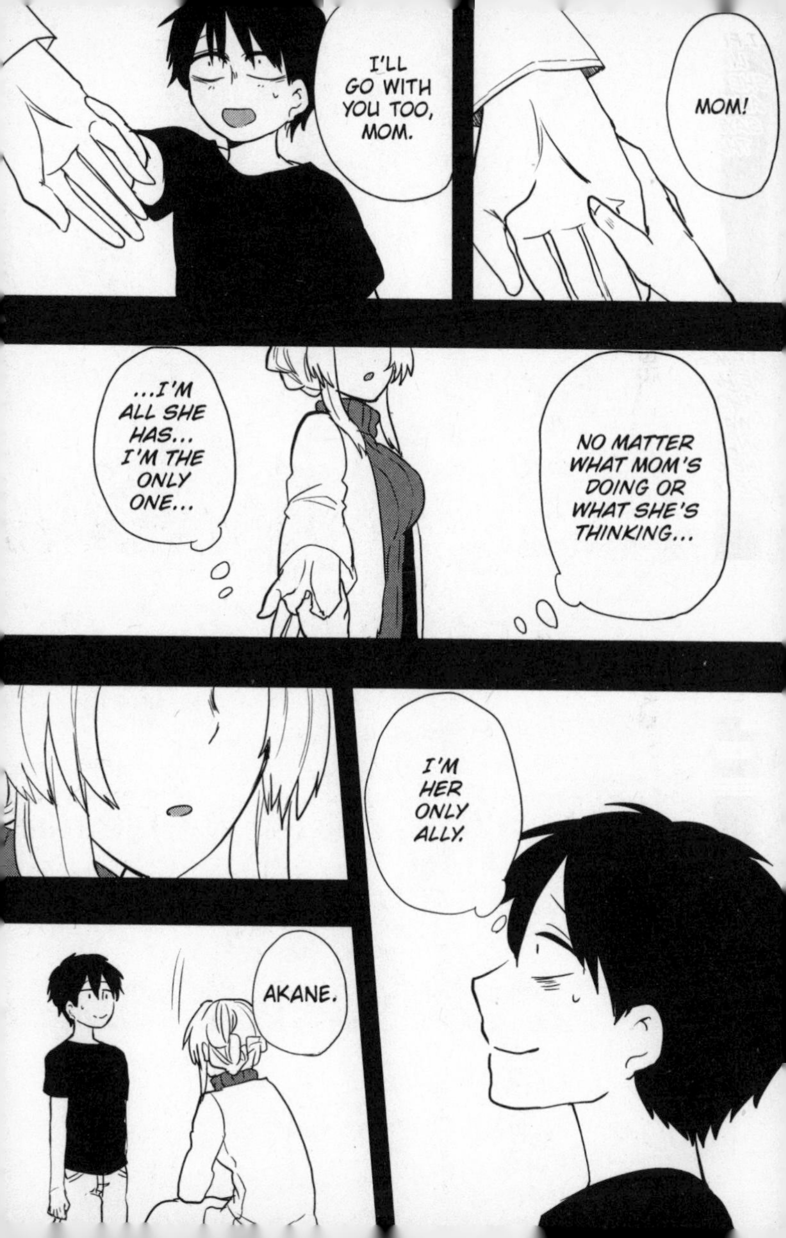
MOM!
I'LL GO WITH YOU TOO, MOM.
NO MATTER WHAT MOM'S DOING OR WHAT SHE'S THINKING...
...I'M ALL SHE HAS... I'M THE ONLY ONE...
I'M HER ONLY ALLY.
AKANE.

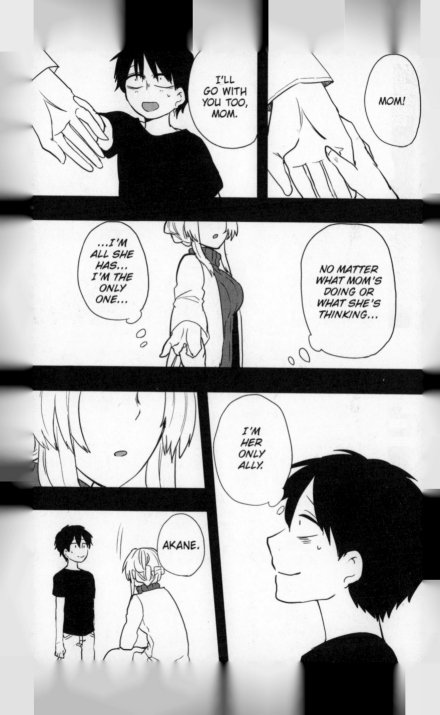

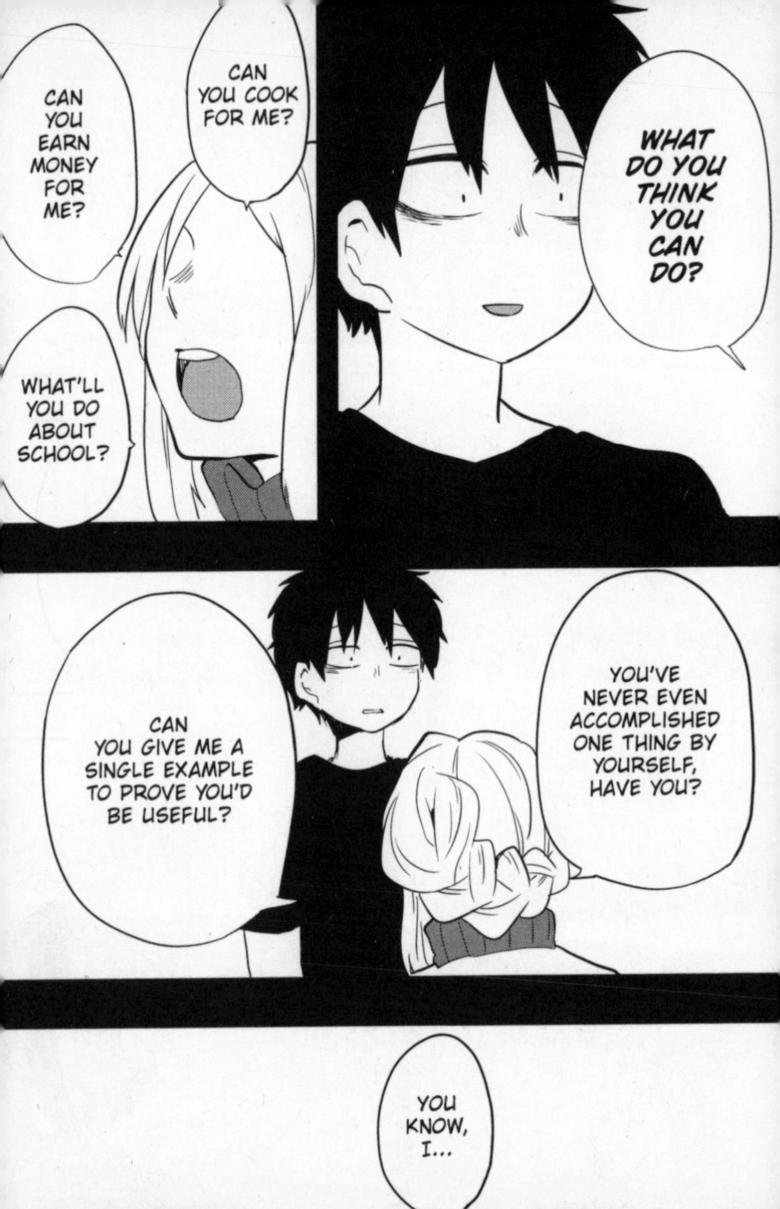
WHAT DO YOU THINK YOU CAN DO?
CAN YOU COOK FOR ME?
CAN YOU EARN MONEY FOR ME?
WHAT'LL YOU DO ABOUT SCHOOL?
YOU'VE NEVER EVEN ACCOMPLISHED ONE THING BY YOURSELF, HAVE YOU?
CAN YOU GIVE ME A SINGLE EXAMPLE TO PROVE YOU'D BE USEFUL?
YOU KNOW, I...

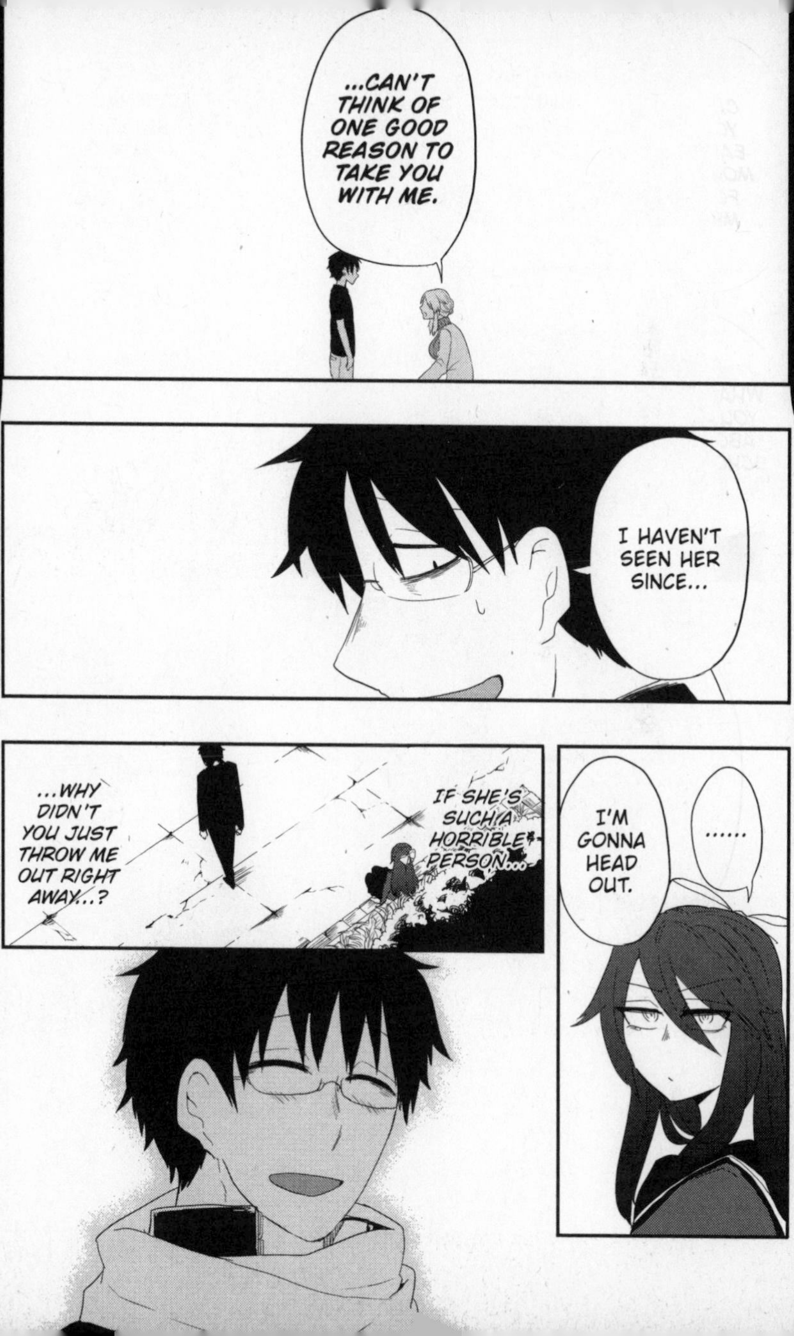

...CAN'T THINK OF ONE GOOD REASON TO TAKE YOU WITH ME.
I HAVEN'T SEEN HER SINCE...
......
I'M GONNA HEAD OUT.
IF SHE'S SUCH A HORRIBLE PERSON...
...WHY DIDN'T YOU JUST THROW ME OUT RIGHT AWAY...?

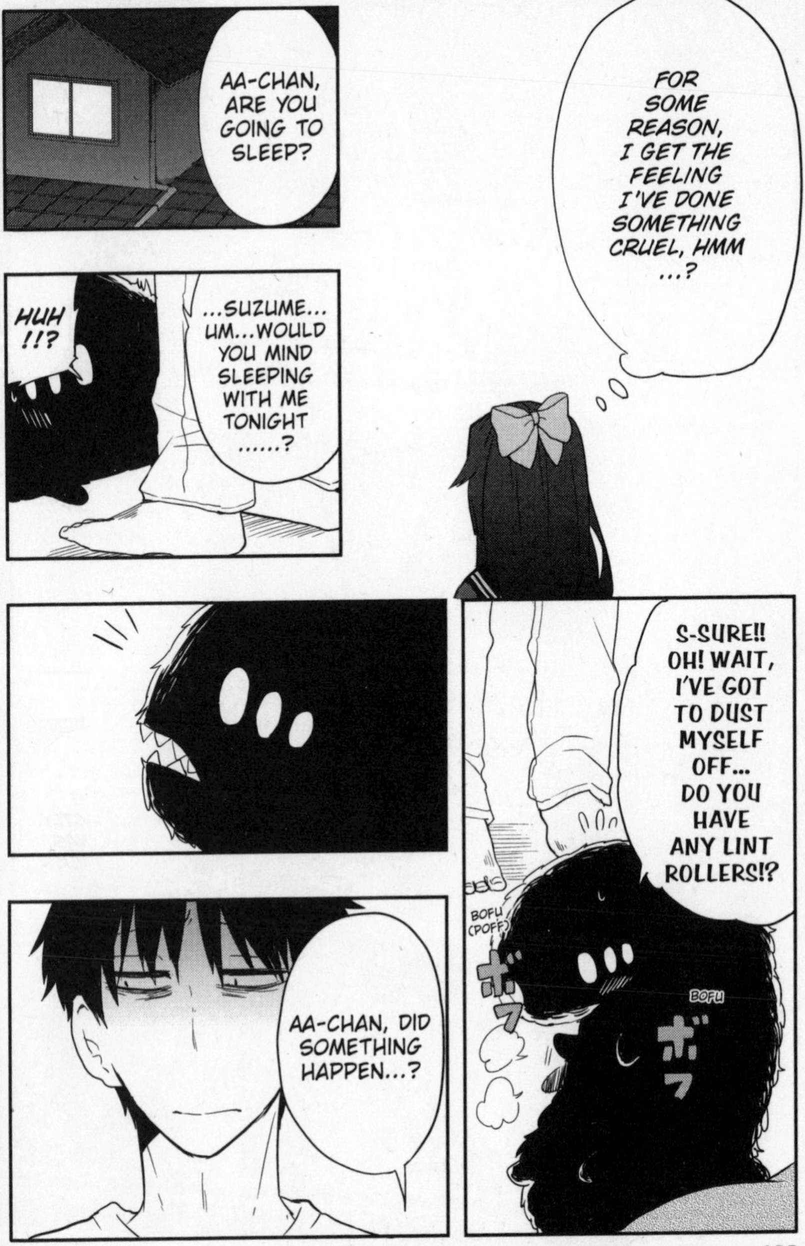

FOR SOME REASON, I GET THE FEELING I'VE DONE SOMETHING CRUEL, HMM ...?
AA-CHAN, ARE YOU GOING TO SLEEP?
...SUZUME... UM...WOULD YOU MIND SLEEPING WITH ME TONIGHT ......?
HUH !!?
S-SURE!! OH! WAIT, I'VE GOT TO DUST MYSELF OFF... DO YOU HAVE ANY LINT ROLLERS!?
BOFU (POFF)
BOFU
AA-CHAN, DID SOMETHING HAPPEN...?

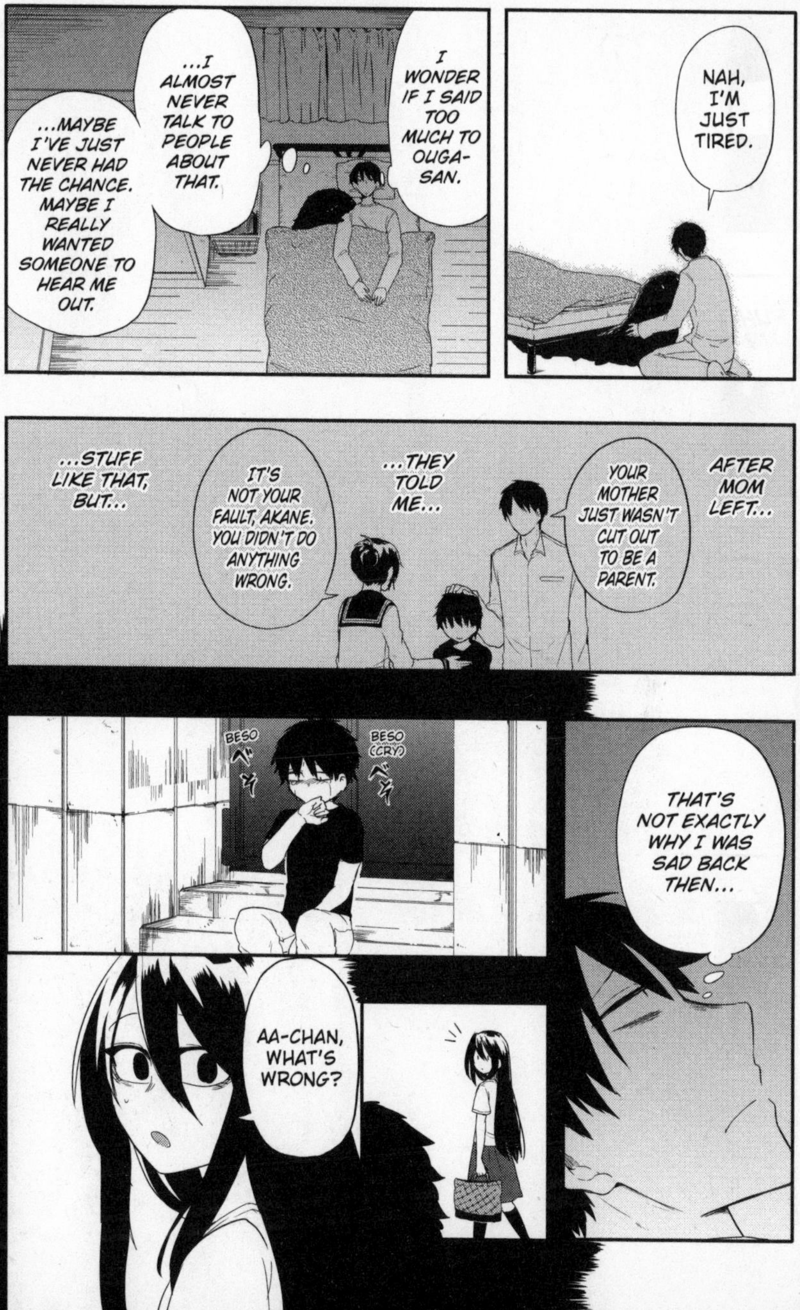
NAH, I'M JUST TIRED.
I WONDER IF I SAID TOO MUCH TO OUGA-SAN.
...I ALMOST NEVER TALK TO PEOPLE ABOUT THAT.
...MAYBE I'VE JUST NEVER HAD THE CHANCE. MAYBE I REALLY WANTED SOMEONE TO HEAR ME OUT.
AFTER MOM LEFT...
YOUR MOTHER JUST WASN'T CUT OUT TO BE A PARENT.
...THEY TOLD ME...
IT'S NOT YOUR FAULT, AKANE. YOU DIDN'T DO ANYTHING WRONG.
...STUFF LIKE THAT, BUT...
THAT'S NOT EXACTLY WHY I WAS SAD BACK THEN...
BESO (CRY)
BESO
AA-CHAN, WHAT'S WRONG?

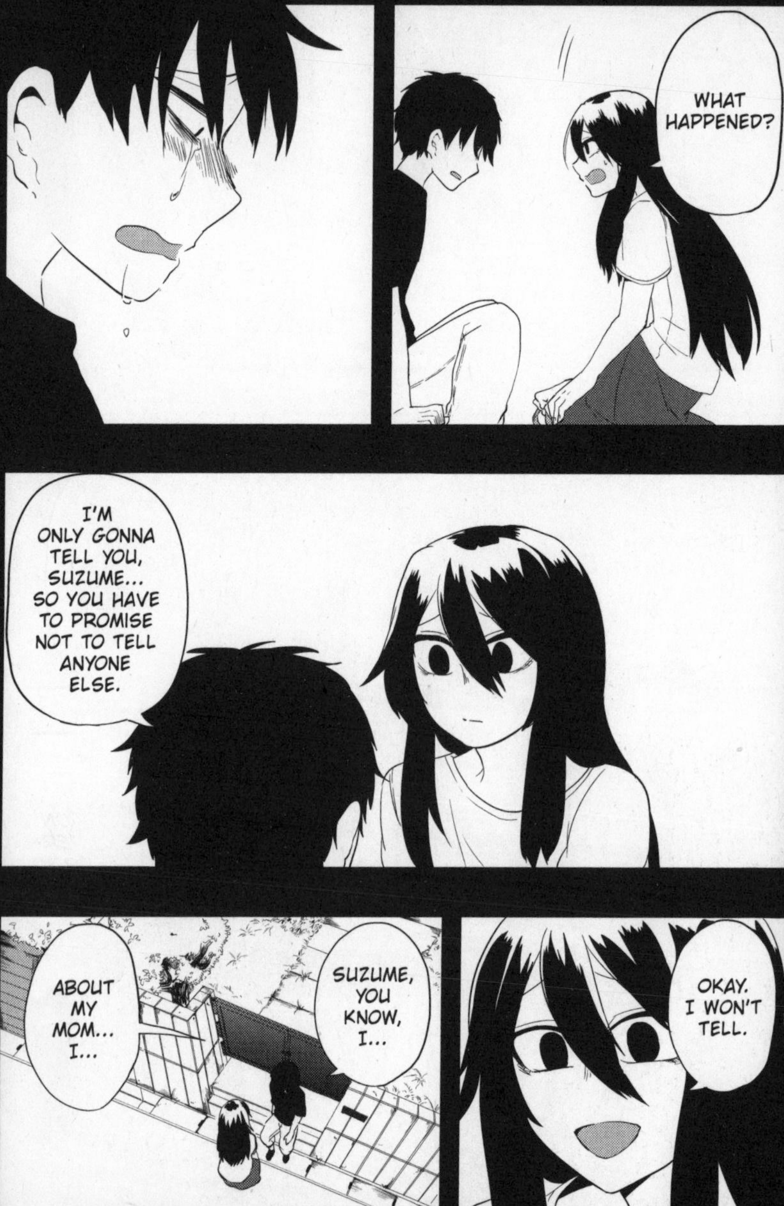
WHAT HAPPENED?
I'M ONLY GONNA TELL YOU, SUZUME... SO YOU HAVE TO PROMISE NOT TO TELL ANYONE ELSE.
OKAY. I WON'T TELL.
SUZUME, YOU KNOW, I...
ABOUT MY MOM... I...

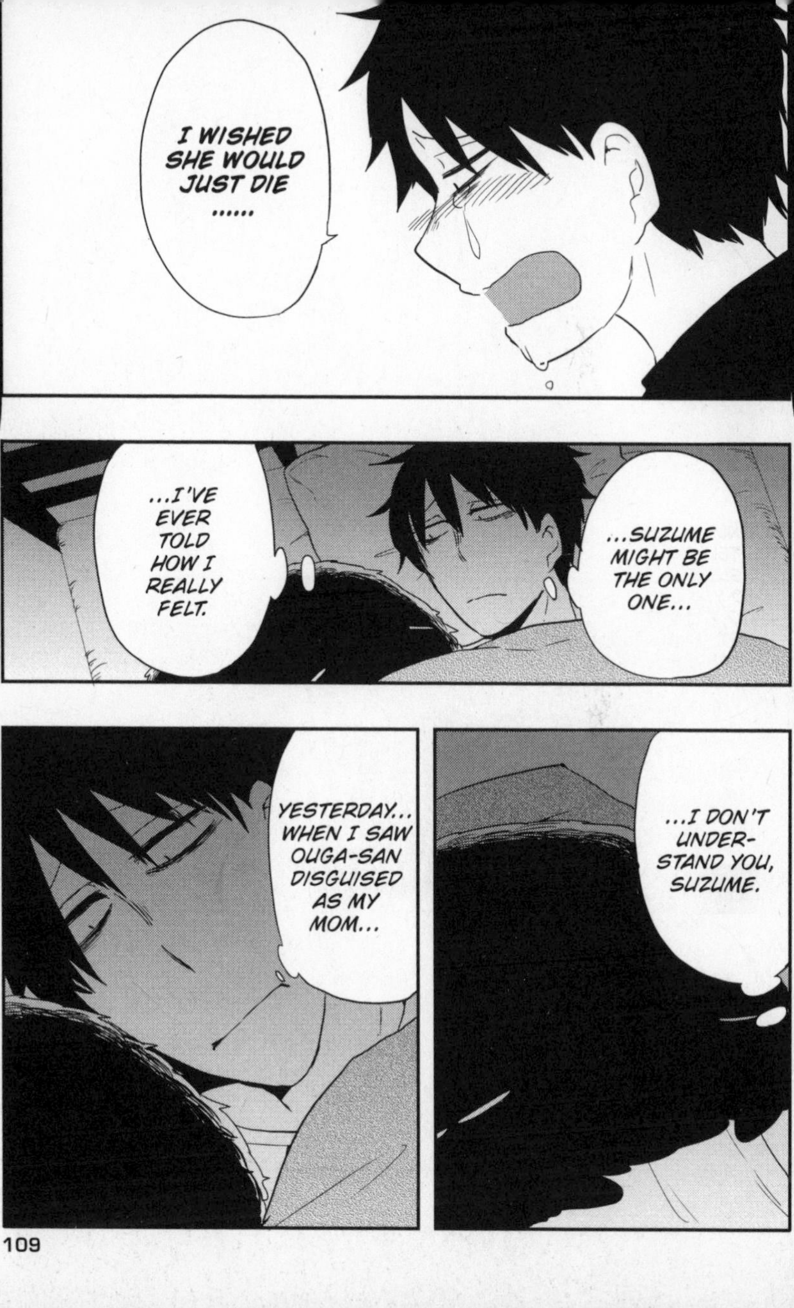
I WISHED SHE WOULD JUST DIE ......
...SUZUME MIGHT BE THE ONLY ONE...
...I'VE EVER TOLD HOW I REALLY FELT.
...I DON'T UNDER-STAND YOU, SUZUME.
YESTERDAY... WHEN I SAW OUGA-SAN DISGUISED AS MY MOM...

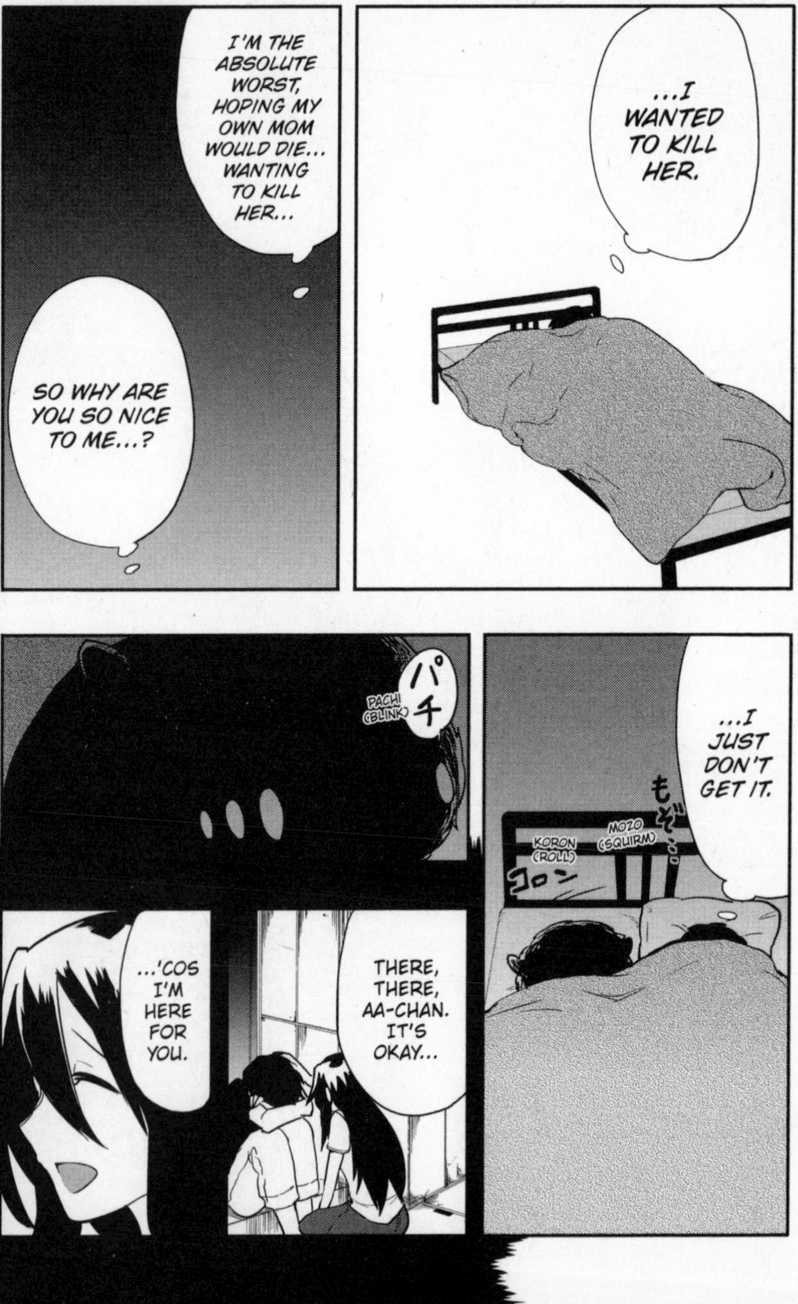
...I WANTED TO KILL HER.
I'M THE ABSOLUTE WORST, HOPING MY OWN MOM WOULD DIE... WANTING TO KILL HER...
SO WHY ARE YOU SO NICE TO ME...?
...I JUST DON'T GET IT.
もぞ...
MOZO (SQUIRM)
コロン
KORON (ROLL)
パチ
PACHI (BLINK)
...
THERE, THERE, AA-CHAN. IT'S OKAY...
...'COS I'M HERE FOR YOU.

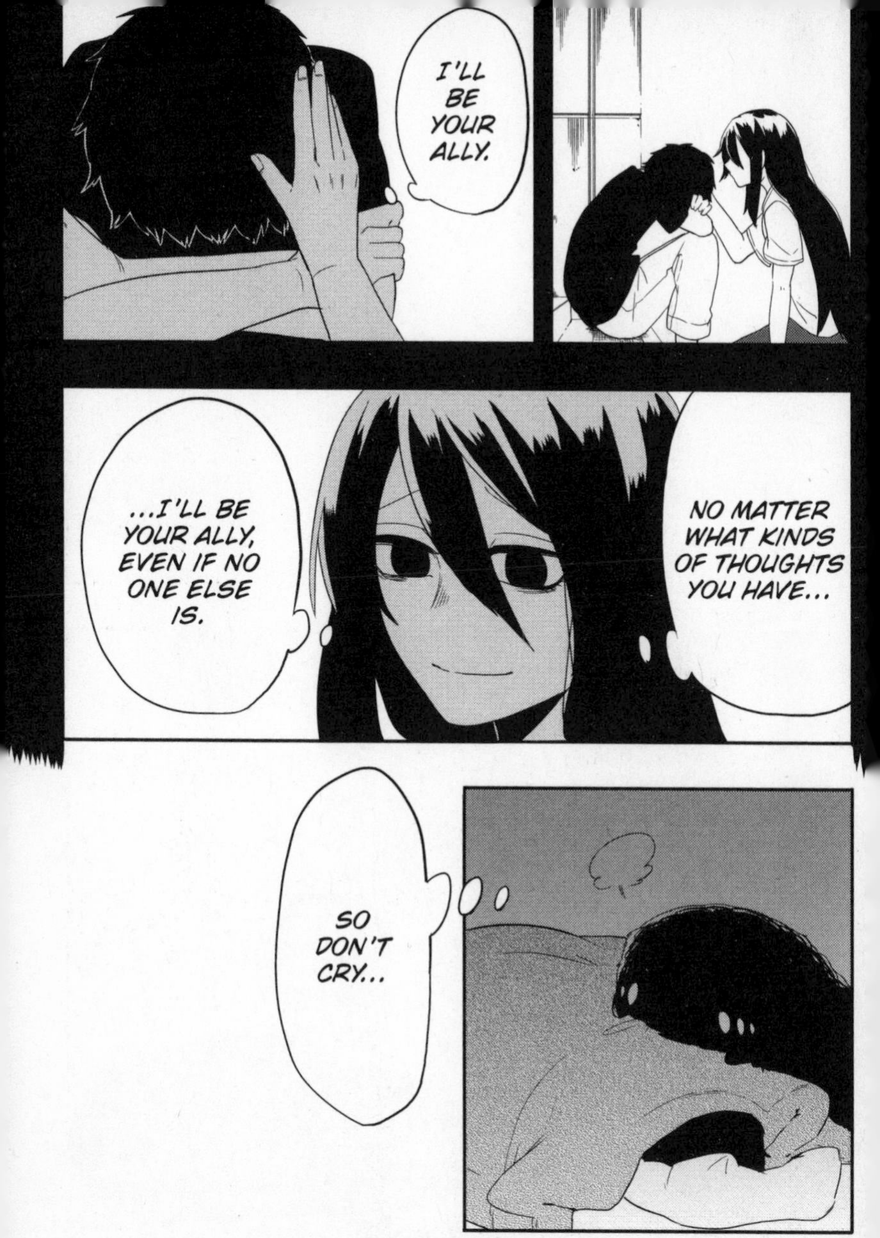
I'LL BE YOUR ALLY.
NO MATTER WHAT KINDS OF THOUGHTS YOU HAVE...
...I'LL BE YOUR ALLY, EVEN IF NO ONE ELSE IS.
SO DON'T CRY...

SENSE OF
RIVALRY

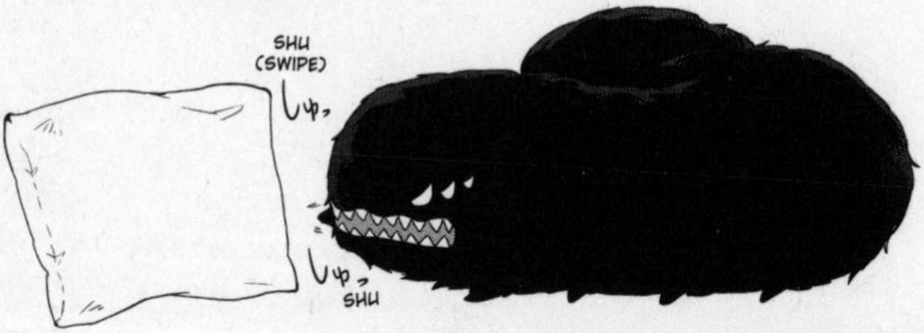
SHU
(SWIPE)
しゅっ
しゅっ
SHU

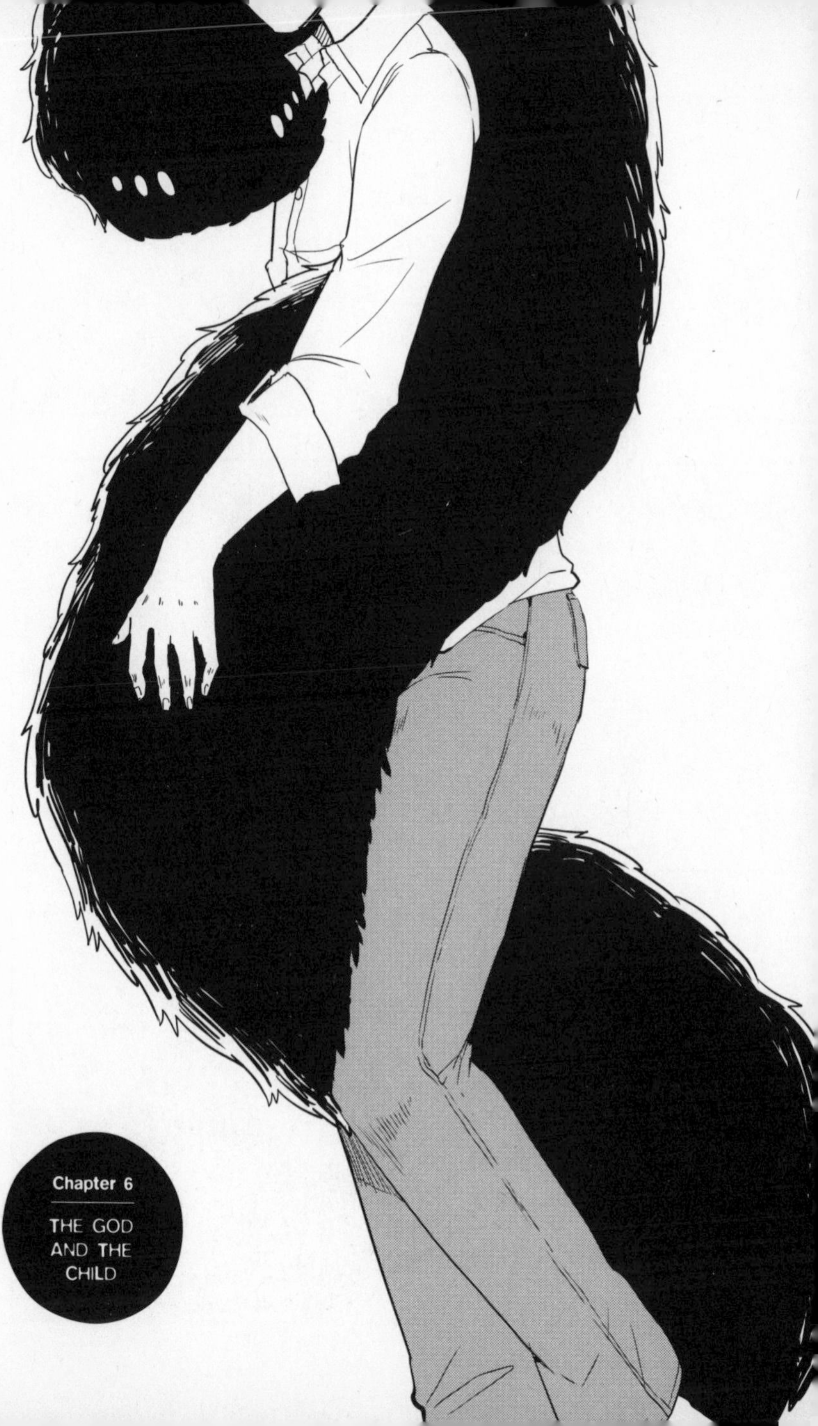
Chapter 6
THE GOD AND THE CHILD

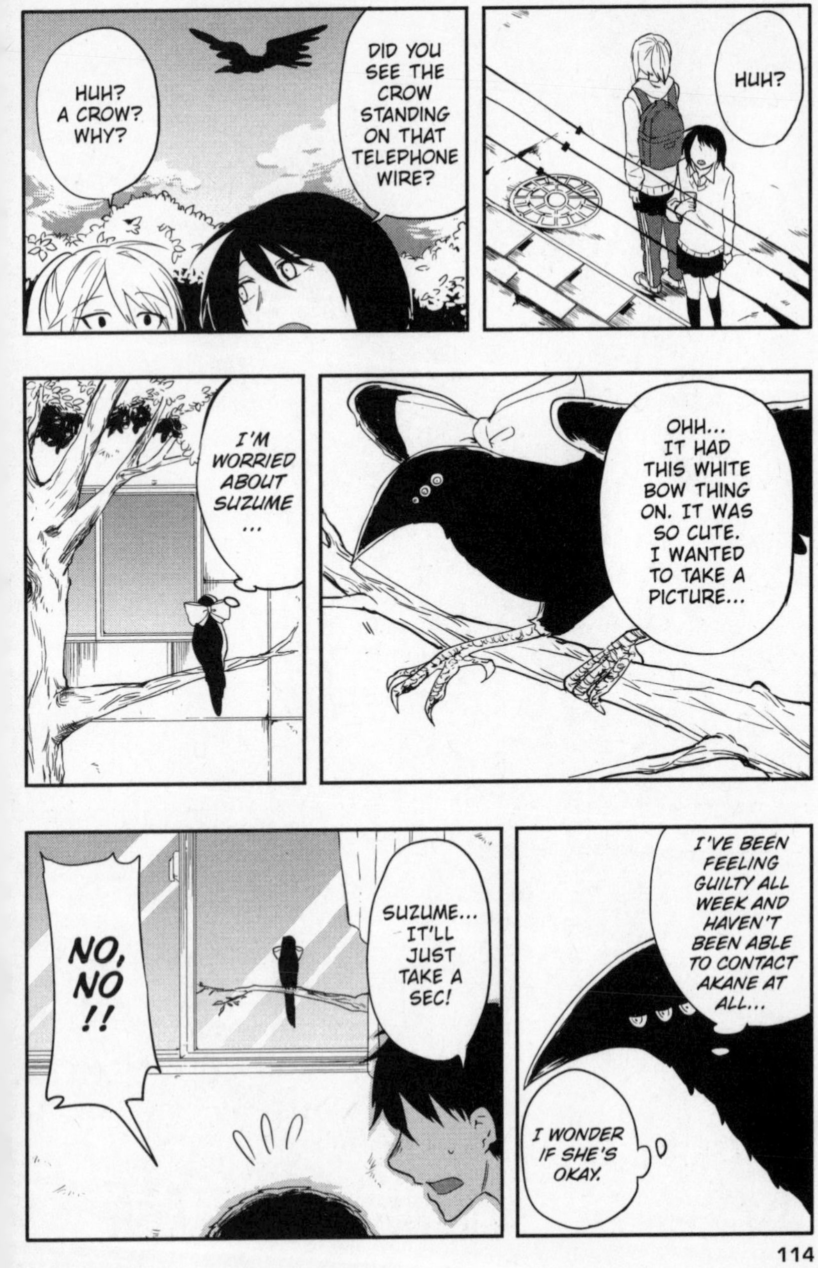
HUH?
DID YOU SEE THE CROW STANDING ON THAT TELEPHONE WIRE?
HUH? A CROW? WHY?
OHH... IT HAD THIS WHITE BOW THING ON. IT WAS SO CUTE. I WANTED TO TAKE A PICTURE...
I'M WORRIED ABOUT SUZUME ...
I'VE BEEN FEELING GUILTY ALL WEEK AND HAVEN'T BEEN ABLE TO CONTACT AKANE AT ALL...
I WONDER IF SHE'S OKAY.
SUZUME... IT'LL JUST TAKE A SEC!
NO, NO !!

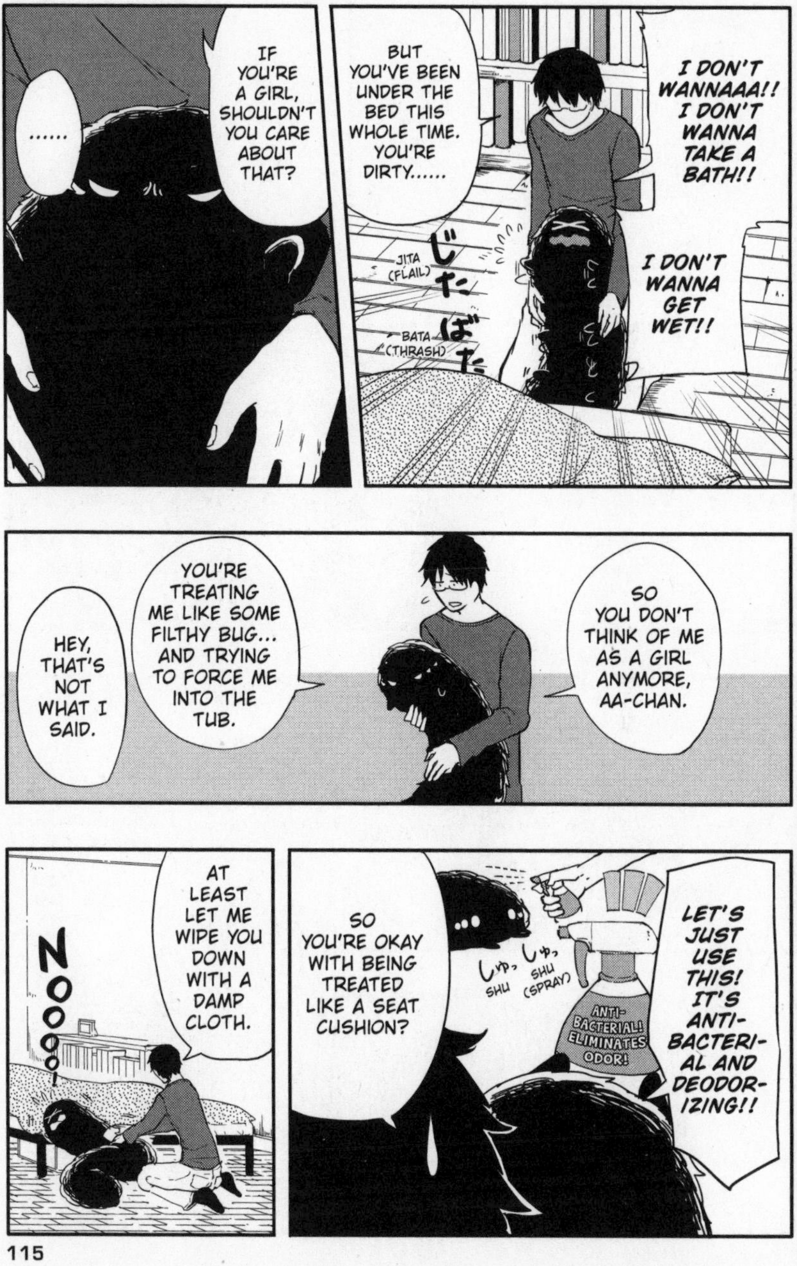
I DON'T WANNAAA!! I DON'T WANNA TAKE A BATH!!
I DON'T WANNA GET WET!!
BUT YOU'VE BEEN UNDER THE BED THIS WHOLE TIME. YOU'RE DIRTY......
じた JITA (FLAIL)
ばた BATA (THRASH)
IF YOU'RE A GIRL, SHOULDN'T YOU CARE ABOUT THAT?
......
SO YOU DON'T THINK OF ME AS A GIRL ANYMORE, AA-CHAN.
YOU'RE TREATING ME LIKE SOME FILTHY BUG... AND TRYING TO FORCE ME INTO THE TUB.
HEY, THAT'S NOT WHAT I SAID.
LET'S JUST USE THIS! IT'S ANTI-BACTERIAL AND DEODORIZING!!
ANTI-BACTERIAL! ELIMINATES ODOR!
しゅっ SHU (SPRAY)
しゅっ SHU
SO YOU'RE OKAY WITH BEING TREATED LIKE A SEAT CUSHION?
AT LEAST LET ME WIPE YOU DOWN WITH A DAMP CLOTH.
NOOOO!

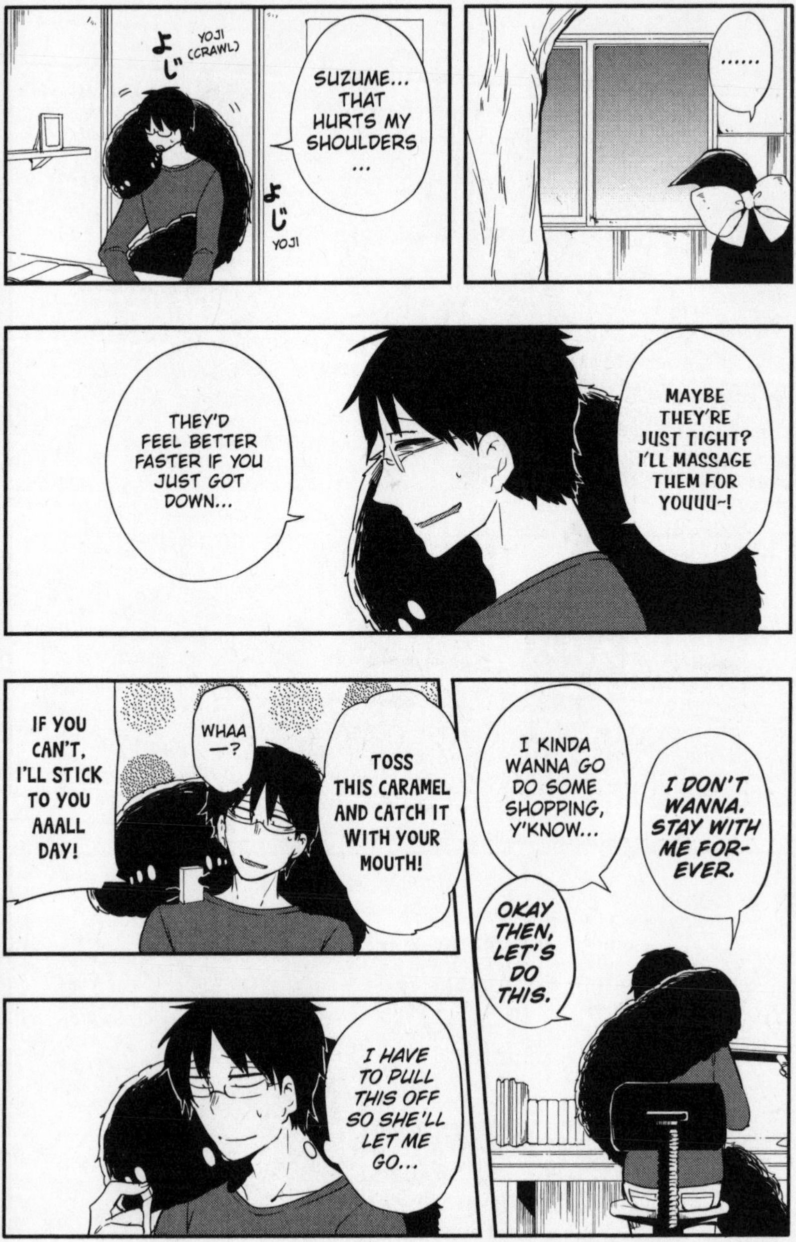
......
SUZUME... THAT HURTS MY SHOULDERS ...
よじ YOJI (CRAWL)
よじ YOJI
MAYBE THEY'RE JUST TIGHT? I'LL MASSAGE THEM FOR YOUUU~!
THEY'D FEEL BETTER FASTER IF YOU JUST GOT DOWN...
I KINDA WANNA GO DO SOME SHOPPING, Y'KNOW...
I DON'T WANNA. STAY WITH ME FOR-EVER.
OKAY THEN, LET'S DO THIS.
TOSS THIS CARAMEL AND CATCH IT WITH YOUR MOUTH!
WHAA—?
IF YOU CAN'T, I'LL STICK TO YOU AAALL DAY!
I HAVE TO PULL THIS OFF SO SHE'LL LET ME GO...

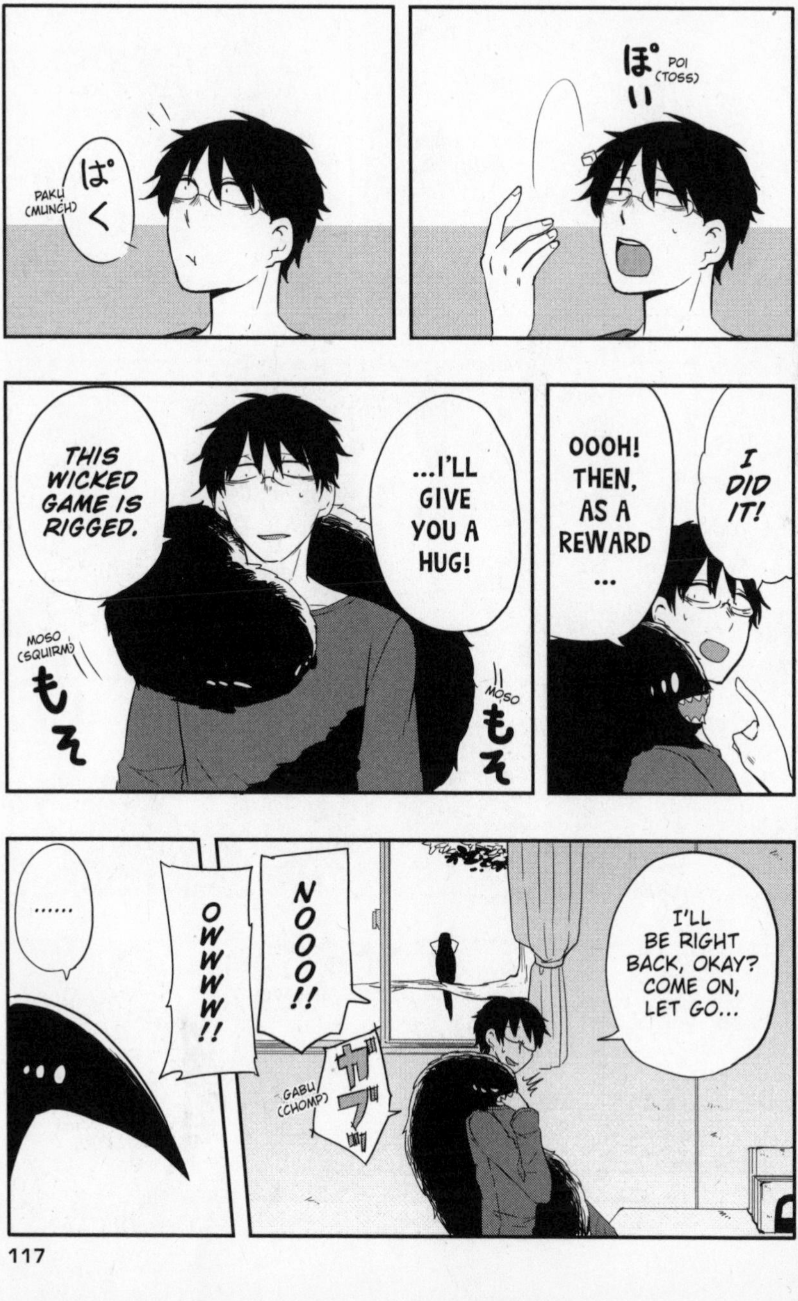
ぽい
POI (TOSS)
ぱく
PAKU (MUNCH)
I DID IT!
OOOH! THEN, AS A REWARD...
...I'LL GIVE YOU A HUG!
もそ
MOSO
THIS WICKED GAME IS RIGGED.
もそ
MOSO (SQUIRM)
I'LL BE RIGHT BACK, OKAY? COME ON, LET GO...
ガブッ
GABU (CHOMP)
NOOOO!!
OWWWW!!
......

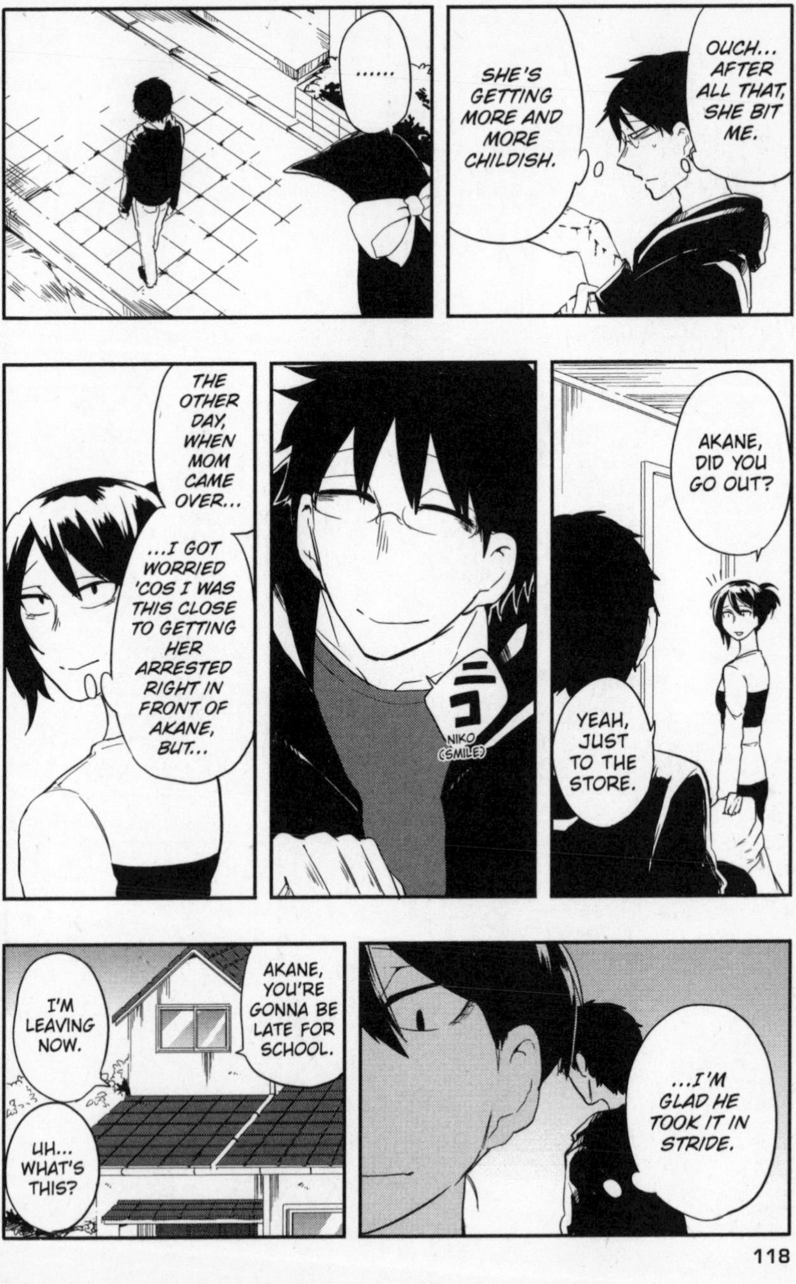
OUCH... AFTER ALL THAT, SHE BIT ME.
SHE'S GETTING MORE AND MORE CHILDISH.
......
AKANE, DID YOU GO OUT?
YEAH, JUST TO THE STORE.
NIKO (SMILE)
THE OTHER DAY, WHEN MOM CAME OVER...
...I GOT WORRIED 'COS I WAS THIS CLOSE TO GETTING HER ARRESTED RIGHT IN FRONT OF AKANE, BUT...
...I'M GLAD HE TOOK IT IN STRIDE.
AKANE, YOU'RE GONNA BE LATE FOR SCHOOL.
I'M LEAVING NOW.
UH... WHAT'S THIS?

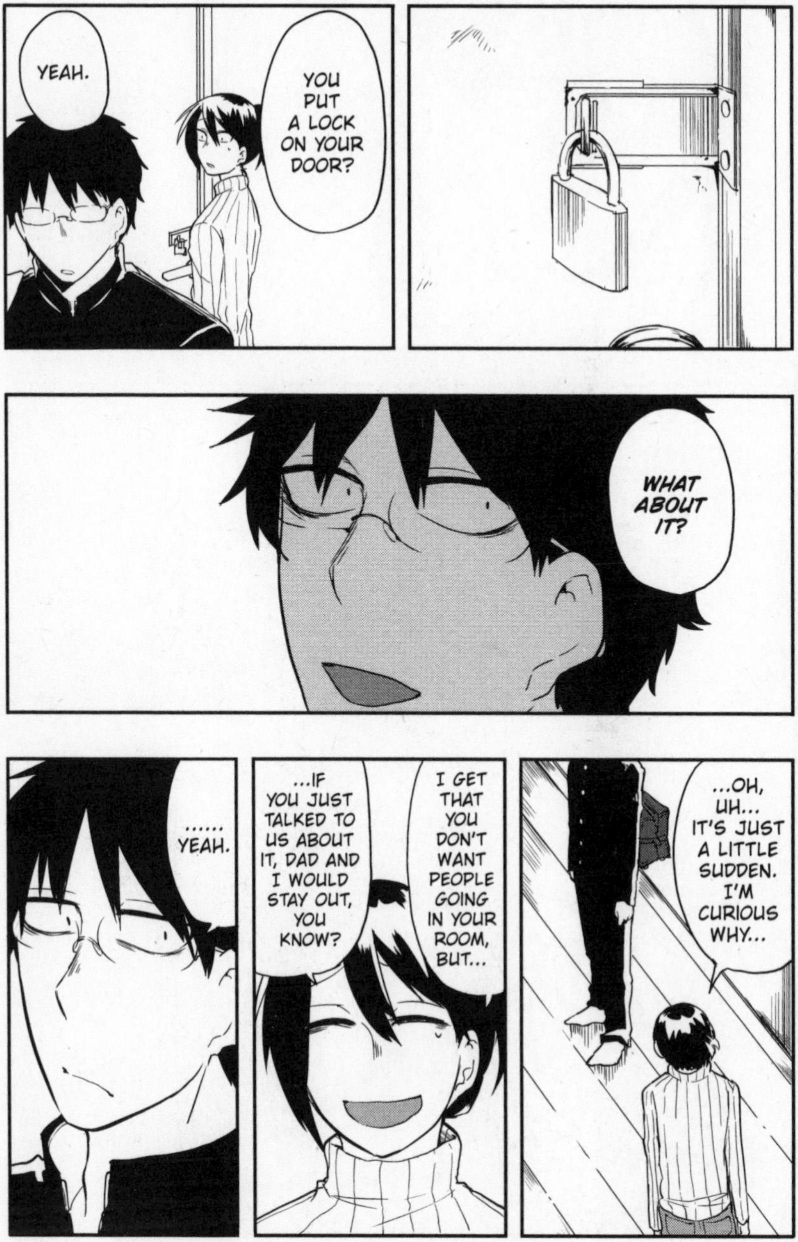
YOU PUT A LOCK ON YOUR DOOR?
YEAH.
WHAT ABOUT IT?
...OH, UH... IT'S JUST A LITTLE SUDDEN. I'M CURIOUS WHY...
I GET THAT YOU DON'T WANT PEOPLE GOING IN YOUR ROOM, BUT...
...IF YOU JUST TALKED TO US ABOUT IT, DAD AND I WOULD STAY OUT, YOU KNOW?
...... YEAH.

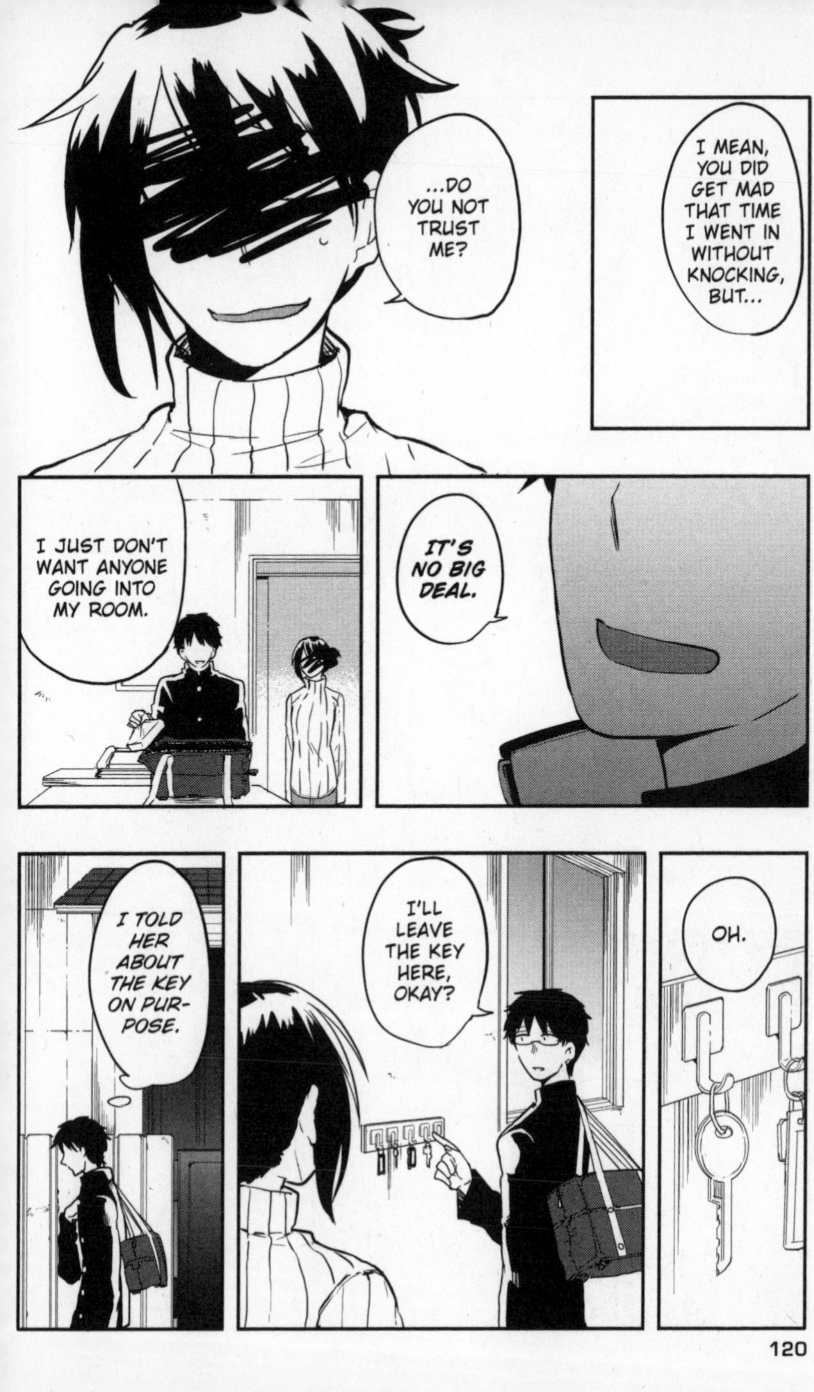
I MEAN, YOU DID GET MAD THAT TIME I WENT IN WITHOUT KNOCKING, BUT...
...DO YOU NOT TRUST ME?
IT'S NO BIG DEAL.
I JUST DON'T WANT ANYONE GOING INTO MY ROOM.
OH.
I'LL LEAVE THE KEY HERE, OKAY?
I TOLD HER ABOUT THE KEY ON PUR-POSE.

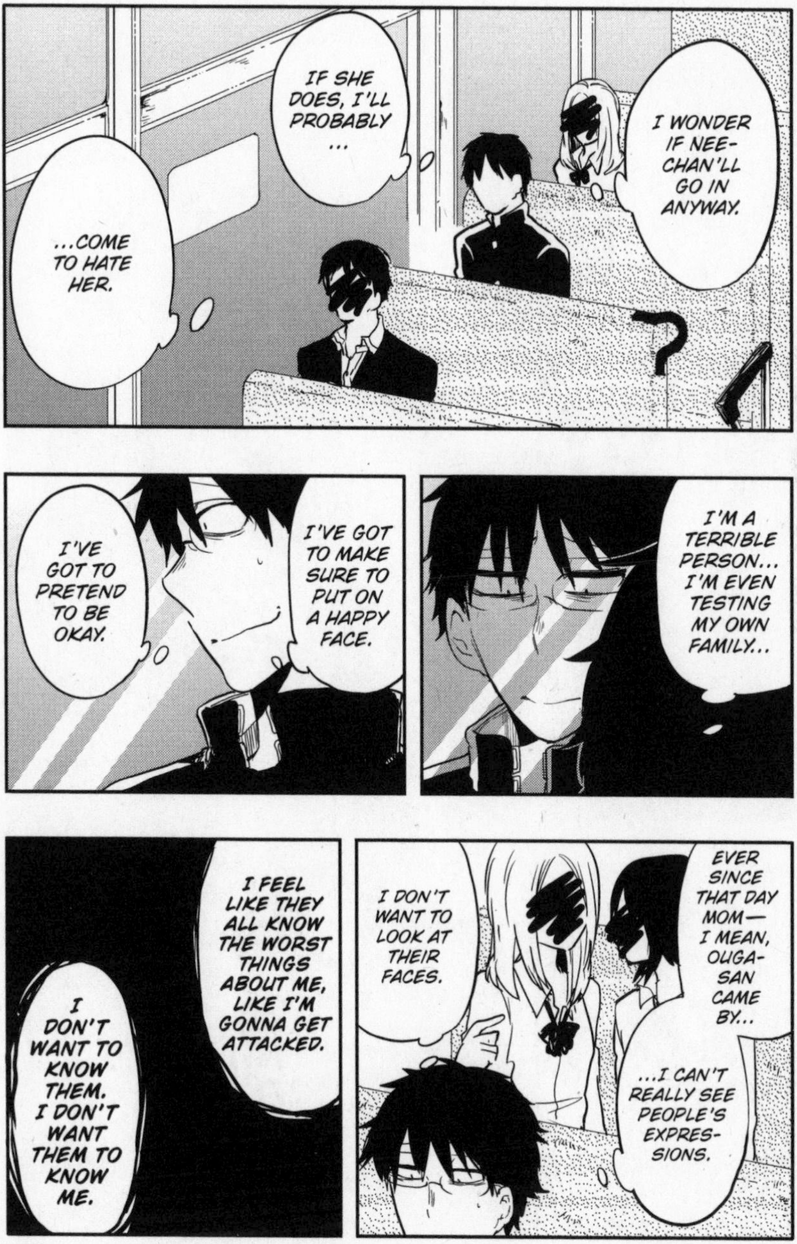
I WONDER IF NEE-CHAN'LL GO IN ANYWAY.
IF SHE DOES, I'LL PROBABLY ...
...COME TO HATE HER.
I'M A TERRIBLE PERSON... I'M EVEN TESTING MY OWN FAMILY...
I'VE GOT TO MAKE SURE TO PUT ON A HAPPY FACE.
I'VE GOT TO PRETEND TO BE OKAY.
EVER SINCE THAT DAY MOM— I MEAN, OUGA-SAN CAME BY...
...I CAN'T REALLY SEE PEOPLE'S EXPRES-SIONS.
I DON'T WANT TO LOOK AT THEIR FACES.
I FEEL LIKE THEY ALL KNOW THE WORST THINGS ABOUT ME, LIKE I'M GONNA GET ATTACKED.
I DON'T WANT TO KNOW THEM. I DON'T WANT THEM TO KNOW ME.

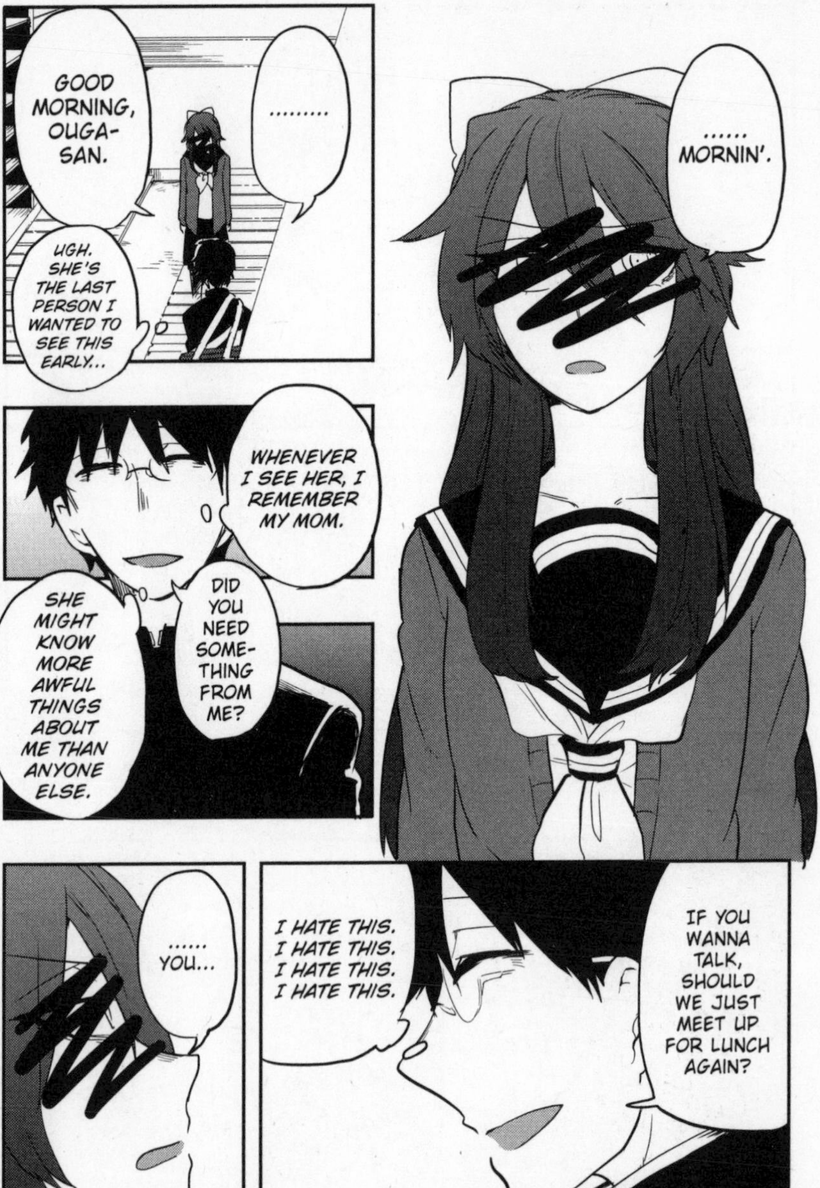
......
MORNIN'.
....
GOOD MORNING, OUGA-SAN.
UGH. SHE'S THE LAST PERSON I WANTED TO SEE THIS EARLY...
WHENEVER I SEE HER, I REMEMBER MY MOM.
DID YOU NEED SOME-THING FROM ME?
SHE MIGHT KNOW MORE AWFUL THINGS ABOUT ME THAN ANYONE ELSE.
IF YOU WANNA TALK, SHOULD WE JUST MEET UP FOR LUNCH AGAIN?
I HATE THIS. I HATE THIS. I HATE THIS. I HATE THIS.
...... YOU...

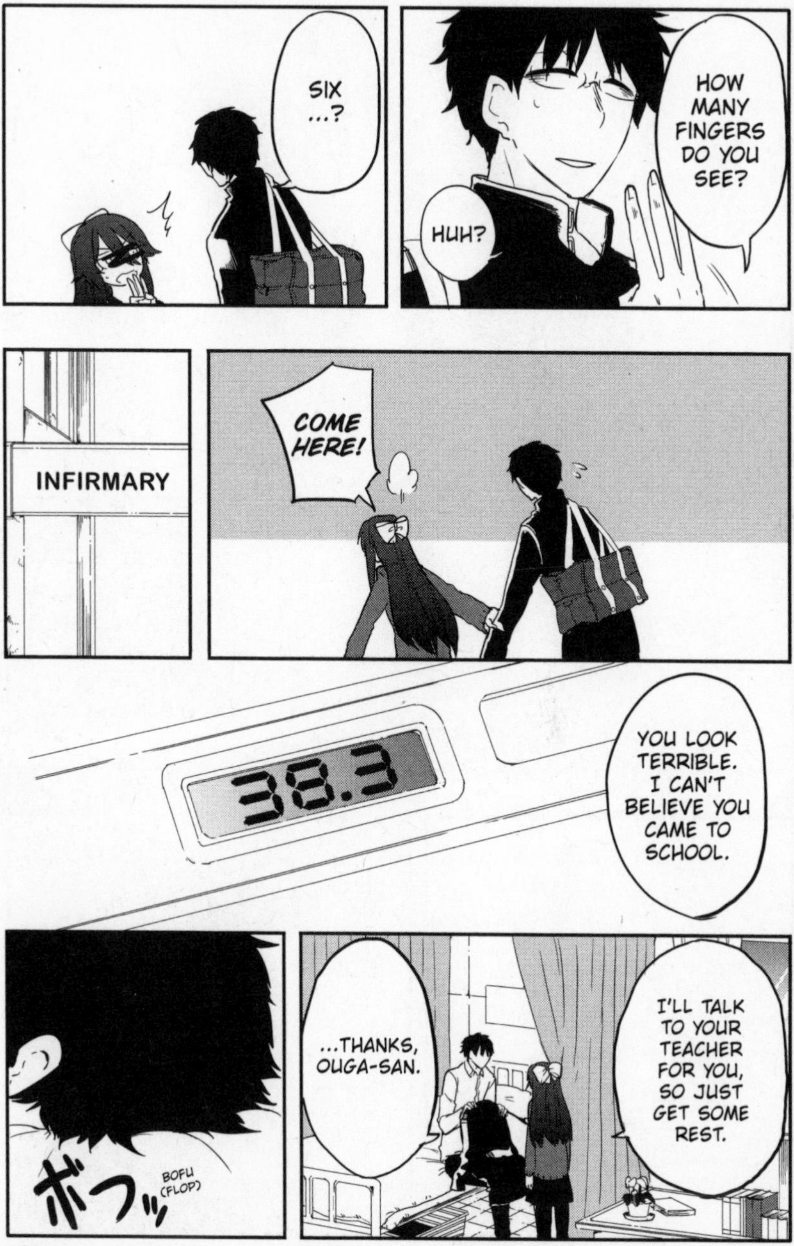
HOW MANY FINGERS DO YOU SEE?
HUH?
SIX ...?
COME HERE!
INFIRMARY
38.3
YOU LOOK TERRIBLE. I CAN'T BELIEVE YOU CAME TO SCHOOL.
I'LL TALK TO YOUR TEACHER FOR YOU, SO JUST GET SOME REST.
...THANKS, OUGA-SAN.
ボフッ
BOFU (FLOP)

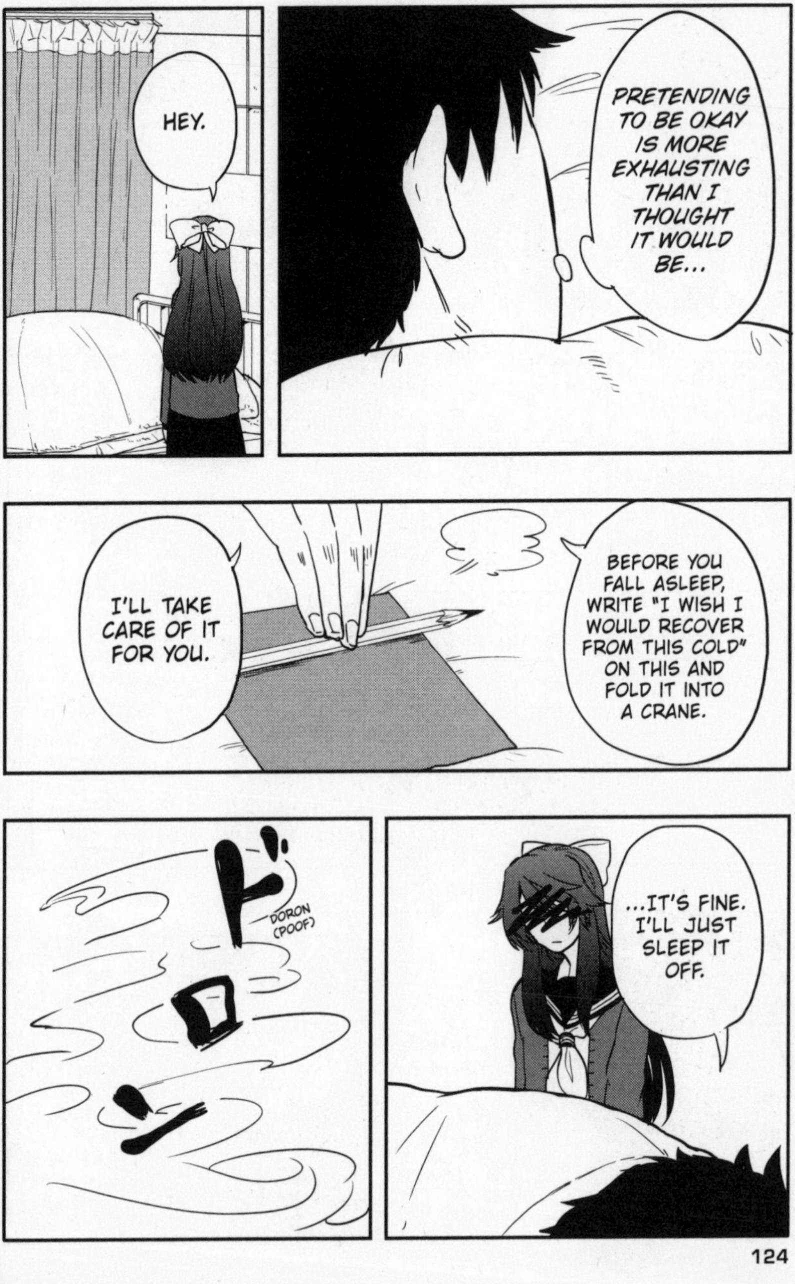
PRETENDING TO BE OKAY IS MORE EXHAUSTING THAN I THOUGHT IT WOULD BE...
HEY.
BEFORE YOU FALL ASLEEP, WRITE "I WISH I WOULD RECOVER FROM THIS COLD" ON THIS AND FOLD IT INTO A CRANE.
I'LL TAKE CARE OF IT FOR YOU.
...IT'S FINE. I'LL JUST SLEEP IT OFF.
DORON (POOF)

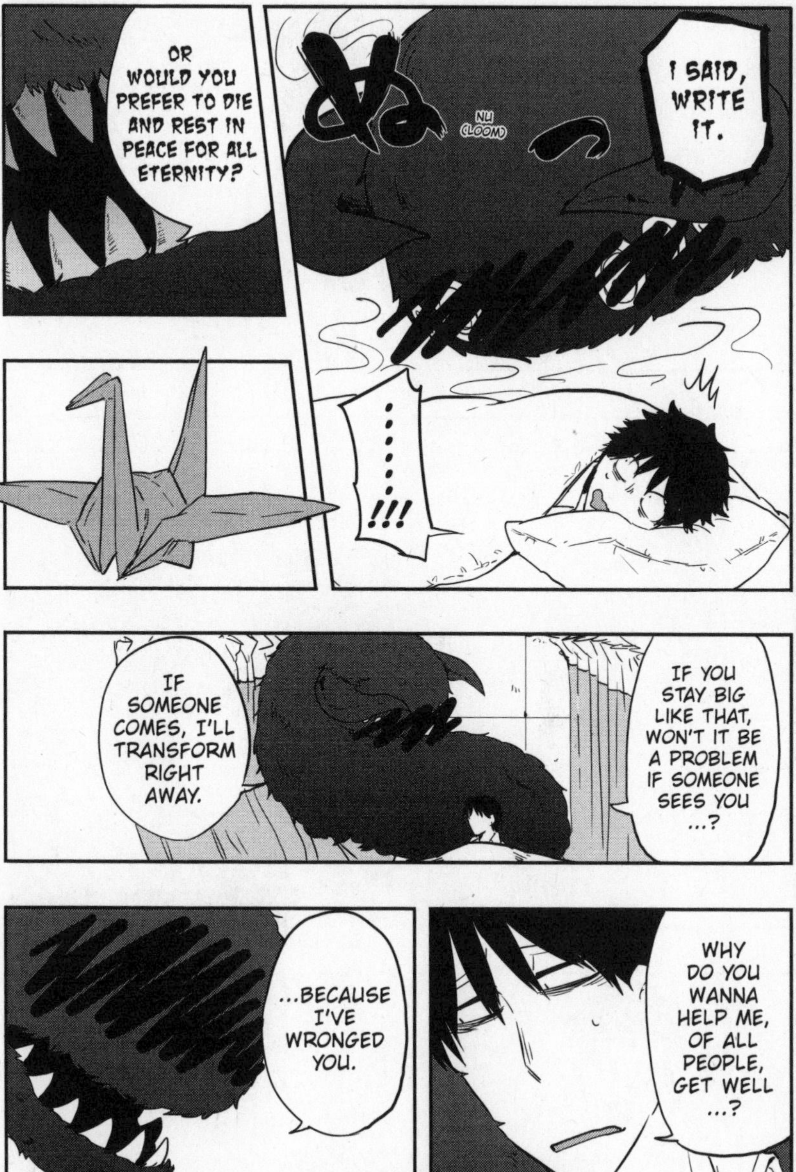
I SAID, WRITE IT.
NU (LOOM)
......!!!
OR WOULD YOU PREFER TO DIE AND REST IN PEACE FOR ALL ETERNITY?
IF YOU STAY BIG LIKE THAT, WON'T IT BE A PROBLEM IF SOMEONE SEES YOU ...?
IF SOMEONE COMES, I'LL TRANSFORM RIGHT AWAY.
WHY DO YOU WANNA HELP ME, OF ALL PEOPLE, GET WELL ...?
...BECAUSE I'VE WRONGED YOU.

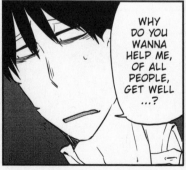

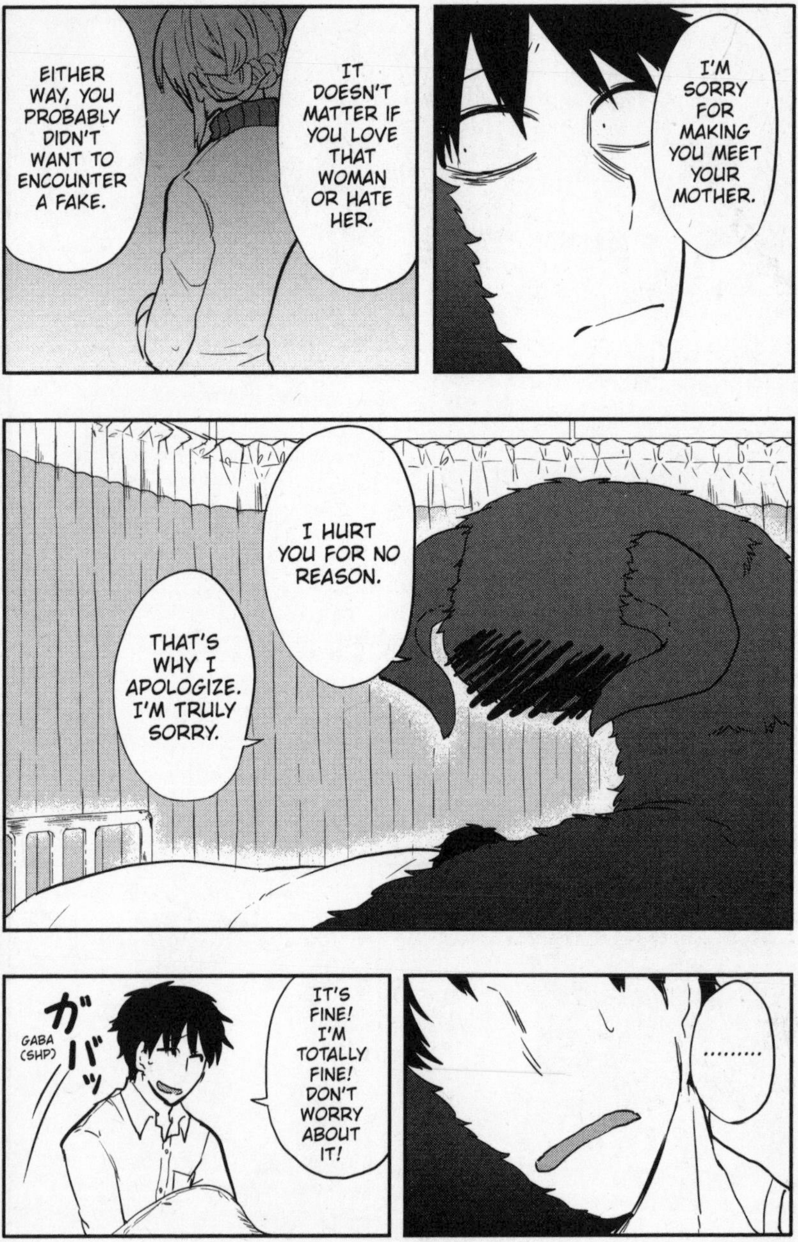
I'M SORRY FOR MAKING YOU MEET YOUR MOTHER.
IT DOESN'T MATTER IF YOU LOVE THAT WOMAN OR HATE HER.
EITHER WAY, YOU PROBABLY DIDN'T WANT TO ENCOUNTER A FAKE.
I HURT YOU FOR NO REASON.
THAT'S WHY I APOLOGIZE. I'M TRULY SORRY.
....
ガバッ
GABA (SHP)
IT'S FINE! I'M TOTALLY FINE! DON'T WORRY ABOUT IT!

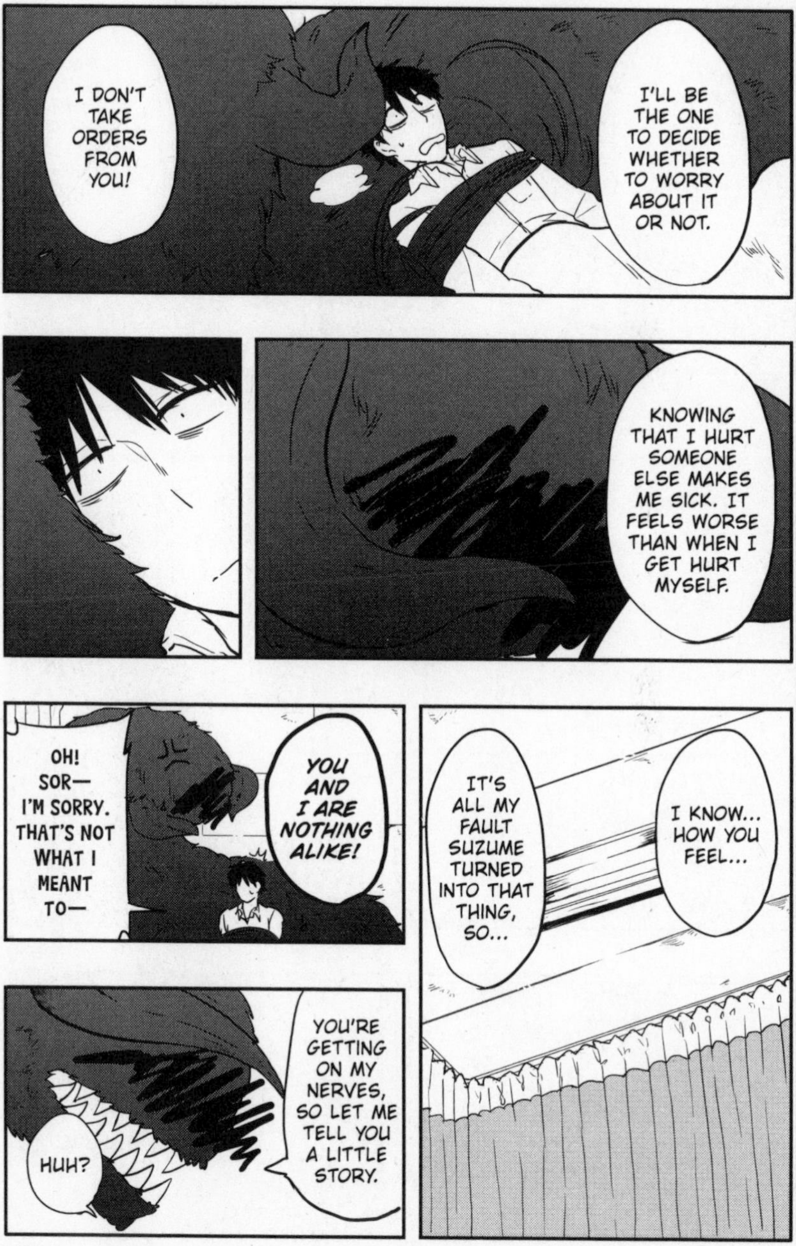
I'LL BE THE ONE TO DECIDE WHETHER TO WORRY ABOUT IT OR NOT.
I DON'T TAKE ORDERS FROM YOU!
KNOWING THAT I HURT SOMEONE ELSE MAKES ME SICK. IT FEELS WORSE THAN WHEN I GET HURT MYSELF.
I KNOW... HOW YOU FEEL...
IT'S ALL MY FAULT SUZUME TURNED INTO THAT THING, SO...
YOU AND I ARE NOTHING ALIKE!
OH! SOR— I'M SORRY. THAT'S NOT WHAT I MEANT TO—
YOU'RE GETTING ON MY NERVES, SO LET ME TELL YOU A LITTLE STORY.
HUH?

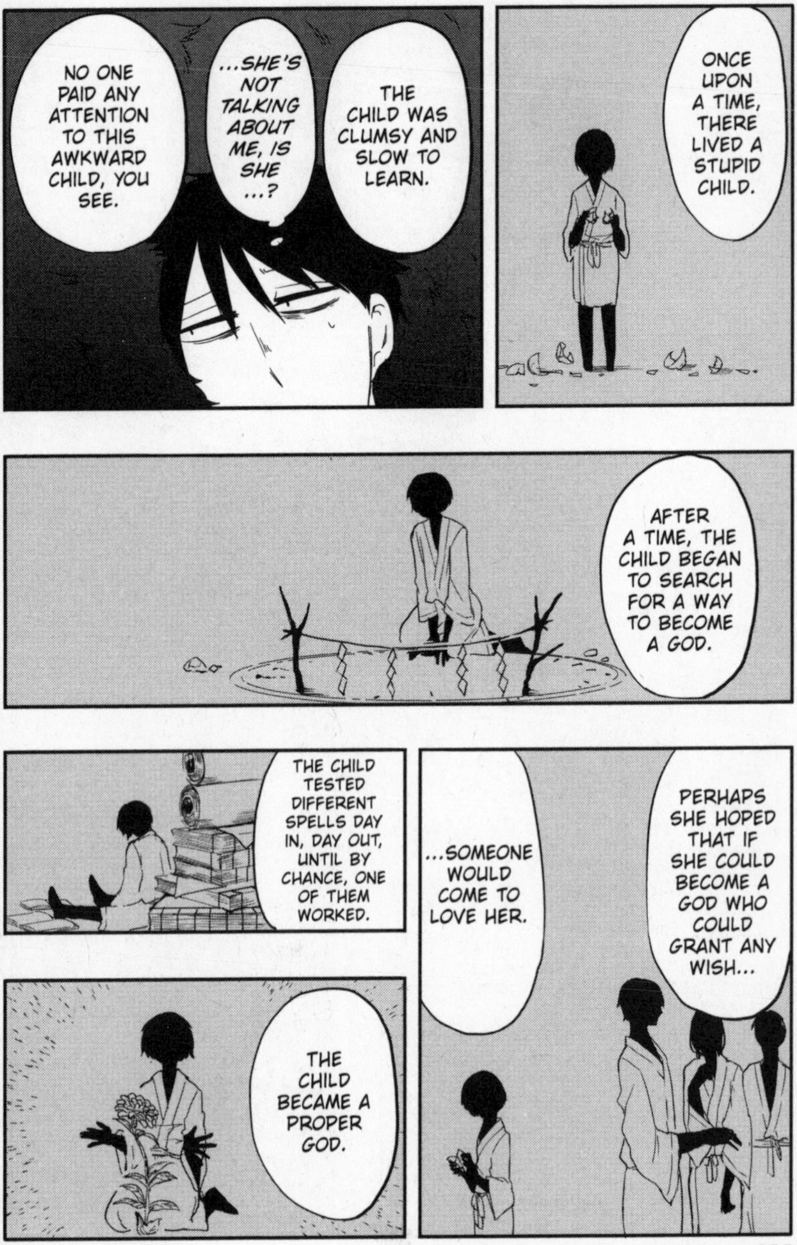
ONCE UPON A TIME, THERE LIVED A STUPID CHILD.
THE CHILD WAS CLUMSY AND SLOW TO LEARN.
...SHE'S NOT TALKING ABOUT ME, IS SHE ...?
NO ONE PAID ANY ATTENTION TO THIS AWKWARD CHILD, YOU SEE.
AFTER A TIME, THE CHILD BEGAN TO SEARCH FOR A WAY TO BECOME A GOD.
PERHAPS SHE HOPED THAT IF SHE COULD BECOME A GOD WHO COULD GRANT ANY WISH...
...SOMEONE WOULD COME TO LOVE HER.
THE CHILD TESTED DIFFERENT SPELLS DAY IN, DAY OUT, UNTIL BY CHANCE, ONE OF THEM WORKED.
THE CHILD BECAME A PROPER GOD.

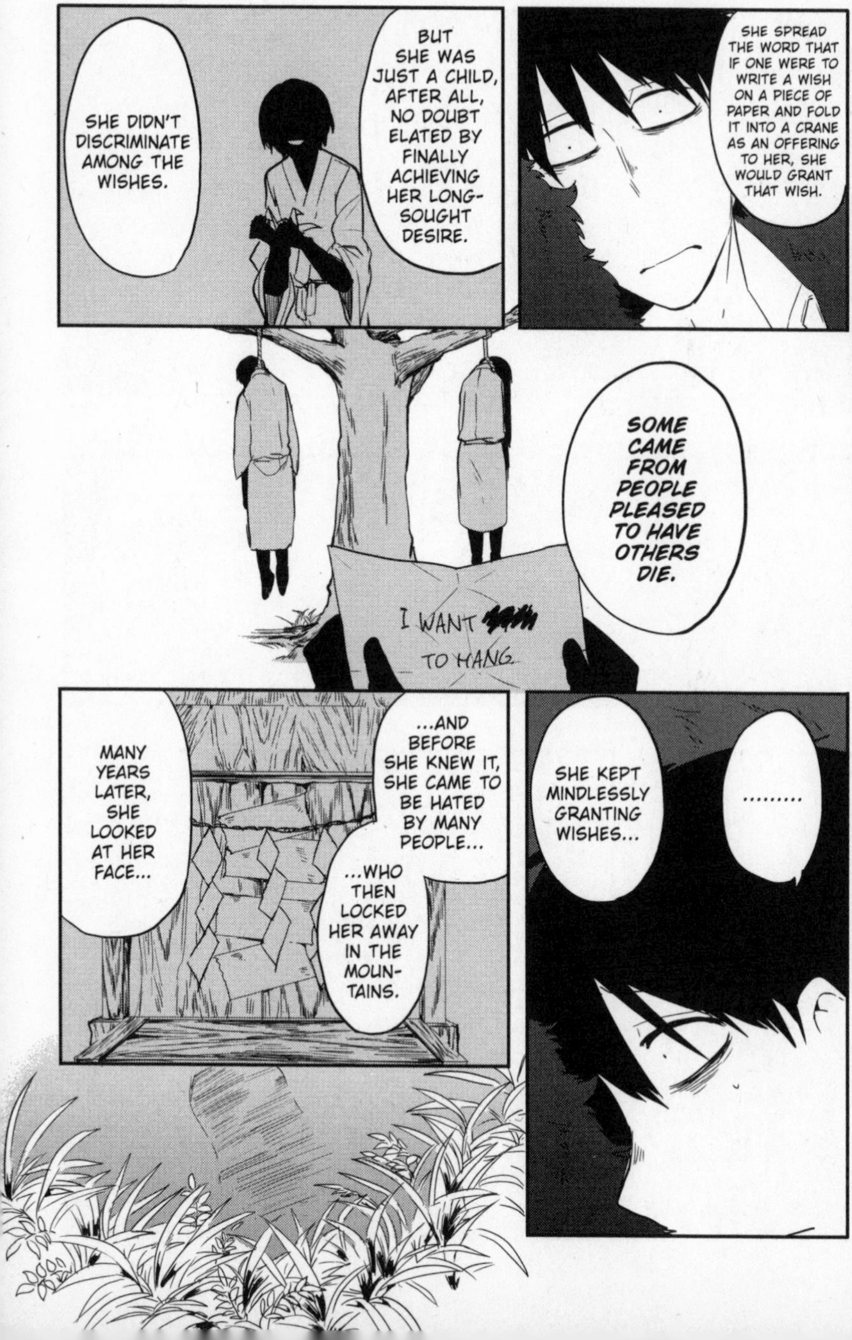
SHE SPREAD THE WORD THAT IF ONE WERE TO WRITE A WISH ON A PIECE OF PAPER AND FOLD IT INTO A CRANE AS AN OFFERING TO HER, SHE WOULD GRANT THAT WISH.
BUT SHE WAS JUST A CHILD, AFTER ALL, NO DOUBT ELATED BY FINALLY ACHIEVING HER LONG-SOUGHT DESIRE.
SHE DIDN'T DISCRIMINATE AMONG THE WISHES.
SOME CAME FROM PEOPLE PLEASED TO HAVE OTHERS DIE.
I WANT [redacted] TO HANG
....
SHE KEPT MINDLESSLY GRANTING WISHES...
...AND BEFORE SHE KNEW IT, SHE CAME TO BE HATED BY MANY PEOPLE...
...WHO THEN LOCKED HER AWAY IN THE MOUNTAINS.
MANY YEARS LATER, SHE LOOKED AT HER FACE...

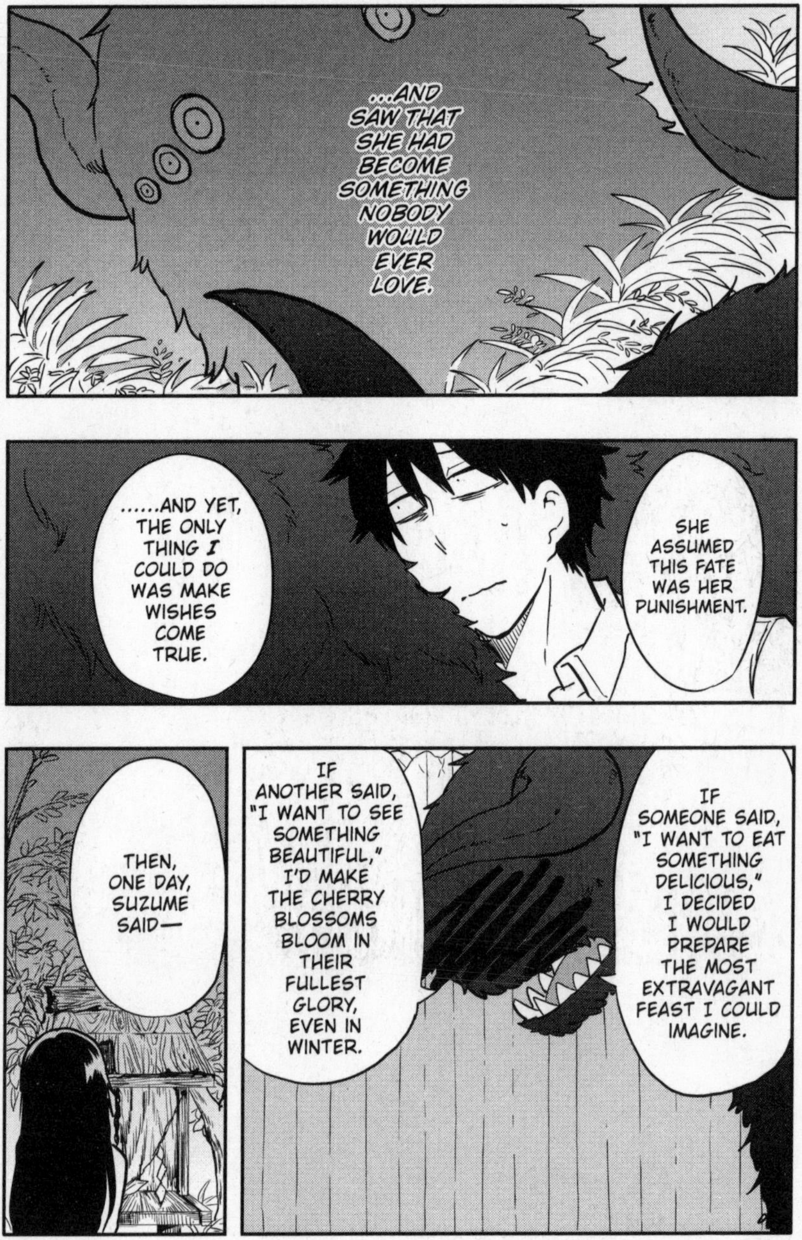
...AND SAW THAT SHE HAD BECOME SOMETHING NOBODY WOULD EVER LOVE.
SHE ASSUMED THIS FATE WAS HER PUNISHMENT.
......AND YET, THE ONLY THING *I* COULD DO WAS MAKE WISHES COME TRUE.
IF SOMEONE SAID, "I WANT TO EAT SOMETHING DELICIOUS," I DECIDED I WOULD PREPARE THE MOST EXTRAVAGANT FEAST I COULD IMAGINE.
IF ANOTHER SAID, "I WANT TO SEE SOMETHING BEAUTIFUL," I'D MAKE THE CHERRY BLOSSOMS BLOOM IN THEIR FULLEST GLORY, EVEN IN WINTER.
THEN, ONE DAY, SUZUME SAID—

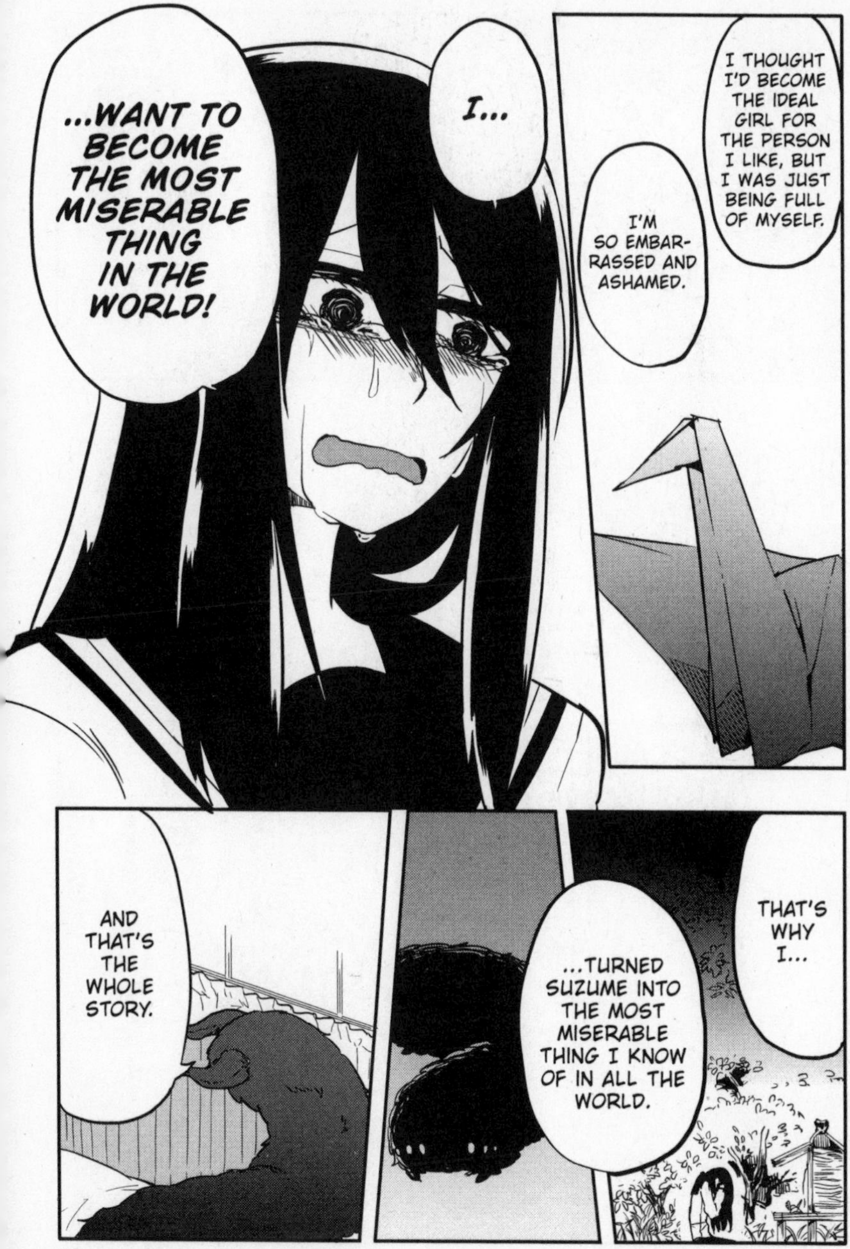
I THOUGHT I'D BECOME THE IDEAL GIRL FOR THE PERSON I LIKE, BUT I WAS JUST BEING FULL OF MYSELF.
I'M SO EMBAR-RASSED AND ASHAMED.
I...
...WANT TO BECOME THE MOST MISERABLE THING IN THE WORLD!
THAT'S WHY I...
...TURNED SUZUME INTO THE MOST MISERABLE THING I KNOW OF IN ALL THE WORLD.
AND THAT'S THE WHOLE STORY.

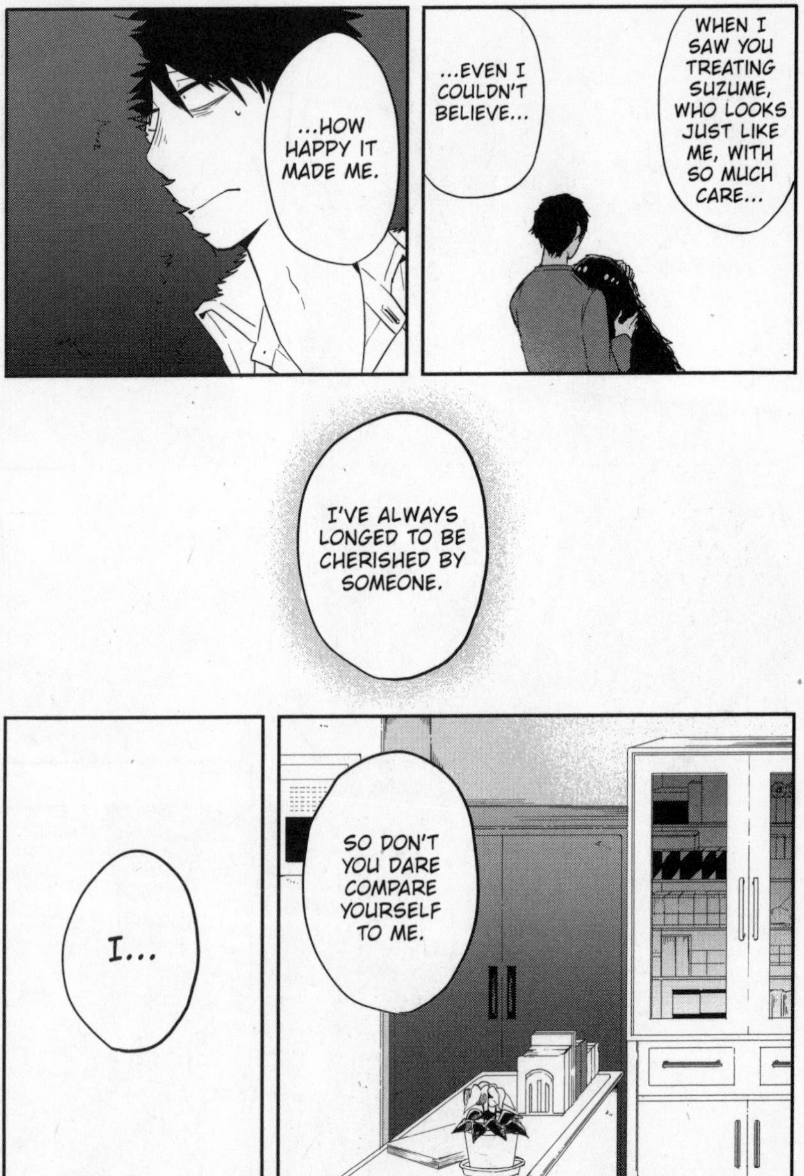
WHEN I SAW YOU TREATING SUZUME, WHO LOOKS JUST LIKE ME, WITH SO MUCH CARE...
...EVEN I COULDN'T BELIEVE...
...HOW HAPPY IT MADE ME.
I'VE ALWAYS LONGED TO BE CHERISHED BY SOMEONE.
SO DON'T YOU DARE COMPARE YOURSELF TO ME.
I...

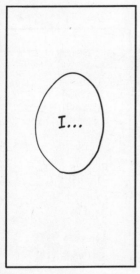

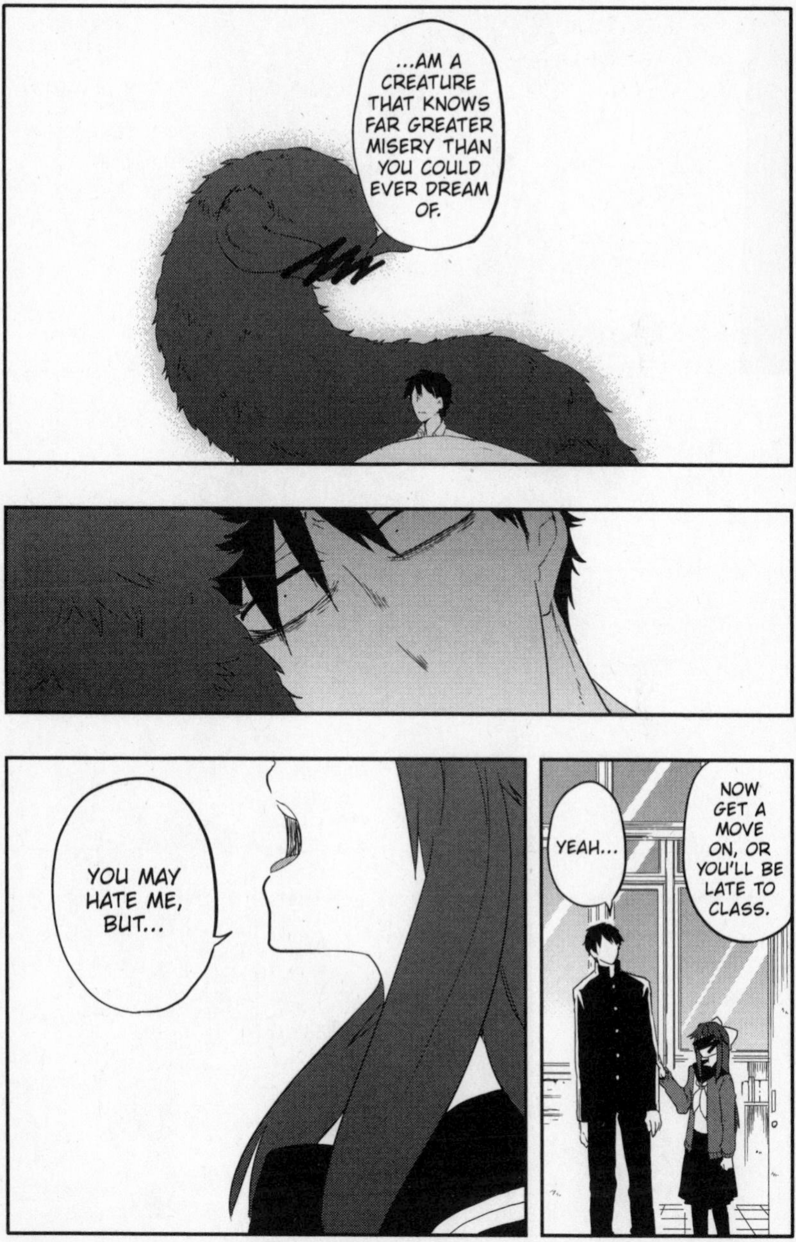
...AM A CREATURE THAT KNOWS FAR GREATER MISERY THAN YOU COULD EVER DREAM OF.
NOW GET A MOVE ON, OR YOU'LL BE LATE TO CLASS.
YEAH...
YOU MAY HATE ME, BUT...

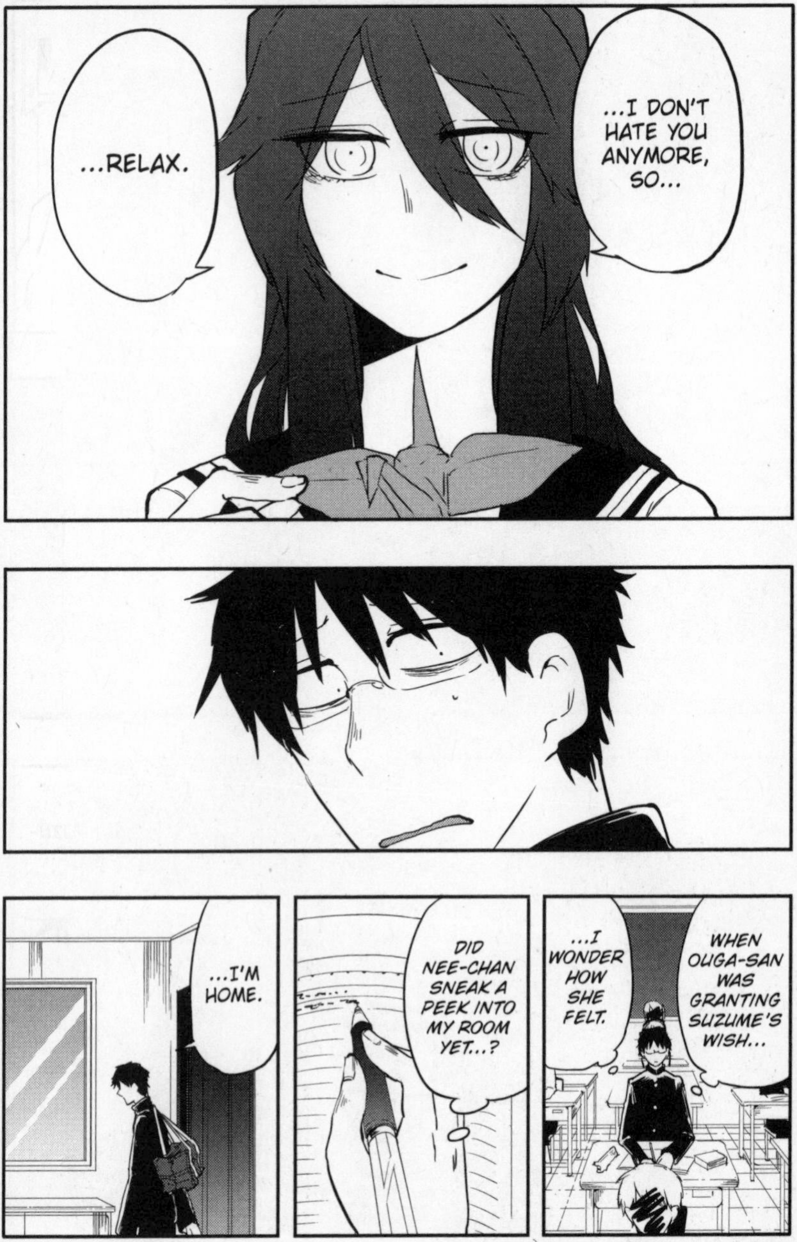
...I DON'T HATE YOU ANYMORE, SO...
...RELAX.
WHEN OUGA-SAN WAS GRANTING SUZUME'S WISH...
...I WONDER HOW SHE FELT.
DID NEE-CHAN SNEAK A PEEK INTO MY ROOM YET...?
...I'M HOME.

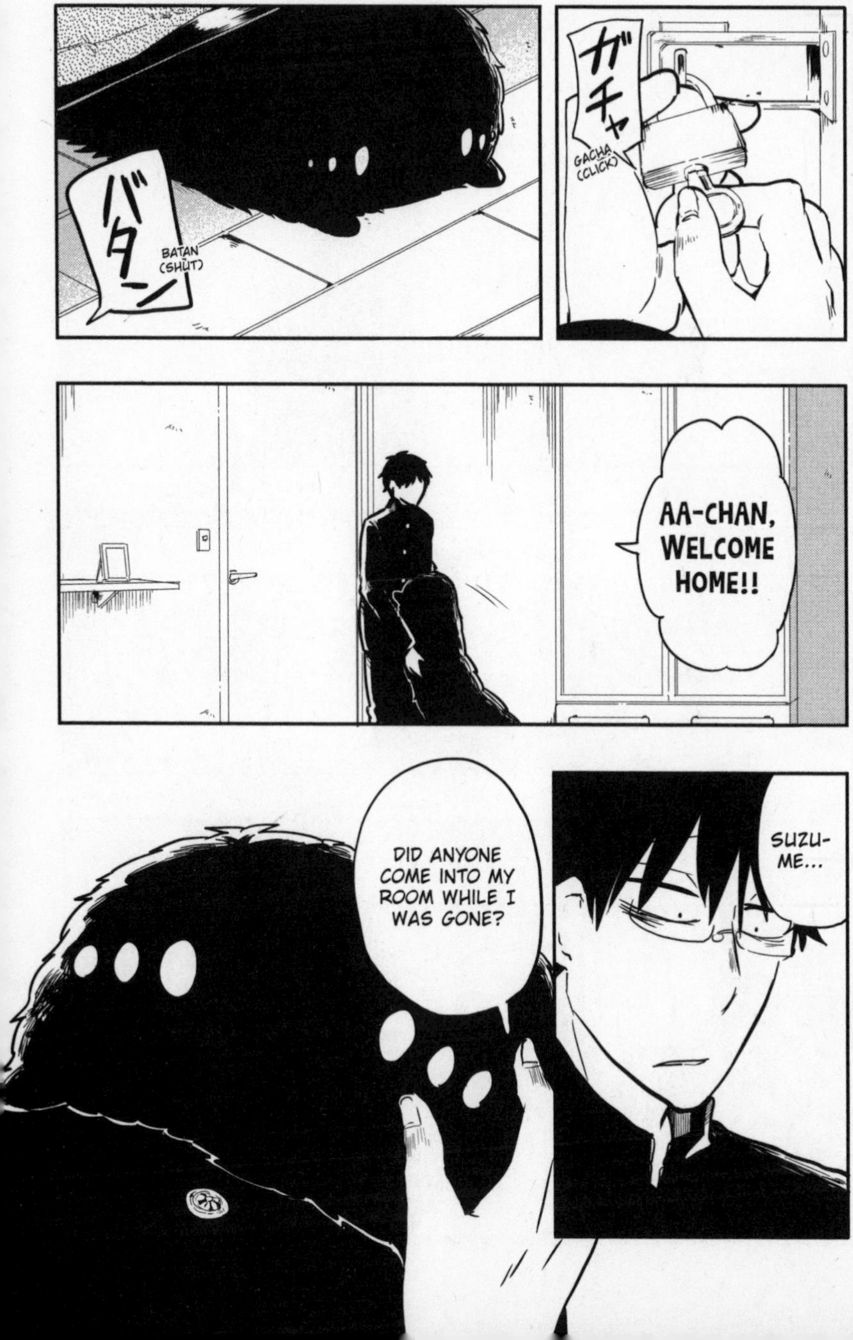
ガチャ
GACHA (CLICK)
バタン
BATAN (SHUT)
AA-CHAN, WELCOME HOME!!
SUZU-ME...
DID ANYONE COME INTO MY ROOM WHILE I WAS GONE?

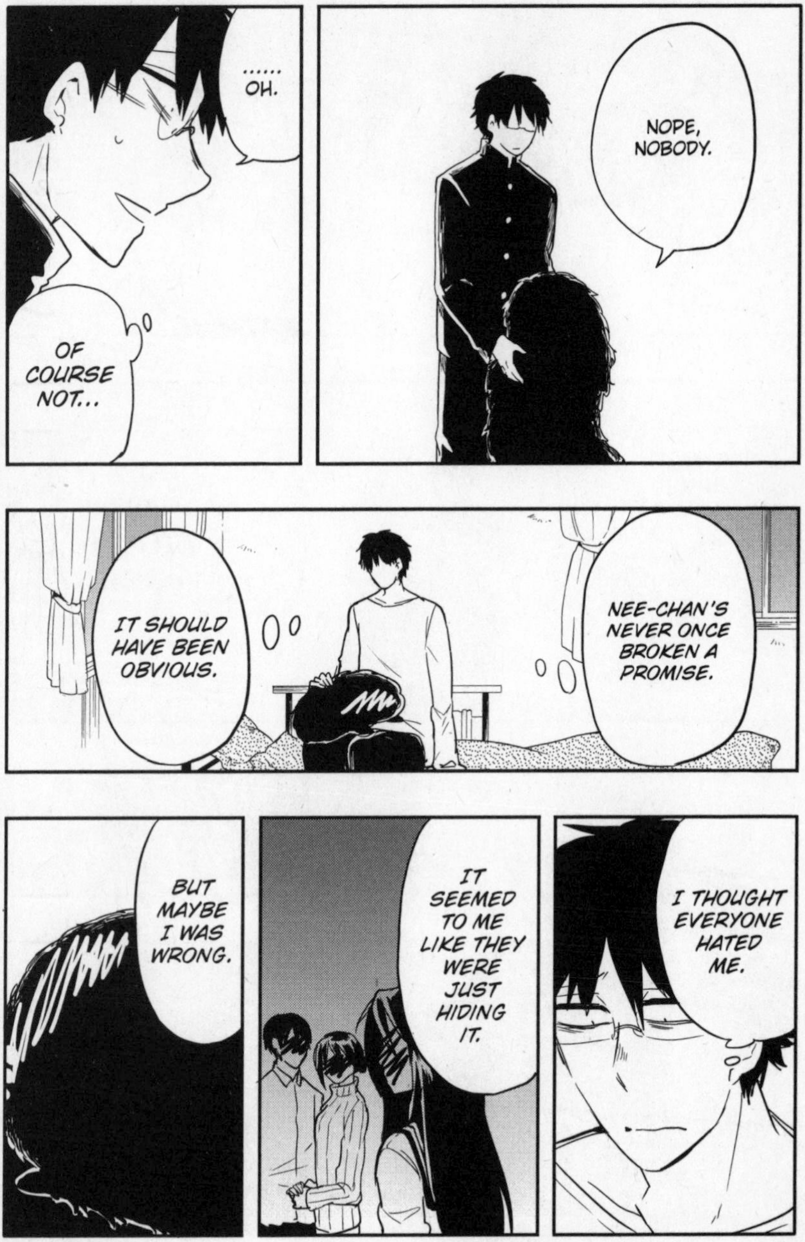
NOPE, NOBODY.
......OH.
OF COURSE NOT...
NEE-CHAN'S NEVER ONCE BROKEN A PROMISE.
IT SHOULD HAVE BEEN OBVIOUS.
I THOUGHT EVERYONE HATED ME.
IT SEEMED TO ME LIKE THEY WERE JUST HIDING IT.
BUT MAYBE I WAS WRONG.

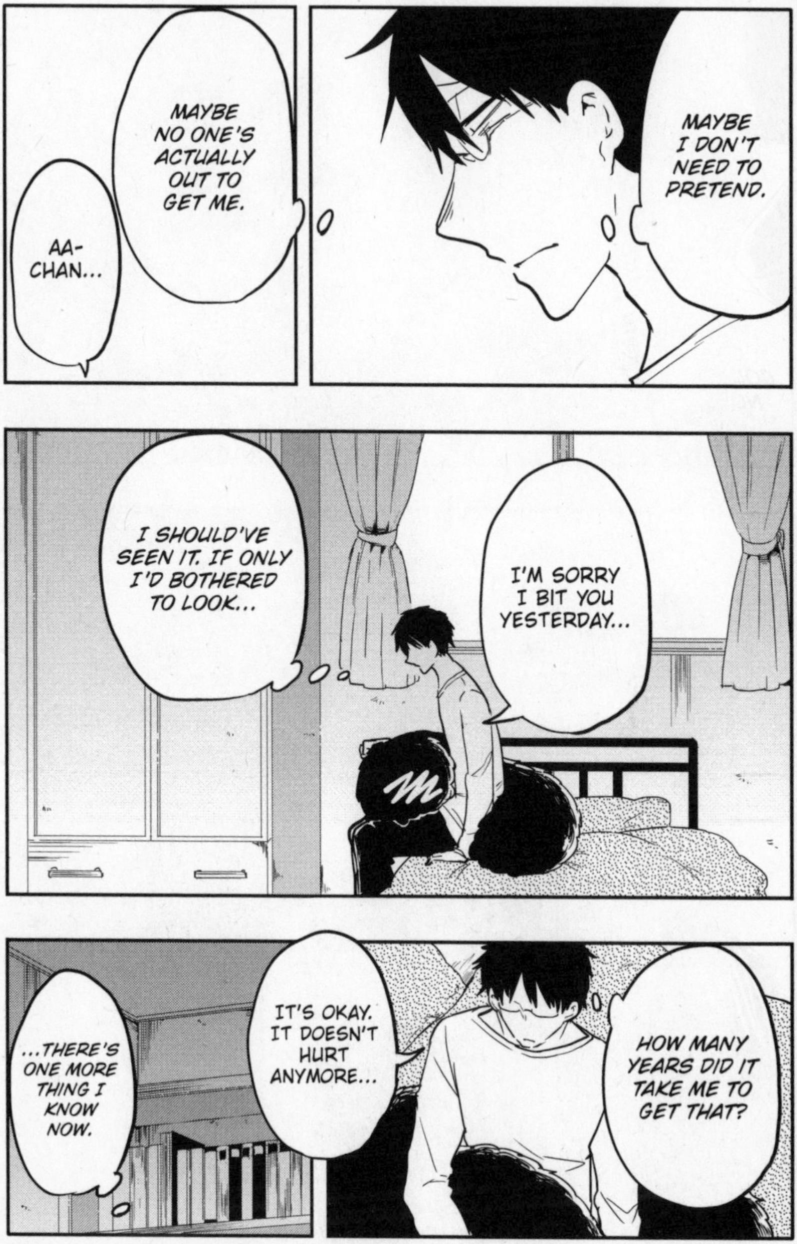
MAYBE I DON'T NEED TO PRETEND.
MAYBE NO ONE'S ACTUALLY OUT TO GET ME.
AA-CHAN...
I'M SORRY I BIT YOU YESTERDAY...
I SHOULD'VE SEEN IT. IF ONLY I'D BOTHERED TO LOOK...
HOW MANY YEARS DID IT TAKE ME TO GET THAT?
IT'S OKAY. IT DOESN'T HURT ANYMORE...
...THERE'S ONE MORE THING I KNOW NOW.

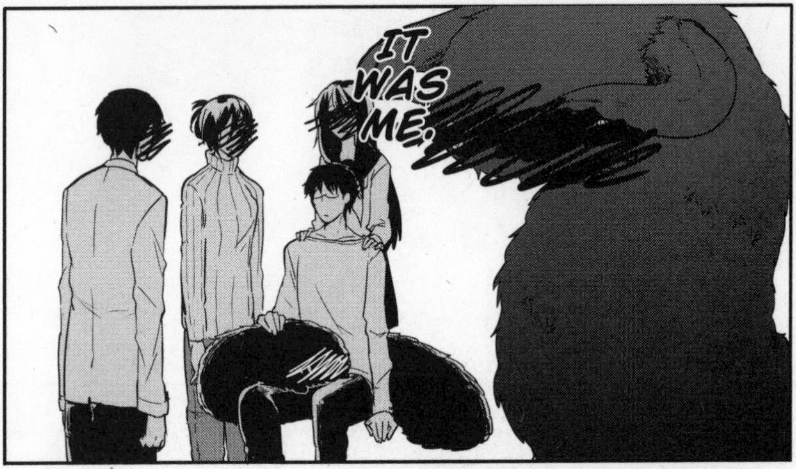
IT WAS ME.

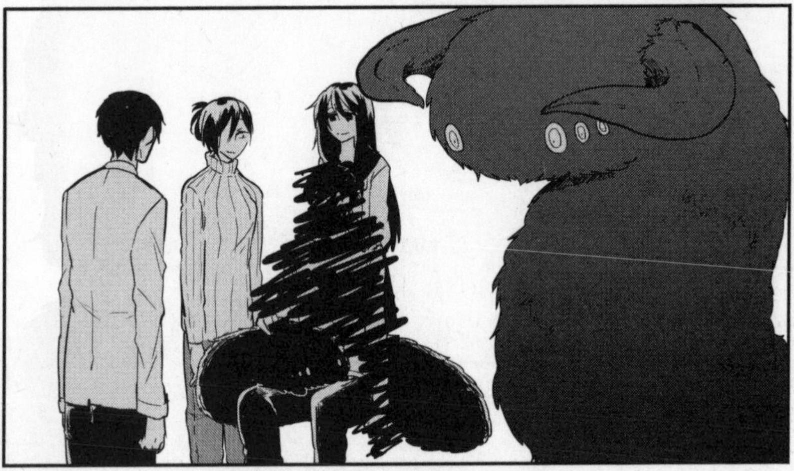

I WAS THE ONE WALKING ALL OVER EVERYONE ELSE'S FEELINGS.

Chapter 7

THE VILLAIN AND HAPPINESS

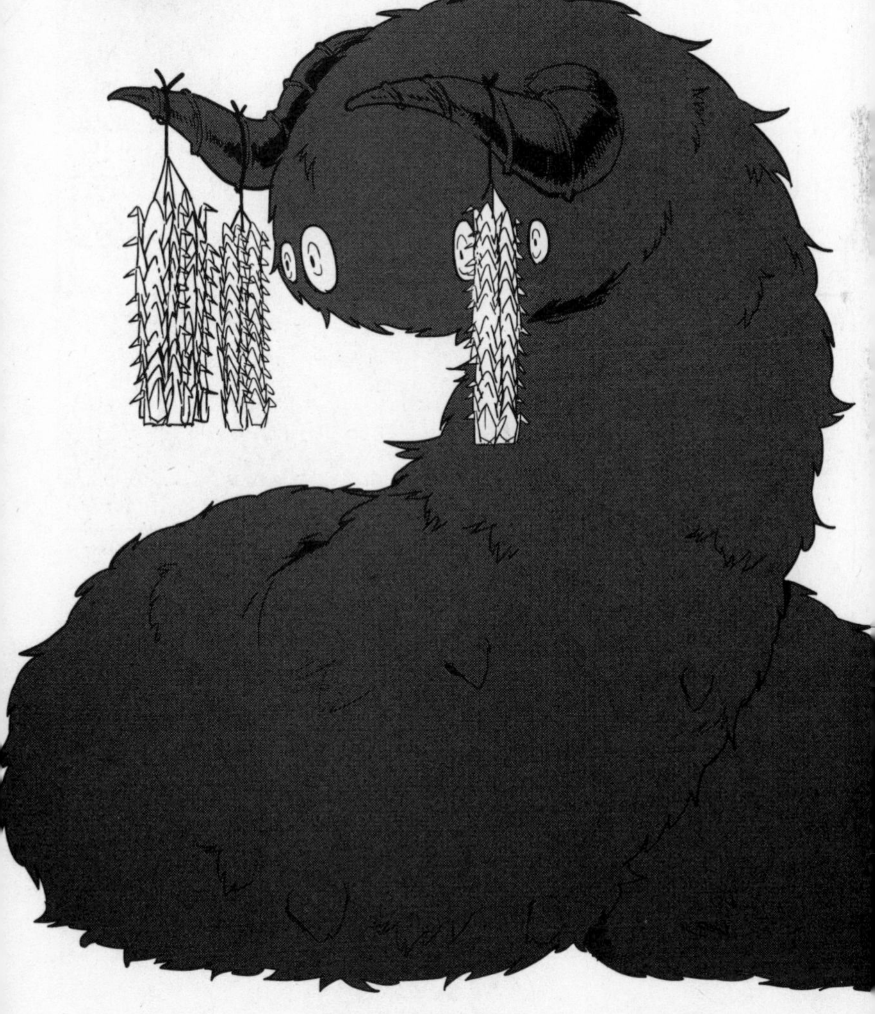

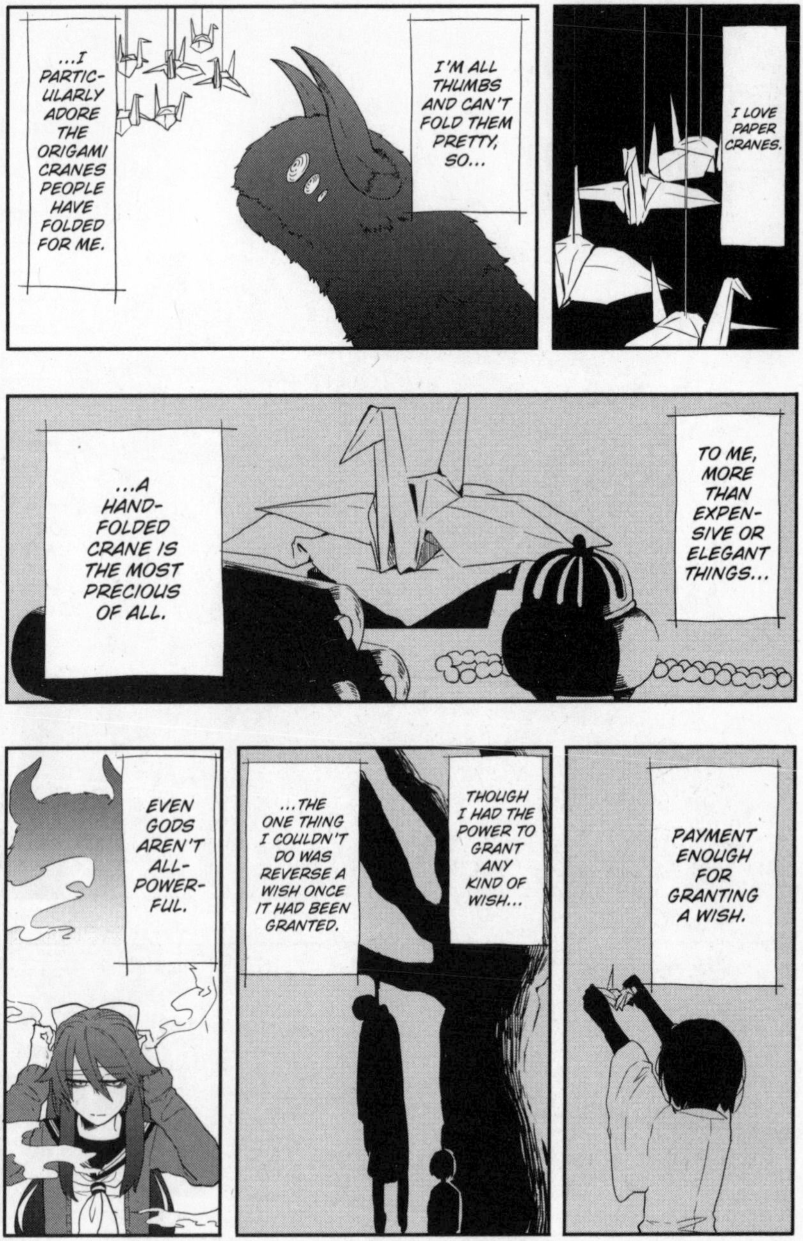
I LOVE PAPER CRANES.
I'M ALL THUMBS AND CAN'T FOLD THEM PRETTY, SO...
...I PARTICULARLY ADORE THE ORIGAMI CRANES PEOPLE HAVE FOLDED FOR ME.
TO ME, MORE THAN EXPENSIVE OR ELEGANT THINGS...
...A HAND-FOLDED CRANE IS THE MOST PRECIOUS OF ALL.
PAYMENT ENOUGH FOR GRANTING A WISH.
THOUGH I HAD THE POWER TO GRANT ANY KIND OF WISH...
...THE ONE THING I COULDN'T DO WAS REVERSE A WISH ONCE IT HAD BEEN GRANTED.
EVEN GODS AREN'T ALL-POWERFUL.

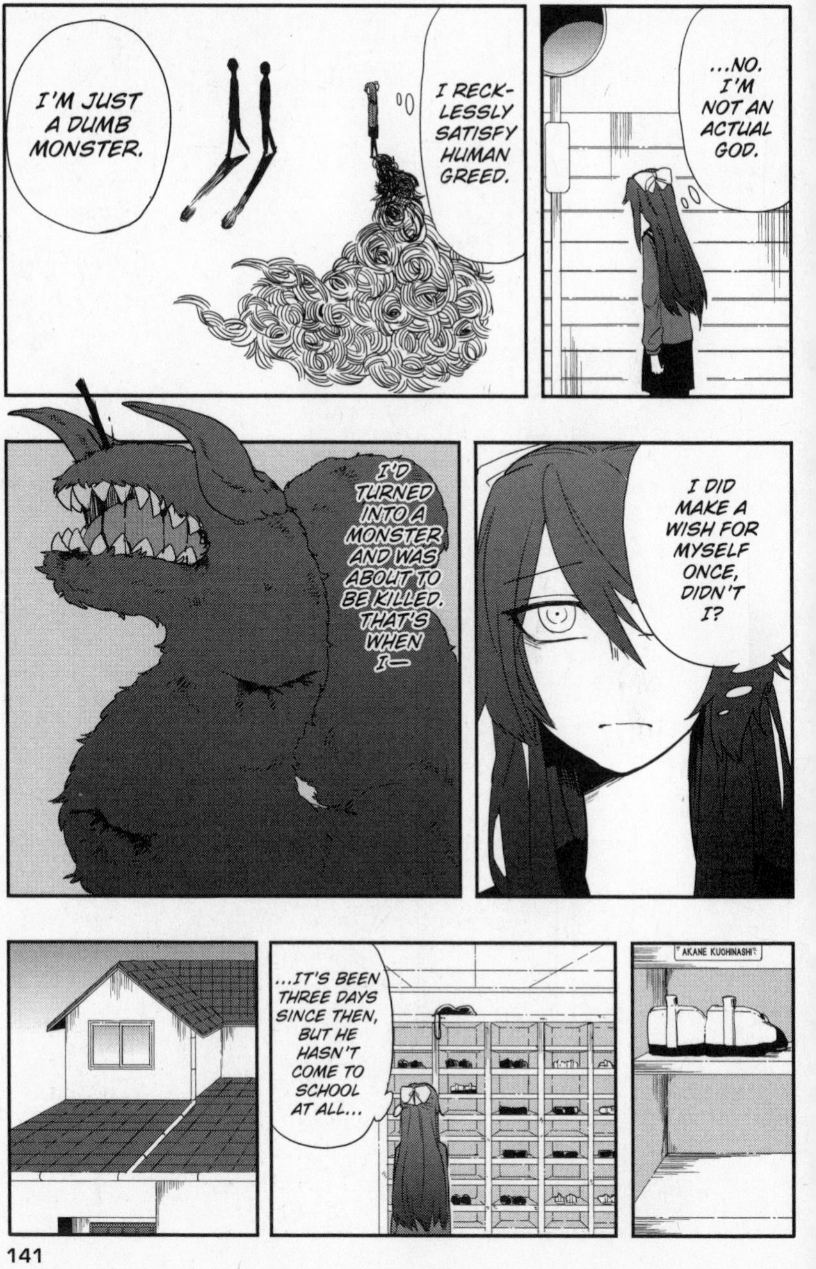
...NO. I'M NOT AN ACTUAL GOD.
I RECK-LESSLY SATISFY HUMAN GREED.
I'M JUST A DUMB MONSTER.
I DID MAKE A WISH FOR MYSELF ONCE, DIDN'T I?
I'D TURNED INTO A MONSTER AND WAS ABOUT TO BE KILLED. THAT'S WHEN I—
AKANE KUOHINASHI
...IT'S BEEN THREE DAYS SINCE THEN, BUT HE HASN'T COME TO SCHOOL AT ALL...

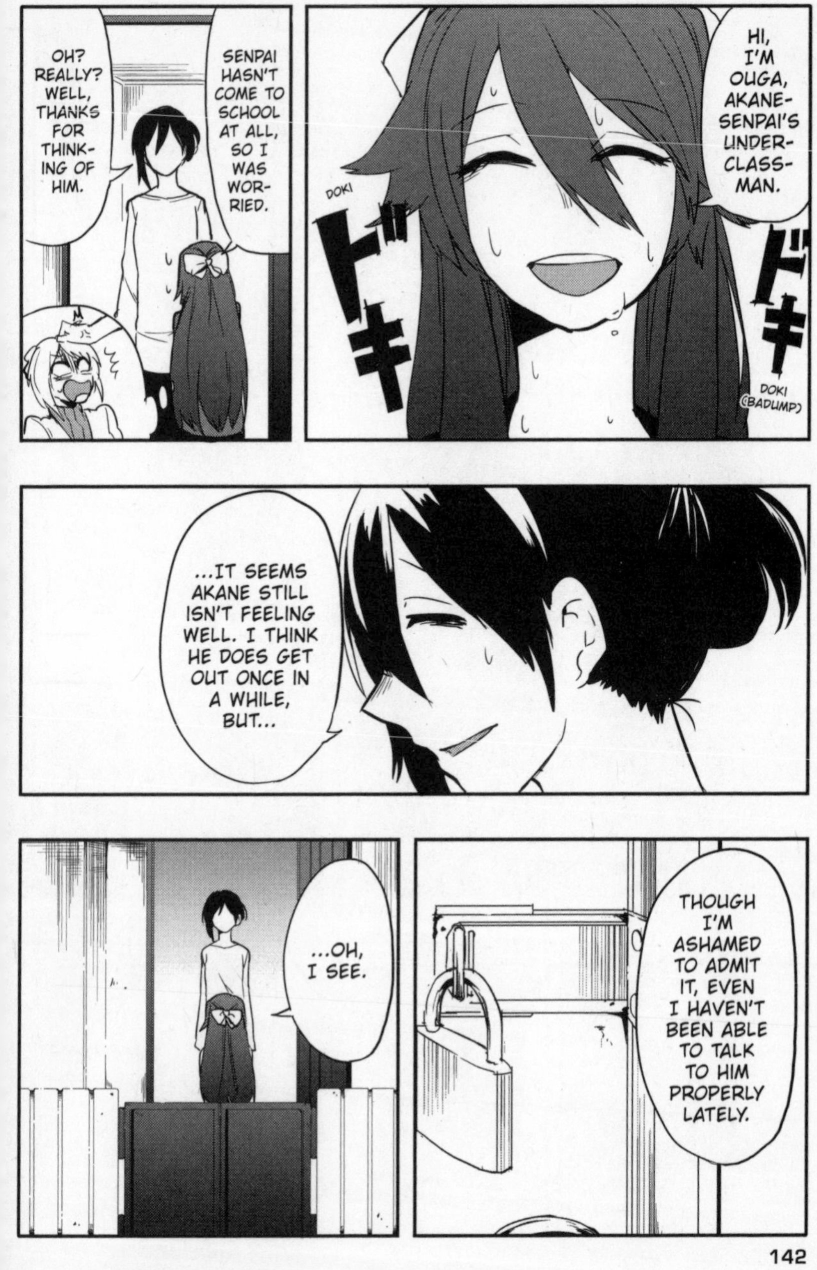
HI, I'M OUGA, AKANE-SENPAI'S UNDERCLASSMAN.
DOKI (BADUMP)
DOKI
SENPAI HASN'T COME TO SCHOOL AT ALL, SO I WAS WORRIED.
OH? REALLY? WELL, THANKS FOR THINKING OF HIM.
...IT SEEMS AKANE STILL ISN'T FEELING WELL. I THINK HE DOES GET OUT ONCE IN A WHILE, BUT...
THOUGH I'M ASHAMED TO ADMIT IT, EVEN I HAVEN'T BEEN ABLE TO TALK TO HIM PROPERLY LATELY.
...OH, I SEE.

I WONDER IF HE'S COME TO HATE BOTH SCHOOL AND HIS FAMILY ...?

BASA (FLAP)
バサッ

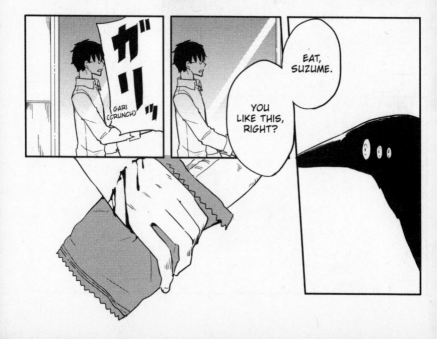

GARI (CRUNCH)

EAT, SUZUME.

YOU LIKE THIS, RIGHT?

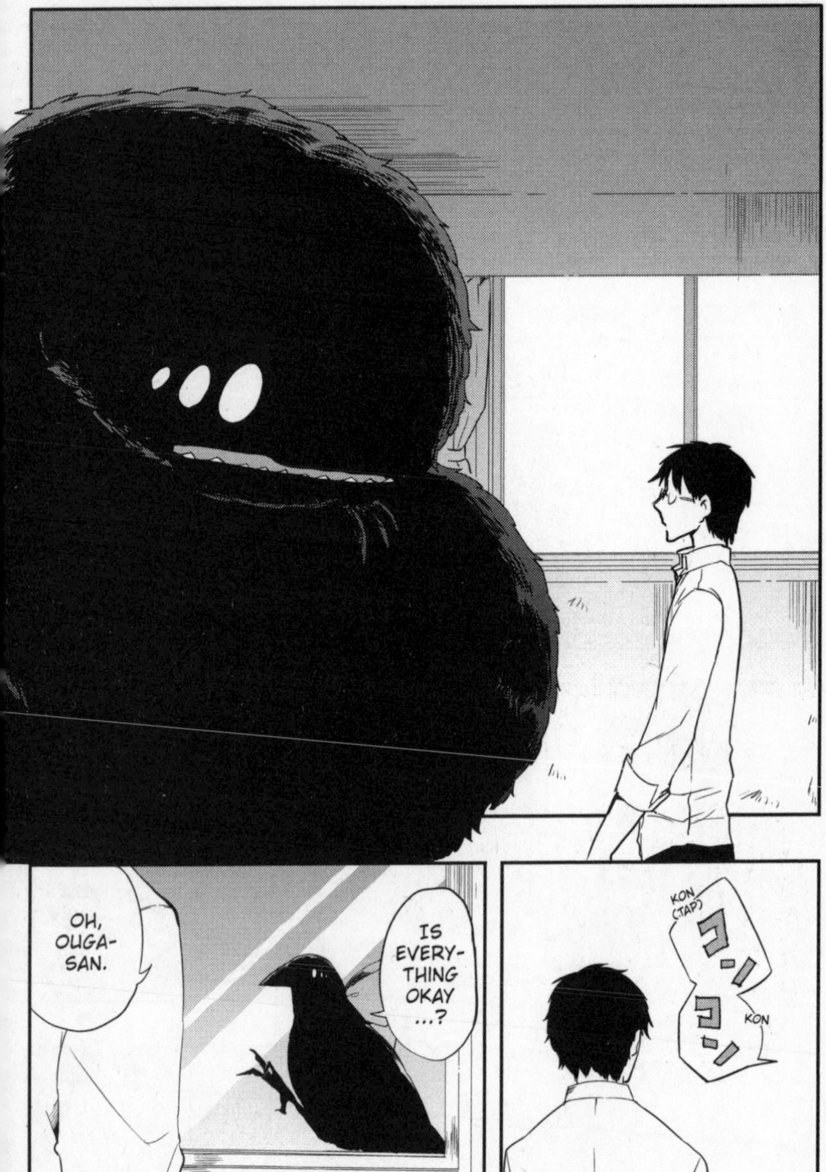
KON (TAP)
KON
IS EVERY-THING OKAY ...?
OH, OUGA-SAN.

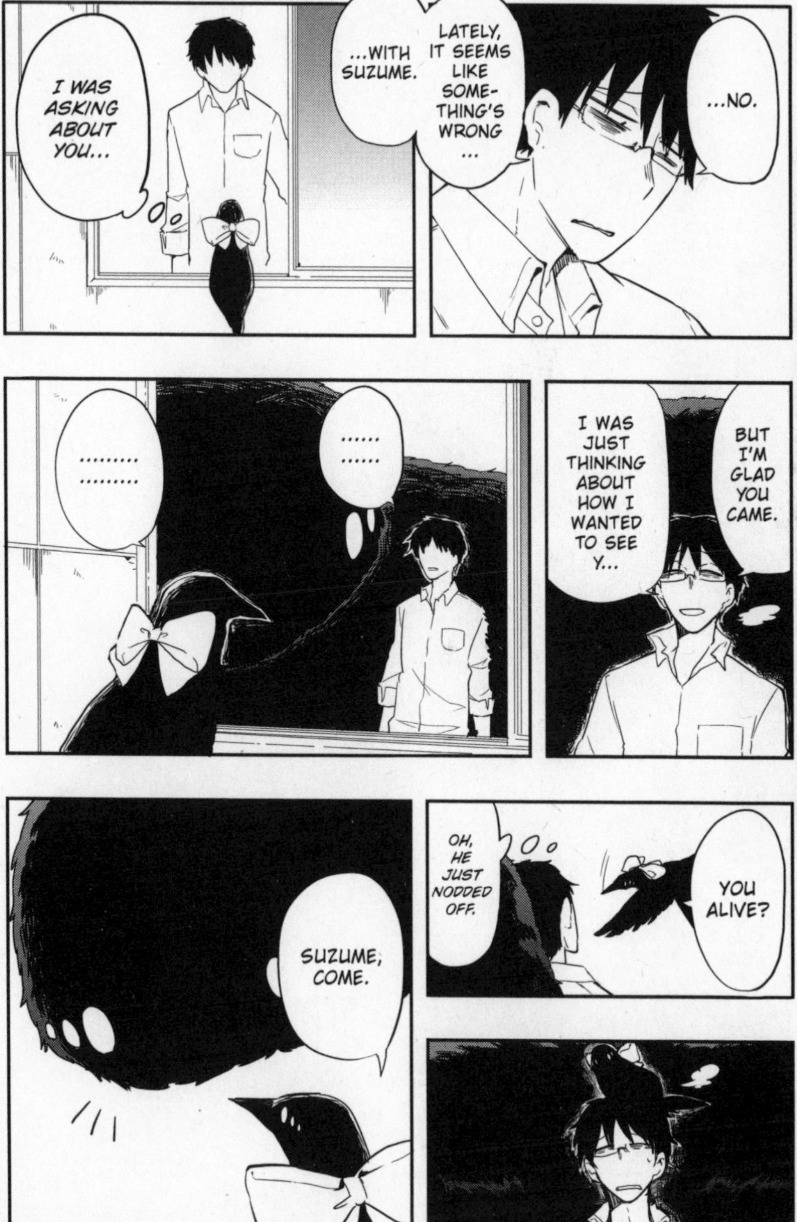
...NO.
LATELY, IT SEEMS LIKE SOME-THING'S WRONG ...
...WITH SUZUME.
I WAS ASKING ABOUT YOU...
BUT I'M GLAD YOU CAME.
I WAS JUST THINKING ABOUT HOW I WANTED TO SEE Y...
......
......
....
....
YOU ALIVE?
OH, HE JUST NODDED OFF.
SUZUME, COME.

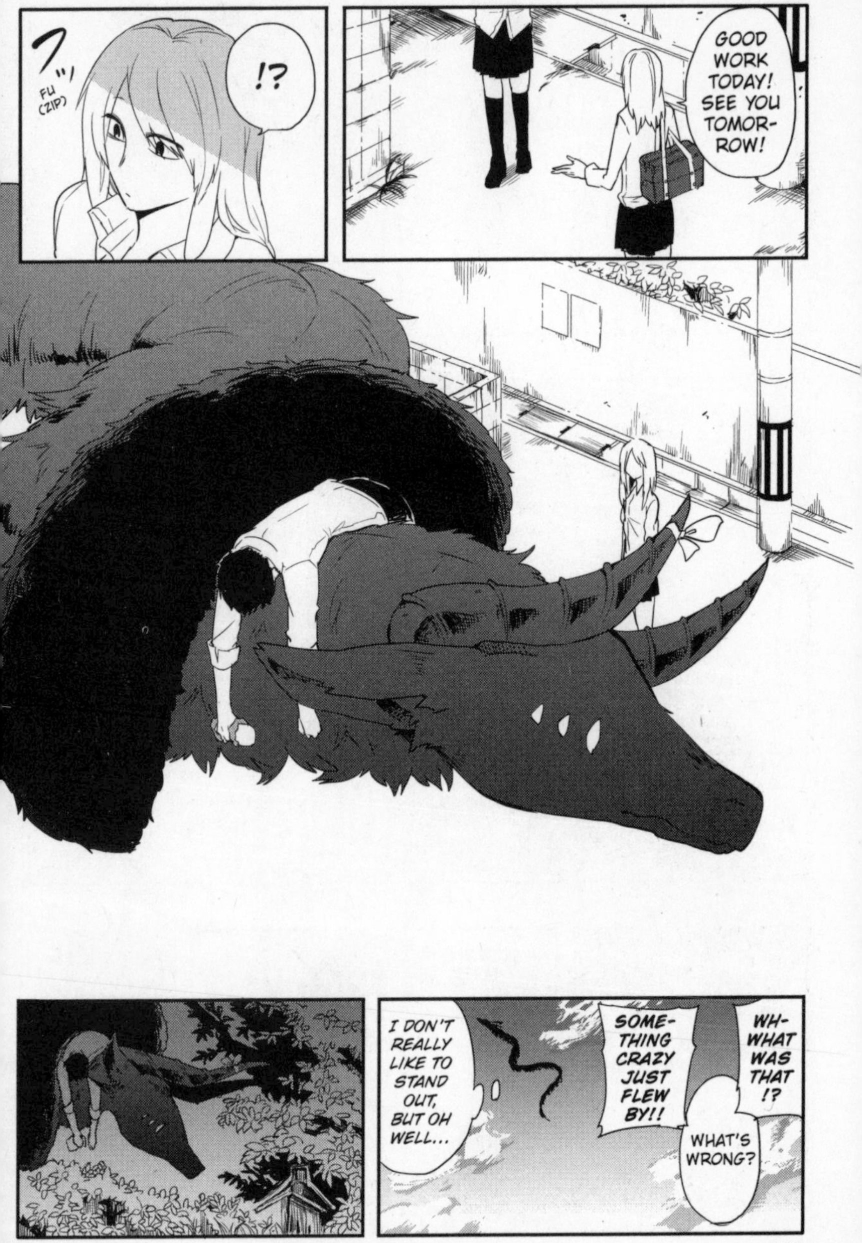
GOOD WORK TODAY! SEE YOU TOMOR-ROW!
!?
FU (ZIP)
WH-WHAT WAS THAT !?
WHAT'S WRONG?
SOME-THING CRAZY JUST FLEW BY!!
I DON'T REALLY LIKE TO STAND OUT, BUT OH WELL...

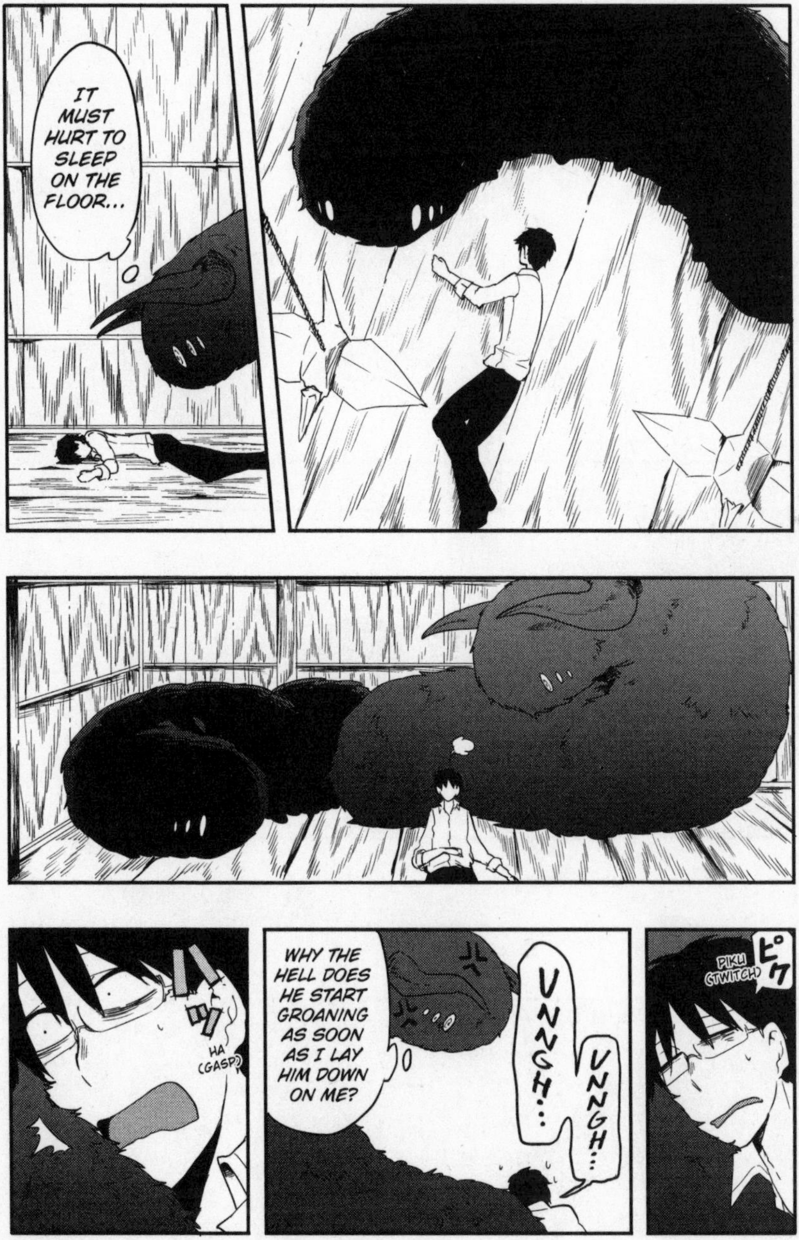
IT MUST HURT TO SLEEP ON THE FLOOR...
PIKU (TWITCH)
ピク
UNNGH...
UNNGH...
WHY THE HELL DOES HE START GROANING AS SOON AS I LAY HIM DOWN ON ME?
HA (GASP)

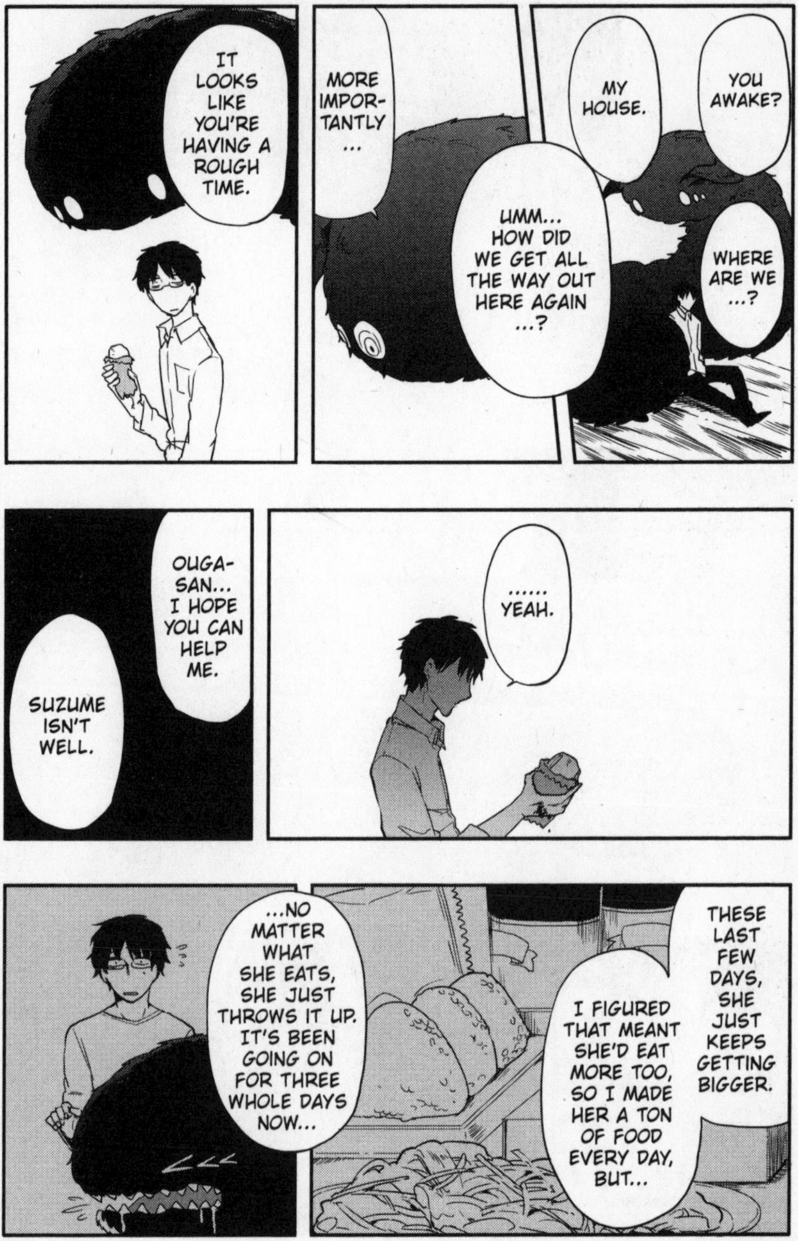
YOU AWAKE?
WHERE ARE WE ...?
MY HOUSE.
UMM... HOW DID WE GET ALL THE WAY OUT HERE AGAIN ...?
MORE IMPORTANTLY ...
IT LOOKS LIKE YOU'RE HAVING A ROUGH TIME.
...... YEAH.
OUGA-SAN... I HOPE YOU CAN HELP ME.
SUZUME ISN'T WELL.
THESE LAST FEW DAYS, SHE JUST KEEPS GETTING BIGGER.
I FIGURED THAT MEANT SHE'D EAT MORE TOO, SO I MADE HER A TON OF FOOD EVERY DAY, BUT...
...NO MATTER WHAT SHE EATS, SHE JUST THROWS IT UP. IT'S BEEN GOING ON FOR THREE WHOLE DAYS NOW...

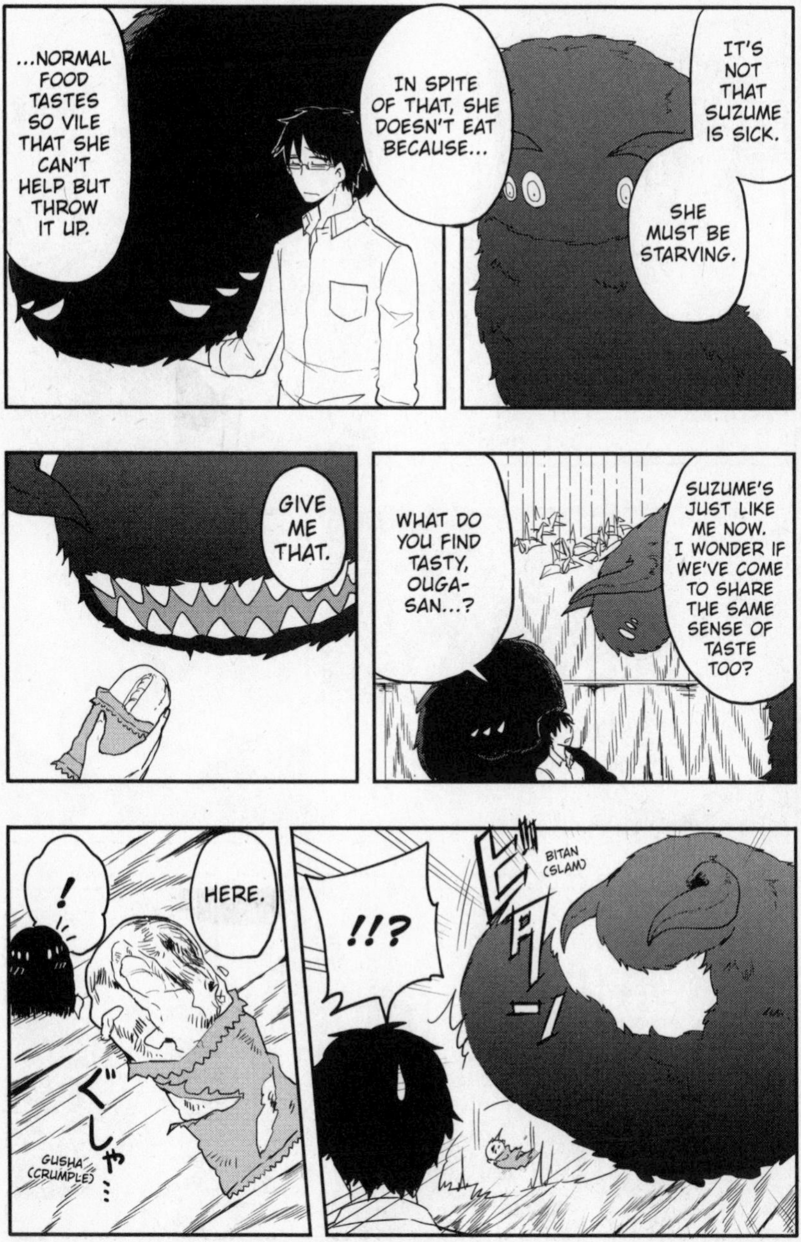
IT'S NOT THAT SUZUME IS SICK.
SHE MUST BE STARVING.
IN SPITE OF THAT, SHE DOESN'T EAT BECAUSE...
...NORMAL FOOD TASTES SO VILE THAT SHE CAN'T HELP BUT THROW IT UP.
SUZUME'S JUST LIKE ME NOW. I WONDER IF WE'VE COME TO SHARE THE SAME SENSE OF TASTE TOO?
WHAT DO YOU FIND TASTY, OUGA-SAN...?
GIVE ME THAT.
BITAN (SLAM)
!!?
HERE.
!
GUSHA (CRUMPLE)

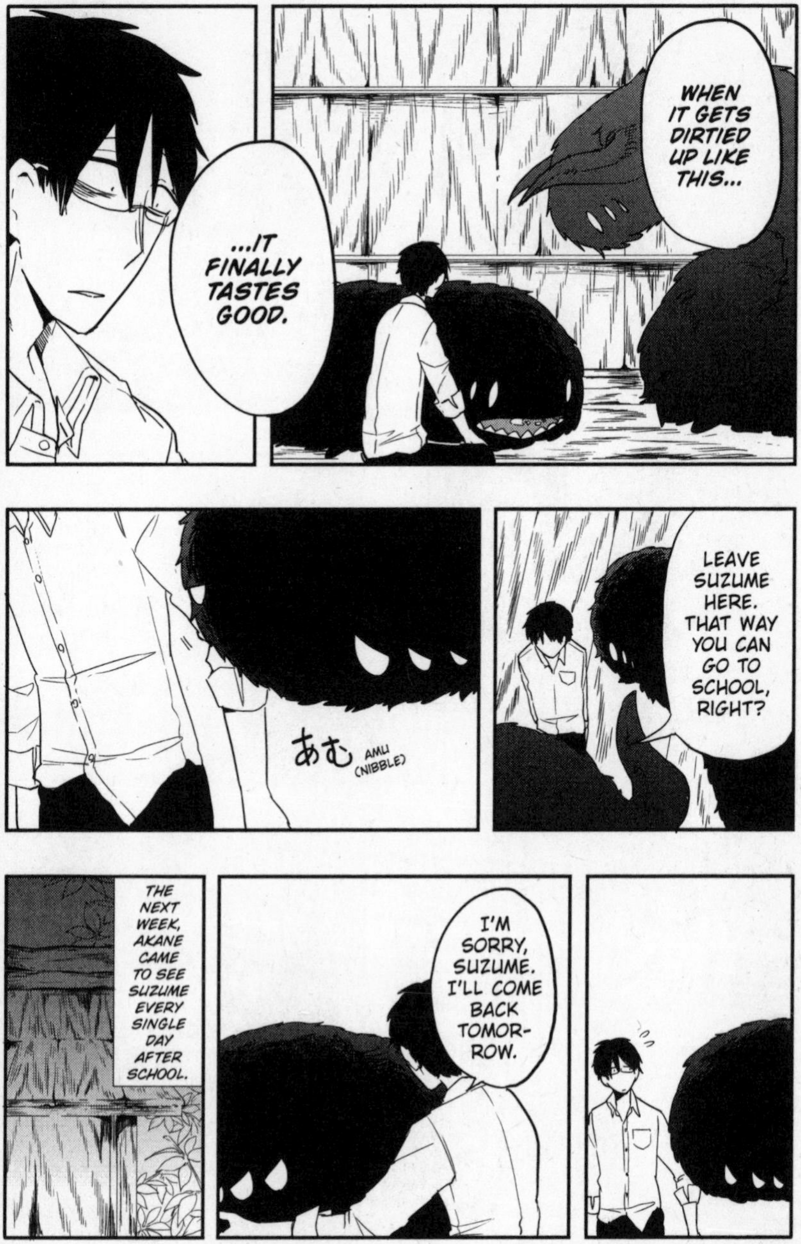
WHEN IT GETS DIRTIED UP LIKE THIS...
...IT FINALLY TASTES GOOD.
LEAVE SUZUME HERE. THAT WAY YOU CAN GO TO SCHOOL, RIGHT?
あむ
AMU (NIBBLE)
I'M SORRY, SUZUME. I'LL COME BACK TOMOR-ROW.
THE NEXT WEEK, AKANE CAME TO SEE SUZUME EVERY SINGLE DAY AFTER SCHOOL.

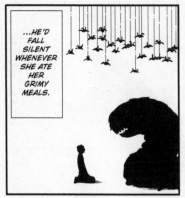

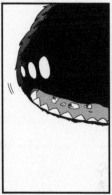

HE'D TALK TO SUZUME FOR HOURS ABOUT THE SILLIEST THINGS, BUT...
...HE'D FALL SILENT WHENEVER SHE ATE HER GRIMY MEALS.
IF... SUZUME KEEPS BECOMING MORE AND MORE LIKE ME...
I'M PRETTY SURE THAT SUZUME...
...WILL CONTINUE TO GET MORE AND MORE UNMANAGEABLE FROM HERE ON OUT.
EVERYTHING SHE SEES WILL OFFEND HER.
EVERYTHING SHE HEARS WILL GRATE ON HER EARS.
SHE'LL GROW TO INCOMPREHENSIBLY HATE EVERYTHING THAT SURROUNDS HER. SHE WON'T BE ABLE TO HELP IT.
DON'T YOU THINK THAT'S UTTERLY DEPRESSING?

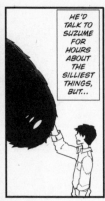

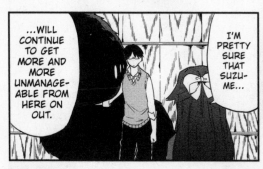

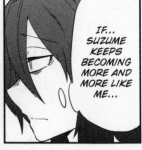

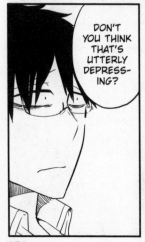

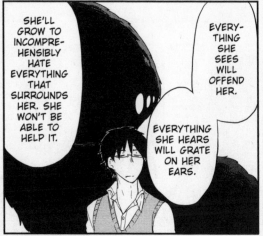

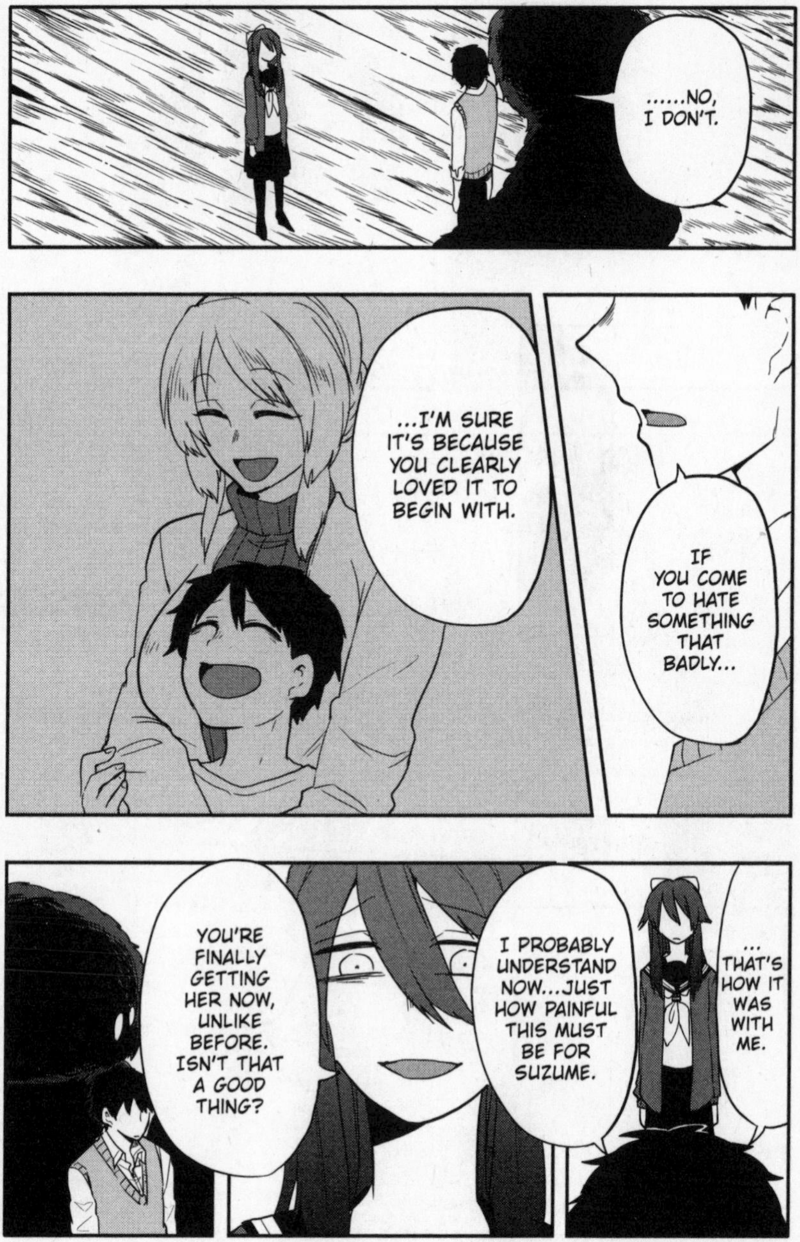

......NO, I DON'T.
IF YOU COME TO HATE SOMETHING THAT BADLY...
...I'M SURE IT'S BECAUSE YOU CLEARLY LOVED IT TO BEGIN WITH.
... THAT'S HOW IT WAS WITH ME.
I PROBABLY UNDERSTAND NOW...JUST HOW PAINFUL THIS MUST BE FOR SUZUME.
YOU'RE FINALLY GETTING HER NOW, UNLIKE BEFORE. ISN'T THAT A GOOD THING?

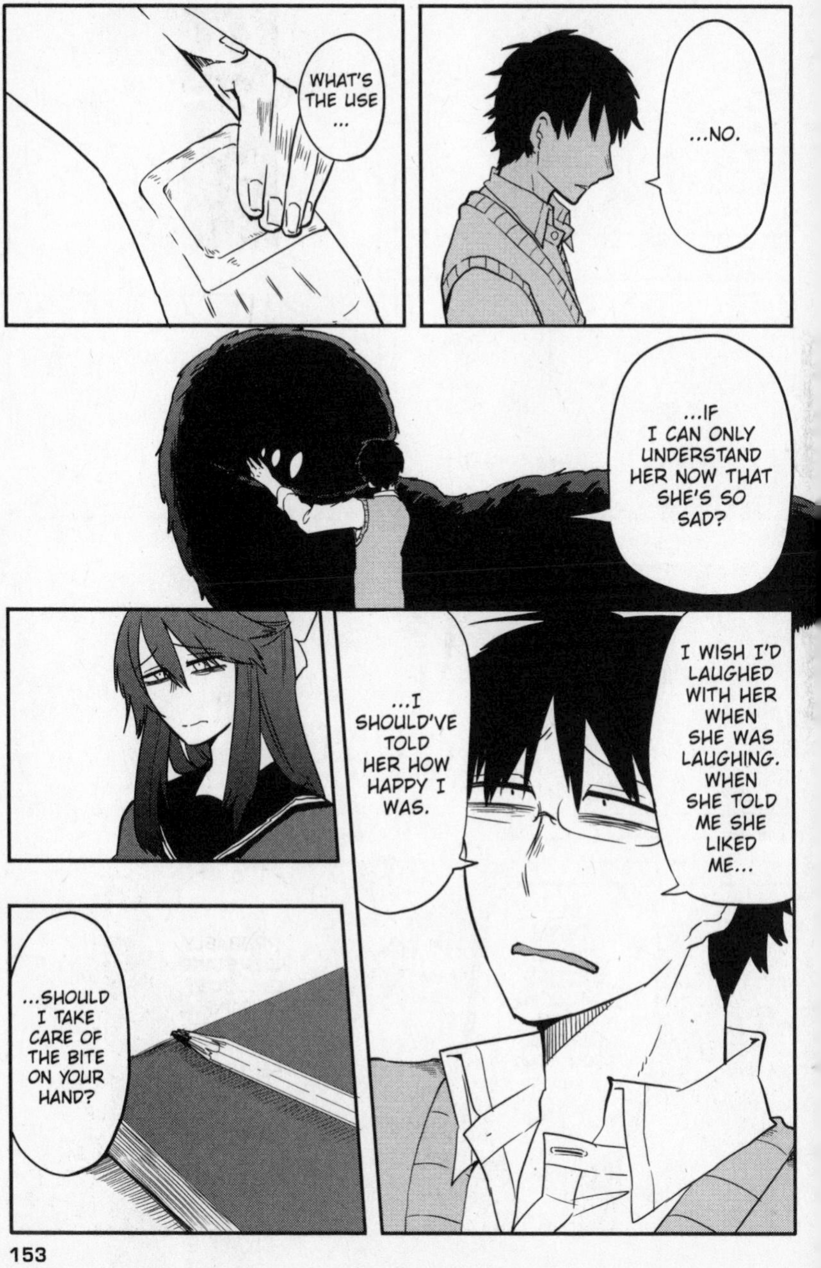
...NO.
WHAT'S THE USE ...
...IF I CAN ONLY UNDERSTAND HER NOW THAT SHE'S SO SAD?
I WISH I'D LAUGHED WITH HER WHEN SHE WAS LAUGHING. WHEN SHE TOLD ME SHE LIKED ME...
...I SHOULD'VE TOLD HER HOW HAPPY I WAS.
...SHOULD I TAKE CARE OF THE BITE ON YOUR HAND?

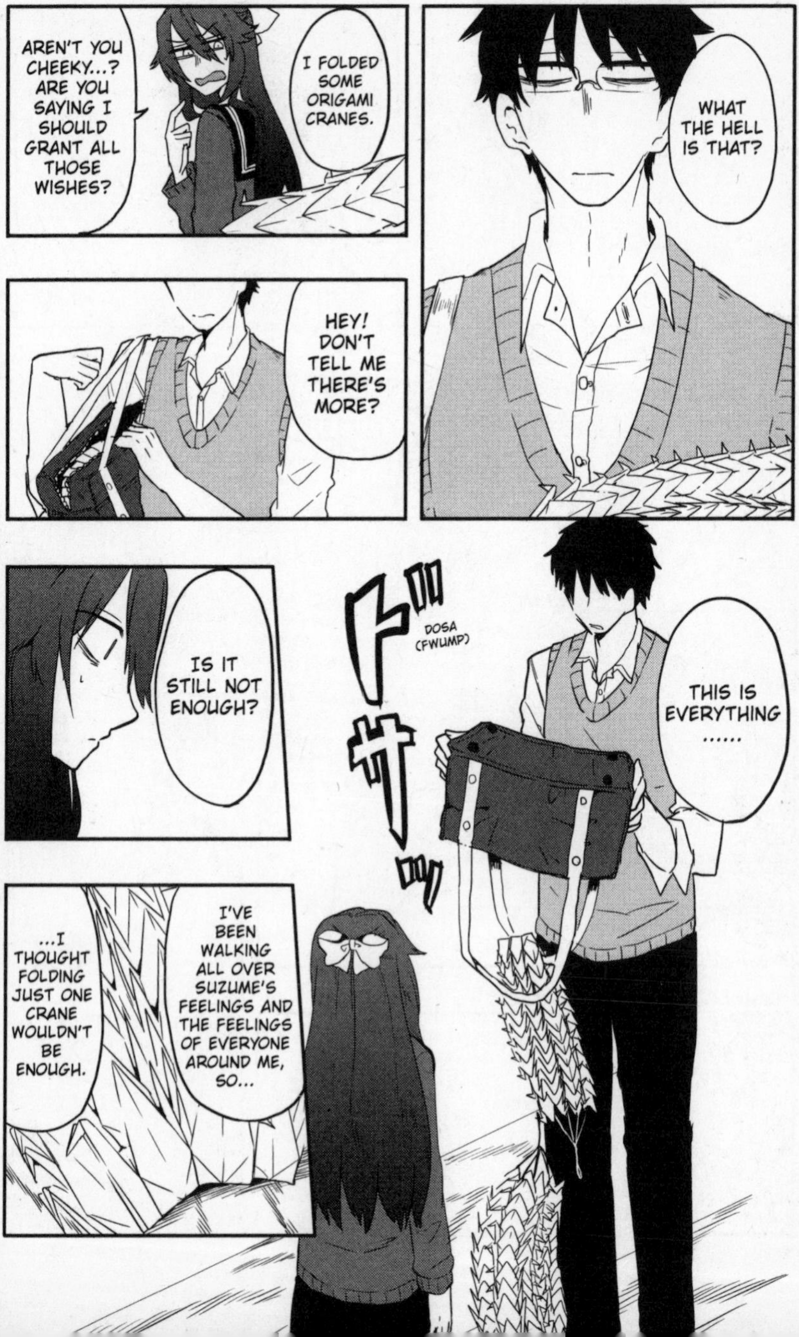
WHAT THE HELL IS THAT?
I FOLDED SOME ORIGAMI CRANES.
AREN'T YOU CHEEKY...? ARE YOU SAYING I SHOULD GRANT ALL THOSE WISHES?
HEY! DON'T TELL ME THERE'S MORE?
DOSA (FWUMP)
THIS IS EVERYTHING ......
IS IT STILL NOT ENOUGH?
I'VE BEEN WALKING ALL OVER SUZUME'S FEELINGS AND THE FEELINGS OF EVERYONE AROUND ME, SO...
...I THOUGHT FOLDING JUST ONE CRANE WOULDN'T BE ENOUGH.

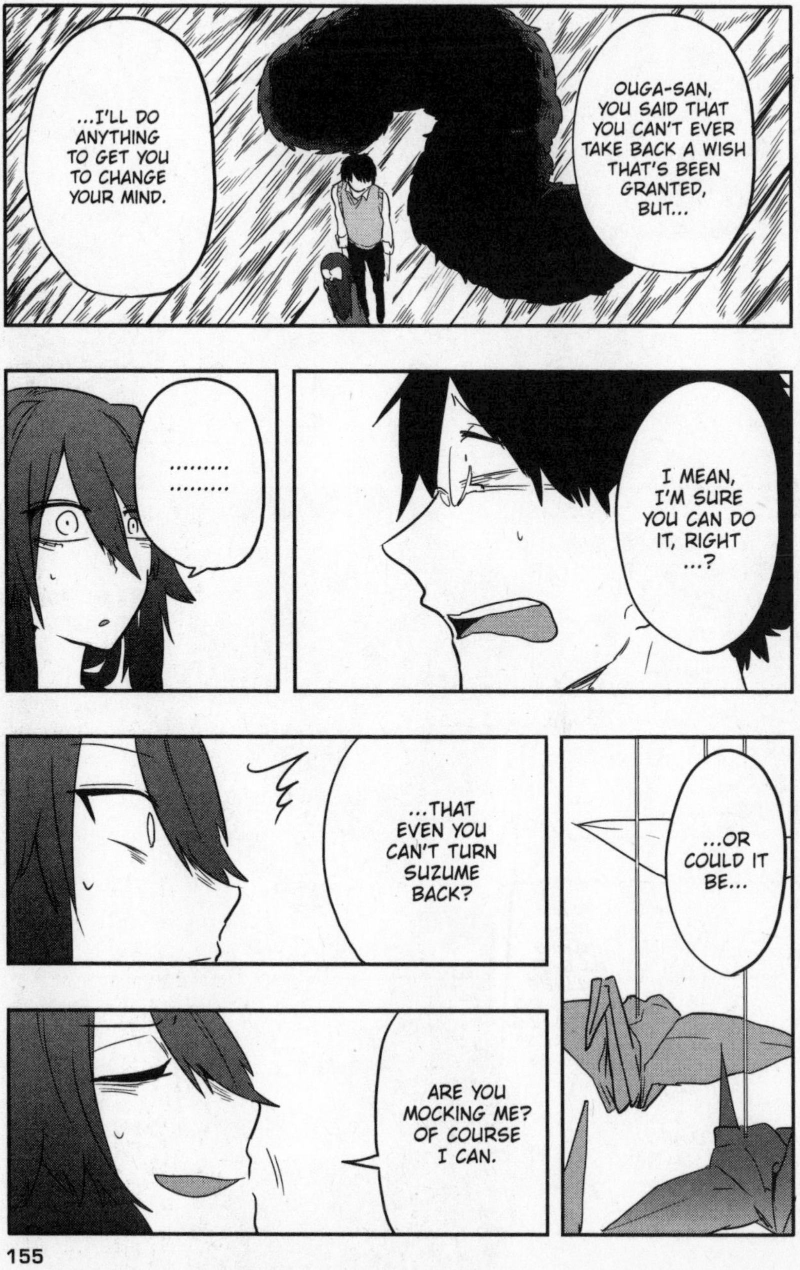
OUGA-SAN, YOU SAID THAT YOU CAN'T EVER TAKE BACK A WISH THAT'S BEEN GRANTED, BUT...
...I'LL DO ANYTHING TO GET YOU TO CHANGE YOUR MIND.
I MEAN, I'M SURE YOU CAN DO IT, RIGHT ...?
....
....
...OR COULD IT BE...
...THAT EVEN YOU CAN'T TURN SUZUME BACK?
ARE YOU MOCKING ME? OF COURSE I CAN.

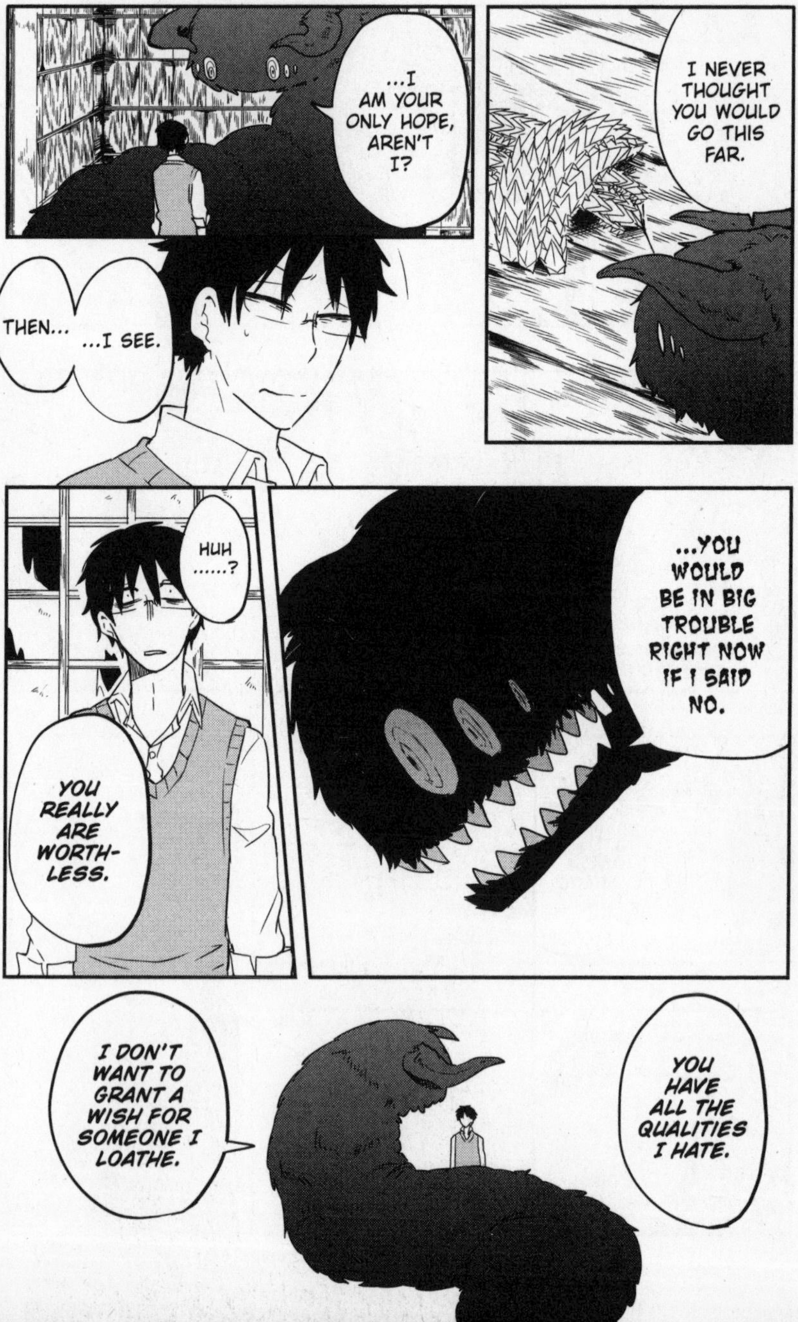
I NEVER THOUGHT YOU WOULD GO THIS FAR.
...I AM YOUR ONLY HOPE, AREN'T I?
...I SEE.
THEN...
...YOU WOULD BE IN BIG TROUBLE RIGHT NOW IF I SAID NO.
HUH ......?
YOU REALLY ARE WORTH-LESS.
YOU HAVE ALL THE QUALITIES I HATE.
I DON'T WANT TO GRANT A WISH FOR SOMEONE I LOATHE.

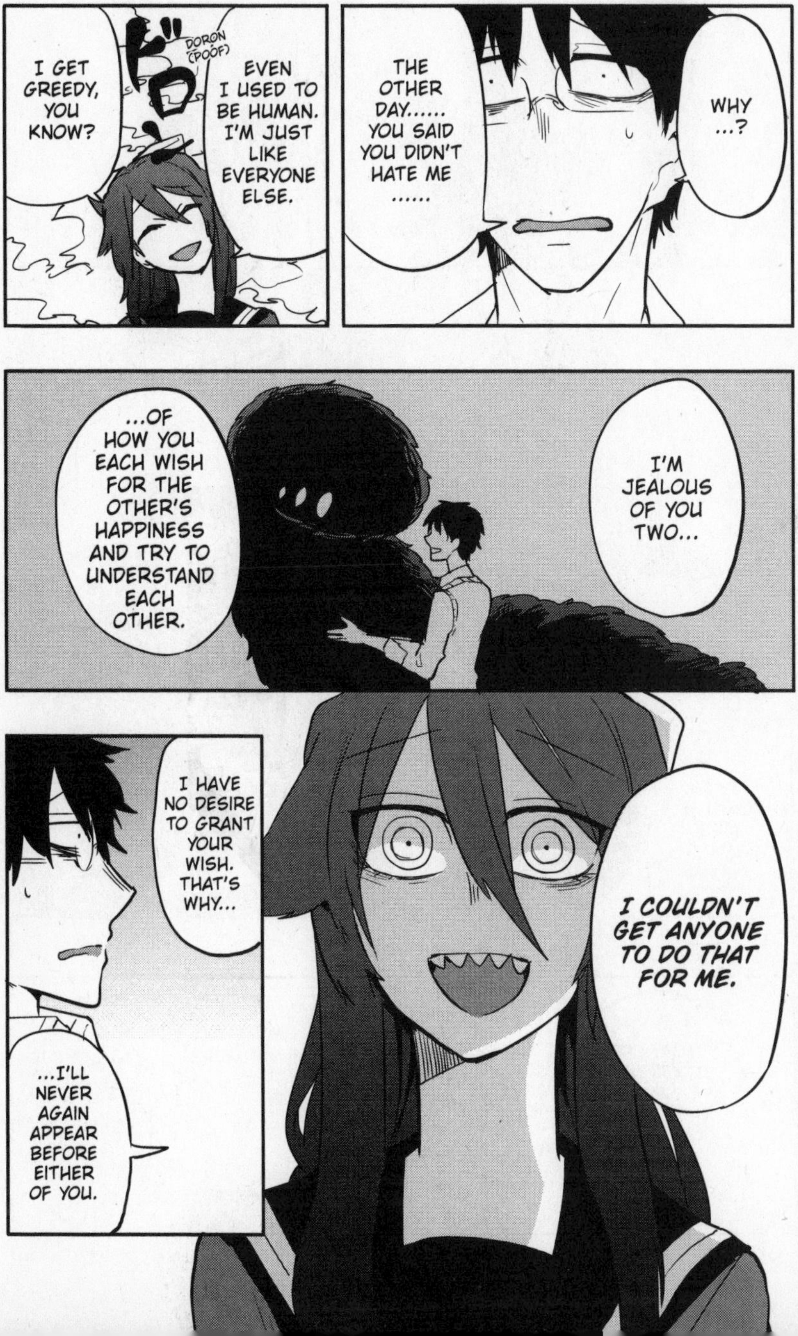
WHY ...?
THE OTHER DAY...... YOU SAID YOU DIDN'T HATE ME ......
EVEN I USED TO BE HUMAN. I'M JUST LIKE EVERYONE ELSE.
DORON (POOF)
I GET GREEDY, YOU KNOW?
I'M JEALOUS OF YOU TWO...
...OF HOW YOU EACH WISH FOR THE OTHER'S HAPPINESS AND TRY TO UNDERSTAND EACH OTHER.
I COULDN'T GET ANYONE TO DO THAT FOR ME.
I HAVE NO DESIRE TO GRANT YOUR WISH. THAT'S WHY...
...I'LL NEVER AGAIN APPEAR BEFORE EITHER OF YOU.

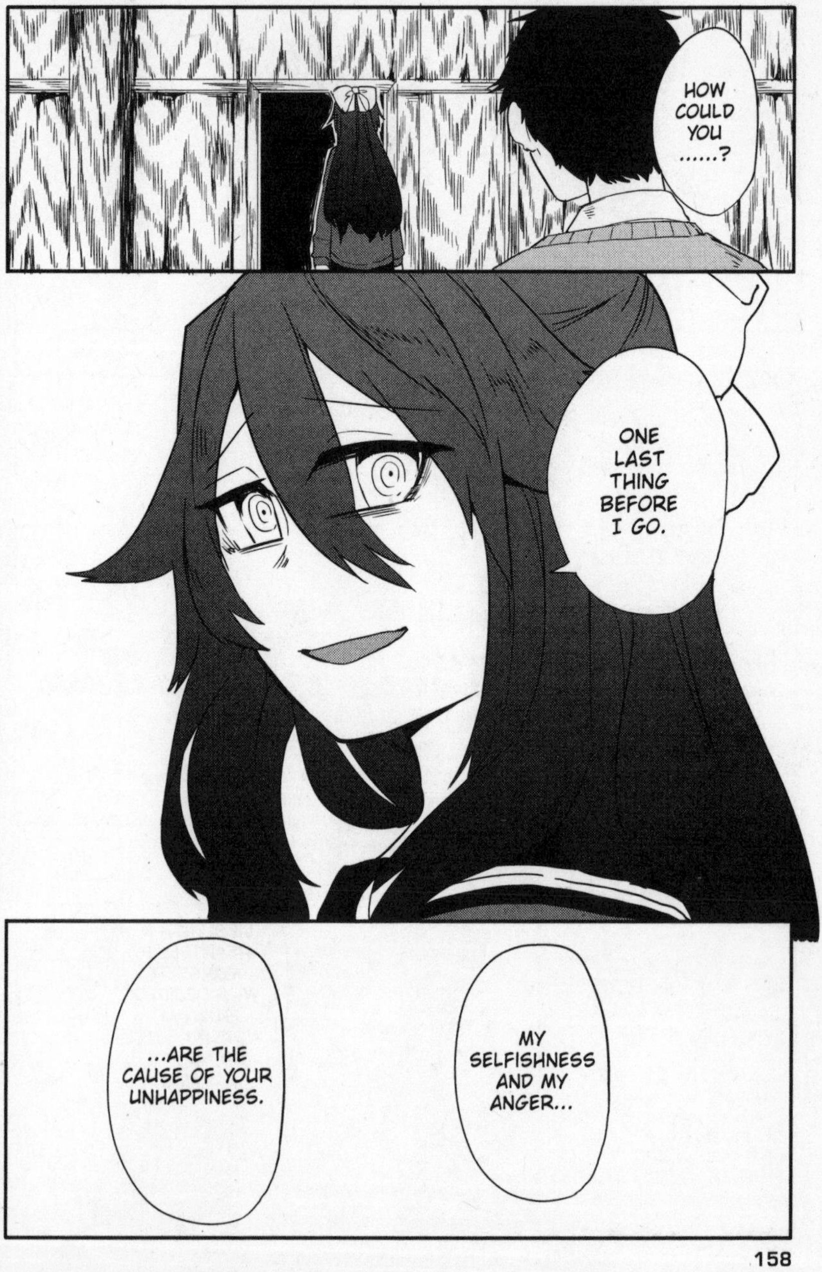
HOW COULD YOU ......?
ONE LAST THING BEFORE I GO.
MY SELFISHNESS AND MY ANGER...
...ARE THE CAUSE OF YOUR UNHAPPINESS.

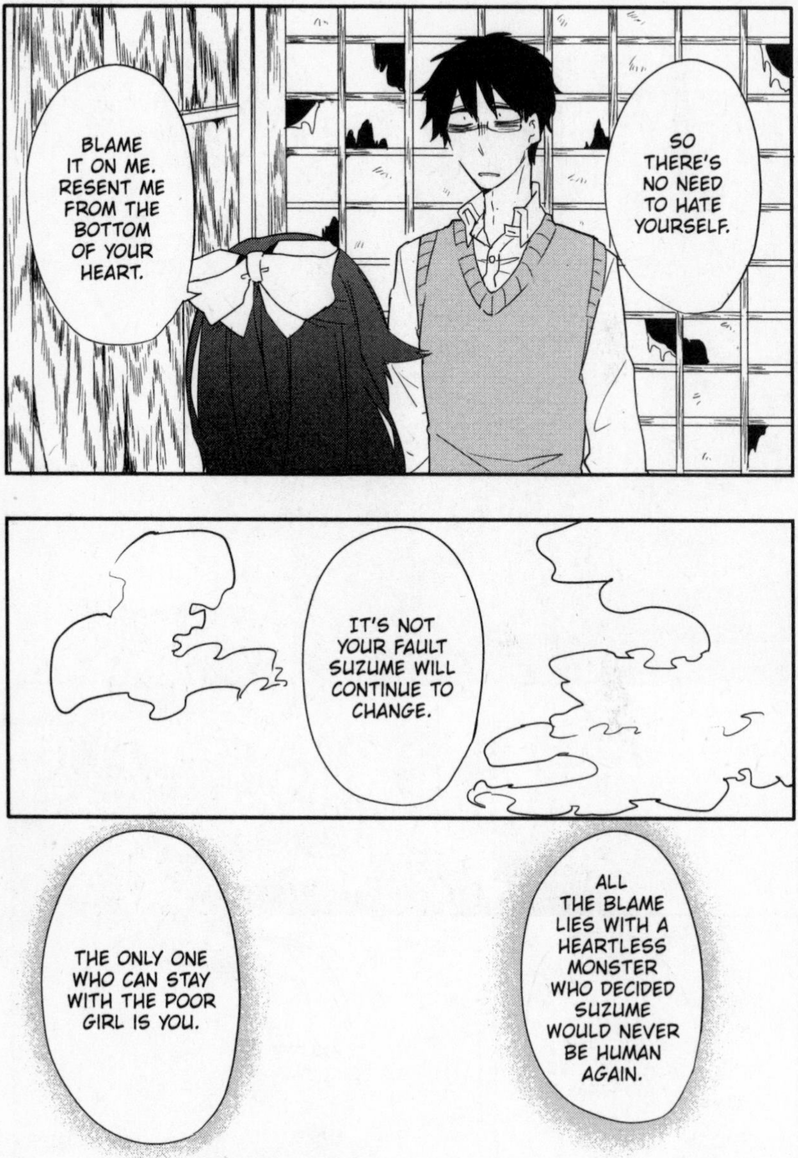
SO THERE'S NO NEED TO HATE YOURSELF.
BLAME IT ON ME. RESENT ME FROM THE BOTTOM OF YOUR HEART.
IT'S NOT YOUR FAULT SUZUME WILL CONTINUE TO CHANGE.
ALL THE BLAME LIES WITH A HEARTLESS MONSTER WHO DECIDED SUZUME WOULD NEVER BE HUMAN AGAIN.
THE ONLY ONE WHO CAN STAY WITH THE POOR GIRL IS YOU.

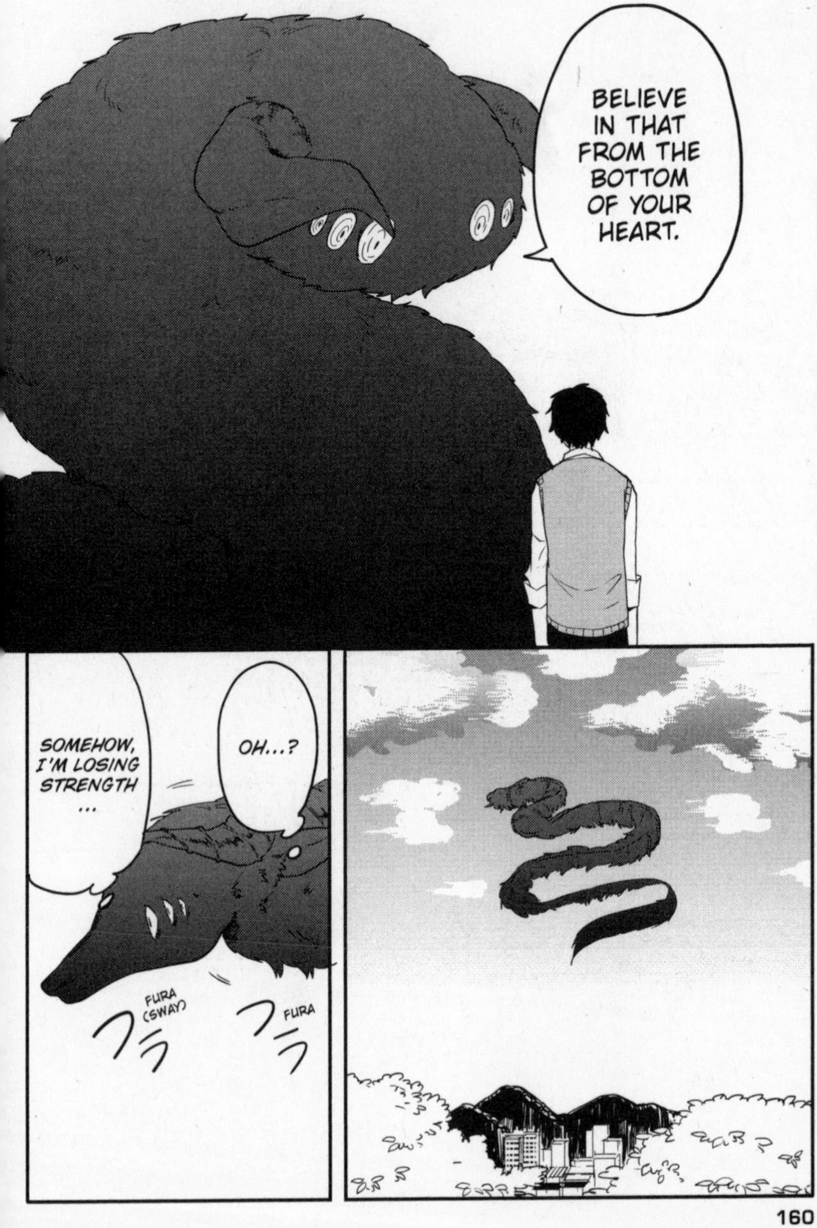
BELIEVE IN THAT FROM THE BOTTOM OF YOUR HEART.
OH...?
SOMEHOW, I'M LOSING STRENGTH...
FURA
FURA (SWAY)

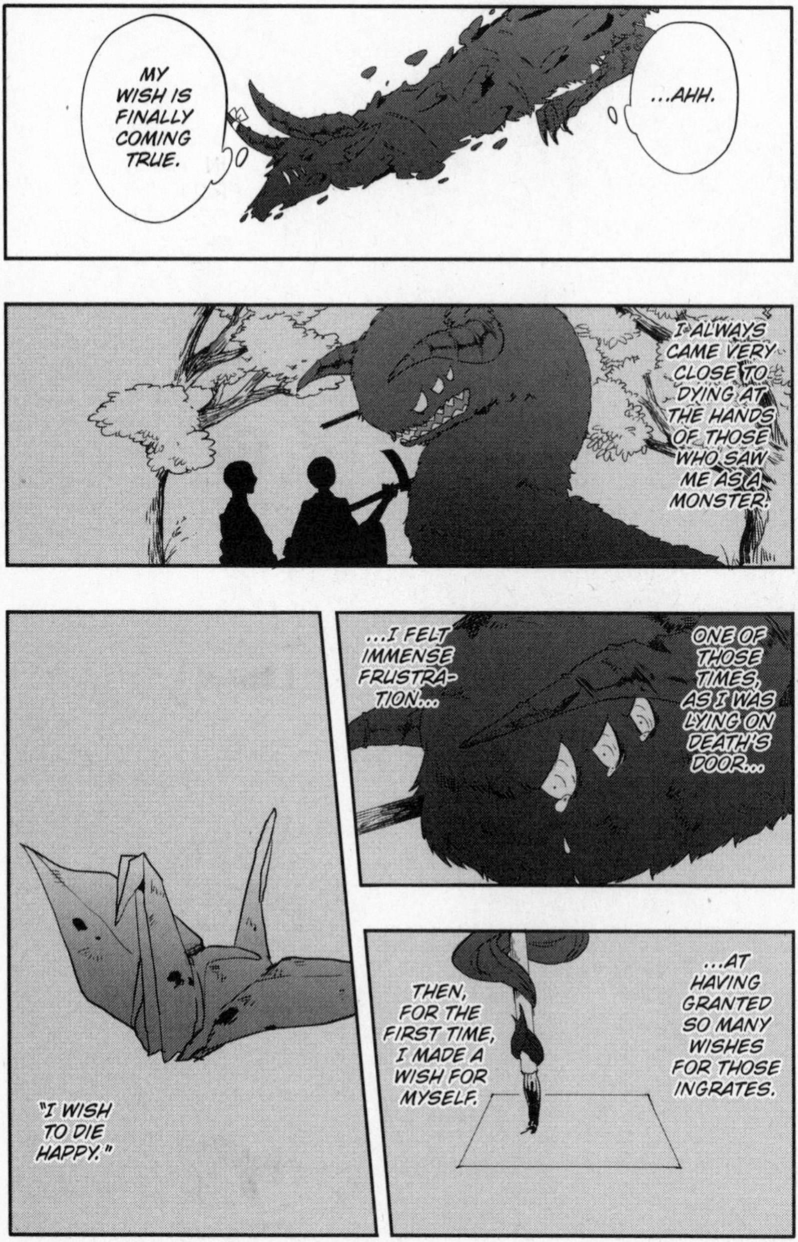
...AHH.
MY WISH IS FINALLY COMING TRUE.
I ALWAYS CAME VERY CLOSE TO DYING AT THE HANDS OF THOSE WHO SAW ME AS A MONSTER.
ONE OF THOSE TIMES, AS I WAS LYING ON DEATH'S DOOR...
...I FELT IMMENSE FRUSTRA-TION...
...AT HAVING GRANTED SO MANY WISHES FOR THOSE INGRATES.
THEN, FOR THE FIRST TIME, I MADE A WISH FOR MYSELF.
"I WISH TO DIE HAPPY."

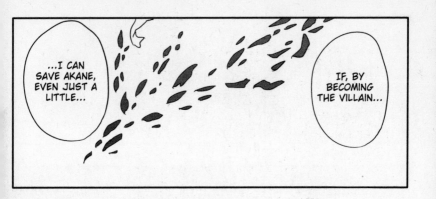

IF, BY BECOMING THE VILLAIN...
...I CAN SAVE AKANE, EVEN JUST A LITTLE...
...THAT WOULD BE MY HAPPINESS.

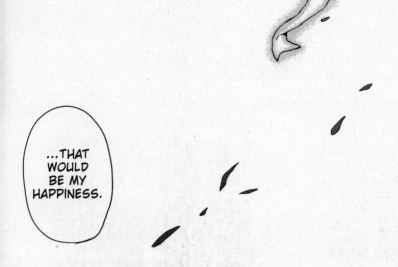

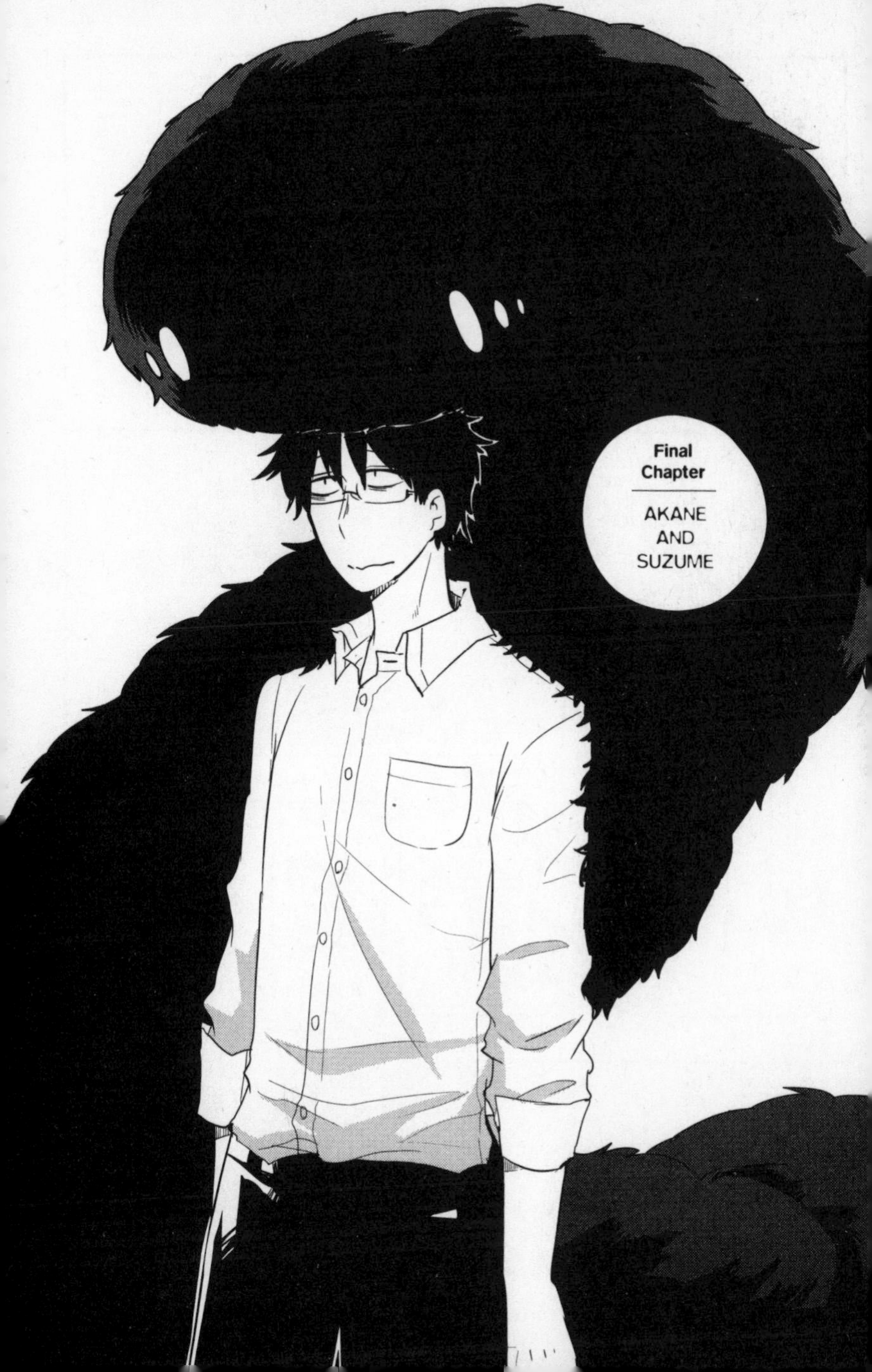
Final Chapter
AKANE AND SUZUME

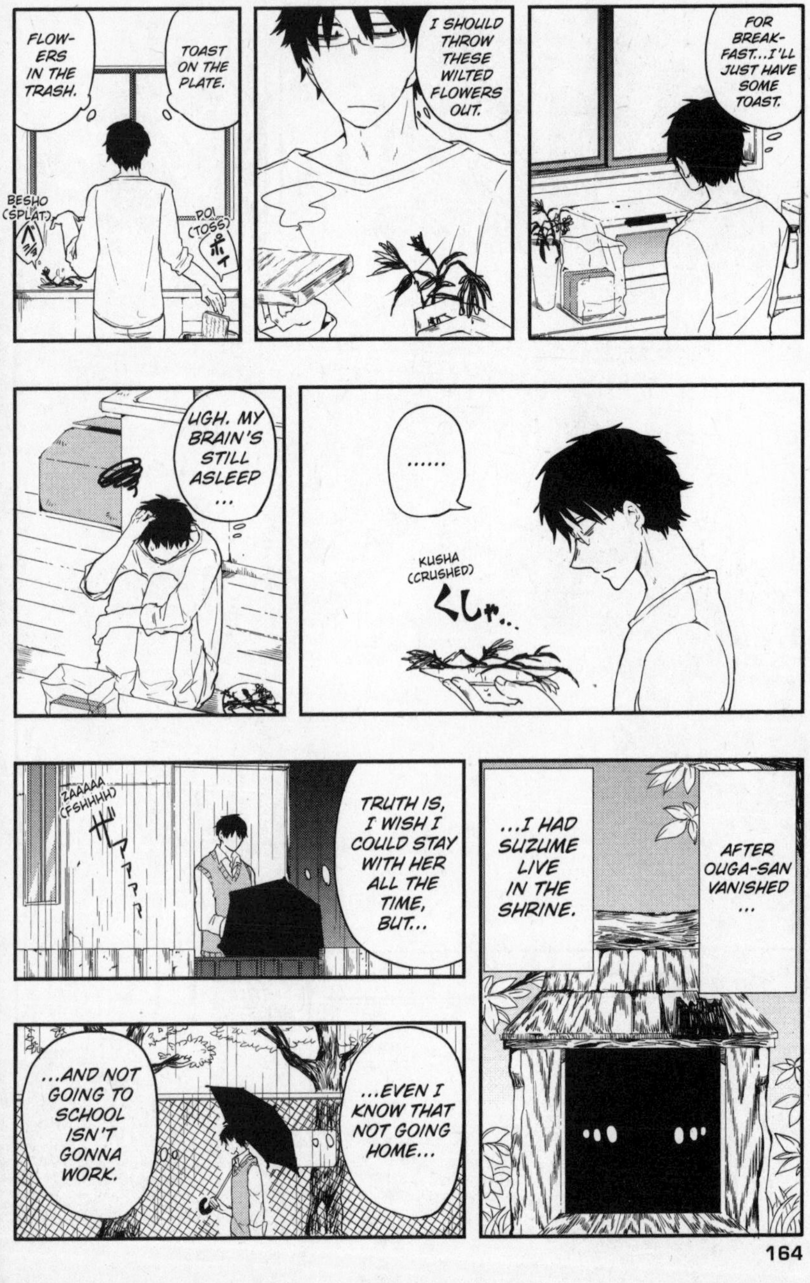
FOR BREAK-FAST...I'LL JUST HAVE SOME TOAST.
I SHOULD THROW THESE WILTED FLOWERS OUT.
TOAST ON THE PLATE.
POI (TOSS)
ポイ
FLOW-ERS IN THE TRASH.
BESHO (SPLAT)
......
KUSHA (CRUSHED)
くしゃ...
UGH. MY BRAIN'S STILL ASLEEP...
AFTER OUGA-SAN VANISHED...
...I HAD SUZUME LIVE IN THE SHRINE.
TRUTH IS, I WISH I COULD STAY WITH HER ALL THE TIME, BUT...
ZAAAAA (FSHHHH)
...EVEN I KNOW THAT NOT GOING HOME...
...AND NOT GOING TO SCHOOL ISN'T GONNA WORK.

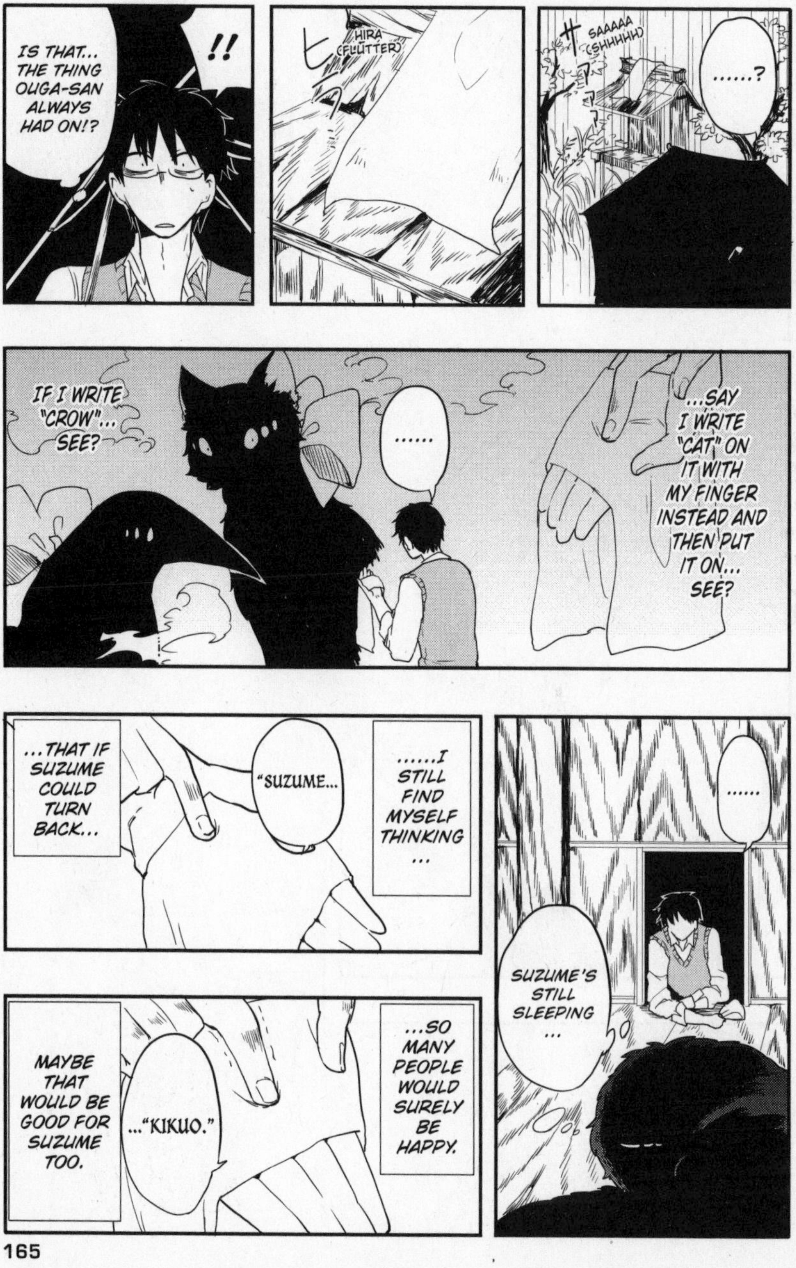
SAAAAA (SHHHHH)
......?
HIRA (FLUTTER)
IS THAT... THE THING OUGA-SAN ALWAYS HAD ON!?
!!
...SAY I WRITE "CAT" ON IT WITH MY FINGER INSTEAD AND THEN PUT IT ON... SEE?
......
IF I WRITE "CROW"... SEE?
......
SUZUME'S STILL SLEEPING...
......I STILL FIND MYSELF THINKING...
"SUZUME...
...THAT IF SUZUME COULD TURN BACK...
...SO MANY PEOPLE WOULD SURELY BE HAPPY.
..."KIKUO."
MAYBE THAT WOULD BE GOOD FOR SUZUME TOO.

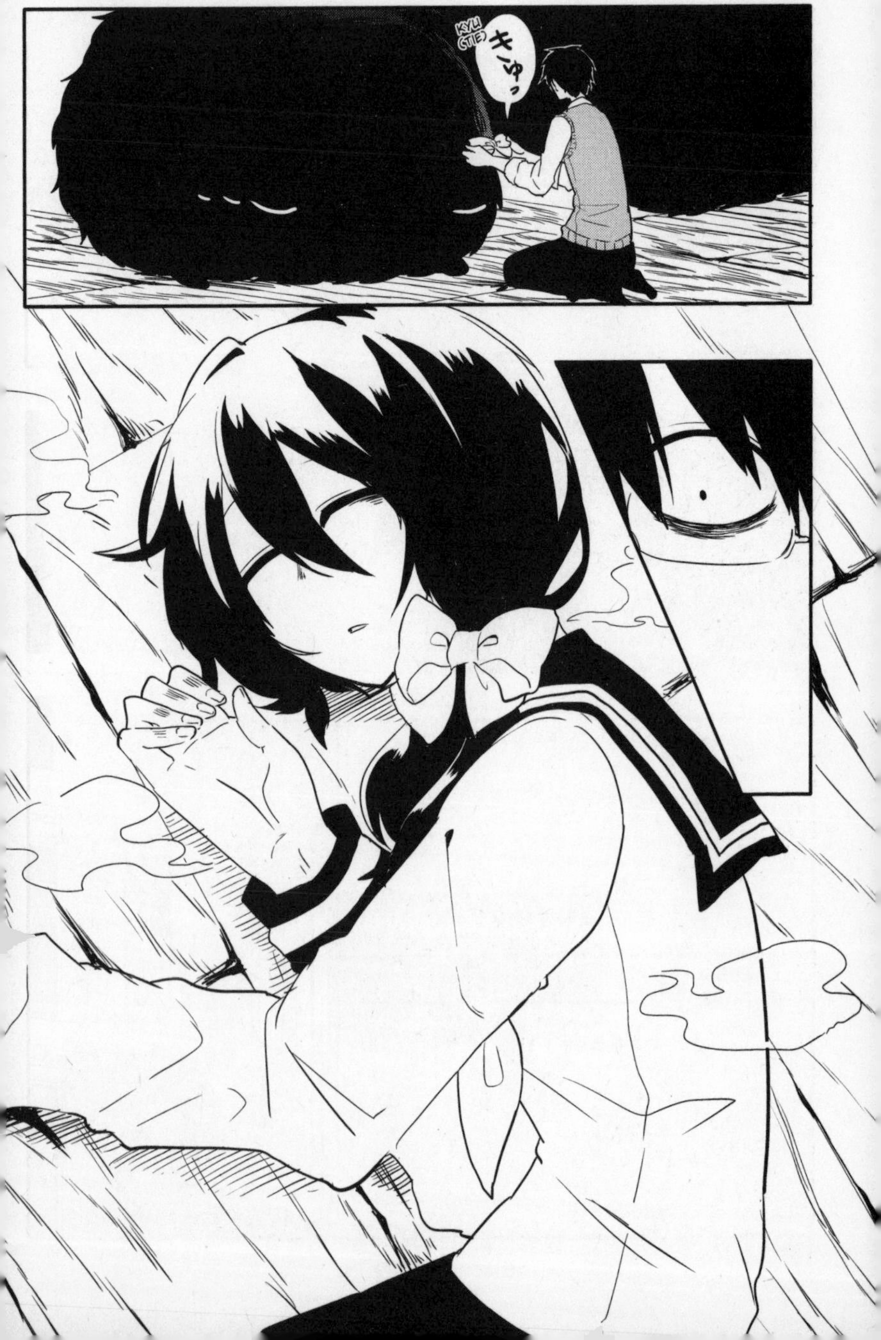
KYU (TIE)
キュッ

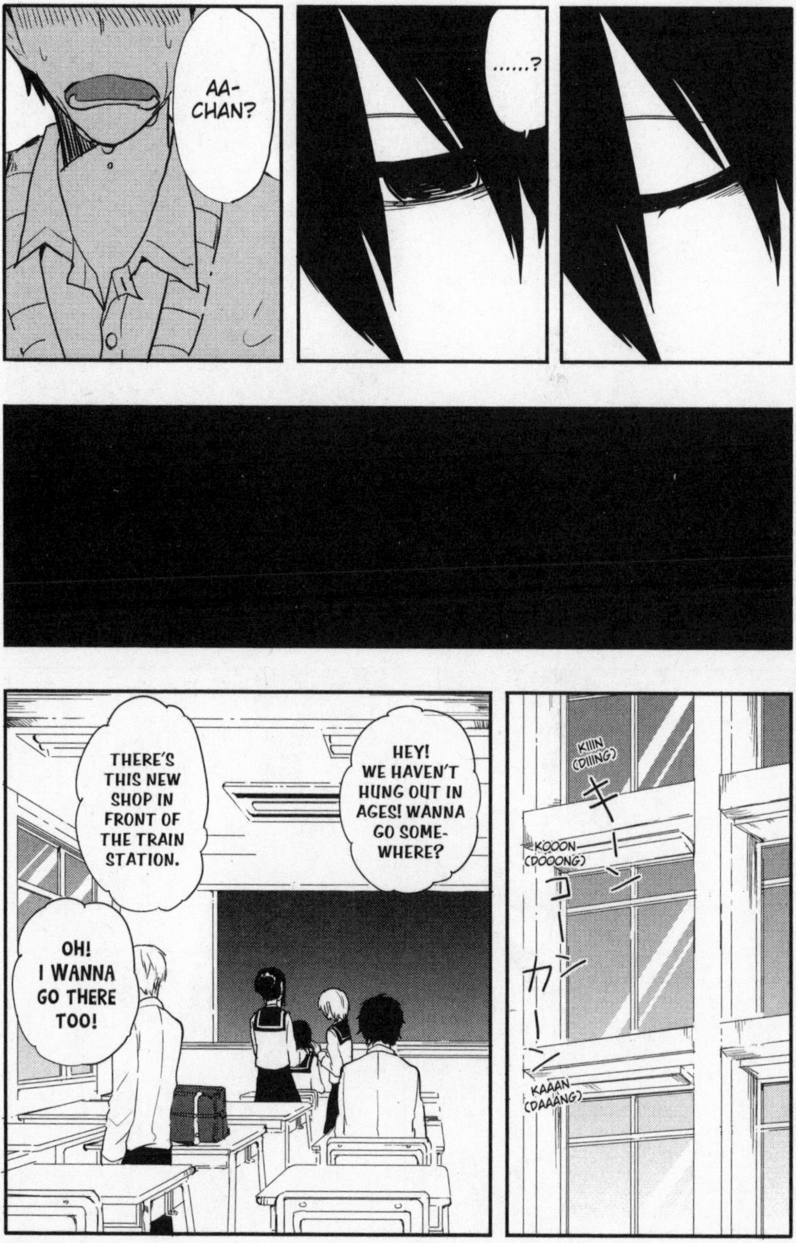
......?
AA-CHAN?
KIIN (DIIING)
KOOON (DOOONG)
KAAAN (DAAANG)
HEY! WE HAVEN'T HUNG OUT IN AGES! WANNA GO SOME-WHERE?
THERE'S THIS NEW SHOP IN FRONT OF THE TRAIN STATION.
OH! I WANNA GO THERE TOO!

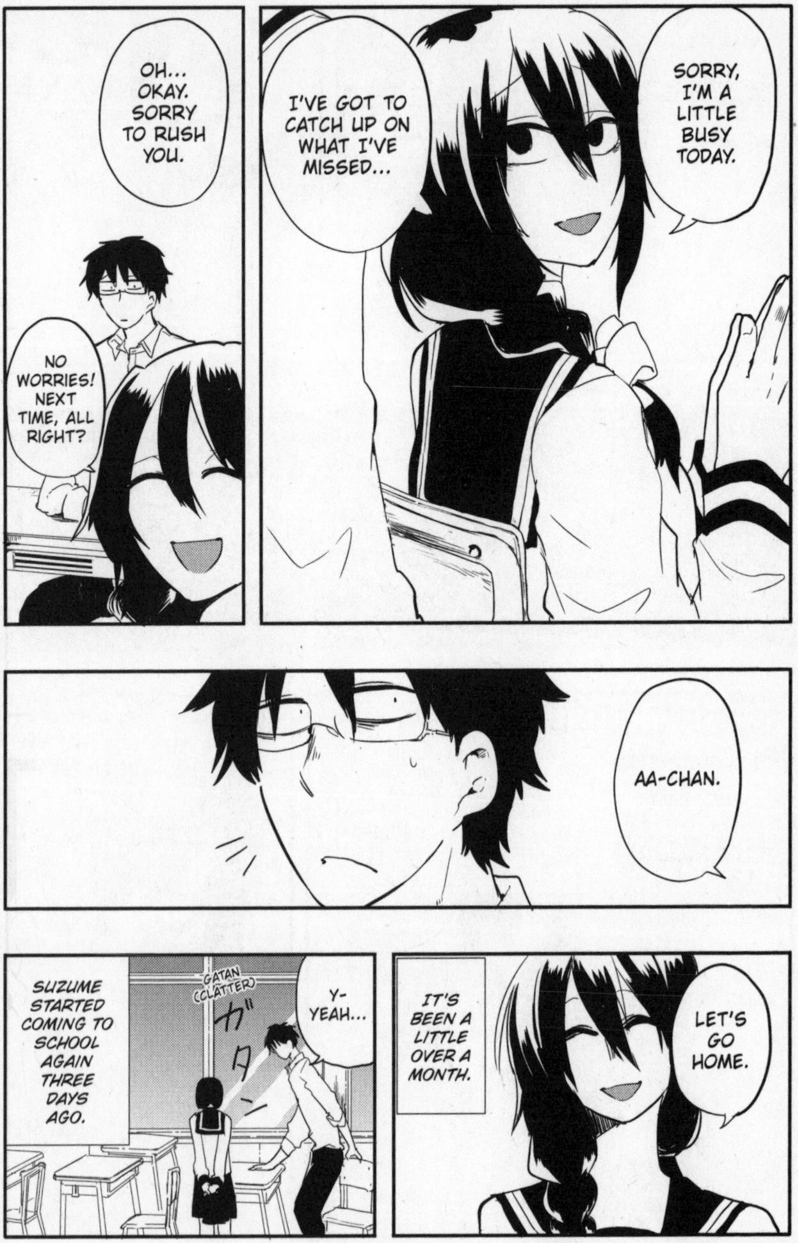
SORRY, I'M A LITTLE BUSY TODAY.
I'VE GOT TO CATCH UP ON WHAT I'VE MISSED...
OH... OKAY. SORRY TO RUSH YOU.
NO WORRIES! NEXT TIME, ALL RIGHT?
AA-CHAN.
LET'S GO HOME.
IT'S BEEN A LITTLE OVER A MONTH.
Y-YEAH...
GATAN (CLATTER)
SUZUME STARTED COMING TO SCHOOL AGAIN THREE DAYS AGO.

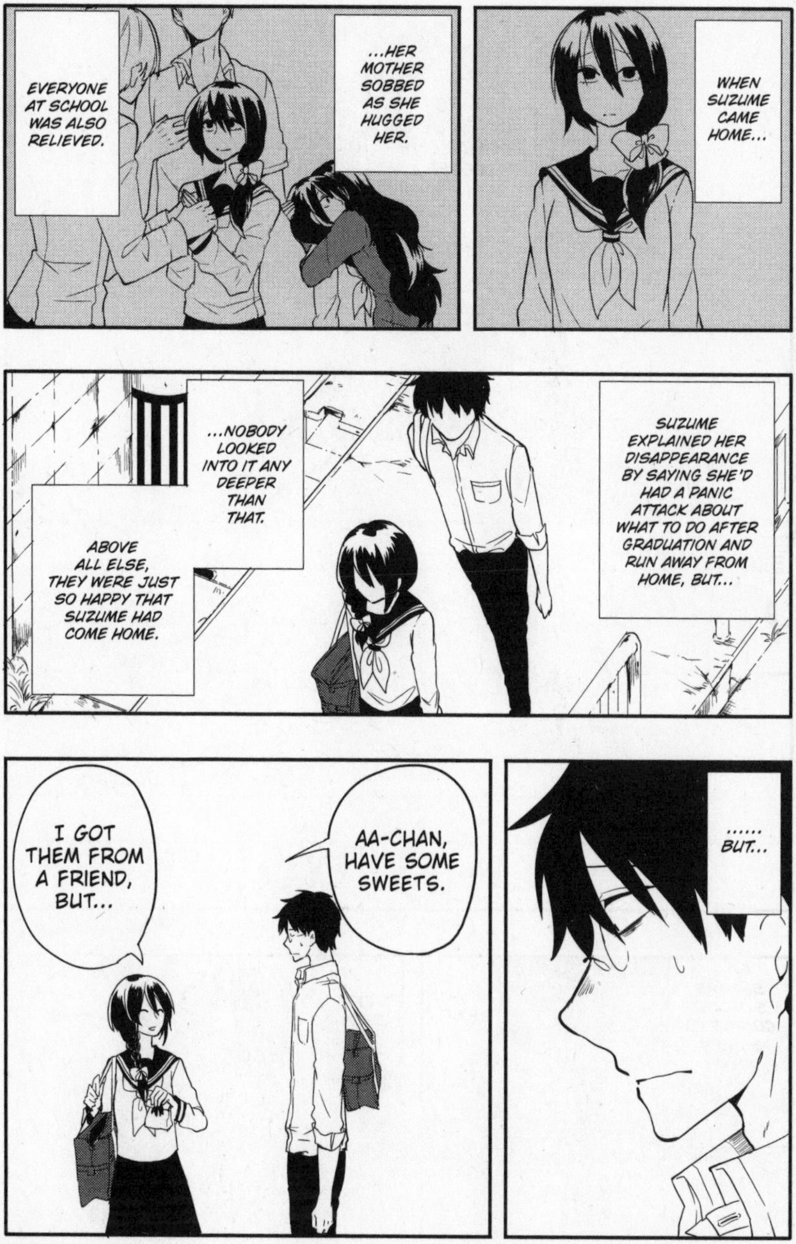
WHEN SUZUME CAME HOME...
...HER MOTHER SOBBED AS SHE HUGGED HER.
EVERYONE AT SCHOOL WAS ALSO RELIEVED.
SUZUME EXPLAINED HER DISAPPEARANCE BY SAYING SHE'D HAD A PANIC ATTACK ABOUT WHAT TO DO AFTER GRADUATION AND RUN AWAY FROM HOME, BUT...
...NOBODY LOOKED INTO IT ANY DEEPER THAN THAT.
ABOVE ALL ELSE, THEY WERE JUST SO HAPPY THAT SUZUME HAD COME HOME.
......BUT...
AA-CHAN, HAVE SOME SWEETS.
I GOT THEM FROM A FRIEND, BUT...

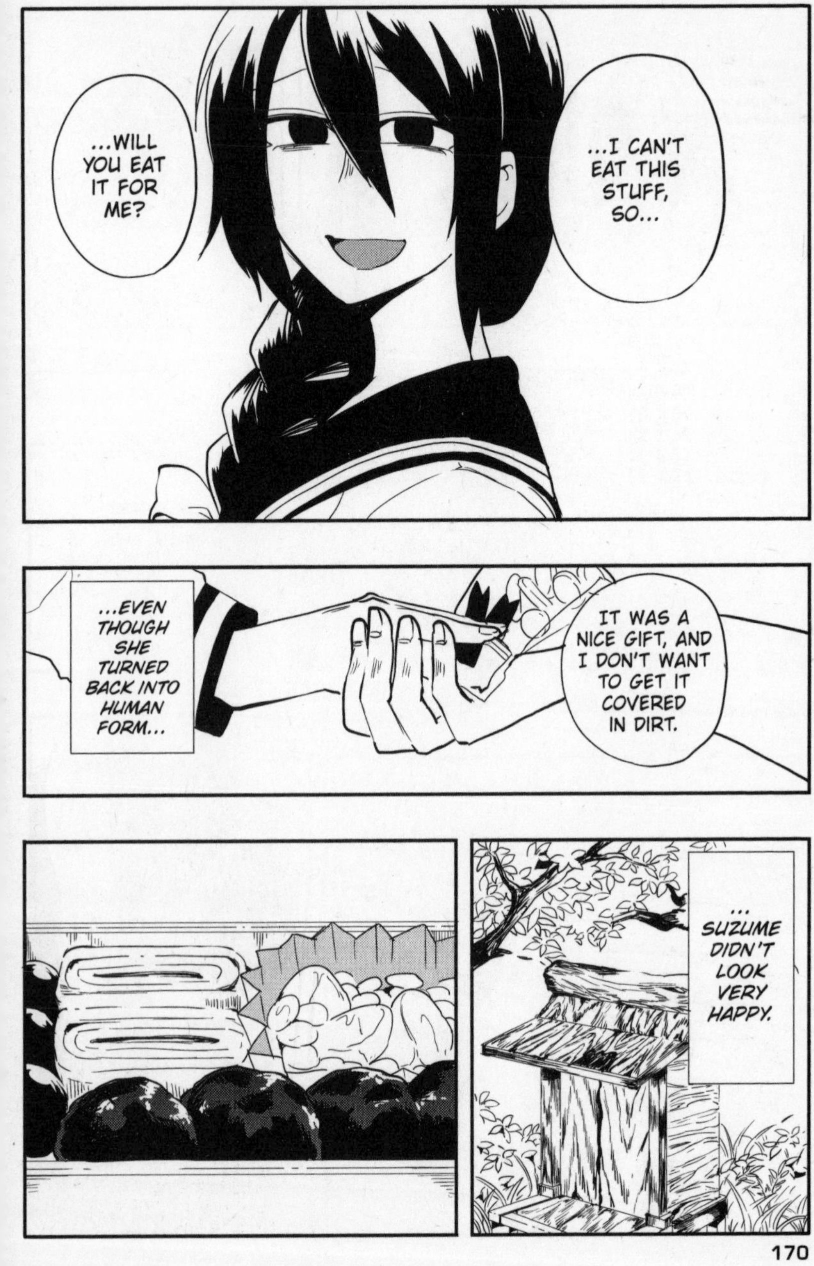
...I CAN'T EAT THIS STUFF, SO...
...WILL YOU EAT IT FOR ME?
IT WAS A NICE GIFT, AND I DON'T WANT TO GET IT COVERED IN DIRT.
...EVEN THOUGH SHE TURNED BACK INTO HUMAN FORM...
... SUZUME DIDN'T LOOK VERY HAPPY.

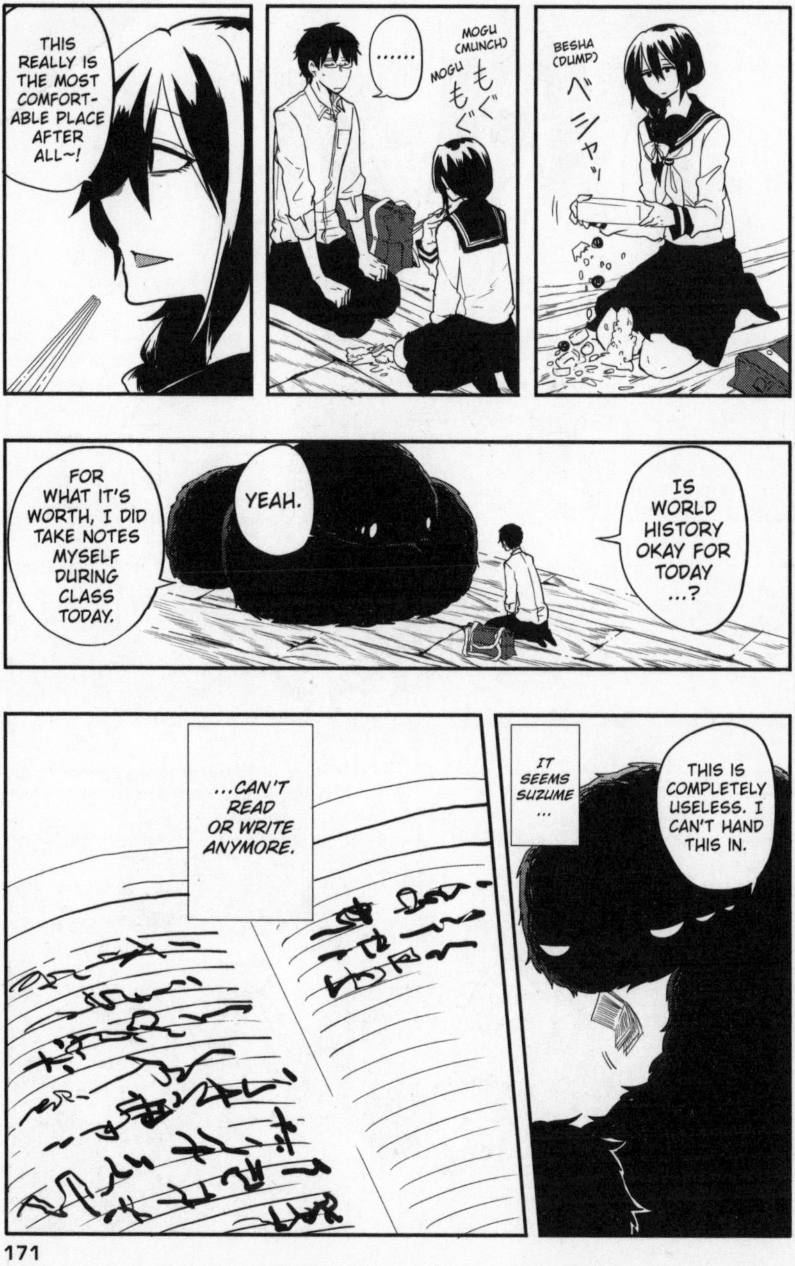
BESHA (DUMP)
ベシャッ
MOGU (MUNCH) MOGU
もぐもぐ
......
THIS REALLY IS THE MOST COMFORTABLE PLACE AFTER ALL~!
IS WORLD HISTORY OKAY FOR TODAY ...?
YEAH.
FOR WHAT IT'S WORTH, I DID TAKE NOTES MYSELF DURING CLASS TODAY.
THIS IS COMPLETELY USELESS. I CAN'T HAND THIS IN.
IT SEEMS SUZUME ...
...CAN'T READ OR WRITE ANYMORE.

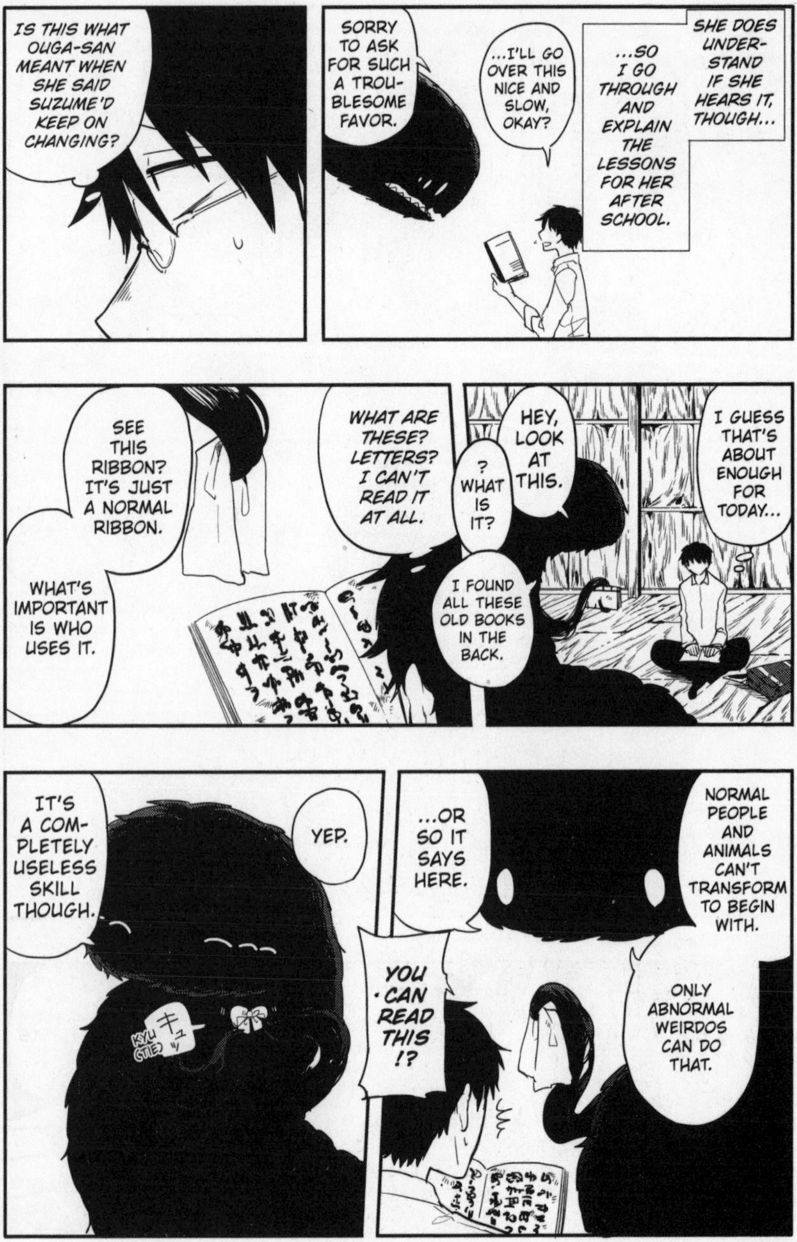
SHE DOES UNDERSTAND IF SHE HEARS IT, THOUGH...
...SO I GO THROUGH AND EXPLAIN THE LESSONS FOR HER AFTER SCHOOL.
...I'LL GO OVER THIS NICE AND SLOW, OKAY?
SORRY TO ASK FOR SUCH A TROUBLESOME FAVOR.
IS THIS WHAT OUGA-SAN MEANT WHEN SHE SAID SUZUME'D KEEP ON CHANGING?
I GUESS THAT'S ABOUT ENOUGH FOR TODAY...
HEY, LOOK AT THIS.
? WHAT IS IT?
I FOUND ALL THESE OLD BOOKS IN THE BACK.
WHAT ARE THESE? LETTERS? I CAN'T READ IT AT ALL.
SEE THIS RIBBON? IT'S JUST A NORMAL RIBBON.
WHAT'S IMPORTANT IS WHO USES IT.
NORMAL PEOPLE AND ANIMALS CAN'T TRANSFORM TO BEGIN WITH.
...OR SO IT SAYS HERE.
ONLY ABNORMAL WEIRDOS CAN DO THAT.
YOU CAN READ THIS!?
YEP.
IT'S A COMPLETELY USELESS SKILL THOUGH.
キュッ KYU (TIE)

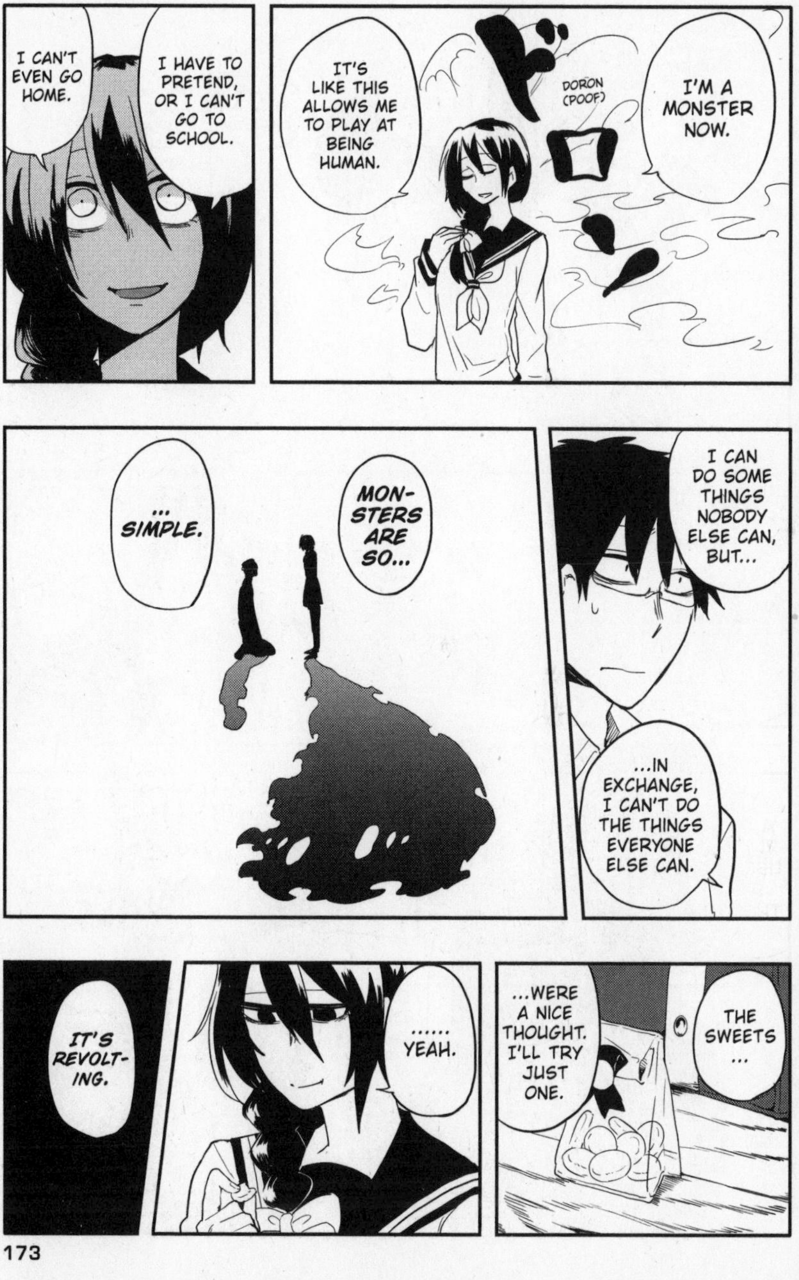
I'M A MONSTER NOW.
DORON (POOF)
IT'S LIKE THIS ALLOWS ME TO PLAY AT BEING HUMAN.
I HAVE TO PRETEND, OR I CAN'T GO TO SCHOOL.
I CAN'T EVEN GO HOME.
I CAN DO SOME THINGS NOBODY ELSE CAN, BUT...
...IN EXCHANGE, I CAN'T DO THE THINGS EVERYONE ELSE CAN.
MONSTERS ARE SO...
...SIMPLE.
THE SWEETS...
...WERE A NICE THOUGHT. I'LL TRY JUST ONE.
......YEAH.
IT'S REVOLTING.

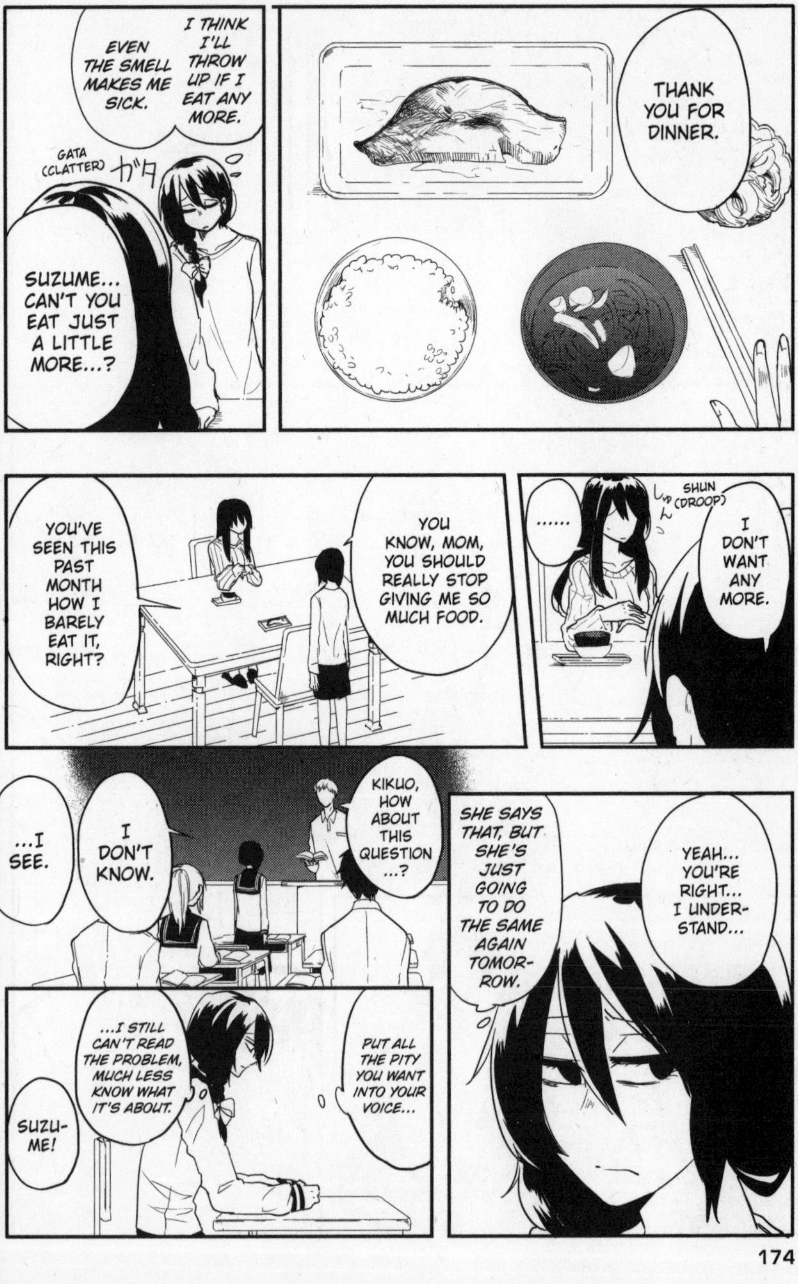
THANK YOU FOR DINNER.
I THINK I'LL THROW UP IF I EAT ANY MORE.
EVEN THE SMELL MAKES ME SICK.
GATA (CLATTER)
ガタ
SUZUME... CAN'T YOU EAT JUST A LITTLE MORE...?
SHUN (DROOP)
しゅん
I DON'T WANT ANY MORE.
......
YOU KNOW, MOM, YOU SHOULD REALLY STOP GIVING ME SO MUCH FOOD.
YOU'VE SEEN THIS PAST MONTH HOW I BARELY EAT IT, RIGHT?
YEAH... YOU'RE RIGHT... I UNDERSTAND...
SHE SAYS THAT, BUT SHE'S JUST GOING TO DO THE SAME AGAIN TOMORROW.
KIKUO, HOW ABOUT THIS QUESTION...?
I DON'T KNOW.
...I SEE.
PUT ALL THE PITY YOU WANT INTO YOUR VOICE...
...I STILL CAN'T READ THE PROBLEM, MUCH LESS KNOW WHAT IT'S ABOUT.
SUZUME!

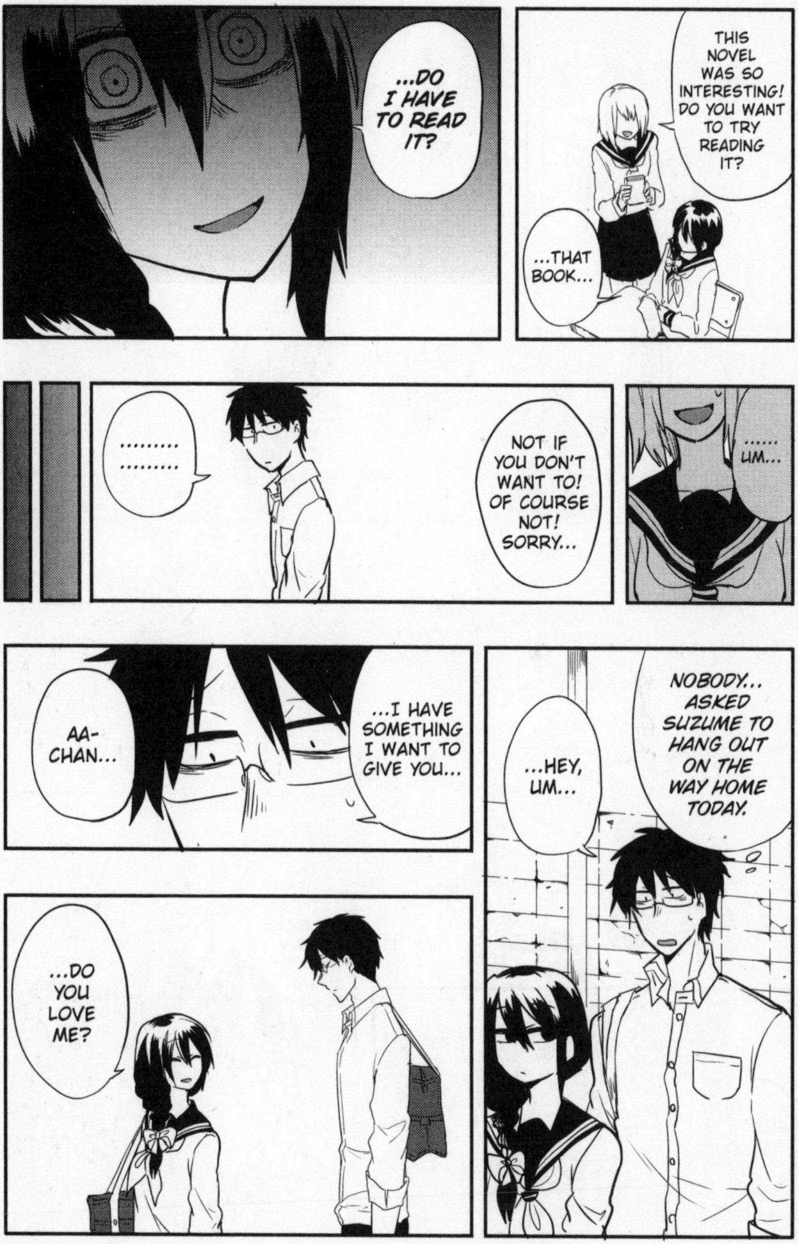
THIS NOVEL WAS SO INTERESTING! DO YOU WANT TO TRY READING IT?
...THAT BOOK...
...DO I HAVE TO READ IT?
..... UM...
NOT IF YOU DON'T WANT TO! OF COURSE NOT! SORRY...
....
NOBODY... ASKED SUZUME TO HANG OUT ON THE WAY HOME TODAY.
...HEY, UM...
...I HAVE SOMETHING I WANT TO GIVE YOU...
AA-CHAN...
...DO YOU LOVE ME?

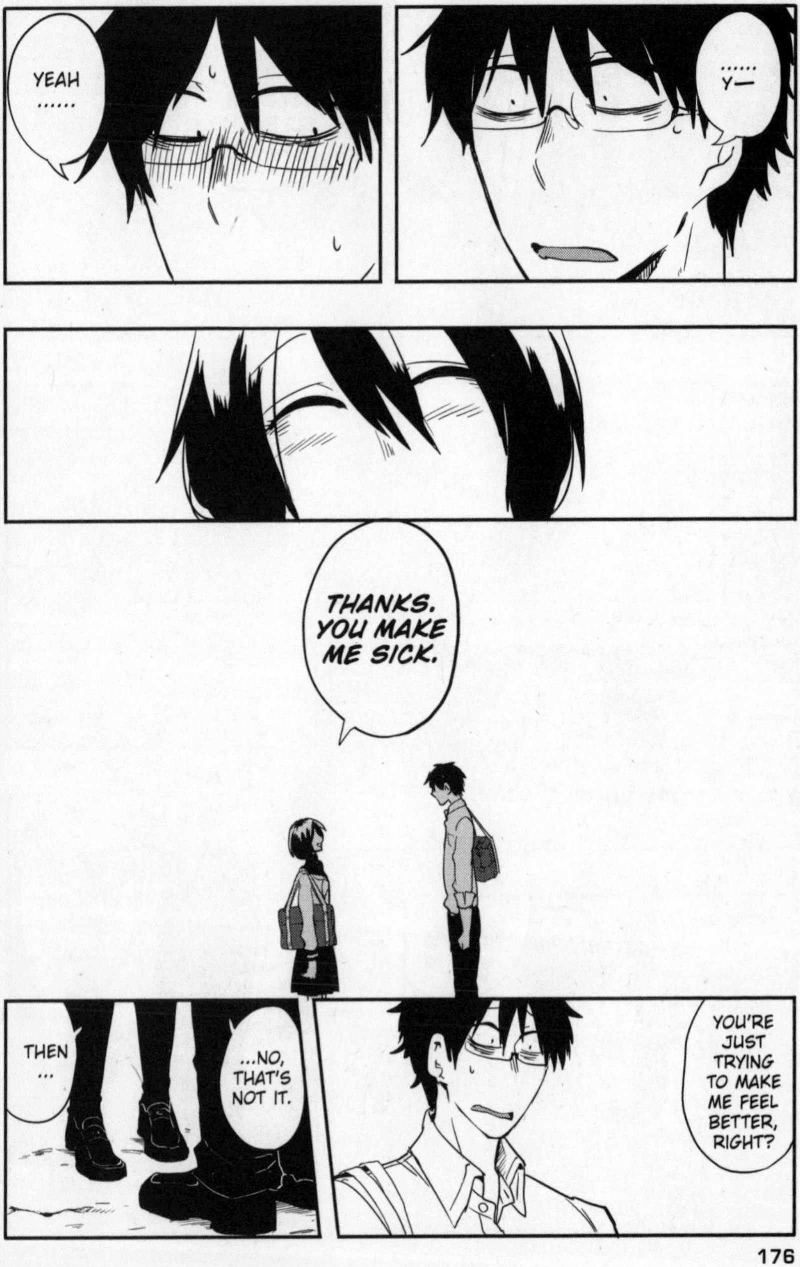

......Y—
YEAH ......
THANKS. YOU MAKE ME SICK.
YOU'RE JUST TRYING TO MAKE ME FEEL BETTER, RIGHT?
...NO, THAT'S NOT IT.
THEN ...

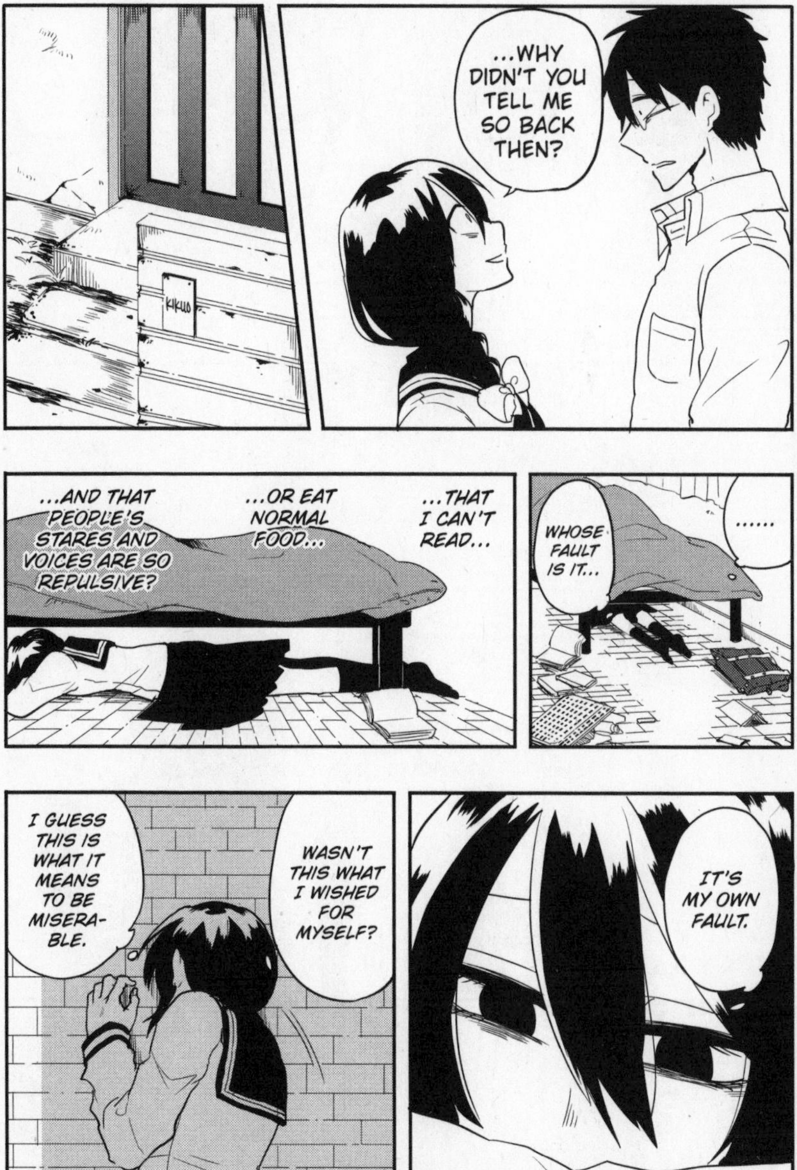
...WHY DIDN'T YOU TELL ME SO BACK THEN?
KIKUO
......
WHOSE FAULT IS IT...
...THAT I CAN'T READ...
...OR EAT NORMAL FOOD...
...AND THAT PEOPLE'S STARES AND VOICES ARE SO REPULSIVE?
IT'S MY OWN FAULT.
WASN'T THIS WHAT I WISHED FOR MYSELF?
I GUESS THIS IS WHAT IT MEANS TO BE MISERA-BLE.

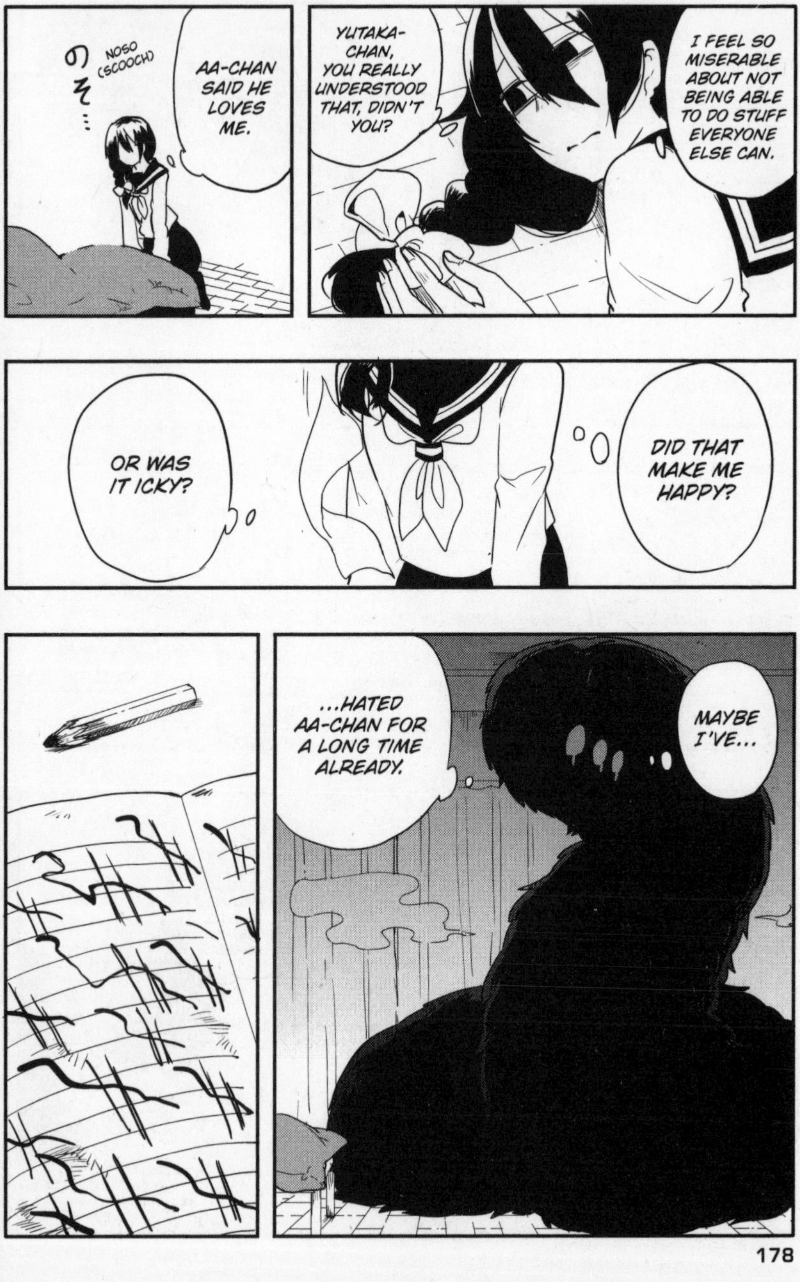
I FEEL SO MISERABLE ABOUT NOT BEING ABLE TO DO STUFF EVERYONE ELSE CAN.
YUTAKA-CHAN, YOU REALLY UNDERSTOOD THAT, DIDN'T YOU?
AA-CHAN SAID HE LOVES ME.
のそ…
NOSO (SCOOCH)
DID THAT MAKE ME HAPPY?
OR WAS IT ICKY?
MAYBE I'VE...
...HATED AA-CHAN FOR A LONG TIME ALREADY.

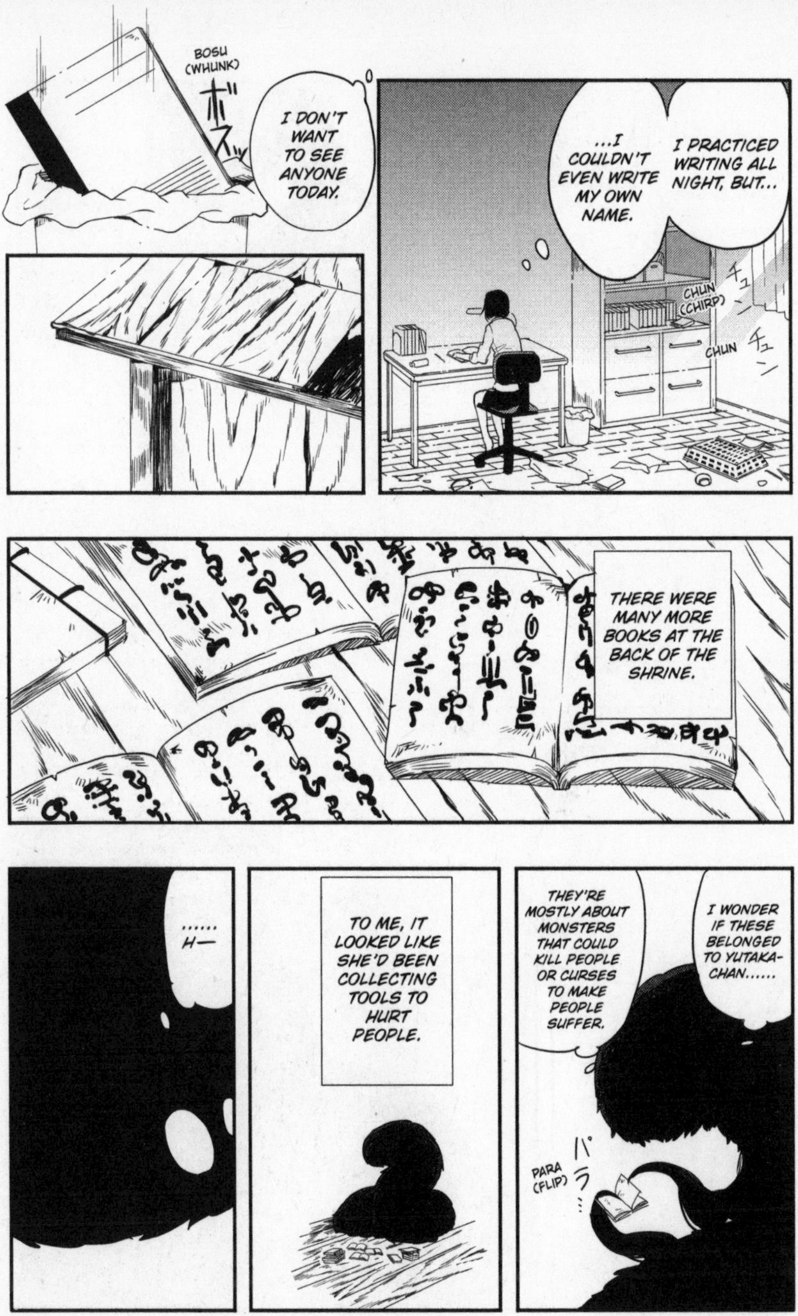
I PRACTICED WRITING ALL NIGHT, BUT...
...I COULDN'T EVEN WRITE MY OWN NAME.
CHUN (CHIRP)
CHUN
BOSU (WHUNK)
I DON'T WANT TO SEE ANYONE TODAY.
THERE WERE MANY MORE BOOKS AT THE BACK OF THE SHRINE.
I WONDER IF THESE BELONGED TO YUTAKA-CHAN......
THEY'RE MOSTLY ABOUT MONSTERS THAT COULD KILL PEOPLE OR CURSES TO MAKE PEOPLE SUFFER.
PARA (FLIP)
TO ME, IT LOOKED LIKE SHE'D BEEN COLLECTING TOOLS TO HURT PEOPLE.
...... H—

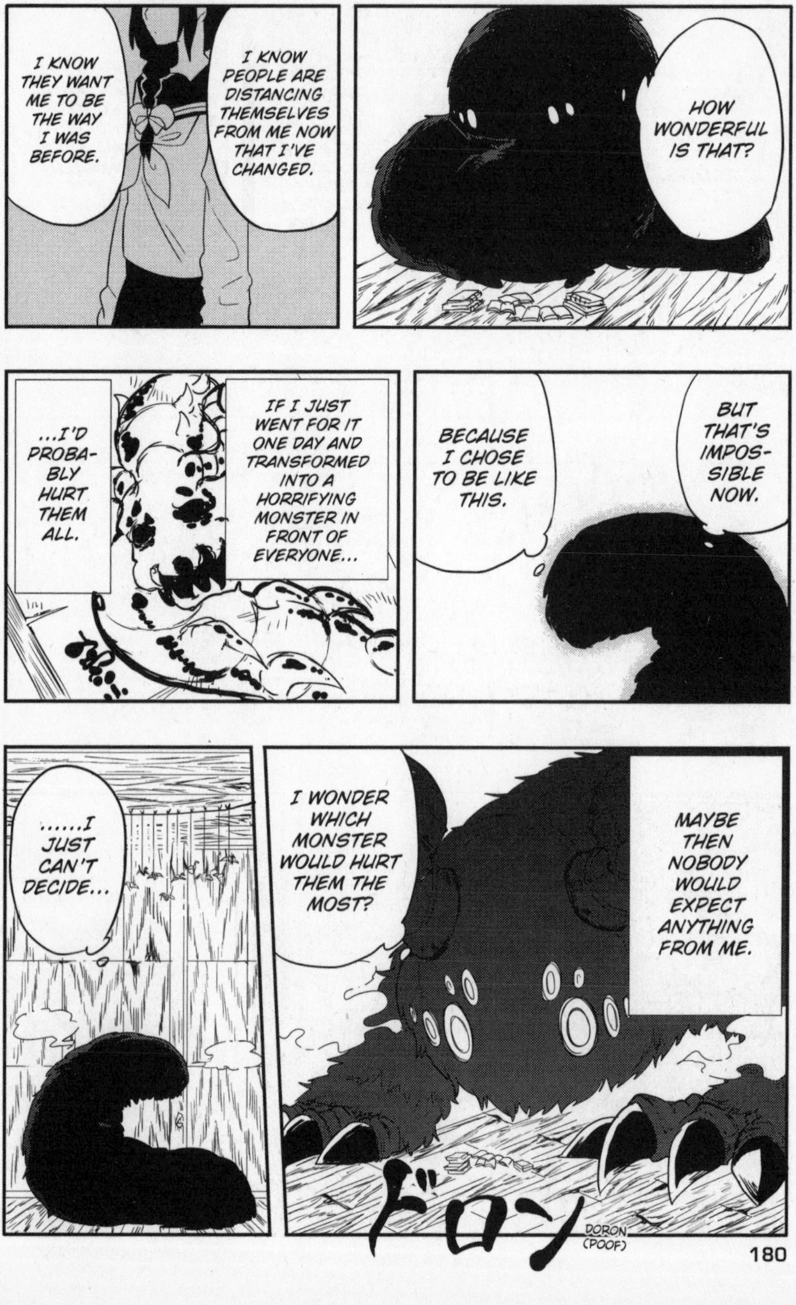
HOW WONDERFUL IS THAT?
I KNOW PEOPLE ARE DISTANCING THEMSELVES FROM ME NOW THAT I'VE CHANGED.
I KNOW THEY WANT ME TO BE THE WAY I WAS BEFORE.
BUT THAT'S IMPOSSIBLE NOW.
BECAUSE I CHOSE TO BE LIKE THIS.
IF I JUST WENT FOR IT ONE DAY AND TRANSFORMED INTO A HORRIFYING MONSTER IN FRONT OF EVERYONE...
...I'D PROBABLY HURT THEM ALL.
MAYBE THEN NOBODY WOULD EXPECT ANYTHING FROM ME.
I WONDER WHICH MONSTER WOULD HURT THEM THE MOST?
ドロン
DORON (POOF)
......I JUST CAN'T DECIDE...

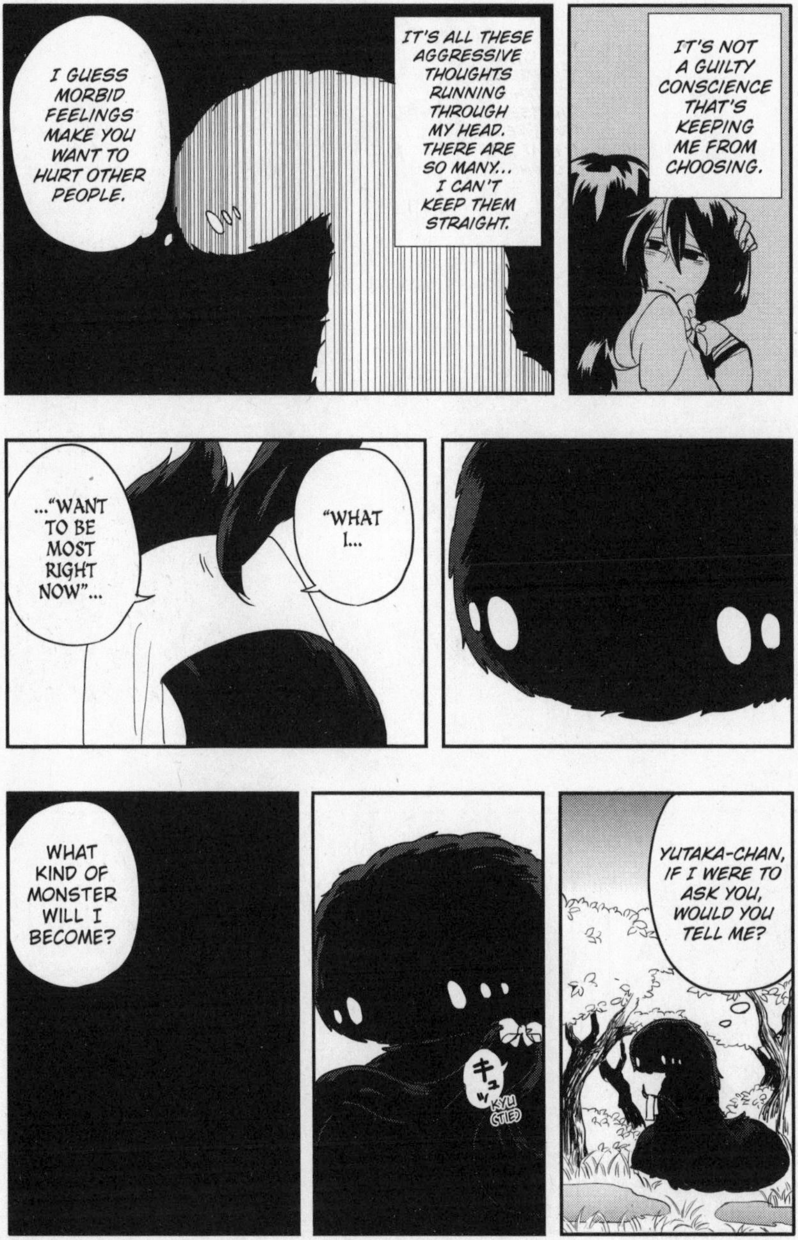
IT'S NOT A GUILTY CONSCIENCE THAT'S KEEPING ME FROM CHOOSING.
IT'S ALL THESE AGGRESSIVE THOUGHTS RUNNING THROUGH MY HEAD. THERE ARE SO MANY... I CAN'T KEEP THEM STRAIGHT.
I GUESS MORBID FEELINGS MAKE YOU WANT TO HURT OTHER PEOPLE.
"WHAT I...
..."WANT TO BE MOST RIGHT NOW"...
YUTAKA-CHAN, IF I WERE TO ASK YOU, WOULD YOU TELL ME?
キュッ
KYU (TIE)
WHAT KIND OF MONSTER WILL I BECOME?

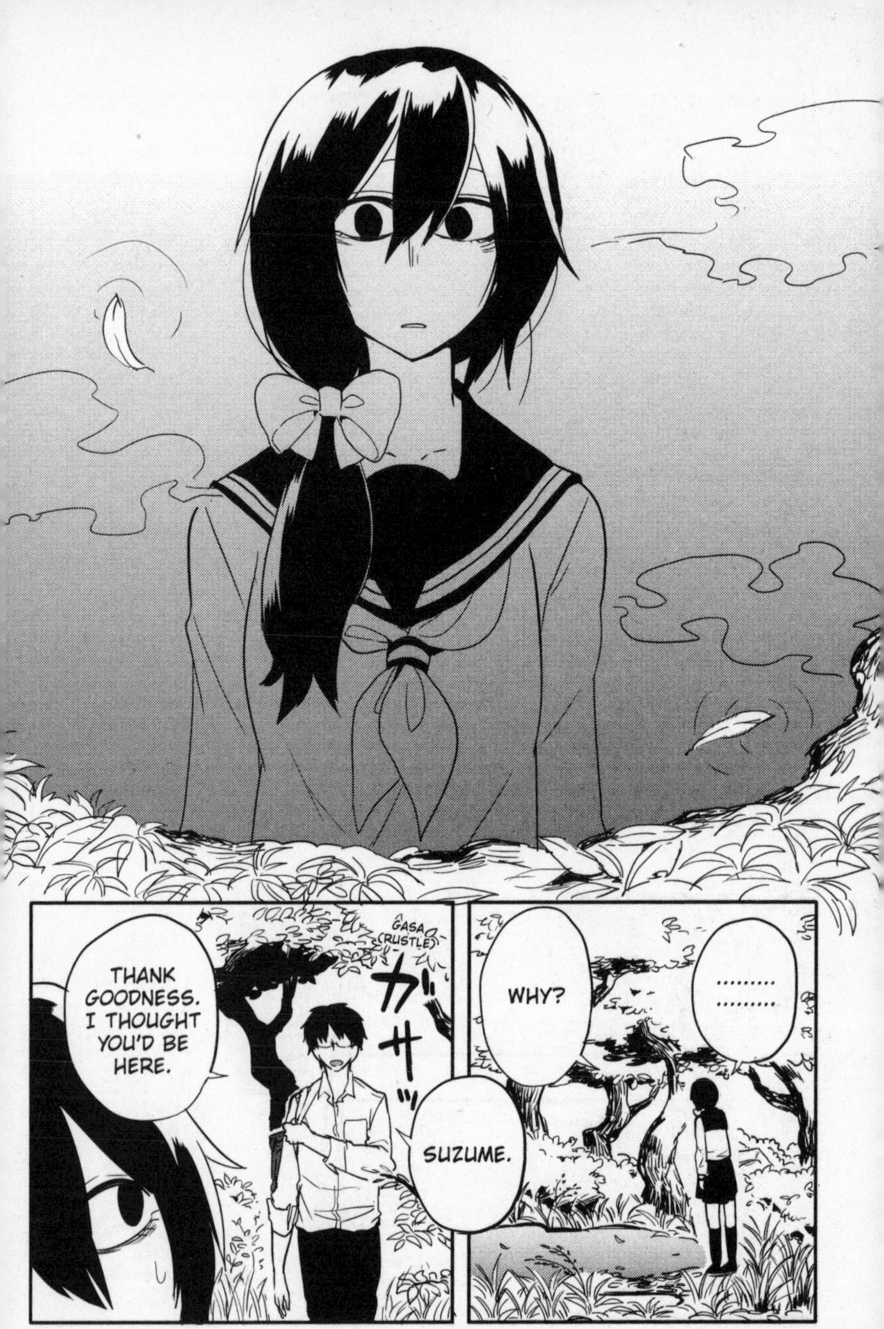

....
....
WHY?
SUZUME.
GASA (RUSTLE)
ガサッ
THANK GOODNESS. I THOUGHT YOU'D BE HERE.

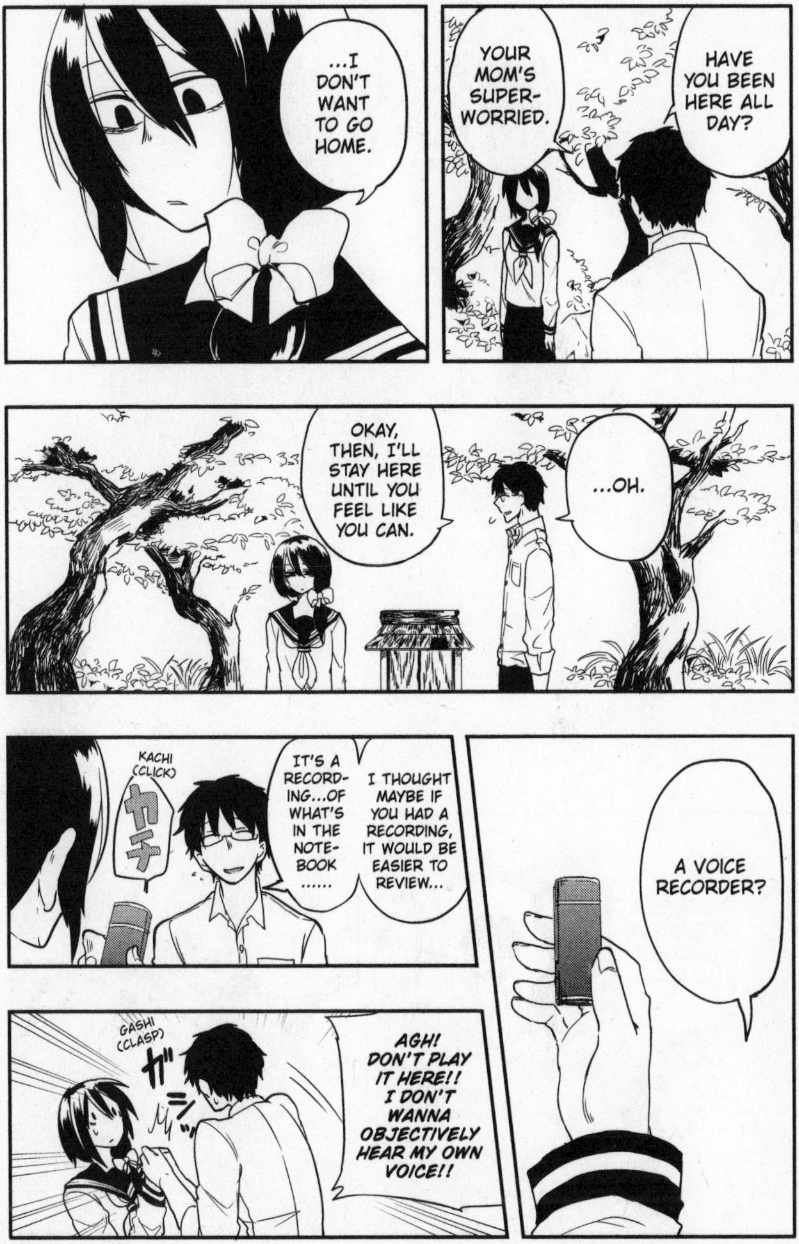
HAVE YOU BEEN HERE ALL DAY?
YOUR MOM'S SUPER-WORRIED.
...I DON'T WANT TO GO HOME.
...OH.
OKAY, THEN, I'LL STAY HERE UNTIL YOU FEEL LIKE YOU CAN.
A VOICE RECORDER?
I THOUGHT MAYBE IF YOU HAD A RECORDING, IT WOULD BE EASIER TO REVIEW...
IT'S A RECORDING...OF WHAT'S IN THE NOTEBOOK......
KACHI (CLICK)
カチ
AGH! DON'T PLAY IT HERE!! I DON'T WANNA OBJECTIVELY HEAR MY OWN VOICE!!
GASHI (CLASP)
ガ

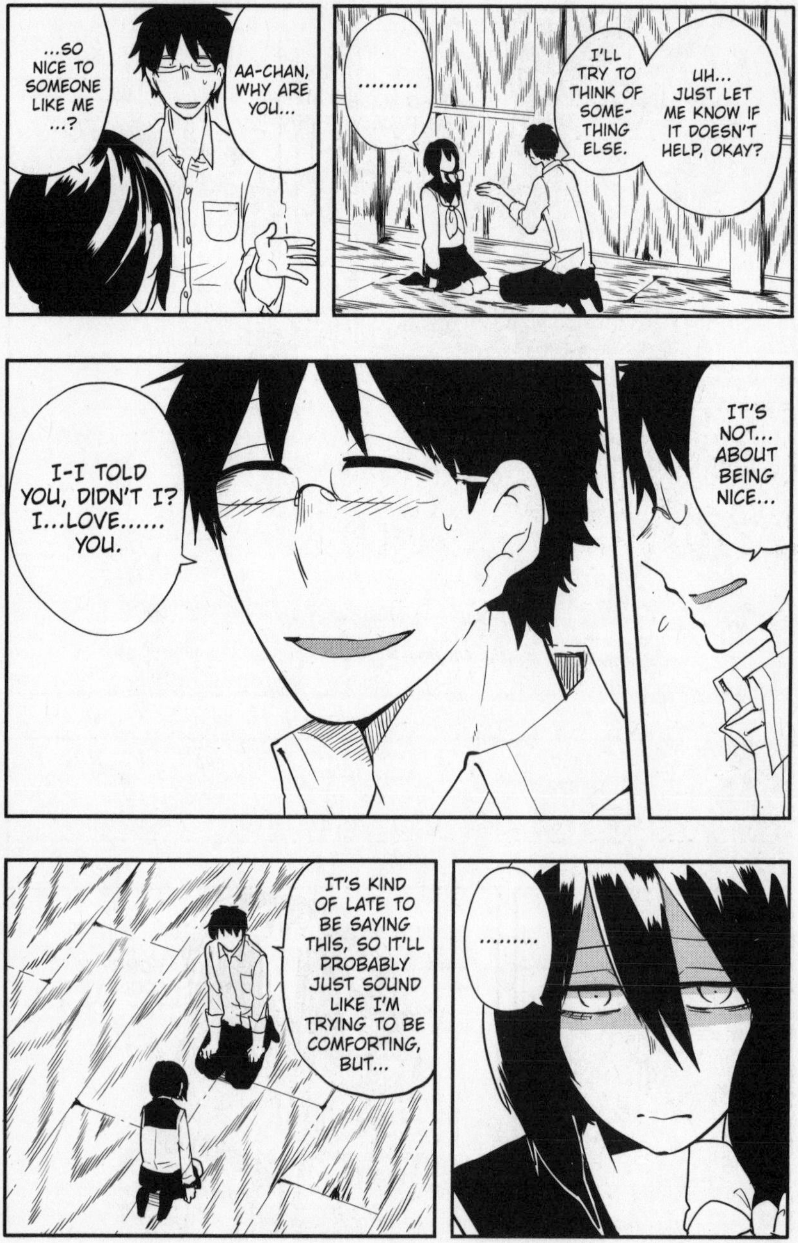
UH... JUST LET ME KNOW IF IT DOESN'T HELP, OKAY?
I'LL TRY TO THINK OF SOME-THING ELSE.
....
AA-CHAN, WHY ARE YOU...
...SO NICE TO SOMEONE LIKE ME ...?
IT'S NOT... ABOUT BEING NICE...
I-I TOLD YOU, DIDN'T I? I...LOVE...... YOU.
....
IT'S KIND OF LATE TO BE SAYING THIS, SO IT'LL PROBABLY JUST SOUND LIKE I'M TRYING TO BE COMFORTING, BUT...

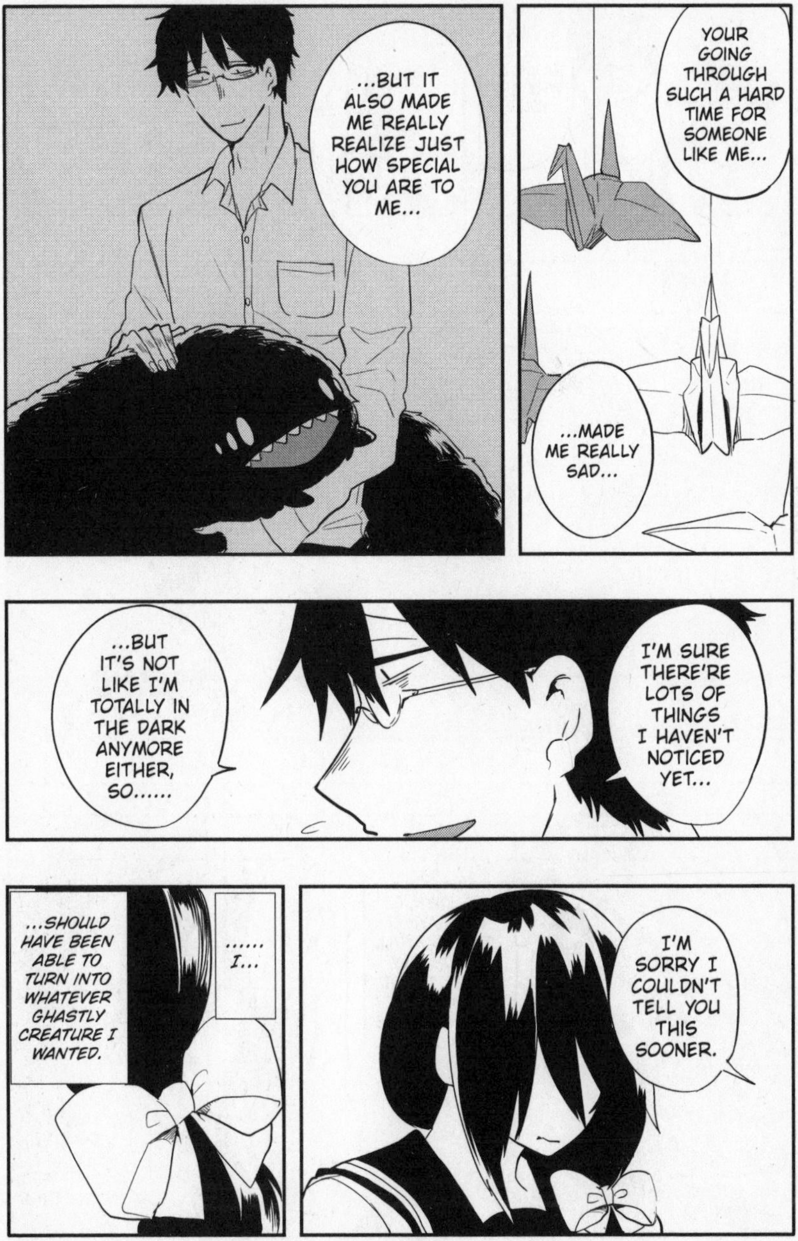
YOUR GOING THROUGH SUCH A HARD TIME FOR SOMEONE LIKE ME...
...MADE ME REALLY SAD...
...BUT IT ALSO MADE ME REALLY REALIZE JUST HOW SPECIAL YOU ARE TO ME...
I'M SURE THERE'RE LOTS OF THINGS I HAVEN'T NOTICED YET...
...BUT IT'S NOT LIKE I'M TOTALLY IN THE DARK ANYMORE EITHER, SO......
I'M SORRY I COULDN'T TELL YOU THIS SOONER.
...... I...
...SHOULD HAVE BEEN ABLE TO TURN INTO WHATEVER GHASTLY CREATURE I WANTED.

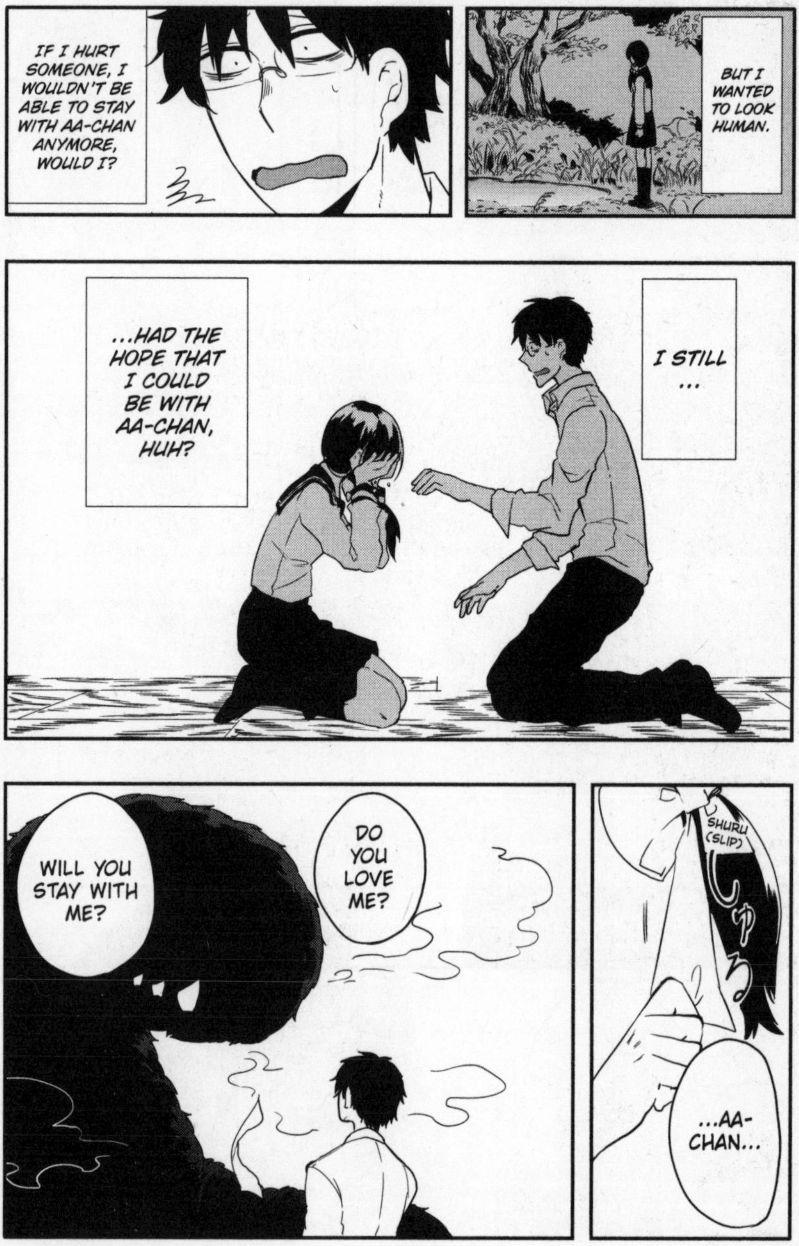
BUT I WANTED TO LOOK HUMAN.
IF I HURT SOMEONE, I WOULDN'T BE ABLE TO STAY WITH AA-CHAN ANYMORE, WOULD I?
I STILL ...
...HAD THE HOPE THAT I COULD BE WITH AA-CHAN, HUH?
SHURU (SLIP)
しゅる
...AA-CHAN...
DO YOU LOVE ME?
WILL YOU STAY WITH ME?

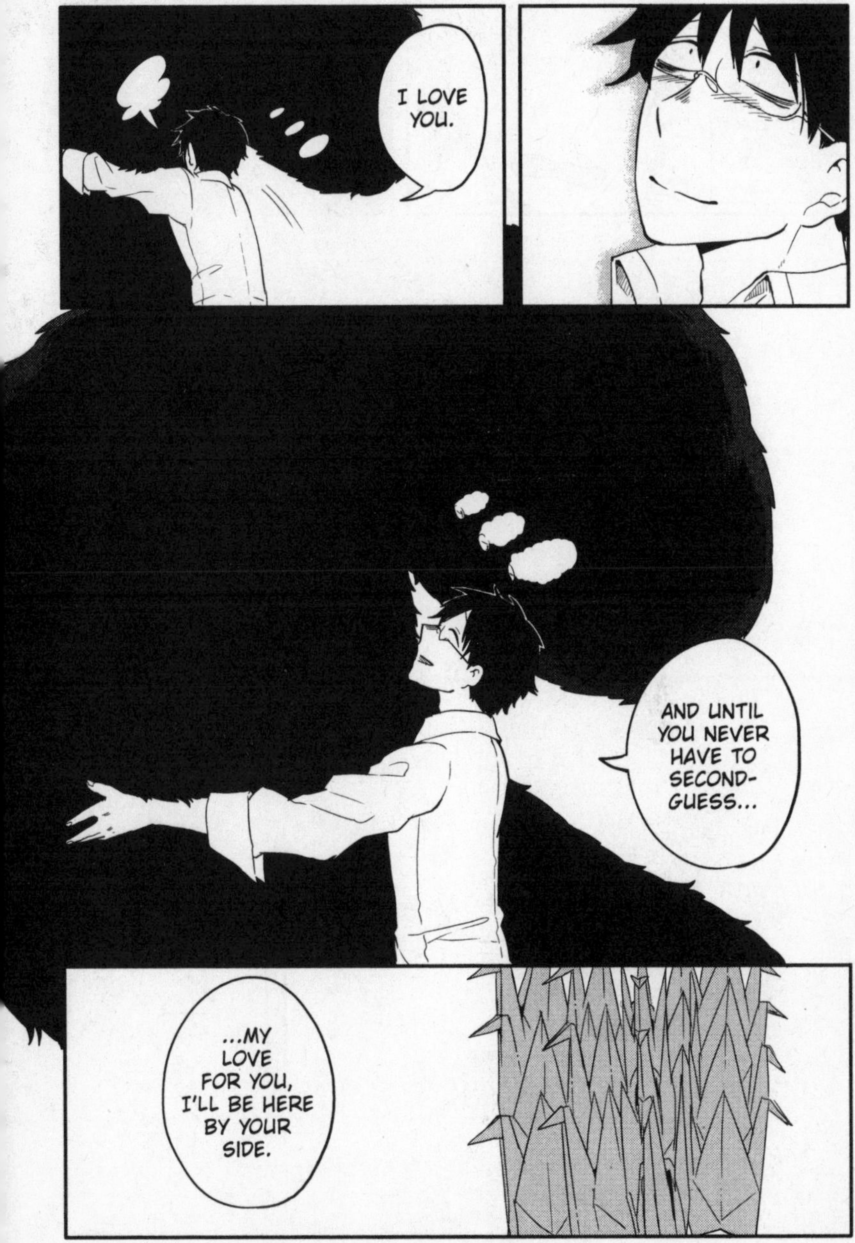
I LOVE YOU.
AND UNTIL YOU NEVER HAVE TO SECOND-GUESS...
...MY LOVE FOR YOU, I'LL BE HERE BY YOUR SIDE.

THE END

AND NOW FOR SOME BONUS MANGA!

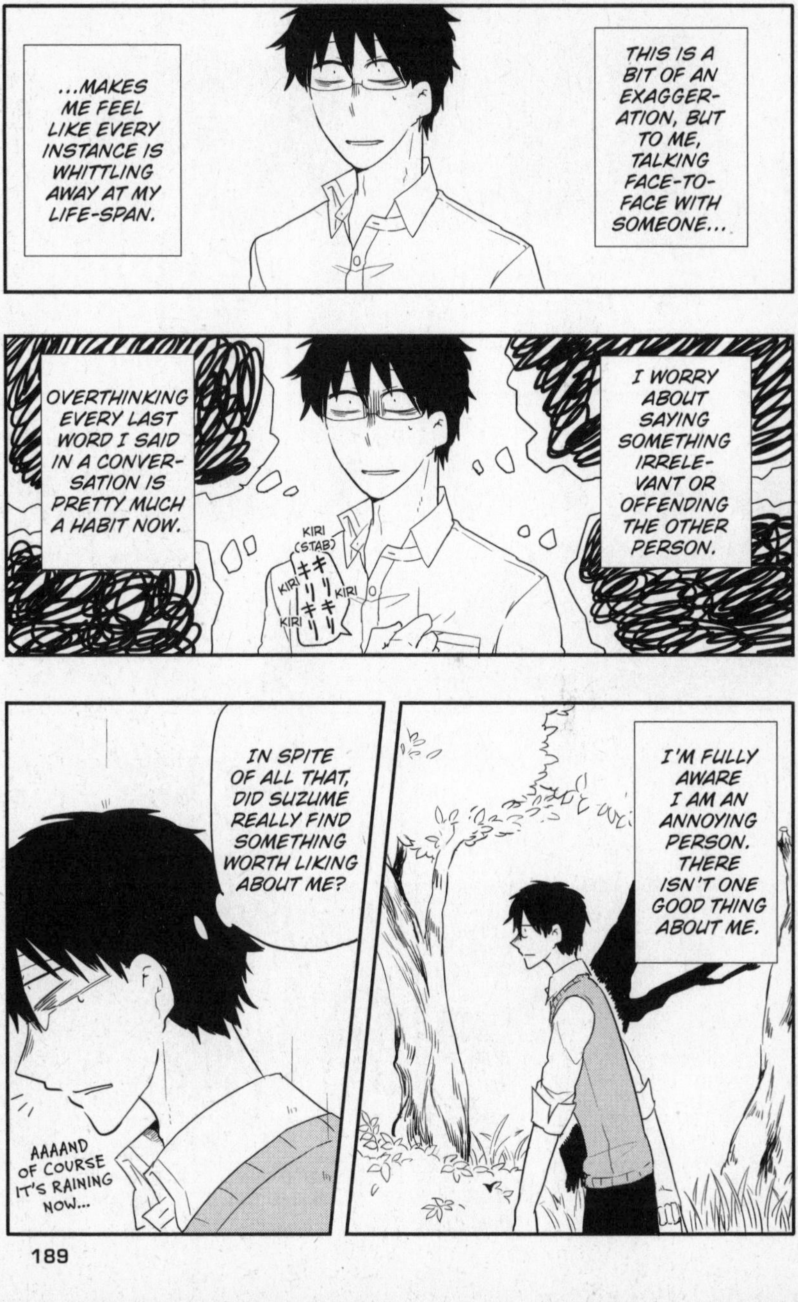
THIS IS A BIT OF AN EXAGGERATION, BUT TO ME, TALKING FACE-TO-FACE WITH SOMEONE...
...MAKES ME FEEL LIKE EVERY INSTANCE IS WHITTLING AWAY AT MY LIFE-SPAN.
I WORRY ABOUT SAYING SOMETHING IRRELEVANT OR OFFENDING THE OTHER PERSON.
OVERTHINKING EVERY LAST WORD I SAID IN A CONVERSATION IS PRETTY MUCH A HABIT NOW.
KIRI (STAB)
キリキリ キリキリ
KIRI KIRI KIRI
I'M FULLY AWARE I AM AN ANNOYING PERSON. THERE ISN'T ONE GOOD THING ABOUT ME.
IN SPITE OF ALL THAT, DID SUZUME REALLY FIND SOMETHING WORTH LIKING ABOUT ME?
AAAAND OF COURSE IT'S RAINING NOW...

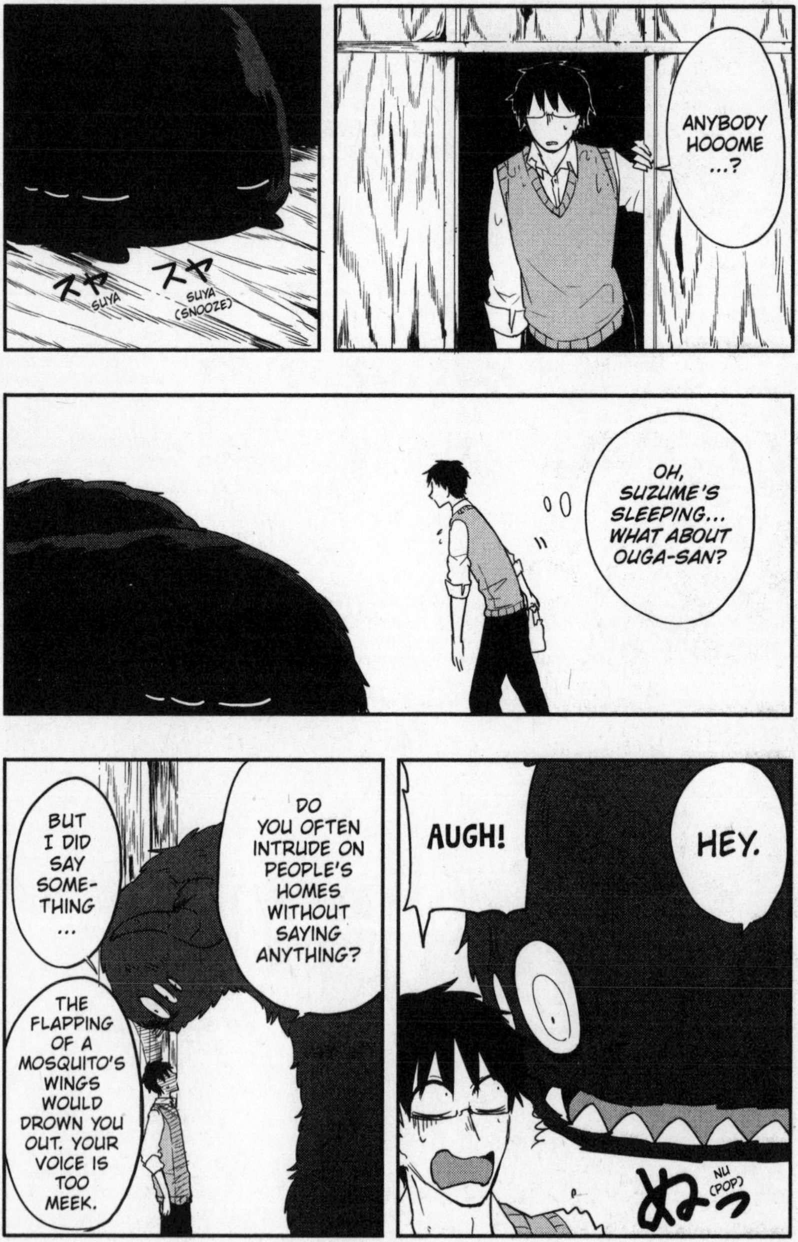
ANYBODY HOOOME ...?
スヤ
SUYA (SNOOZE)
スヤ
SUYA
OH, SUZUME'S SLEEPING... WHAT ABOUT OUGA-SAN?
HEY.
AUGH!
ぬっ
NU (POP)
DO YOU OFTEN INTRUDE ON PEOPLE'S HOMES WITHOUT SAYING ANYTHING?
BUT I DID SAY SOME-THING ...
THE FLAPPING OF A MOSQUITO'S WINGS WOULD DROWN YOU OUT. YOUR VOICE IS TOO MEEK.

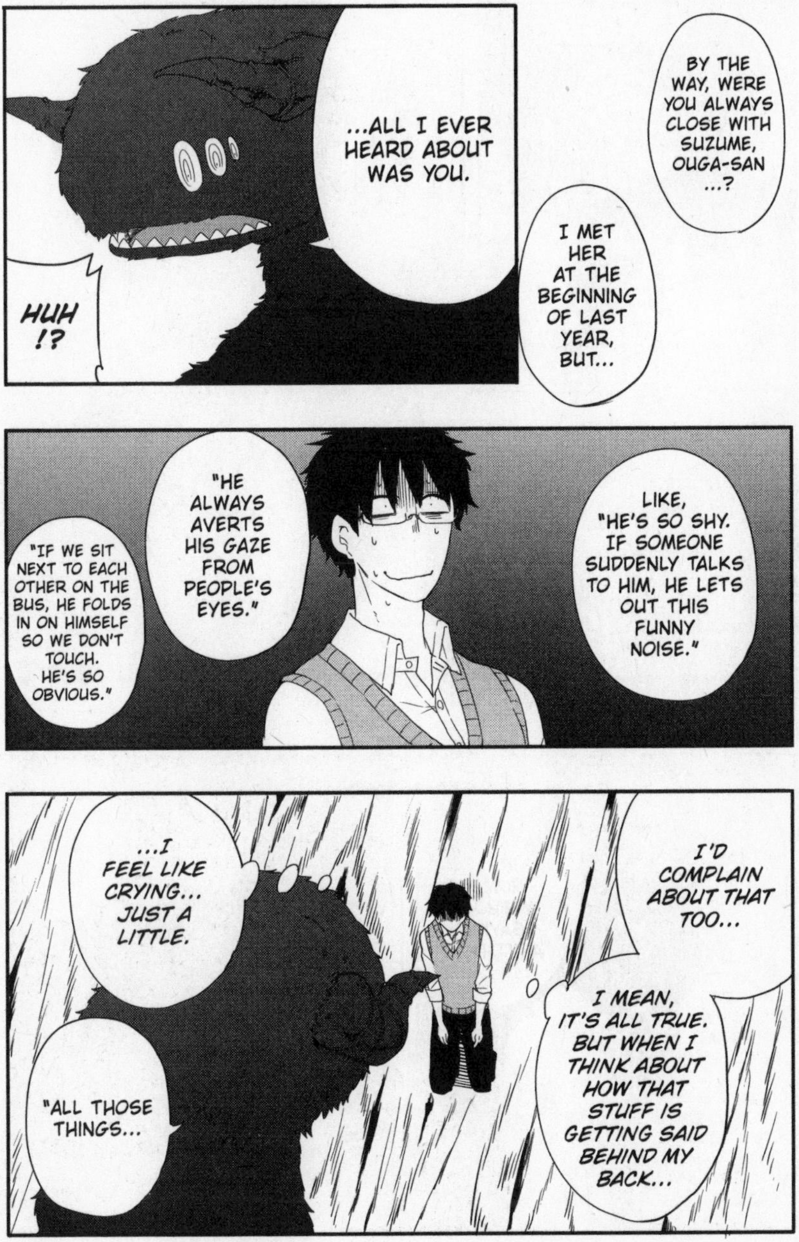
BY THE WAY, WERE YOU ALWAYS CLOSE WITH SUZUME, OUGA-SAN ...?
I MET HER AT THE BEGINNING OF LAST YEAR, BUT...
...ALL I EVER HEARD ABOUT WAS YOU.
HUH !?
LIKE, "HE'S SO SHY. IF SOMEONE SUDDENLY TALKS TO HIM, HE LETS OUT THIS FUNNY NOISE."
"HE ALWAYS AVERTS HIS GAZE FROM PEOPLE'S EYES."
"IF WE SIT NEXT TO EACH OTHER ON THE BUS, HE FOLDS IN ON HIMSELF SO WE DON'T TOUCH. HE'S SO OBVIOUS."
I'D COMPLAIN ABOUT THAT TOO...
...I FEEL LIKE CRYING... JUST A LITTLE.
I MEAN, IT'S ALL TRUE. BUT WHEN I THINK ABOUT HOW THAT STUFF IS GETTING SAID BEHIND MY BACK...
"ALL THOSE THINGS...

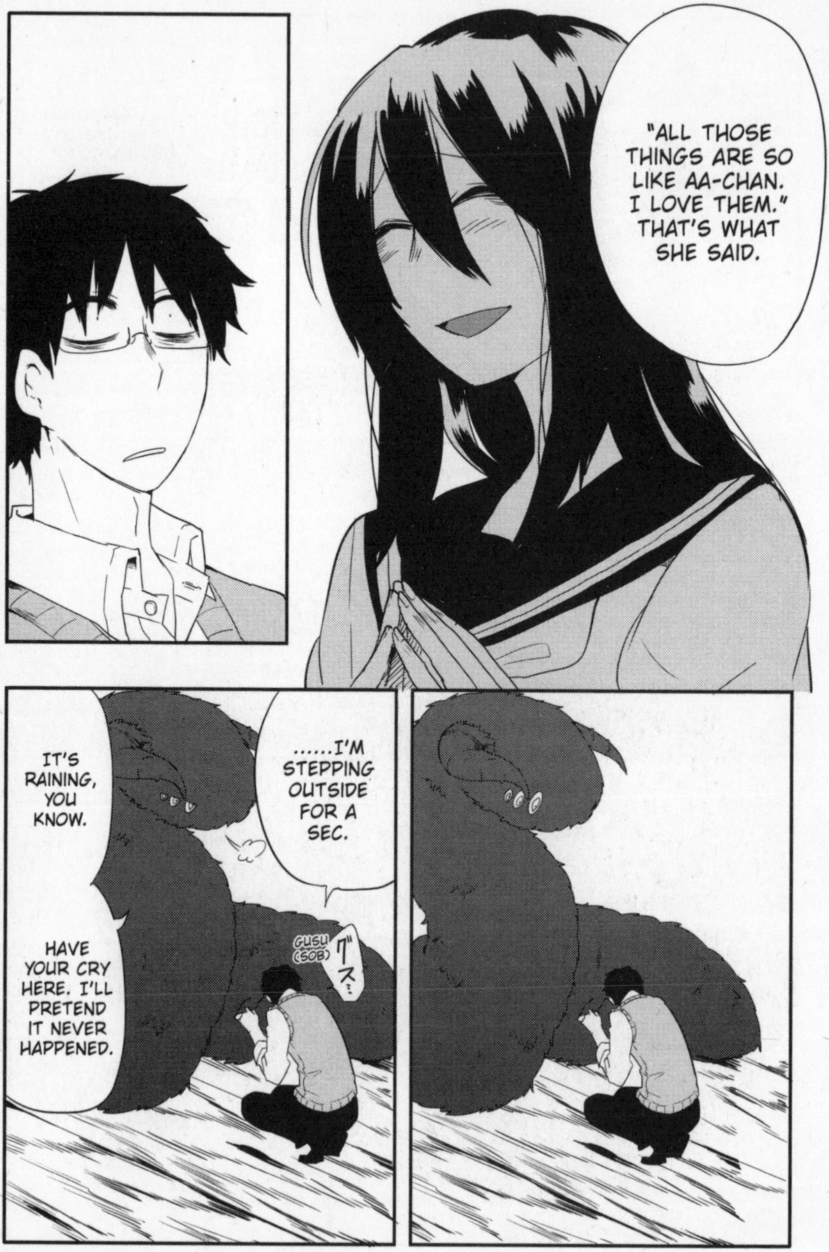
"ALL THOSE THINGS ARE SO LIKE AA-CHAN. I LOVE THEM." THAT'S WHAT SHE SAID.
......I'M STEPPING OUTSIDE FOR A SEC.
グス
GUSU (SOB)
IT'S RAINING, YOU KNOW.
HAVE YOUR CRY HERE. I'LL PRETEND IT NEVER HAPPENED.

CATERPILLAR GIRL AND BAD TEXTER BOY

THIS PROJECT TROUBLED PEOPLE FAR AND WIDE, BUT WE MANAGED TO MAKE IT TO THE END IN ONE PIECE! THANK YOU EVERYONE FOR PUTTING UP WITH MY PROBLEMATIC ATTACHMENT TO THIS BLACK BALL OF FUR! —SANZO

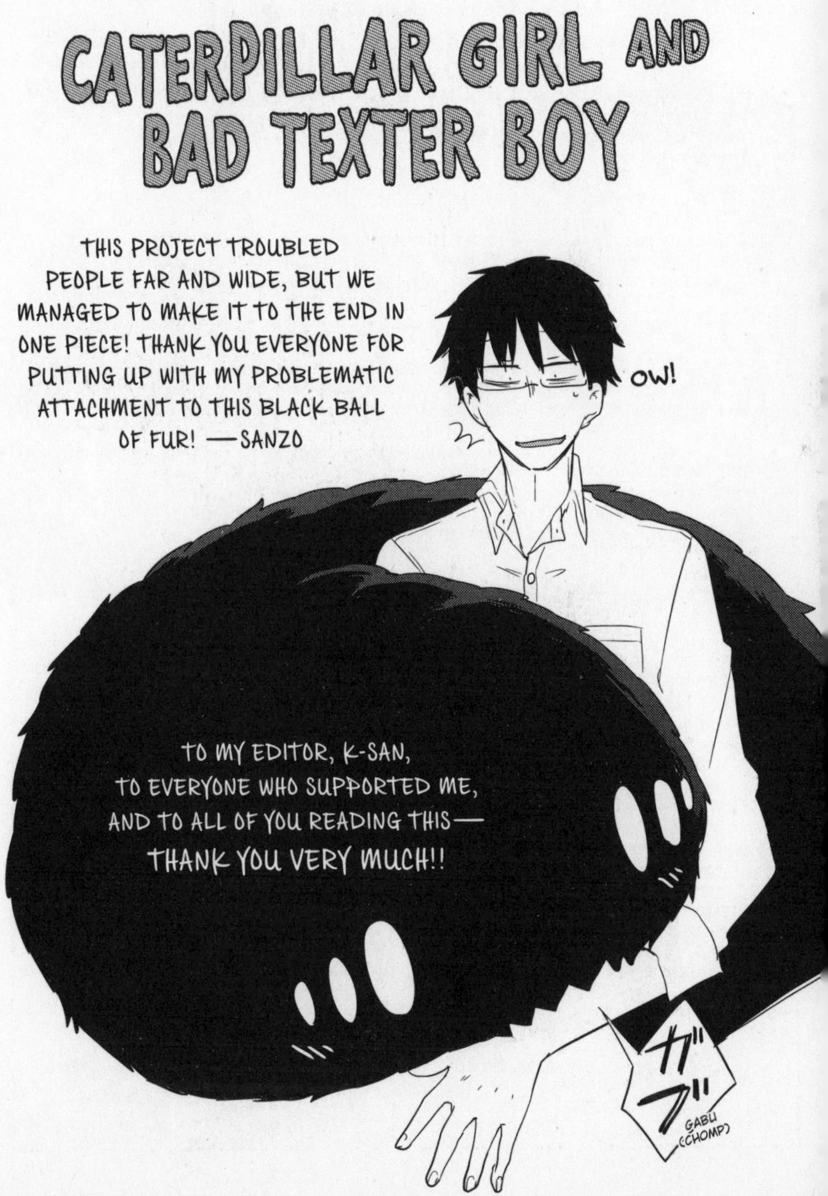
OW!
TO MY EDITOR, K-SAN,
TO EVERYONE WHO SUPPORTED ME,
AND TO ALL OF YOU READING THIS—
THANK YOU VERY MUCH!!
ガブ
GABU (CHOMP)

Caterpillar Girl and Bad Texter Boy

SANZO

Translation/Adaptation: **Alexandra McCullough-Garcia**
Lettering: **Takeshi Kamura**

IMOMUSHISHOJO TO KOMYUSHODANSHI
©Sanzo 2017
First published in Japan in 2017 by KADOKAWA CORPORATION, Tokyo. English translation rights arranged with KADOKAWA CORPORATION, Tokyo through TUTTLE-MORI AGENCY, INC., Tokyo.

English translation © 2018 by Yen Press, LLC

Yen Press
1290 Avenue of the Americas
New York, NY 10104

Visit us!
yenpress.com
facebook.com/yenpress
twitter.com/yenpress
yenpress.tumblr.com
instagram.com/yenpress

First Yen Press Edition: June 2018

Yen Press is an imprint of Yen Press, LLC.
The Yen Press name and logo are trademarks of Yen Press, LLC.

The publisher is not responsible for websites (or their content) that are not owned by the publisher.

Library of Congress Control Number: 2018935617

ISBNs: 978-1-9753-2748-4 (print)
       978-1-9753-5425-1 (ebook)

10 9 8 7 6 5 4 3 2 1

WOR

Printed in the United States of America